GUIDE TO MODERN ENGLISH

FOR GRADE NINE

RICHARD K. CORBIN

*Chairman of the English Department, Hunter
College High School, New York City*

MARGUERITE BLOUGH

*Head of the English Department, East High
School, Waterloo, Iowa*

HOWARD VANDER BEEK

*Chairman of the Language Arts Department
of the Malcolm Price Laboratory School, Iowa State
Teachers College, Cedar Falls*

Editorial Advisor:
JOHN C. GERBER, *State University of Iowa, Iowa City*

GUIDE

TO MODERN

ENGLISH

Scott, Foresman and Company

Chicago   Atlanta   Dallas   Palo Alto   Fair Lawn, N. J.

ILLUSTRATED BY FRAN FOLEY

CONTENTS

1

2

3

4

5

6

7

CHAPTER 1

WRITING

GOOD

PARAGRAPHS

Anyone who knows how to saw wood and pound nails can build a chair—that is, he can turn out a piece of furniture that others would recognize as a "chair." But it takes quite a bit more skill to build a *good* chair, one that others would find not only useful and comfortable, but attractive as well.

Anyone who knows how to write sentences can write paragraphs. All he has to do is to indent the first lines of several groups of sentences, and he has what others would recognize as "paragraphs." But again—it takes a lot more skill to write *good* paragraphs, paragraphs that others would find not only interesting and enjoyable, but worth reading.

Though it takes skill to write good paragraphs, it is a skill that all of you can acquire. The first step in gaining this skill is learning what you should do and what you should not do. This chapter will help you acquire paragraph "know-how." It will show you what you must put into a paragraph to make it good and will provide exercises to get you started right. The rest is up to you.

WHAT A PARAGRAPH IS

Perhaps the main reason why some people cannot write good paragraphs is that they do not really know what a paragraph is. Oh, they know what a paragraph looks like, of course; they can tell you how many paragraphs there are on a particular page or in a certain article. They can tell this much without even reading the page or the article; they simply look for the outward signs. They know that every group of sentences that begins with an indention is called a "paragraph."

But what makes a group of sentences a paragraph? Why does a writer group certain sentences together in a particular paragraph? Why are there three paragraphs on one page? Why not four or five, as on the next page? How does the writer know where to indent for a new paragraph? Does he just put in an indention wherever he thinks it will look attractive?

You can answer these questions only if you know what a paragraph is—and not merely what a paragraph looks like.

A paragraph is a group of sentences that work together to make clear one central idea, one phase of the subject that the writer is discussing in his paper. Because the sentences work together to make this one idea clear to the reader, they belong together—in a paragraph. The writer does not indent for paragraphs just to break up a page of writing into sections; he indents to show his readers that he is going to discuss a new idea, to move on to a new phase of his subject.

In any well-written paper there are as many paragraphs as the writer needs to give a clear picture of his subject. Before he starts writing the paper, the writer decides what main topics he will cover. If, for example, he is planning a short article about the career of baseball's famous Lou Gehrig, he may decide to discuss such main topics as these:

1. Gehrig's amazing record as a baseball great
2. His unusual courage in spite of serious physical handicaps
3. The tragic illness that put an end to his baseball career
4. The public's farewell on Lou Gehrig Appreciation Day
5. Gehrig's last job as a New York parole commissioner

For each of the main topics the writer decides to include in his article, he will write a number of sentences to tell his readers about that particular point. For example, he might write the following sentences to explain the second of the topics in the list—Gehrig's courage as a player:

Lou played despite colds. He played despite fevers. He played so doubled over with lumbago that it was impossible for him to straighten up; and bent over at the plate, he still got himself a single. One year he fractured a toe. He played on. Again, knocked unconscious by a wild pitch, he suffered a concussion that would have hospitalized the average man for two weeks. He was at his position the next day—and collected four hits. When, late in his career, his hands were X-rayed, the doctors found seventeen fractures that had healed by themselves. He had broken every finger on both hands—some of them twice—and hadn't even mentioned the fact to anyone.— Paul Gallico, "Lou Gehrig—An American Hero." Copyright © 1942 by Paul Gallico. Reprinted by permission of Harold Ober Associates Incorporated.

Since all of these sentences written by Paul Gallico (a former sports editor and columnist) work together to make one particular topic clear, *they form a good paragraph.* Gallico indents the first sentence in the group to show his readers that he is beginning a new topic at this point.

Remember: Indenting the first word of a group of sentences does not *make* a paragraph; the indention merely shows where the paragraph begins. The paragraph itself is made by writing a group of sentences that belong together because they work as a unit to make one idea or topic clear.

EXERCISE (1) The following passage (taken from the book *Insect Allies*) was originally published as two paragraphs, each covering a different phase of the subject. Read the passage and decide where the indention for the second paragraph should be. On a sheet of paper, write the first three words of the sentence that should be indented. Then explain why you would start the second paragraph at this point.

Termites do about forty million dollars' worth of damage a year. One reason that they can do so much damage is that many of our buildings are poorly constructed. Where wood is placed directly on the ground, termites can enter it. Telephone posts that have not been treated with coal tar or creosote appeal to them as much as a tree stump in a field—they don't know the difference. In their search for a place to live they invade ships, bridges, grain elevators, stored material such as books; and they have even been known to attack linen, shoes, trees, plants, and flowers. Railway ties are seldom bothered by them—they are creosoted, and roadbeds are usually well drained. Man is the termites' greatest enemy. We can build our houses and other buildings more carefully, putting them on concrete or other foundations that the termites cannot penetrate. The termites also have some natural enemies. They are subject to a disease caused by molds and bacteria that kills a great many of them. Spiders, toads, frogs, lizards, wasps, snakes, and ants prey on them. And many birds help keep them under control—especially the woodpecker, English sparrow, road-runner, and flicker.—Eleanor King and Wellmer Pessels, *Insect Allies.* Copyright 1938 by Harper & Brothers, New York.

EXERCISE (2) The following passage (taken from an article by Donald Culross Peattie) was originally published as three paragraphs, each covering a different phase of the subject. Read the passage and decide where the indentions for the second and third paragraphs

11

should be. On a sheet of paper, write the first three words of the two sentences that should be indented. Then explain why you would indent at these points.

Half a lifetime ago things were still serene, as I remember. The biggest bang in my childhood was a "giant cracker" on the Fourth of July. In that placid world of yore a boy could rejoice in the flashing rattlety-clack of the train as it tore through the edge of town. Or there was the rare fun of galloping horses pulling the fire engine with its bell giving iron tongue. Otherwise the days were long with quiet, from cockcrow to twilight. A generation later we are drowned in decibels. A baseball game played in Yankee Stadium comes across the continent to California so loud and clear that a deaf neighbor of mine, by turning up his radio, can hear it all while he works in his garden. So, alas, can I. Children today protest that they can't do their homework without the accompaniment of jazz from their personal sets. If you visit friends, you're more likely to get TV gunfire than talk. The roar of traffic has grown so overwhelming that now they are soundproofing cars. So, of course, they have to make auto horns louder for the motorist to hear them. Here and there, efforts are made to fight noise. Industries employ technical researchers who come up with the profound discovery that people work better when they are not deafened or driven crazy by racket. Communities struggle valiantly—and, for the most, vainly—with the problem. There are anti-noise leagues, and I heartily wish them well. But the screeches, the bangs, roars, snorts, honks, thundering, bellowing, and pneumatic drilling are more and more forced upon us. —Donald Culross Peattie, "Tune in on Quiet," in *The Reader's Digest,* June 1957. Copyright © 1957 by The Reader's Digest Assn., Inc.

WRITING GOOD PARAGRAPHS

A good writer, as you have seen, *plans* before he starts the actual writing of a paper. The reason he plans is that he usually has several ideas (or topics) to present to his readers. Unless he figures out *beforehand* just what the ideas are and in what order he should present them, he will very likely set down on paper a confused— and confusing—jumble.

But once he has his ideas sorted out and knows which he should present first and which next, chances are that what he writes will be clear and interesting to his readers—particularly if he knows ways to make his paragraphs good.   Let's look at some of these ways.

A GOOD PARAGRAPH MAKES
THE TOPIC CLEAR TO THE READER

No matter what your purpose is in writing a theme—to tell about something that happened, to explain how to do something, to persuade others to think as you do, or simply to entertain your readers with an amusing story—your chief concern should be to make your ideas clear.   It is not enough for *you* to know what you mean; your job is to make your meaning clear to your readers.   How can you do this?

SUPPLYING DETAILS

The best way to make your meaning clear is to make sure that each paragraph you write contains enough specific details to show the readers exactly what you have in mind.   The details may be of various kinds, depending on what the topic of the paragraph is.

Suppose, for example, that you are writing a report about an American scientist, Karl August Steinmetz (known as Charles P. Steinmetz).   One of the topics that you have decided to include in your report is Steinmetz's amazing scholastic ability.   You yourself are quite impressed with his ability; you have read several stories that showed how exceptional a student he was.   Naturally you want your readers to share your admiration for him.

Now you certainly won't arouse in your readers the same admiration for Steinmetz that you feel if you write a vague, general paragraph of this sort:

> In college Karl Steinmetz was an unusually bright student. Not only his professors, but all his friends, admired his scholastic ability.   He was considered outstanding even among other good students.

How could your readers be impressed by what this paragraph says about Steinmetz?   There is nothing in it that would help them understand exactly *why* you think he was so unusual.

13

Give examples.   To make clear to your readers *why* you admire Steinmetz, you must supply details—details that give **examples** of his unusual ability.   See how well the writer of the following paragraph has done this:

> Karl's ability amazed everyone. He knew so much about so many subjects, and he had a remarkable memory. He could recite whole sections of many books by heart. Friends would give mathematics problems to him that would take them a long time to do, even on paper and with books of tables. Karl would just close his eyes for a moment, then give the right answer. The other students soon nicknamed him "Proteus," after a character in Greek legends who was able to answer many questions.—Dan Murdoch, "Steinmetz—A Wizard of Electricity," in *Jack and Jill*, April 1950. Copyright 1950 by The Curtis Publishing Company, Philadelphia.

The central idea that the writer of the following paragraph wants to get across is that all animals, even the lowliest, seem to have the ability to learn from experience. To make sure that his readers will clearly understand what he means, he provides a specific **example**. The example is so unusual that most of his readers will probably never forget it—or the idea it makes clear.

> All animals, even the most humble, appear to have some ability to learn from experience. An earthworm can learn to turn to the right or the left when it is placed in a maze in which it receives an unpleasant electric shock when it makes a wrong turn. Its nervous system records the lesson thus learned and the earthworm will even continue to make the correct turn after its head has been cut off.—Edwin Way Teale, *The Lost Woods*, published by Dodd, Mead & Co., Inc., New York. Copyright 1945 by Edwin Way Teale.

Give reasons.   Suppose you are writing a theme comparing independent stores and chain stores. If in one of the paragraphs you merely state that in your opinion the independent store has many advantages and that therefore people should trade there, you will not be very convincing to your readers. But if you add details that give specific **reasons** to back up your opinion, as is done in the following paragraph, your readers will understand why you think as you do.

> The small independent store has many advantages. It is often located near your home, perhaps just around the corner. You can get there within a few minutes if you need a loaf of

bread or a few pounds of potatoes. Sometimes the independent store gives you the privilege of running a charge account, allowing you to pay your bill at the end of the week or month. Or it may deliver your groceries and meats to your home after you have phoned in your order. Often the small retail shopkeeper knows you and your family personally. He knows your likes and dislikes and will try to give you what he knows you want, whether it is lean meat or large brown eggs.—Lawrence V. Roth and Stillman M. Hobbs, *Your World and You.* Copyright 1954 by Laidlaw Bros., River Forest, Illinois.

Point out similarities and differences. Sometimes the best way to make a topic clear is to give details that point out specific **similarities and differences**, as the writer of this paragraph has done:

Parties for young people in Latin America are more or less like those in our own country, except that they are more formal. Girls in the elementary schools and high schools entertain each other with teas which are not very different from those their mothers give. There are many more preliminaries for parties at which there will be both boys and girls. Of course there must be one chaperon or several. Usually the boys and girls do not go together. The father or an elder brother will take the girl of the family and call for her again. The boys go alone or in groups. The food is as important a part of the party as it is in our own country, although there usually is more of it. Salad, cold cuts, sandwiches, jellies, fruit, ice cream, and fancy cakes may all be served.—Delia Goetz, "Boy Meets Girl," in *Other Young Americans*, published by William Morrow & Co., Inc., New York. Copyright 1948 by Delia Goetz.

15

Tell an incident. At other times the best way to make a topic clear is to give the details of an **incident** that illustrates the point you want to make. For example:

Mexicans are patient with our little peculiarities, such as our love of warmth and comfort. On a beautiful summer day I went on an expedition which meant a return trip by bus. Setting out at midday, I foolishly forgot that it would be cold if I should be out after sunset. Sunset found me shivering in my thin dress, even before a driving rain caught up with us in the open bus. The other passengers were all Indian folk, who seem practically immune to cold. I was growing more miserable by the minute, when suddenly a tall peon rose from the back of the bus, came to my seat, and without a word put a woolen serape over me. How comfortable that felt, and how grateful

I was! But when at the journey's end I tried to thank him, he only smiled indulgently and said, "I had no use for it, but *Norteamericanos* [people from the U.S.] are always so cold!" —Montanye Perry, "I Like Mexicans," in *The Pan American*, December 1947.

Being able to name the *kinds* of details you use to "develop" the topics of your paragraphs is not especially important. What is important is that you *use* details—to give the specific examples, reasons, illustrations, or facts which the reader will need if he is to understand what you have in mind. Without details, he can get only a vague idea of what you mean.

EXERCISE (3) All the details in each of the following paragraphs help make clear the particular topic the writer is discussing. Read each paragraph carefully and decide which of the three topics listed below it most accurately tells the central idea of the paragraph. Write the topics you choose on a sheet of paper, and be ready to explain why they are the right ones.

1   All bottles containing poisonous ingredients should be labeled with a red label. This plan, however, is not really safe unless one can see which bottle he is about to use. It has been recommended that such bottles have a small bell attached to them, so that even at night when one is sleepy, he will know when he has the wrong bottle in his hands. Wrapping a piece of sandpaper around the bottle is a good idea. Some pins stuck in the cork is another way to indicate that a bottle contains poison. —William A. Evans, *Everyday Safety*. Copyright 1952 by Lyons & Carnahan, Chicago.
   The topic of the paragraph is:
   a) People often accidentally drink poison.
   b) Poison should be kept in bottles with a red label.
   c) Various ways to prevent people from drinking poison by mistake.

2   Grant Wood soon became known in Cedar Rapids as the "boy who minds the doctor's horse." He rode in the doctor's buggy, after school hours, and held the horse while the doctor, satchel in hand, went into a house to visit a sick patient. But he needed more money than the doctor could pay, to support his mother and the three younger children, so he took every job the town had to offer him. He mowed lawns in summer and shoveled snow in winter, and he milked the neighbor's cows in the early morning before he went to school, and again in the late afternoon when he had returned. And for the food the

family ate, he raised sweet corn and potatoes and tomatoes in the backyard.—Charlie May Simon, "Grant Wood," in *Art in the New Land.* Copyright 1945 by E. P. Dutton & Co., Inc., New York.

The topic of the paragraph is:

a) Grant Wood was well known by all the people in Cedar Rapids.

b) How Grant Wood managed to support his family.

c) Grant Wood's great love for horses.

3   There is no insect better known and more hated than the mosquito. The male mosquito is a peaceful creature, a poet in his small way, for his mouth is made for sucking nothing stronger than honey. He neither bites nor buzzes. A very ladylike person. Not so his wife! Mrs. Mosquito's mouth is made for a deadly purpose, and she is so literally bloodthirsty that she will drink until she is swollen to the point that she can hardly lift the red bag of her body on her frail wings. What is more than this, she squirts poison into the bite she makes to keep the blood flowing freely past her beak—so afraid she's going to miss something! But almost the worst thing about this gluttonous lady is her song, piped through her many breathing holes. —Julia Closson Kenly, *Children of a Star.* Copyright 1935 by Appleton-Century-Crofts, Inc.

The topic of the paragraph is:

a) The female mosquito, not the male, is a dangerous and annoying pest.

b) The mosquito's buzz is worse than its bite.

c) The male mosquito does not bite or buzz.

EXERCISE (4) Prepare (for a class discussion) a list of specific details that a writer might use to make clear his thoughts about each of the following topics. As suggestions are made in the discussion, jot them down on a sheet of paper in as brief a form as possible. After all the topics have been discussed, write a paragraph on the topic of your choice, using whichever of the details you like best.

1 Our town has a number of interesting places for tourists to see.

2 Tornadoes often cause freakish damage.

3 Is traveling by air better than traveling by train?

4 What should you expect from a friend?

5 One's tone of voice may give the same words different meanings.

6 The proverb "Where there's smoke, there's fire" is not always a reliable guide.

7 Little League baseball isn't all it's cracked up to be.

8 Many people deny they are superstitious, yet show by their actions that they are.

9 If I had to decide which three books should be required reading in all ninth-grade English classes, I would choose _____, _____, and _____. [Here you may name specific books or tell the type of book—with reasons for the choices.]

10 People living in different sections of our country often use different words for the same thing.

EXERCISE 5 Choose one of the following sentences to use as the opening sentence of a paragraph of from 100 to 150 words. The way each sentence is worded shows you what the topic of the paragraph is to be. Think over the topic and decide what specific details you will use to develop it in your paragraph. Write the paragraph on scratch paper first. After revising this first draft, copy it in ink on theme paper. Hand in both your first draft and the revision.

(If none of the suggested topics interests you, use one of your own; or change one of the topics so that it does interest you.)

1 Being a baby sitter is not always an easy job.
2 You can tell quite a bit about people's character by the way they dress.
3 If I were a dog, I'd hate to live in a city.
4 Miss _____, my history teacher, has a fine sense of humor.
5 I never let bad weather interfere with my plans, as some people do.
6 Many high-school students don't know how to study.
7 Last week I learned the importance of "A stitch in time saves nine."
8 High school is more interesting than junior high.
9 Being the baby of the family is not always an advantage.
10 A bargain is not always a bargain.

A GOOD PARAGRAPH
STICKS TO THE TOPIC

All of us joke about the absent-minded professor—the fellow who is so intent on a particular thought that he does such ridiculous things as leaving the house wearing a black shoe and a brown one, or walking through a heavy rain with his umbrella under his arm instead of over his head. No wonder we tell jokes about him.

Yet many of us could learn a lesson from the professor, a lesson on the value of *sticking to the main thought*—especially in writing paragraphs. The professor doesn't let even a heavy downpour distract his mind from his thoughts on a particular topic. But many of us seem unable to keep our minds on a particular topic even for the length of a paragraph.

Has this ever happened to you? You start writing a paragraph, fully intending to make a certain topic clear to your readers. You write two or three sentences that are closely related to the topic. And then, suddenly, a word you have written reminds you of something else—and you veer off the main topic into something that has no connection with it. Your paragraph turns out something like this:

> Girls differ widely in their ideas about what types of boys are the most desirable dates. Some girls will not go out with a boy unless he is good-looking, has a good line, and knows the latest dance steps. Any fellow who is really interested can learn to do the latest dances. Even if he can't afford to take lessons at Arthur Murray's, there is always someone who would be willing to teach him. They wouldn't even have to have a lot of records, because they could always turn on the radio to a disk-jockey program. The disk jockeys all keep up with the latest hit tunes. . . .

What a confusing and disappointing paragraph! The reader is all set to learn what the writer has to say about the different types of boys that girls prefer as dates. And what does he get? Just one type is described. The rest of the paragraph has nothing to do with the topic. Interesting as the reader may find the part about dancing lessons and disk jockeys, it doesn't satisfy his curiosity about the types of boys. *The paragraph is poor because it does not stick to the topic.*

Keeping to the topic. How can you avoid disappointing or confusing your readers with paragraphs that do not stick to the topic? Perhaps the best way is to *plan* your paragraphs carefully beforehand. Before you start writing, figure out not only what main topic you are going to cover in each paragraph, but exactly what details you are going to use to develop that topic.

In other words, *think through* the topics to make sure you know what to do when you start the actual writing. If, for example, the topic of one paragraph is to be the various types of boys that different girls prefer to date, think over the types and sort them out—in your mind or, better, on a sheet of scratch paper. Once you have the types clearly thought out, you can more easily curb any tendency to wander away from the topic while you write. With a plan to guide you, you can turn out a paragraph like this, in which each sentence sticks to the topic:

> Similarly, among girls you will find a wide range of ideas about the kind of boys who are "good dates." Some girls like boys who are attentive and who treat them as if they were fragile creatures. Other girls prefer to date boys who treat them more casually and who will play tennis or go ice-skating with them. Still other girls think a good date is one who shares in common an interest such as dramatics or the school newspaper.—Gladys Jenkins, W. W. Bauer, and Helen Shacter, *Teen-Agers*. Copyright 1954 by Scott, Foresman and Co.

EXERCISE (6) In each of the following paragraphs one sentence that is not closely related to the main topic of the paragraph has been added. Read each paragraph carefully. On a sheet of paper, write (1) the topic presented in each paragraph and (2) the added sentence.

1   The country offers no escape from accidents. In fact, the farm offers an exceptional variety of possible mishaps, some of them with very serious possibilities. Many accidents have resulted from the use of power or horse-drawn machinery. The modern farmer could not get along without tractors and other farm machines, for they have made it possible to produce tremendous crops with a minimum of hired hands. Occasionally the farmer or one of his family is seriously injured by livestock. The danger of infection through cuts or other such injuries is especially great on the farm, and calls for immediate and thorough disinfection, and in many cases an injection of serum to ward off the deadly disease tetanus. Drowning is another serious menace in the country.—Howard E. Brown, *Your Life in a Democracy*. Copyright 1949 by J. B. Lippincott Co., Philadelphia.

2   He [George Washington Carver, a distinguished American scientist] continued to live in the simplest style. Two small rooms in a dormitory, a mile and a half from his laboratory, were all that he ever wanted. Year in and year out he wore the same old alpaca jacket. When it wore out in a new spot, he patched it. Very few young men of today would even know how to sew patches, and most of them would refuse to wear mended clothes except while working around the yard. He patched his own shoes. Every morning he still rose early to go hunting in the woods and fields, returning to his classroom with a few flowers in one hand and a bundle of stocks and weeds in the other. His only love affair came to nothing as a

result of this habit. "I won't play second fiddle to a handful of weeds and flowers," the girl said, and that was the end of the romance.—Alice Cecilia Cooper and Charles A. Palmer, *Twenty Modern Americans.* Copyright 1942 by Harcourt, Brace and Company, Inc., New York.

3   Tools employed by the beaver are as efficient as they are simple. Four curved front teeth are the principal instruments, with the clever forepaws playing second part. These front teeth are some two and one-half inches long, from base to tip, including the part within the jaw. They grow constantly and the cutting edge is replaced as wear occurs, an ideal arrangement for an animal that will bite through a four-inch tree in twenty minutes. Grinding teeth, farther back, complete the dental equipment and are employed to crush the bark before it is swallowed. Beavers never eat fish, fowl, or insects; they are vegetarians.—William Henry Carr, "Beaver, Builder of Empire," in *Natural History Magazine*, September 1938. Copyright 1938 by American Museum of Natural History, New York.

EXERCISE (7) Each of the following numbered items is the main topic for one of the paragraphs in a theme. After each topic are listed five details. Three of these details stick to the topic and should be used in developing the paragraph. The other two are not *closely* related to the topic and should not be used.

On a sheet of paper, copy each topic. Under it, list the three details that should be used in the paragraph to make the topic clear.

1 Topic: Neighborhood pests
    a) The borrowers who forget to return what they borrow
    b) The sloppy ones who let their property get run-down
    c) Many beautiful, well-kept homes in our neighborhood
    d) The back-fence gossipers who criticize everyone else
    e) Attractive fences add to the appearance of the yards
2 Topic: The advantages of shopping at chain stores
    a) Prices usually lower than in small independent stores
    b) Quicker service because shopper helps himself
    c) First grocery chain was started by the A & P Company
    d) Wider selection of brands of canned goods
    e) Tin cans are made mostly of steel
3 Topic: How the average person can help conserve wildlife
    a) Being careful with fire—in parks, forests, and on highways
    b) By not picking or destroying wild flowers
    c) Importance of feeding birds and building homes for them
    d) Song birds that are found in the South
    e) The mystery of migration

4 Topic: The causes of soil waste in our country
   a) Soil from dry plains, prairies, and sandy regions carried away by wind
   b) Soil in hilly regions carried away by heavy rains
   c) Poor farming leads to loss of fertility, making soil worthless
   d) American farmers are interested in scientific farming
   e) Large farms are rare in European countries like Italy
5 Topic: The beneficial results of advertising
   a) Advertising calls attention of people to new products and improved labor-saving devices
   b) By increasing sales, advertising leads to lower prices
   c) TV commercials are improving
   d) Advertising is expensive; total cost ranges between five and six billion dollars a year
   e) Spreads useful information about developments in science and medicine

THE TOPIC SENTENCE

To make it easy for readers to know what topic is going to be discussed in a certain paragraph, writers sometimes begin the paragraph with a **topic sentence**. The topic sentence states the main thought of the paragraph in general terms. For example:

> *This formidable creature [the octopus] has three distinct methods of locomotion.* He can crawl nimbly, like a huge spider, on the bottom or over rocks, with his eight flexible arms moving like walking snakes. He can paddle or swim through the water, using his arms with a kind of rowing motion. But above all, when he is attacking, he can shoot himself backward like a rocket, fifty to a hundred feet, almost faster than the eye can follow him. It seems to be a trick he uses for attack, and it is a tiger's spring—the fastest movement I have seen in the water world.—Victor Berge and Henry Wysham Lanier, *The Pearl Diver*, published by Doubleday & Co., Inc., New York. Copyright 1930 by H. W. Lanier.

Sometimes writers use a topic sentence at the end of a paragraph, to summarize the main thought of that paragraph for the reader before he moves on to the next. For example:

> Think of the things that you use from day to day. You may be awakened in the morning by the ringing of an alarm clock manufactured in New Haven, Connecticut. You wash with

soap that was perhaps made in Cincinnati, Ohio. You may eat cereal that was packed in Iowa, and spread your toast with butter from a dairy in Wisconsin. Your toast is made on an electric toaster manufactured in Schenectady, New York. You eat grapefruit from Florida or drink orange juice from California or pineapple juice from Hawaii. The tin for the cans in which the fruit juice was packed came from Bolivia or Malaya. You may put on a pair of shoes made in St. Louis and a suit made in Chicago. You may ride to school in a bus manufactured in Detroit or on a bicycle made in England. *And so all day long you use things from all corners of the world.*—Lawrence V. Roth and Stillman M. Hobbs, *Your World and You.* Copyright 1954 by Laidlaw Bros., River Forest, Illinois.

Many paragraphs do not have a topic sentence; often the writer can make the main thought of a paragraph clear without expressing the topic in specific words. For example, no one sentence in the following selection states that the paragraph is about the great caution necessary in handling radium. But even without such a sentence, careful readers would easily understand the central idea of the paragraph.

An ounce of it [radium], if carried in a glass tube in a man's hip pocket, would kill the carrier in ten hours. Its rays would destroy bone and tissue alike. The careless handling of even a small quantity—two or three particles the size of the head of a pin—would also cause serious burns. Scientists early learned this, and, ever since, they have taken extreme precautions in handling it. The substance is never kept in even so large a quantity as a gram. Tiny glass tubes are made to hold about twenty-five milligrams each, and these tubes are handled with long pliers in gloved hands. The tray or container for these tubes has lead sides three inches thick.—J. Walker McSpadden, "The Discoverer of Radium," in *How They Blazed the Way.* Copyright 1939 by Dodd, Mead & Co., New York.

23

Using topic sentences. Topic sentences are useful to you in two ways. First, they help you as a reader, since they let you know in a few words the central idea of the paragraphs you read. Second, and more important, they are useful to you as a writer. Writing paragraphs that stick to the topic is not easy, especially for a beginning writer. So while you are learning to write good paragraphs, you will find it helpful to use topic sentences frequently. They will remind you what the central idea of the paragraphs should be and will keep you from straying from the topic while you are writing.

EXERCISE 8 Read each of the following paragraphs, noticing how well the writer has stuck to the topic stated in the topic sentence. Be ready (1) to point out the topic sentence of each paragraph and (2) to tell several of the details the writer uses to make the topic clear.

1   [J. Edgar] Hoover's training program is rigid. It includes lectures by the country's foremost criminal lawyers and psychologists; expert photography; and handling the intricate devices which draw clues from such trivial things as used papers, tool marks, tire tracks, bits of fabric, and even dust. An almost invisible particle of dust found on a crook's clothing may destroy the best-laid alibi. In the FBI laboratories men learn to trace bullets to the very guns which fired them, and to prove their conclusions to skeptical juries. They learn fingerprinting by exploring the smudged and battered fenders and the interior of Beulah, an old car. They practice jujitsu with one another and with Oscar, a beloved dummy which has been thrown by the law more times than any living jail-breaker. They are taught to shoot standing up, lying down, running, from a moving running board at a moving target. And, whether their weapon is an indictment, a microscope, or a gun, they don't miss.—Alice Cecilia Cooper and Charles A. Palmer, *Twenty Modern Americans*. Copyright 1942 by Harcourt, Brace and Company, Inc., New York.

2   I noticed that the [Eskimo] adults trained their children to perform manual tasks, even from very early childhood. I saw boys four to five years of age punching holes in sealskins so as to facilitate the sewing of these when the women were making boots. When a boy reached the age of seven, he would be regarded as old enough to help in lashing crossbars to komatics [sledges], making harpoons, and taking his first lesson in throwing the spear and paddling a kayak. Ten years old, and he would be hunting seals with his father. The girls would start work at an early age also. As soon as they had teeth strong enough, they would learn the best way of softening skins by chewing them. At eight they would be regarded as old enough to help with the fishing.—Bruce D. Campbell, *Where the High Winds Blow*. Copyright 1946 by Charles Scribner's Sons, New York.

3   The camel is a treacherous, bad-tempered creature, with affection for no one. He is always waiting to bite the man who looks after him. He is as revengeful as the elephant and will kill anyone who has ill treated him, if he gets the chance. This he does by catching the victim with his hideous teeth, flinging him on the ground, and then battering him to pulp with a kind

of pad which grows between his front legs, on the breastbone. If a load is badly tied, he will wait till the whole caravan is on the move to throw it. If not watched, he will overeat and give himself such bloat that he is out of commission for days. The Arabs say that when a camel suddenly decides to die on the line of march, he does it from spite.—R. V. C. Bodley, *Wind in the Sahara,* published by Coward-McCann, New York. Copyright 1944 by R. V. C. Bodley.

EXERCISE (9) Choose one of the following topic sentences and write a paragraph that makes the topic clear. Feel free to use any of the details given in the quoted paragraphs in Exercise 8, but state the details *in your own words.* Make sure that every sentence in your paragraph sticks to the idea stated in the topic sentence.

1 The men of the FBI go through a rigorous training program.
2 Eskimo boys and girls are taught to do many jobs that we would consider strange.
3 The camel is not a kindly, even-tempered, willing beast of burden.

IN A GOOD PARAGRAPH
THE THOUGHT IS EASY TO FOLLOW

When you write, one of your main goals should be to make it as easy as possible for your reader to follow the thought in each paragraph. You can achieve this goal if you see to it—

1) That the details in each paragraph are arranged in a "sensible" order
2) That the ideas are linked together in such a way that the reader can move smoothly from one sentence to the next

Let's see exactly what each of these means.

PUTTING DETAILS IN ORDER

Time order. In many paragraphs the most sensible order to use for the details is a time order. Suppose that the topic of a paragraph you are writing is how to make or do something—how to make fudge, for example, or how to tool leather. Unless you present the steps in the order in which they should be done, your paragraph will not be very helpful to the reader. A paragraph with the steps given in a hodgepodge order may seem clear to you, since you already know what to do. But it won't make sense to anyone else. Make it easy for your readers: tell them *first* what they should do first. Then tell the rest of the steps in the right time order.

In paragraphs that tell *what happened,* a time order is the easiest order to follow—not only for your readers, but for you as a writer. After all, whatever incident you are telling about happened in a certain order. First one thing occurred, then another, and still another. What, then, is more natural than to write the details in the order in which they took place?

Order of importance, interest, or difficulty. Now suppose you can't use a time-order arrangement; suppose the details you want to tell have nothing to do with time. For example, you may be writing a paragraph on one of the following topics:

> Nylon has many uses.
> Report cards should be abolished.
> Customers that clerks hate to wait on.

For each of these topics, you have several details to tell: (1) four different uses of nylon, (2) your three reasons for abolishing report cards, or (3) examples of four types of pesky customers.

In what order should you give these details? There is no set answer; the best order to use in such paragraphs is a matter of personal opinion. Most good writers think over the details and arrange them in the order of importance, moving from the detail they think least important to the one they consider most important. Or they use the order of interest, starting with the most commonplace detail and ending with the one they think will most impress the readers. Another commonly used order is to move from the details that are easiest to understand to those that are harder to understand.

EXERCISE (10) Suppose that each of the following numbered items is the topic of a paragraph you are to write. After each topic are listed several details to be used in the paragraph. Copy each topic on a sheet of paper. Below the topic (and indented one inch), list the details in what you consider the most sensible or effective order. Compare lists in class and be ready to give reasons for the order you used.

1 Why my first baby-sitting job was my last
    a) Sleeping soundly while the boys damage the upstairs rooms
    b) Being awakened by the Martins at midnight
    c) Phone call from a Mrs. Martin, mother of two boys, offering me a job

d) Meeting the children and getting instructions for the evening's work
e) Troubles in getting the children to go to bed
f) Settling down in the Martin living room to enjoy favorite TV shows
g) Long streetcar and bus rides to get to Martins' house
h) Falling asleep during a long TV commercial
i) The endless ride home in car driven by an angry and silent Mr. Martin
j) Apologizing to the horrified Martins for what had happened

2 How to wallpaper a room
a) Let filler coat dry thoroughly—a matter of about 24 hours
b) Apply paste to strips of paper (one strip at a time)
c) Fill cracks with plaster of Paris
d) Sandpaper edges of cracks to remove excess plaster
e) Smooth paper with wall brush, slowly working out wrinkles and bumps
f) Brush filler coat over the walls
g) Remove old wallpaper and wash off old paste
h) Paste strips on wall, using plumb line to get them hung straight
i) Cut paper into strips of right length, making sure pattern matches at edges

3 Sure ways to lose friends
a) Be moody or overeager to argue when with them
b) Say mean things about them in their presence
c) Never laugh at the jokes they tell
d) Say mean things about them behind their backs
e) Borrow money often and be slow in returning it
f) Be late for dates with them
g) Break dates with them to go with someone else

4 Qualities of an ideal teen-age student
a) Understands and believes in American democracy
b) Keeps himself and his clothes clean and neat
c) Is a good citizen of his school, community, and country
d) Is free from prejudice and intolerance
e) Faithfully does his school assignments to best of his ability
f) Respects the property of others
g) Assumes responsibility of doing what is expected of him and a little more
h) Coöperates with others in work and in play
i) Is always courteous and polite—in the home, in and out of school
j) Is honest in his dealings with others

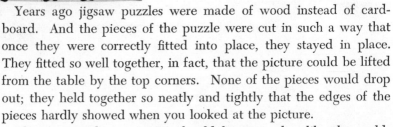

Years ago jigsaw puzzles were made of wood instead of cardboard. And the pieces of the puzzle were cut in such a way that once they were correctly fitted into place, they stayed in place. They fitted so well together, in fact, that the picture could be lifted from the table by the top corners. None of the pieces would drop out; they held together so neatly and tightly that the edges of the pieces hardly showed when you looked at the picture.

The paragraphs you write should be somewhat like these old-fashioned jigsaw pictures. The pieces of the paragraph picture are the details and ideas you put in the sentences to develop the main thought of the paragraph. In order to give the reader a clear picture, you must fit the sentences together neatly, linking one to the other in such a way that there are no gaps or holes in the thought to puzzle the reader.

Direct links. One of the ways to link the sentences together is to use *direct links*—specific connecting words that show how one detail is related to another. Suppose, for example, you were writing a paragraph about how firemen rescued a baby from a flaming house. Many things happened before and during the rescue. And they happened fast, one thing leading to another until the baby was carried out to safety. To give your readers an accurate picture of what occurred, you should, of course, present the ideas in a time order. And to help your readers keep the details straight, you should make use of such connecting words as:

At first . . .	Soon . . .
Then . . .	A little later . . .
Next . . .	Meanwhile . . .
At last . . .	*When* the firemen chopped . . .
After that . . .	Finally . . .
Before long . . .	Afterward . . .

In paragraphs explaining the steps in doing or making something, linking expressions like the following will help your reader follow your thought smoothly from one sentence to the next:

First . . .	In the meantime . . .
Second . . .	*After* sanding the surface . . .
Last . . .	*As soon as* the varnish is dry . . .
At the same time . . .	The *next* step is . . .

And in paragraphs in which you use details giving reasons for an opinion or giving examples or illustrations to make a topic clear, **you** can show the reader how one detail is related to another by using such linking words as these:

For example . . .	However . . .
To begin with . . .	And . . .
But . . .	As a result . . .
On the other hand . . .	In the second place . . .
For this reason . . .	Finally, and most important . . .
In addition . . .	Years ago . . . Now . . .
Also . . .	In spite of this . . .
Therefore . . .	Even so . . .

Keep your reader in mind as you write your paragraphs. You, as the writer, know how your details and ideas are related; you know how one detail leads into another and how one idea grows out of another. But your reader, who doesn't know the topic as you do, may not know *unless you use specific linking words* to show him the connection between one sentence and the preceding or following one.

EXERCISE (11) The sentences in the following groups are linked together by specific connecting words that show how the details are related. On a sheet of paper, write the number of each group. After it, write the direct linking word or words that are used in the group.

Example: Neilsville, like other industrial towns in our state, enjoys prosperity. Years ago very few families in town owned an automobile. Now three out of seven families have two cars, both of recent make.

Linking words: Years ago
Now

1 Obviously something must be done to encourage students to attend these plays. To begin with, the Little Theater Group should cut the admission price for students.

2 Large-scale production brings many advantages to the public. For example, it makes available at a low price many articles that people could not otherwise afford to buy.

3 In contour farming, the furrows and rows run across the slopes of the hills instead of up and down the hillsides. Therefore they form many little dams to hold back the water when it rains. As a result, the water can soak into the ground instead of sliding downhill and washing away the valuable topsoil.

4 Jerry unfolded the letter and began reading. At first he seemed puzzled. Then an angry look came into his eyes. Before long he was sputtering with rage.

5   The parking meters are, I will admit, a nuisance to shoppers, who do not always have change with them. On the other hand, having the meters has kept people from leaving their cars parked for unnecessarily long periods in busy shopping districts.

6   Some materials, such as metals, are better conductors of heat than others. For this reason, metals are used for cooking utensils, stoves, and radiators.

7   Many people and industries play a part in getting your beef roasts to the restaurant owner who serves them to you. First there are the farmers who raised the steers and the cowboys who helped out on the range. Then there are the railroads that transport the cattle to the stockyards.

8   Liquids evaporate at all temperatures, high or low. However, the hotter a liquid becomes, the faster the rate of evaporation.

9   Phil tugged hard at the ladder, trying to lift it so that Bob could crawl free. Meanwhile I ran to the tool shed to get help. A minute later I was back, Mr. Evans only a step behind me.

10   Weather forecasts are far more important than many of us realize. Power companies, for instance, depend on forecasts to inform them of a coming ice storm so they can provide crews to repair wires with a minimum of delay. And farmers in all sections of the country must know the forecasts to determine the best time for harvesting and shipping their crops.

Indirect links. A paragraph in which every sentence is joined to the one before by direct linking words would be tiresome to read. Such a paragraph would not only sound unnatural, but it would be unnatural. Useful as direct linking words are, they are *not* needed for every sentence and should not be used unless they are needed. There is a simpler and more natural way to join sentences together —making use of "indirect" links.

The sentences in the following paragraph, for example, are neatly linked together by the pronoun *He*, which refers, of course, to the "Willie" mentioned in the first two sentences.

> To me the most dangerous character we can find on the highway is Two-Wheel Willie. Willie is always trying to get just a little bit more of a thrill. *He* is usually a first-class show-off. *He* takes all corners on two wheels to see if he can't lean the car just a little bit more without rolling it. *He* takes every risk he can think of and then some. *He* is usually the one involved in a drag or some other game which involves risk to him, to his car, and to others.—Harold Schlachtenhaufen, "Trail Threats," in *The Wooden Horse*, No. 1, 1957. Sponsored by Quill and Scroll, East High School, Waterloo, Iowa.

Another effective way to link sentences together is to repeat an important, or *key*, word from sentence to sentence, as in the following paragraph:

> While it is true that I cannot walk a block from my home free of any *rule*, it is also true that I cannot sit down to eat without profiting by *rules*. A farmer, a laborer in a meat-packing plant, and a clerk in the corner grocery store all must obey *rules*— *rules* that are enforced to assure me of the purity and quality of my breakfast bacon. An insurance company obeys *rules* that are designed to protect my home and the security of my dependents. A worker in an automobile plant and a tire manufacturer obey *rules* that contribute to the safety of my wife and boy when we're going around the sharp curve on the road to Grandma's.—Hudson Nix, "I Like to Obey the Rules." Reprinted from THIS WEEK *Magazine*. Copyright 1940 by the United Newspapers Magazine Corporation.

Often instead of repeating a key word itself, a synonym is used or a word that has a similar meaning. Notice how the writers of the following paragraph tie the sentences together by referring constantly to the "gangsters" mentioned in the topic sentence. They use both synonyms and pronouns.

> Early in the hand-to-hand battle with the *gangsters*, J. Edgar Hoover had sensed a strange thing. These cruel, ruthless *murderers* whom he was bringing to justice were public heroes! *Their* names and deeds got big, black headlines in the papers because the people wanted to learn more about *them*. Movies glorified *them*. Admiring stories were written about *them*. The public was actually thinking of *these sneaking robbers and murderers* as modern Robin Hoods.—Alice Cecilia Cooper and Charles A. Palmer, *Twenty Modern Americans*. Copyright 1942 by Harcourt, Brace and Company, Inc., New York.

By using these indirect links to join the sentences, the writers make it easy for readers to follow the main thought of the paragraph from beginning to end. When you write your paragraphs, try to make it as easy for your readers to go from sentence to sentence without losing track of the main thought. You can do this by providing indirect links to hold the sentences together in a simple, natural way.

EXERCISE (12) The sentences in the following groups are held together by indirect links: a pronoun (like *he*, *they*, *those*, *some*, *several*, *one*, etc.), a repetition of a key word, the use of a synonym of a key

31

word. On a sheet of paper, write the number of each group. After it, write the word or words providing the indirect links for the sentences.

Example: There are many kinds of deserts. Some, like the Sahara, are very hot. Others, like the vast treeless plains of the Arctic Zone, are exceedingly cold.
Indirect links: Some
Others

1 Unfortunately, Mrs. Blair's favorite pastime was criticizing her neighbors. Criticism, if it is meant kindly and is constructive, can be valuable. Mrs. Blair's criticism was not meant to be kind.

2 It was ten hours later, and the rain still showed no signs of abating. The torrent came pouring down, harder than ever. The downpour turned the creeks into rivers and the streets into canals.

3 The writer of the article about juvenile delinquency acts as if all young people were the same. Teen-agers are individuals, each different from the other. Not all youngsters are as irresponsible and troublesome as the writer seems to think.

4 Martha spent her whole allowance on a silver fountain pen for her dad. He would have been just as pleased with a two-dollar can opener. A mechanical device always fascinates him.

5 Ten or twelve women were crowded around the entrance. The little group had been waiting patiently and silently since news of the cave-in had broken. Their silent wait continued through the night and well into the next day.

6 A person could live for a month without food. Without water, he could not live for more than three or four days. Without oxygen, he could not live for more than seven minutes.

7 During his first year at Lincoln High, Gerald won a college scholarship, broke two track records, won a tennis award, and was elected president of his class. These achievements would have made most boys conceited. They did not seem to impress Gerald as important or unusual. He kept on being as modest, friendly, and democratic as ever.

8 Many of my friends have interesting and rewarding hobbies. Several are interested in photography and have won prizes in various contests. One raises rabbits, many of which he sells to an experimental laboratory at the college. Another collects autographs of authors and jazz musicians. He has been offered as much as twenty dollars for one of the autographs and five dollars for another.

EXERCISE (13) The sentences in each of the following paragraphs have been put in a hodgepodge order. Read the sentences and decide in what order they would have to be arranged so that the main thought could easily be followed. Copy the paragraphs on a sheet of paper, putting the sentences in the right order. Then draw a circle around all the direct linking words and the indirect links that you can find to show that the order you used is the order the writers used.

1. (a) At six and seven, young Bobby Feller talked about becoming a ballplayer the way other kids talk about growing up to be a fireman, a cop, a cowboy. (b) Bob still has the essay. (c) When Bobby was three years old, the farmhouse began to fill up with all the books on baseball that Bill Feller could buy. (d) At eight, when asked to write an essay about a tree, the Feller boy's words told how an oak could be made into home plate.—Jack Sher, "Bill Feller's Boy." Copyright © 1947 by The American Legion. By permission of the author.

2. (a) If he finishes the job, he will have each size of every kind in a little box by itself. (b) Then he will go back and separate the square-cut, iron nails from the round steel ones, after which he will make separate piles for each size, from the little twopenny fellows up to the big twentypenny spikes. (c) And one of the rainy-day jobs for the farm boy is to sit down beside such a box and sort out its contents. (d) Around any carpenter shop there is likely to be a box into which all sorts of odd nails, tacks, screws, nuts, and bolts are tossed. (e) Probably he will start by throwing all the nails into one pile, the screws into another, and so on.—Paul Bigelow Sears, "No Two Are Alike," in *Who Are These Americans?* Copyright 1939. Used with the permission of The Macmillan Company, New York.

3. (a) It means that you must be careful in the excitement of an English game not to shout out remarks which everyone in America would understand but which the British might think insulting. (b) In America the crowd would probably shout, "Take him out!" (c) If a fielder misses a catch at cricket, the spectators will shout, "Good try," even if it looks to you like a bad fumble. (d) This contrast should be remembered. (e) The Briton's character is clearly seen at sports contests. (f) The English crowds at football or cricket matches are more orderly and more polite than American fans.—*A Short Guide to Britain*, prepared by the United States Office of Armed Forces Information and Education, Department of Defense, Washington 25, D.C.

4   [Note: The "prisoner" in this paragraph is a cat that had been trapped in a broken barrel over which sand had been piled by the wind.]   (a) For three days the prisoner kept up her intermittent appeals for help.   (b) When she withdrew it again, the hole was considerably enlarged.   (c) Eagerly the cat stuck her paw through the hole.   (d) On the third day the wind changed, and presently blew up a gale.   (e) She took the hint and fell to scratching.   (f) In a few hours it had uncovered the barrel.   (g) At one corner a tiny spot of light appeared. (h) At first her efforts were rather aimless; but presently, whether by good luck or quick sagacity, she learned to make her scratching more effective.   (i) The opening rapidly enlarged, and she squeezed her way out.—Sir Charles G. D. Roberts, "How a Cat Played Robinson Crusoe," in *Neighbors Unknown*.   Copyright 1911, 1938 by The Macmillan Company, New York.   By permission of the author.

5   (a) When you did, you found that there were three things involved that were not involved in the spoken language. (b) Sometime between the age of four and eight, you began to try to learn for yourself the secret of writing.   (c) The next step was learning how to combine these separate letters to form pictures of the noises known as words.   (d) You found that this process was called "spelling."   (e) First, you had to learn how to make the little individual marks that were called letters. (f) This involved things called sentence structure (or grammar) and punctuation.   (g) You discovered that these letters, of which there were twenty-six in all, were called the alphabet. (h) Then, after you had learned to make the letters and form the words, you had to learn to put the words down on paper in such a way that they would say exactly what you meant. (i) These three things you had to learn and master, if you were to be able to use the written language to your advantage.— Eloise Lambert, *Our Language*.   Copyright 1955 by Lothrop, Lee & Shepard Co., Inc., New York.

EXERCISE 14   Choose one of the following topics (or substitute one of your own) as the topic for a paragraph of from 150 to 200 words.   As you write, refer to the three main points summarized on the next page.

1   The importance of patience in getting along with people
2   How to *use*—not *waste*—leisure time
3   Advertisements that promise the impossible
4   Learning from our mistakes
5   A secret ambition
6   Apologizing without using words

The main points in this chapter can be summarized in very brief form:

1 **A good paragraph makes the topic clear.**
You can make the topic of each paragraph clear to the reader by supplying enough specific, concrete details to show him exactly what you mean.

2 **A good paragraph sticks to the topic.**
Thinking through a topic *before* you start writing will keep you from including sentences that have nothing to do with the topic. Expressing the main thought in a topic sentence will help you stick to the topic while writing.

3 **In a good paragraph the thought is easy to follow.**
To make it easy for your reader to follow the thought, present the details in a sensible order, and use direct linking words and indirect links to tie the sentences together.

This summary, like the chapter, emphasizes the importance of keeping the reader in mind when you write. Writing is for the reader; you write to make your ideas clear to others. The ideas in your paragraphs will be clear if you stick to the topic and use enough details, neatly linking them together in the right order.

EXERCISE (15) Exchange the paragraph you wrote for Exercise 14 with that of a classmate. Read his paragraph carefully. On a sheet of paper, write the answers to the following questions. Then return the paragraph, with your answers, to the owner.

1 What is the topic of the paragraph? Is the topic specifically stated in a sentence? If so, what is the sentence? Does it come at the beginning or end of the paragraph?

2 Do all the sentences stick to the topic? Which, if any, do not?

3 Do you think the writer has used enough details to make the topic clear? Would you like more details? Of what kind?

4 Did you find it easy or hard to follow the thought from sentence to sentence? What direct linking words and indirect links did the writer use to tie the sentences?

5 What suggestions can you make that would help the writer improve the paragraph?

CHAPTER 2

CLEAR

THINKING

"The only good Indian is a dead Indian." These words, or words very similar to them, have been uttered time after time on television by a type of rugged frontier character we are all familiar with. We learn during the course of the program that when this character was a little boy his parents had been scalped in front of his eyes by five Indians. From that moment on, his life is devoted to punishing "bad" Indians—which to him means *all* Indians. Of course as the program ends, he is shown his mistake by a band of obviously "good" Indians, who rescue him from the hands of some murderous white claim jumpers, take him to the tribal camp, nurse him back to health, and send him safely home. He sees at last that Indians differ just as much from one another as white men do. Unfortunately, before he learns this lesson, he has killed a number of innocent Indian bystanders.

Like this frontier character, many people permit certain experiences to influence their thinking in a mistaken way about a great variety of things. For example, they think that all policemen, all

bank presidents, all Negroes, Catholics, Jews, Baptists, Englishmen, Puerto Ricans, and so on, are exactly alike. They see all housing developments as identical with the one development in which they once lived. They think that all politicians are crooked, because one or two politicians they have known or heard about were crooked. Having had a strict, crabby teacher in the first grade, they never get over the notion that all teachers are strict and crabby—even though every teacher they have had since has been pleasant and understanding. And a long time ago, a good many people who had been told that the world was "flat" found it difficult to believe otherwise, even after several explorers had sailed *around* it.

This kind of mistaken thinking is widespread. Even people who are on their guard against it get trapped by it sometimes. A very important part of a person's education, then, is learning what traps to avoid in thinking. Just as important are the aids a person can use to help himself think clearly. The most essential aids are facts. All clear thinking begins with them.

IS THAT A FACT?

When someone says, "The survival of the human race depends on science," we are all likely to nod our heads in solemn agreement. At the mention of the word *science*, we visualize chemistry laboratories with rack after rack of shining test tubes, or smoking factories and mills, or great medical centers filled with white-clad researchers and doctors. We deeply respect science because in all of its activities it is based on *facts*, we commonly think. And we are right; science *is* based on facts. But how many of us stop to consider what facts are? And how many of us try to use facts in our own, everyday lives as skillfully as scientists do in their laboratories?

A fact is a thing or event that people agree has been or now is. It may be a person, place, or process that people see, hear, feel, taste, or smell. To the frontiersman it was a fact that five Indians had killed his parents; he had seen them do it. To you it is a fact that you live in a certain building on a certain street, attend a certain school, and have certain physical characteristics; you have observed these things for as long as you can remember. The Empire State Building is a fact because millions of people have seen it and agree that it exists. It is also a fact that on Saturday morning, July 28, 1945, a fogbound B-25 Mitchell bomber crashed into the 79th floor of the Empire State Building; this event was observed by reliable people who recorded it in writing and pictures. No one disagreed about the circumstances of the accident. No reliable witness declared that it was the RCA Building, or that it was a B-29 instead of a B-25.

In other words, we recognize something as a fact when we have observed it ourselves and/or when people agree generally that it exists or has existed.

Facts are vital. They comprise what we call knowledge. Our frontier character knew one fact when he saw it: five Indians had scalped his parents. There was no doubt about it. But even though he started his career of revenge with this fact firmly in mind, he went wrong. Why?

KINDS OF STATEMENTS

"Now, what I want is Facts. Teach these boys and girls nothing but Facts. Facts alone are wanted in life."
"In this life, we want nothing but Facts, Sir."

These statements, with which many people would heartily agree, were made by Thomas Gradgrind, a leading character in Dickens's novel *Hard Times*. Gradgrind served as a school superintendent— a mean one, as his name suggests. In the course of the novel, his demand for facts, and nothing but facts, from his scholars landed him in a lot of trouble.

Like many people today, Gradgrind had to learn the hard way that important as facts are, mere facts alone will not do anybody much good. Nothing but facts is hardly better than nothing at all. In order to be *useful*, facts must be thought about and talked about.

When we talk about facts, our statements are generally of two kinds—(1) statements-of-fact, and (2) statements of opinion. On the surface, these two kinds of statements often seem to be identical. Actually, however, they are quite different. Unless we know the difference between them, we will not be able to talk, listen, write, or read intelligently.

STATEMENTS-OF-FACT

A **statement-of-fact** is a statement that can be proved true or false. It is a statement about something that can be or has been observed. Everyone who reads or hears a statement-of-fact will agree on what its words mean. But often there will be disagreement about whether the statement-of-fact is true or false. Each of the following four sentences is a statement-of-fact; each is verifiable:

Centerville City Hall is surrounded by elms.
Centerville City Hall is surrounded by oaks.

The Pirates won the National League pennant in 1958.
The Braves won the National League pennant in 1958.

Obviously, one sentence in each pair is definitely false. Both sentences may be false. One may be true. Yet all four are statements-of-fact because they *can be proved true or false.*

It is important to note that a *fact* and a *statement*-of-fact are not the same thing. Facts are so important today and so widely respected that many people accept anything having to do with facts as automatically true. This is a mistake. Facts themselves are neither true nor false; they either exist or do not exist, existed or did not exist. The Empire State Building is either there, or it is not there. A *statement*-of-fact, on the other hand, *is* either true or false. It can be *proved* true or false by checking to see whether the facts it tells about exist or do not exist, existed or did not exist.

39

Whether a statement-of-fact is true or false is, of course, very important. Suppose, for example, that someone tells us these statements-of-fact:

"Your new neighbor is a convicted arsonist."

"Your father's 'new' car is actually a second-hand one. The dealer turned back the mileage and painted the tires."

"None of the other history teachers gives as much homework as Mr. Wood does."

We cannot brush aside statements like these. If they are true, it may be important to us to do something about them. If they are false, we will not want to accept them blindly and take some kind of foolish action based on them.

CHECKING STATEMENTS-OF-FACT

The truth or falseness of statements-of-fact can be checked in two general ways. Suppose, for example, that someone tells us, "The Bon Ton is selling $10 sweaters for $5.98 today" or "That first-base line is two feet shorter than the third-base line." We can check the truth of these statements-of-fact by *direct personal observation*. We can hop on a bus and go directly to the store to see for ourselves if the report is true; we can measure the base lines with a tape.

The same is true with a statement like "Chameleons change color according to the color of their surroundings." We can get a chameleon—or, preferably, several—and experiment to see under what circumstances they do or do not change color. There is no more reliable proof or disproof than this. This *direct* method is the basic one used by a scientist in his laboratory.

If it is inconvenient or impossible for us to experiment with statements-of-fact like the one about chameleons, we can still check the statements for truth. We can refer to reports of reliable people who have made the observations. A good place in which to look for these reports is a library. Its encyclopedias contain articles on chameleons, and we can probably find a book or two on lizards for more detailed reports. This is an example of the *indirect* method of checking the truth of statements-of-fact.

The indirect method is especially useful in checking statements-of-fact about the past. If we have a misinformed friend who insists that the Pittsburgh Pirates won the National League pennant in 1958, we cannot take him back to observe the pennant race and discover his error for himself; as yet, time machines exist only in

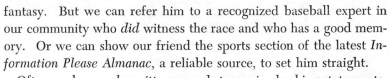

fantasy. But we can refer him to a recognized baseball expert in our community who *did* witness the race and who has a good memory. Or we can show our friend the sports section of the latest *Information Please Almanac*, a reliable source, to set him straight.

Often we have *only* written records to use in checking statements-of-fact. None of us can go back to Gettysburg on November 19, 1863, to see if Lincoln really did give his famous address on that day. But none of us doubts it either. Many people who *were* in Gettysburg that day have left us records of the event—in diaries, letters, newspapers, and other written reports of various kinds. In checking these records, we find that they agree on the date of the address and that Lincoln himself did give it. Therefore we accept the statement that "Lincoln made the Gettysburg Address on November 19, 1863" as a true statement-of-fact.

Few of us can blast off into space with the latest rocket or missile. But we can read about space exploration in the reports of rocket experts and reliable journalists. As we compare their reports, we usually notice that they agree on many or most statements-of-fact. We then accept these statements as true. If the experts make conflicting statements-of-fact, we must wait for more evidence before deciding which are true.

On the basis of this indirect method, we are able to check and make use of countless facts reported by men since the invention of writing—without having to observe the facts for ourselves. That is why the indirect method of checking statements-of-fact is so important today. It is also, incidentally, one reason why teachers constantly urge students to do more than the minimum amount of reading.

41

Our frontier character, of course, did not need to use this indirect method. He had observed the scalping for himself. We shall have to look elsewhere for his mistake.

EXERCISE (1) Imagine that you have heard or read the following statements-of-fact. They may be true, or they may be false; you do not know, but you would like to find out. On a sheet of paper, write the number of each statement. After each number, tell in complete sentences what steps you would take to check the truth of the statement *directly* for yourself.

Example: Joe can't sit still when he hears calypso records.
            I would play some calypso records and watch Joe to see whether he can sit still or not.

1   Cats eat catnip.
2   Red paint plus blue paint equals brown paint.

3　Hap Bell has replaced Marty James on the Teen-Hop show.

4　There's a man down on Oak Street selling midget missiles that really work.

5　If you handle a toad, you get warts.

6　Charles Sweetland has a sea story in the May *Boys' Life*.

7　Even when filled with water, a rowboat will not sink.

8　You can't get FM beyond those hills west of town.

9　Dusty buried the purse just north of the rosebush in the back yard.

10　The Ajax Auto Supply Company has a new tire that is guaranteed never to blow out.

11　If pressed with a hot iron, rayon fabric will shrivel.

12　The path of a boomerang is elliptical.

EXERCISE (**2**)　Some of the following statements-of-fact are true, and some are false.　All must be checked by the indirect method.　Check each statement by consulting an encyclopedia or an almanac, as indicated in the brackets after each statement.　Use any one of three encyclopedias: *World Book*, *Compton's*, or *Britannica Junior*; and either the *World* or the *Information Please* almanac.　On a sheet of paper, write "True" after the number of each true statement-of-fact.　Correct and rewrite the false statements.

1　The third President of the United States was Andrew Jackson. [Encyclopedia.]

2　The first submarine ever to pass under the North Pole was the *Nautilus*.　[Almanac.]

3　Adolf Hitler died in a bunker at his mountain hide-out during one of the last air raids of World War II.　[Encyclopedia.]

4　Scientists cannot make protoplasm.　[Encyclopedia.]

5　It has been proved that Spanish agents were responsible for the destruction of the battleship *Maine*, an event which touched off the Spanish-American War.　[Encyclopedia.]

6　Sculptured on Mount Rushmore in the Black Hills of South Dakota are the heads of Washington, Jefferson, Lincoln, and Franklin Roosevelt.　[Almanac.]

7　Maxwell Anderson won the Nobel prize for literature in 1936. [Almanac.]

8　In 1956 Brooklyn won the National League pennant and the World Series.　[Almanac.]

9　English is classified as a Germanic, or Teutonic, language.　[Encyclopedia.]

10　The Hall of Fame for great Americans is in Washington, D.C., two blocks east of the Lincoln Memorial.　[Encyclopedia.]

A **statement of opinion**, unlike a statement-of-fact, can *not* be proved either true or false. It is a personal reaction to facts, usually an expression of approval or disapproval. Let's take a simple example:

"Vanilla ice cream is better than chocolate ice cream."

A person making this statement is expressing his opinion about two kinds of ice cream. Before making the statement, he had to have some facts at hand, of course: vanilla and chocolate ice cream exist; they have different flavors. Then, after tasting the two, he found that the vanilla pleased him more than the chocolate. So, to him, the vanilla is "better" than the chocolate.

Now if we consider this opinion carefully, we see that it cannot be proved true or false. The word "better"—the opinion word—does not state any fact about ice cream; it simply expresses the speaker's attitude. Some people will agree that vanilla ice cream is "better," and others will not. And some people do not like either vanilla *or* chocolate. Even if we could take a vote among all the people who eat ice cream, the result would not prove that one flavor is "better" than the other. It would simply show that one flavor is more popular among the voters than the other.

Statements like the one we have been considering are the simplest kind of opinion that we can give. They express approval or disapproval of something, based solely on the way we feel about it. In our example, the word *better* expressed the person's approval of vanilla ice cream. Some other opinion words like *better* are *good*, *bad*, *pleasant*, *unpleasant*, *best*, *satisfactory*, *poor*, and *great*. Statements of opinion that contain words of approval or disapproval like these are often called judgments.

Other statements of opinion say that something is an obligation or is desirable. These statements contain words like *should*, *ought to*, and *must*. If we say, for example, "High-school students should take mathematics," our statement is an opinion and cannot be proved true or false. Why? Because it is based on our judgment that mathematics is "good" for high-school students. But that too is an opinion and cannot be proved true or false. Not everyone will agree that high-school students should take mathematics, because not everyone will agree that mathematics is "good" for high-school students. In fact, some people might even argue that mathematics isn't "good" for anybody!

Predictions are a third kind of opinion. Predictions contain such words as *will*, *shall*, and *is sure to*. Statements containing these

43

words are opinions because we have no way now of seeing, hearing, smelling, tasting, or touching events in the future. Therefore, we have no way of knowing *for sure* that the events will occur. We cannot even be sure, for example, that the sun will rise tomorrow. The chances are overwhelmingly in favor of its rising, of course, but there is always the slight chance that it will not. It could blow up tonight. The odds against an oyster egg's growing to maturity are approximately 2,000,000 to 1. Yet, obviously, many oyster eggs do grow to maturity. The odds against human quintuplet births are about 54,000,000 to 1. Yet quintuplets are born despite the odds. Nine people out of ten may predict that our team will win this Saturday. These are pretty good odds. Yet, if quints can be born, the team *could* lose—despite the odds.

EXERCISE (3) The ability to distinguish between a statement-of-fact and a statement of opinion is a key to clear thinking. Yet many people confuse the two kinds of statements. These people tend to accept as a statement-of-fact any opinion that sounds important or agrees closely with what they already think. In other words, they let their hopes or prejudices trap them into accepting as true or false something that cannot be proved true or false.

To sharpen your own skill in distinguishing between statements of opinion and statements-of-fact, study the following sentences carefully. Fourteen of them are statements of opinion; six are statements-of-fact. On a sheet of paper, write the number of each statement and the kind of statement that it is. (Write "Statement of opinion" or "Statement-of-fact.") Be ready to explain why you classify the statements as you do.

1 Every student should have a part-time job.
2 Liver may not taste good, but it's good for you.
3 Russian dentists are smarter than American dentists.
4 Russian dentists use stainless steel for filling teeth.
5 Children learn many valuable lessons from games.
6 "I must go down to the seas again. . . ."—Masefield
7 The doctor will be there in five minutes, Mrs. Harper.
8 Sue is 5 feet 2 inches tall, weighs 105 pounds, has blond hair, brown eyes, freckles, and a Southern accent.
9 Sue is cute.
10 Our rent is high.
11 Our six-room furnished apartment rents for $110 a month.
12 Jim wasted his money on a sleazy flannel jacket.
13 You should take a serious interest in student government.
14 The doctor has given Jones six months to live.

15 Jones will die within six months.
16 Mom is the best cook in the world.
17 Boy Scouts make the best leaders.
18 Last night Ed's scout troop broke six chairs in the basement.
19 On June 15, 1957, Scout I. W. Washington of Troop 432, Houston, Texas, rescued six children from a flaming apartment.
20 "People do not deserve to have good writing, they are so pleased with bad."—Emerson

THE IMPORTANCE OF OPINIONS

It may seem that, since opinions cannot be proved true or false, they are not very important. Actually, however, they are. They are important for at least two reasons: (1) They are indispensable in our thinking, speaking, and writing. (2) They are indispensable when we have to make decisions about matters for which we have no facts.

1) We cannot do without statements of opinion in our thinking, speaking, and writing. Even if we could, we would not want to. How poverty-stricken our conversation would be if we could not praise (or condemn) a team despite its record and the odds on next Saturday's game. How unpersuasive election campaigns would be if we had to stick strictly to statements-of-fact in building up our candidate and could not even tell people they "should" vote for him. How dull our letters, book reports, and papers of all kinds would be without our judgments of the present and our predictions of things to come.

2) To help us make decisions, we often seek out expert opinions on matters for which we do not have the facts. Before scheduling a picnic on a certain day, we consult the weather forecast (a prediction). Before deciding to undergo surgery, we seek out a doctor's advice and accept his judgment about our case. When choosing a summer camp we have never visited, we consult, in an interview or through reading, the opinions of others who have the facts about camps we are interested in. When we want to know the best way to reach a destination, we rely on the opinions of others who have tried various routes.

The only catch in using opinions in thinking, speaking, and writing and in reaching decisions is that the opinions must be *sound*. Sound opinions are opinions that are backed up with adequate facts. If we can support our opinions with adequate facts, people will rely on them. If we cannot support them with adequate facts, people will reject them. And, for our own protection, we must have some way of evaluating the opinions of others.

Making our opinions sound. Here is a headline similar to one we could find in almost any newspaper any summer:

BOY BUMPS HEAD; DROWNS

In reading the story, we learn that the victim dived into a strange pond, cracked his skull on a submerged rock, and drowned. And, if we think a moment, we realize that the boy was the victim of an unsound opinion. He evidently dived into the strange pond *feeling* that it was perfectly safe to do so, but without checking to see if his opinion was sound.

We resolve, therefore, not to make the same mistake the next time *we* go for a swim in the country. We will gather facts about the depth of the water, possible submerged rocks, hidden currents, and the like. These precautions will take time and effort, and they will delay our fun, but they will make our opinion about the safety of diving into the pond *sound*. They will *not* make it *foolproof*. We may miss some facts in our survey—the presence of impetigo staphylococci, for example. But by gathering all the facts we can before forming our opinion, we will make it worth a great deal more, both to ourselves *and to anyone else who is depending on it*.

Now consider the sad case of Joe Baxter, who went home from a meeting of the Varsity Club feeling hurt and silly. During a discussion of the best place to hold the club's spring banquet, everyone but Joe favored a new restaurant that had recently opened in town. Joe was against it. But when his fellow athletes asked him why, he said only, "I know we shouldn't; that's all. We wouldn't like it; that's all." Unimpressed by this argument, the club members voted 38 to 1 in favor of the restaurant.

This is a very sad story because, of all the fellows in the club, Joe alone had eaten at the new restaurant. The other fellows wanted to banquet there simply because it was new. Only Joe knew the sad facts: He had had to put his coat and hat over a chair because the single clothes tree had been filled. Prices for ordinary customers —not banqueters—were at a $3 minimum. Three waitresses took care of thirty-six tables. Joe had waited forty minutes for his meal. His meat was burned. The potatoes were cold. His ice cream had ice in it. And his parents had had similar experiences the two times that they had tried the restaurant.

This story is even sadder because Joe *had* a sound opinion. But he did not *make* it sound to the fellows in the Varsity Club. All he needed to do was to support his opinion by telling the fellows the facts of his and his parents' experiences. Why didn't he? Only Joe knows, but it looks like a case of cowardice. Everyone was against him, so his nerve failed.

Evaluating the opinions of others.   In addition to making our opinions as sound as possible, we must check the opinions of others to see whether they are as sound as possible. If they are, we can accept them and use them to help us make decisions. If they are unsound, we can reject them. To check the soundness of an opinion that we have heard or read, we should consider these three things about it: (1) the *facts* on which it is based, (2) the *authority* of the person who spoke or wrote it, and (3) the amount of his *self-interest*.

1) "Mr. Perez is a better Spanish teacher than Mrs. Smith." Before we accept an opinion like this and decide to try to get the "better" teacher, we should ask the speaker what facts he has to support his opinion. If he gives such a vague answer as "Oh, I don't know—Mr. Perez just seems nicer than Mrs. Smith," his opinion is not very worth while. It is certainly not a good basis for trying to get into Mr. Perez's class and avoid Mrs. Smith's. But if the person gives us adequate facts to back up his opinion, then we can take it seriously. Such facts might be these:

47

MR. PEREZ	MRS. SMITH
Has ten years of teaching experience	Has two years of teaching experience
Gives students individual help after school	Does not give students any individual help
Always arrives on time for class and always presents a complete lesson	Is often late for classes and often dismisses her classes early
Is a native of Mexico and was educated there	Has never visited a Spanish-speaking country

2) "The Wildcats are sure to win this Saturday." If we are Wildcat fans, it may seem almost treason to question such a prediction when we read it in the sports section of our favorite paper. But, as we have already seen, no prediction is 100 per cent foolproof, much as we might like it to be. We can say, however, that the prediction is *sound* and *reliable* if the person making it is an *authority* on the subject. Is he a person who has had considerable training and experience in sports? Does he know the facts about the Wildcats and their opponents? Does he compare the win and loss records of the two teams for the past few seasons? The skills and records of the

various players? The odds quoted by other professional sports writers? If, instead of writing authoritatively about the two teams, he bases his opinion-prediction merely on how he feels about them, we would be foolish to put much confidence in it.

3) "The Democrats are ruining the country." If a Republican candidate says this in the heat of a campaign, we can dismiss it almost automatically as an unsound opinion. We can do the same if a Democratic candidate says that the Republicans are ruining the country. A candidate of any political party will gain much personal advantage if he can convince us that everything his party does is good for the country and everything his opponents do is bad. It is the same with sales of all sorts. It is in the salesman's own *self-interest* to convince us that his product is the best we can possibly buy. His commission will rise if we accept uncritically *his* words of praise for *his* product. If he is trying to sell us a camera, for example, we should be skeptical of his calling it "the most beautiful camera made," "the choice of professionals," and "a real bargain." But if, on the other hand, he gives some facts about the camera, if he explains carefully the kind of pictures we can take with it and how it compares in cost and performance with other cameras, then we can take his opinion seriously. After comparing it with the opinions and supporting facts of other camera salesmen, we can make our decision.

Note: There is, of course, self-interest in almost any statement of opinion. Even the person who tells us that vanilla ice cream is "better" than chocolate would be happy if we accepted his opinion. It is the *amount* of self-interest in *important* statements of opinion that we have to watch out for. We should stop to consider the purpose of the person expressing the opinion. If his only or primary interest is in what *he* stands to gain from our accepting his opinion, it would be foolish to base a decision on his opinion alone. On the other hand, if in spite of some measure of self-interest, a person can back up his opinion with statements-of-fact that can be verified, then his opinion is well worth considering seriously.

Our frontier character had the opinion that all Indians were bad. To support his opinion, he could point to the fact that five Indians had scalped his parents. We can now begin to see where his thinking went wrong. Were his facts *adequate*? Isn't there a considerable difference between *five* Indians and *all* Indians?

EXERCISE (4) Each of the following numbered statements-of-fact summarizes a large number of facts. The first one, for example, summarizes the facts that high school A, high school B, high school C, and so on, offer at least one foreign language. Assume that the numbered statements-of-fact are true. Each of them is followed by two statements of opinion (*a* and *b*). Decide which statement of opinion seems to be the sounder. It will be the one that is better supported by the statement-of-fact. Be ready to explain your choice in class.

1 Most high schools in the United States offer at least one foreign language.
   a) Most high-school graduates in the United States speak at least one foreign language fluently.
   b) The study of a foreign language is a valuable part of a person's education.

2 Penicillin and other newly discovered drugs have reduced the number of deaths from pneumonia.
   a) Penicillin is remarkably effective in fighting flu.
   b) The discoverers of penicillin were great servants of man.

3 An Austin A35 costs $1465 and gets 45 miles per gallon; a Volkswagen Deluxe costs $1495 and gets 32 miles per gallon.
   a) Advertising should stress the economy of buying and operating an Austin.
   b) Everyone ought to buy an Austin.

4 Americans, on the average, are taller today than they were fifty years ago.
   a) Clothmakers should be doing better business now than they were fifty years ago.
   b) Americans are better basketball players today than they were fifty years ago.

5 The majority of fatal highway accidents are due, directly or indirectly, to speeding.
   a) Speeding is unethical.
   b) People who do not speed will not be involved in fatal highway accidents.

6 Millions of copies of Hemingway's books have been sold.
   a) Hemingway is a good writer.
   b) Hemingway is a popular writer.

7 Carrots contain vitamin A, which is essential to developing night sight.
   a) People who eat carrots will have good night sight.
   b) Carrots are better for one's health than leafy vegetables.

8 Cigarette smoking impedes the night sight of drivers.
   a) A person should not smoke while driving at night.
   b) It is all right to smoke while driving at night if you eat a carrot stick after each cigarette.

EXERCISE (5) Write three reasons why each of the following predictions may not come true.

Example: By 1970 there will be more cars than people in the United States.

Population may increase at a rate greater than expected.

Helicopters may replace cars for personal transportation.

A war might shift production from cars to weapons.

1 Tonight I will watch my favorite television show.
2 If I study hard, I am sure to make good grades.
3 Aunt Clara is coming to visit us this Christmas.
4 The heavily favored Wildcats will win this Saturday.
5 If a person drinks plenty of milk—preferably a quart a day— he will have strong teeth and bones.

EXERCISE (6) The following fifteen statements are opinions about important matters that you might want to make a decision about sometime. Since the matters are important, you will, of course, want to make the right decision. Each opinion is followed by a list of three persons who you are to imagine made the statement. Be ready to discuss in class whether the opinion—coming from each person—is likely to be reliable or not *and why*. Remember to consider the person's authority, the amount of his self-interest, and the facts he would give to support his statement.

1 This record player is the finest you can buy for the money. (a) a record-player salesman, (b) a music teacher, (c) a disk jockey
2 Hemingway's stories are more interesting than Faulkner's. (a) an English teacher, (b) a blurb writer for Hemingway's publisher, (c) a classmate
3 Schools should have codes of dress to govern what students may wear to class. (a) the principal, (b) the president of the P.T.A., (c) a classmate
4 Of all groups in a typical community, the police have the most difficult and trying work to do. (a) the police commissioner, (b) the fire chief, (c) a social worker
5 This used car will last you another fifty thousand miles. (a) the original owner, (b) the salesman, (c) a mechanic friend you have asked to examine the car
6 Alaska is as fine a state as any other. (a) a citizen of Alaska, (b) the governor of Kentucky, (c) a widely traveled Peruvian diplomat

7   If he wants to excel in his sport, an athlete should keep in training.   (a) Bill Stern, famous sportscaster, (b) Mickey Mantle,
baseball star, (c) Branch Rickey, baseball executive

8   Dogs are more useful pets than cats.   (a) a veterinarian,
(b) the mailman, (c) Amos Bark, owner of Keno Kennels

9   Brushing your teeth after each meal will help keep them free of
cavities.   (a) an announcer giving a spot commercial for Dr.
Pullem's Tooth Powder, (b) the director of research of the
American Dental Association, (c) your family dentist

10 Mastery of English grammar and composition is a key to success
in any field.   (a) an English teacher, (b) a professor of electrical engineering, (c) the president of General Motors

11 The President should declare a "National Wildlife Conservation Week."   (a) a professor of biology, (b) your congress-
man, (c) a fur trapper

12 Man will reach Mars before the year 2000.   (a) a writer of
science fiction, (b) the Secretary-General of the United Nations, (c) a manufacturer of jet fuel

13 Unless you use live bait, you will not catch anything in Star
Lake.   (a) an Indian guide, (b) a live-bait seller, (c) the
manager of the Star Lake Lodge

14 Our community cannot afford to build a new junior high school.
(a) an architect hired by the board of education, (b) the
mayor, (c) a taxpayer

15 People ought not to smoke cigarettes.   (a) an officer of the
United States Public Health Service, (b) a pipe manufacturer,
(c) a coach

51

GENERALIZATIONS—

FAIR AND FAULTY

When a person makes a broad statement that is based on a number of instances, his statement is called a **generalization**. If we have
seen wrens eat spiders, phoebes eat flies, orioles eat beetles, and
crows eat grasshoppers, we can generalize from these detailed observations and say "Birds eat insects." Even though some kinds of
birds eat more insects than others, and a few birds eat no insects
at all, we are justified in making our statement because, *generally speaking*, most birds are known to eat insects.

By observing in detail *some* examples of any group or class of
things, we can make fairly reliable generalizations about *all* members of the group or class. If, for example, we have discovered that

most of the time when we switch on the television during the summer months we find repeated or second-rate programs, we can generalize fairly that "Summer television shows aren't very good." But are there *no* good summer television programs? Of course there are—occasionally. Still, from the sum total of our disappointments, we feel perfectly justified in our generalization. And most people hearing our complaint will agree with us *in general*.

It is important, however, always to keep the exceptions in mind when we generalize. We can say, "People don't get very far these days without a high-school education," and almost everyone will be inclined to agree with our statement. Looking about us, we note that most of the people we know who are considered successful have graduated at least from high school. On the other hand, most of those not considered successful left school without graduating. But—and this is a very important *but*—here and there we may see a successful person who did not finish high school or one who did but is not a success in his work. Does this make our generalization untrustworthy? No. Enough people's experiences bear out the statement so that we can regard it as a fair one—one that is *generally* true. If someone challenges it, we will gladly say that of course we know there are exceptions.

Often, however, we make generalizations which, if we stopped to think about them, would appear most untrustworthy. If we are walking down the street of a strange town and observe three banks in one block, we express our surprise by saying, "Nothing but banks in this town!" If we snap a shoestring while rushing to dress for an appointment, we complain angrily, "Every time I'm in a hurry, my shoestrings snap!" If we have a neighbor who practices the trombone loudly and regularly, we are likely to tell a guest, "That fellow never does anything but practice the trombone!" Exaggerations like these are a useful kind of small talk; they help us express surprise or relieve irritation. We do not intend them to be taken at face value. They are usually quite harmless.

But it is only a step from this kind of harmless small talk to faulty generalizations that can be quite harmful. Perhaps we have bought a pair of shoes in a certain shop for the first time. When we get home, we find that they are the wrong size. Immediately we begin to advise our friends, "Don't buy any shoes at those Trot-About Shops. They never give you the right size!" Although we did not get a good fitting, we have no information about the kind of fitting hundreds of other Trot-About customers are getting. There is absolutely no basis for saying that people "never" get fitted correctly in these shops or even that "many" Trot-About customers are sold shoes that do not fit. In complaining to our friends as we did,

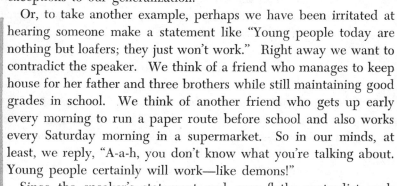

we may have unfairly damaged the Trot-About's reputation. Even though we were exaggerating, our friends are likely to be so sympathetic with our complaint that they will forget the hundreds of exceptions to our generalization.

Or, to take another example, perhaps we have been irritated at hearing someone make a statement like "Young people today are nothing but loafers; they just won't work." Right away we want to contradict the speaker. We think of a friend who manages to keep house for her father and three brothers while still maintaining good grades in school. We think of another friend who gets up early every morning to run a paper route before school and also works every Saturday morning in a supermarket. So in our minds, at least, we reply, "A-a-h, you don't know what you're talking about. Young people certainly will work—like demons!"

Since the speaker's statement and ours flatly contradict each other, which one is right? As it happens, the speaker has a son who refuses to get a job, preferring to spend his time with the "boys on the corner." Also in his office he employs a girl who constantly "watches the clock" and takes every opportunity to avoid unpleasant but necessary chores. So both statements are based on actual cases.

The trouble is, of course, that while each statement is based on some evidence, neither has *enough* evidence supporting it to make it a fair, dependable generalization. A careful thinker would not accept either statement, because he could not be sure which is the more accurate description of how young people *in general* feel about work. Knowing from his observations that some are lazy and others not, he would delay making up his mind until he had gathered more evidence.

But how will he know when he has sufficient evidence to make up his mind? How many instances do we need before we can make a fair generalization? How can we tell when a generalization is *faulty* because it is a sweeping statement based on too few instances? To answer these very important questions, consider for a moment the difference between one misfitted pair of shoes and hundreds of pairs of correctly fitted shoes, between five Indians and all Indians. The answer seems to be that a generalization is fair when it is based on *as many instances as can be gathered* and when both the speaker and the listener keep in mind that for every generalization there are *a number of exceptions*.

The sampling process. What happens in our minds when we generalize should be similar to the sampling process used in industry. Suppose a machine in a certain factory can turn out a thousand ball bearings an hour. If each ball bearing is checked

53

individually to make sure that it matches specifications, it will either take one man so long or else so many men will have to be hired for this one operation that there will be no advantage in having such an efficient machine. But technologists discovered long ago that this costly, time-consuming step could be simplified by applying the "generalizing" principle—or what they call the "sampling process."

The technologists discovered that there was no need to check each ball bearing, since by checking at given intervals—perhaps every fiftieth bearing—they could be fairly certain that the unchecked ones would be similar. That is, from the quality of the sample ball bearings that were checked, they could safely generalize about the quality of all the ball bearings that the machine was producing. Of course a few faulty ball bearings would slip through. However, without the discovery of this sampling principle, mass-production methods in modern industry would be almost impossible. Without applying the same principle in our own lives, clear and efficient thinking would be almost impossible.

Now let's see how this sampling process works in two other random examples of generalizations that we make or hear scores of times every day.

"People respond pleasantly to friendly acts." We can make a generalization like this because we have observed that most of the people we have known behave this way. One or two persons here or there may have been mean when we were friendly; but by and large, our neighbors, relatives, and even chance acquaintances have been pleasant. Since the vast majority of our "samples" have responded pleasantly to friendly acts, our generalization is a fair one.

According to a driver-education textbook, cars traveling at 50 miles per hour can stop in 193 feet. But can *every* car stop within 193 feet, traveling at 50 miles per hour? What if the brakes are worn? What if the road is slippery? What if the car has six heavy people in it? Under these conditions, cars may well require more than 193 feet to stop. Yet the textbook can make its generalization because, after testing thousands of cars, experts found that *most* cars traveling 50 miles per hour can, *under average conditions*, stop within 193 feet.

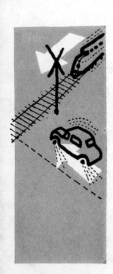

Each of these two generalizations is based on a fair sampling of actual instances. There are many cases of people responding pleasantly or unpleasantly to friendly acts. Many cars were actually checked on testing grounds for their braking ability. When enough instances point in one direction, we generalize—we say that a thing *is* this way or that, even though we are aware of exceptions. This kind of generalization is fair, reliable, and useful.

As we have seen, dependable generalizations play a very important role in our speaking and writing. They are helpful, too, in listening and reading if we develop the habit of watching for topic sentences, many of which are generalizations that tie together the details. For example, the reader of a paragraph about skin irritation caused by laundry soap would be helped by this topic sentence: "Laundry soaps irritate the skin." The writer would be entitled to use this generalization if he supported it with a fair sampling (in this case, statistics) of actual instances. He would not be entitled to use it if he could offer only one or two instances.

We have all seen or heard advertisements claiming that a certain product will or will not do something for us. The only "proof" that is offered for these generalizations is the testimony of one or two users of the product. Generalizations like these are faulty and undependable. They are a real hazard to communication. We should avoid them, especially in writing, in which we should make statements that are as dependable as possible.

Qualifying generalizations. One safeguard against misleading people when we generalize is to limit our idea by adding qualifying words or phrases to our statements. Such expressions are *some, several, almost, apparently, probably, usually, seems to,* and *in my opinion.* Qualifying expressions like these notify the reader that there may be exceptions, that we are generalizing, that he should check our statement against his own observations. Compare these sets of statements to see how qualifying works:

UNQUALIFIED	QUALIFIED
American students don't want to learn.	*Some* American students *apparently* don't want to learn.
Every student should be made to take part in intramural sports.	*In my opinion,* every student should be made to take part in intramural sports.
He never hires high-school students.	He never hires high-school students *so far as I know.*
Statistics never lie.	Statistics *don't usually* lie.
Summer television programs are not very good.	*Most* summer television programs are not very good.

Ideally, all generalizations should be qualified. Instead of saying "Birds eat insects" we should say "Most birds eat insects," if for no other reason than to show that *we* know that for every generalization there are exceptions. Yet in practice we do not qualify generalizations like "Birds eat insects." We feel that it would be awkward and self-conscious to do so. When there are only a very few exceptions to a generalization, or when it will harm no one to leave it unqualified, qualifying it is generally unnecessary.

EXERCISE (7) Be ready to take part in a class discussion in which you may be called on to label the following generalizations *fair*, *faulty but harmless*, or *faulty and harmful* and to explain the reasons for your labels. If you are dissatisfied with a classmate's reasons, feel free to criticize them. Expect criticism yourself.

1 The products of the _____ Company are no good.
2 Meat left for several hours in the sun will spoil.
3 Every time I get in the tub the telephone rings.
4 Eating too many hot dogs gives people indigestion.
5 Ads, ads, nothing but ads in our mailbox!
6 No other teachers ever give as much homework as Mr. Evers.
7 Boys who talk only about themselves are boring dates.
8 People who eat balanced meals are healthy.
9 Americans laugh too much and treat everything as a joke.
10 People who write letters to the editor are show-offs.

EXERCISE (8) Rewrite each of the following generalizations, adding **one or** more qualifying words or phrases to make it more reliable.

1 Animals have an instinct to hoard food for the future.
2 Girls are better in history and foreign languages, and boys excel in mathematics and science.
3 Football is the roughest of all sports.
4 Small cars are more practical than large cars.
5 People without high-school diplomas are poorly educated.
6 All people with red hair have bad tempers.
7 Teen-agers are delinquency prone.
8 People who think clearly succeed.
9 Students who don't behave in school should be expelled.
10 In two years schools in our state will be badly overcrowded.

EXERCISE (9) Recently a group of seventeen thousand teen-agers were polled on their views on current affairs by Purdue University. Part of the poll asked for views on foreign aid. Twenty-five per cent of the teen-agers said that foreign economic aid should be increased. Twelve per cent would boost military aid. Twenty-seven per cent favored increases in both economic and military aid. Seventeen per cent would decrease foreign aid. Ten per cent would cut it off.

We can assume that seventeen thousand teen-agers are a fair sampling of all American teen-agers. And on the basis of the views of the seventeen thousand, we can formulate a sound, dependable generalization about the views of all American teen-agers: *American teen-agers **generally** favor increased foreign aid.*

Using this example as a guide, you are to write one sound, qualified generalization and the instances that support it. You may get the instances through research in the library or through personal observation. Your generalization may be about a group as small as your own family or as large as American teen-agers as a whole. Just make certain that your generalization is based on a fair sampling of actual instances.

STEREOTYPES

The "bad" Indians slain by our vengeful TV frontiersman were obviously victims of his very faulty generalization: "Five Indians equal all Indians"—or, to put it another way, "All Indians are bad like the five that scalped my parents." Faulty generalizations like these, which are used mostly for members of certain races, religions, professions, or nationalities, are called **stereotypes**. You have no doubt heard many of them: "All policemen are dull and have flat feet"; "Orientals are sneaky"; "Every Italian is fat, temperamental, and musical"; "Professors are absent-minded"; "The Scotch are stingy"; "Quakers are old-fashioned"; and so on and on.

Of all faulty generalizations, stereotypes are the most unfair—as anyone who has known a fair sampling of policemen, Orientals, Italians, and so on, will tell you. The trouble is that people who think in stereotypes are often the people who have had the *least* fair sampling of the objects of their stereotypes.

And stereotypes are tenacious. Once they have got hold of a person's thinking, they are very difficult to shake off. An idea about librarians, say, or Southerners, or movie actresses, may become so fixed in our minds that it sticks even when there are new facts that are quite different from those on which our stereotype is based. Think of what it took to change our frontiersman's notion about Indians. It took a serious attempt on his life by white claim jumpers and the healing efforts of a whole tribe of Indians to make him see the light!

Stereotype thinking may be set off by any number of things. The blue of a policeman's uniform which we have caught out of the corner of our eye may remind us that we have heard that all policemen are dull and have flat feet. "Aha," we think to ourselves, "another

57

flatfoot." Having seen a movie in which the villain was a sneaky Oriental, we hurriedly clutch our pocketbooks when an Oriental enters the restaurant where we are eating. Loving our recordings of Perry Como or Arturo Toscanini and knowing that these men are Italians, we expect every Italian we meet to burst into song or to talk authoritatively about music.

Merely hearing or reading the WORD that names the kind of persons or things we have a stereotype for will make us react unfairly. If we have the stereotype that everybody from Boston is snooty, and we hear that our new neighbors are from Boston, we will be dead certain that they are snooty before we even meet them. The moment the word *union* (or *management*) is introduced into a conversation, people with stereotypes about unions (or management) will get furious, start shouting, or go home. They are quite like the irate father who stormed into the office of the Dean of Students in a small Pennsylvania college and demanded to know what labor union his son was being forced to join. The father's expensive trip to the college had been set off by this item on his son's bill: **Union fee.....$3.50**. The "Union" was the Student Union—a recreational *building*. This fact was explained in detail in the college catalogue. The father could have saved himself considerable expense, not to mention embarrassment, if he had simply checked his stereotype against the available facts.

58

REVIEW

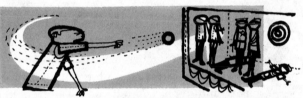

Let's review the thinking of our frontier character to fix in our own minds where he went wrong. His first step was right. He began with the fact that five Indians had scalped his parents. But on the basis of this fact he leaped to a faulty generalization: "All Indians are bad." He allowed this faulty generalization to become frozen into a stereotype, which caused him to kill all the Indians he could before they had a chance to show him that they were not necessarily "bad." Not until he was rescued and healed by a tribe of "good" Indians did he discover his error. In the meantime, he had killed a number of innocent people. The best we can say for him is "better late than never."

Most people who think in stereotypes are honest people. They do not realize that their thinking is not clear. They sincerely believe that they are right; and they will try very hard to convince us that they are right. By keeping in mind the case of our frontiersman, we can avoid being trapped by their stereotype, whatever it may be. And, without raising our voices, we might be able to point out quietly how they themselves have been trapped.

EXERCISE (10) Be ready to tell the class a personal experience in which a stereotype once blocked your own clear thinking. If you wish, you may tell how a stereotype blocked the clear thinking of someone else, whose name you will not mention.

EXERCISE (11) Read each of the following selections at least twice—once fast for fun and once slowly for full meaning. Discuss each of them in detail in class. Be ready to point out the stereotype or stereotypes in each and tell how they block clear thinking.

1 Man's work lasts till set of sun;
    Woman's work is never done.

2 Once I came back with a delicious kind of white meat in a can with a Spanish label that neither of us could read. The meat was so good that I went back to the store and bought three or four cans more, and Frau Schultz made sandwiches of it at coffee time in the afternoons. Finally, one day it occurred to me to look up the delicacy's name in my Spanish-English dictionary. It turned out to be eel. I didn't mind, since I have no prejudice against eels. But when, in the English-German dictionary, Frau Schultz saw the frightful word in her own tongue, she almost died, declaring she'd as soon have eaten a snake! But by then we had both consumed several pounds of eel.—Langston Hughes, *The Big Sea*. Copyright © 1940 by Alfred A. Knopf, Inc., New York.

3 In cafeteria lines [at Pomona College] it was like meeting so many hundreds of deans. No sooner would I enter the room than, although I was quite capable of finding the line myself, all the men standing would start directing me, and once at the counter, would get the tray, silverware, and even the food. Sometimes, when they put my milk on their own tray, they would drink it for me also. And if I did manage to ignore or slip through these scrutinizing eyes, find a tray, get my food, and at random sit down at a table, all of a sudden the conversation would cease, and after a while, when I was no longer an object of curiosity to be stared at—not for being an Indian, but for being blind—people would ignore my existence at the table altogether, and would carry on talk unaware of my very presence.—Ved Mehta, *Face to Face*. Copyright © 1957 by Little, Brown & Company, Boston.

59

THE AMERICAN INDIAN:

STEREOTYPES VERSUS REALITY

The frontiersman described in the preceding chapter
is, of course, just a fictitious character; he
exists today only in television dramas.   Unfortunately,
however, he has many counterparts in real life.
There are hundreds of people who, like him, let mental
stereotypes interfere with clear thinking.

   To these people, all members of a particular group
are the same—all are cast from the same mold.
A first experience with one or two members of the
group sets the pattern; and from then on,
they think that all other members of the group have
been cut from that same pattern.   To see how
inaccurate this sort of thinking is, let's contrast
some stereotypes of the American Indian
with the real Indians of the present day.

The stereotypes . . .
From reading in American history about
Indians like Massasoit, who helped
the Pilgrims (or in fiction about heroic
Indians like those in James Fenimore
Cooper's novels), many people think
of every Indian as a noble brave—
wise, courageous, remote, dedicated
to a strict code of honor.

Three Lions

Some of the Western movies they saw as children have given others just the opposite idea. To them, the word *Indian* immediately brings to mind a picture of tomahawk-twirling savages—bloodthirsty, cruel, preying on defenseless women and children.

Visiting certain resort areas where Indians provide a great part of the entertainment has given many people the notion that *all* Indians are characters who wear a costume of feathered headdress, beaded moccasins, and deer-hide clothing, and perform native dances to entertain audiences.

Each of these notions is a stereotype—a faulty generalization based on too few instances. None of the stereotypes, as you will see, gives an accurate idea of even one member of the American Indian group—let alone all members.

H. Armstrong Roberts

The reality . . .

American Indians, like people of any other racial or
national background, differ greatly from one another. No two are
exactly alike—in appearance, intelligence, physical strength,
skill, artistic ability, personality, or in any other respect.
They can no more be fitted into a single pattern than
can all Irishmen, all Germans, all Australians. They live
in all parts of our country and work at as many different
kinds of jobs as do citizens who are descended from English or
Dutch or Polish or Chinese immigrants to this country.

Some Indians live on reservations, lands set aside for them
long ago by the government. Here are a few of the many
activities—both work and recreation—you would see Indians
engaged in if you visited a reservation in the Southwest.

George C. Hight

Hand weaving beautiful rugs of intricate pattern

Three Lions

Guarding

a flock

of sheep

Teaching and

attending school

Sand painting,

creating colorful

designs in sand

64

Alfredo Valente

Other Indians do not live on reservations but in cities
and towns and on farms all over the United States. Some of these
Americans of Indian heritage have become famous. For example—

Maria Tallchief, an Osage princess, is a famous dancer whom
thousands have seen perform both in Europe and in America.
She has danced with the Ballet Russe de Monte Carlo and has been
prima ballerina of the New York City Ballet Company.

Jim Thorpe, a Sauk and Fox Indian from Oklahoma and a descendant
of the courageous chief Blackhawk, has often been
called the greatest athlete of all time. He excelled in baseball,
football, and all kinds of track events.

Still other Indians, not so well known as Jim Thorpe
and Maria Tallchief, are absorbed in a wide variety of interesting
and worth-while occupations. Among them you can find—

A chef at a famous restaurant—

Henrici's in Chicago—who, like Jim

Thorpe, is a Sauk and Fox Indian

A television technician

who is a Sioux Indian

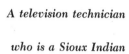

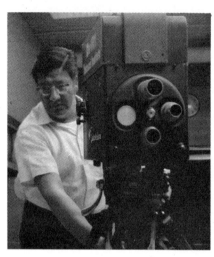

65

A jazz musician who is

a member of the Pima tribe

An assistant book buyer for a

large wholesale dealer, also a Sioux

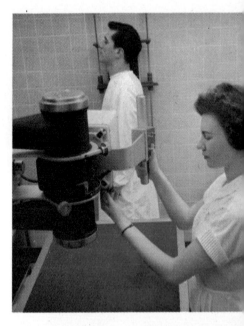

Operators of heavy earth-moving

equipment, a Navaho and a Chippewa

A hospital x-ray technician,

a Chippewa Indian

A beauty operator,

a member of

the Sioux tribe

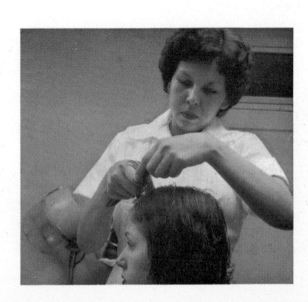

Just like your parents and neighbors, Indians who
work at daily jobs also have absorbing hobbies and interests.

A Pueblo lithographer who is also an artist

A baker, a member of the

Apache tribe, who performs difficult

Indian hoop dances expertly

and professionally

Clothes courtesy of Seventeen *magazine*

A teen-age fashion model in New York, a Mohawk Indian, who is studying dancing and hopes some day to be an actress

CHAPTER 3

GROUP

DISCUSSION

70

Dave Martin, the president of the Hill School Model-Airplane Club, has what he thinks is an excellent idea—the club should make a trip by bus to International Airport to see real planes in action. He realizes, however, that there is not enough money in the treasury to pay for such a trip. Therefore he talks it over with the vice-president, and they decide that the members will sell pencils with the school's name on them to raise money for the trip. Without consulting the other members, they order five hundred pencils.

At the special meeting they call to inform the members of what has been planned for them, only a few show up, unfortunately. And those who do come to the meeting balk not only at selling pencils but also at the idea of the excursion. The matter finally ends with an embarrassed president canceling an order for five hundred unwanted pencils.

The president of a similar club in nearby Summit School has somewhat the same idea. But before taking any action, Bill proposes the idea at a regular meeting of the club. The members dis-

cuss the proposal, finally deciding that it is too expensive a trip. However, one member suggests a less expensive trip—to the Westchester Airport, which is only half as far away as International Airport. Another member suggests that to pay for the bus trip, the club should sell pencils bearing the school name. After a thorough discussion, the proposal is unanimously agreed upon, and the president is authorized to order the pencils. Everyone coöperates; the pencils are sold; and the following month, the club spends a memorable day examining the planes at Westchester.

These stories illustrate two ways in which decisions affecting groups of people may be made. Dave's method may, at first thought, seem the quicker and more efficient one, but it is a far from satisfactory or wise method. In the first place, it is not likely that one person (or even two) will think of all the phases of a problem that need to be considered in making a decision for a group. In the second place, most groups of people resent having their decisions made for them.

Bill, on the other hand, realized these important points about group decisions. Although he personally would have preferred to visit the International Airport, he knew that it was up to the club to make its own decision. With a number of people offering ideas and suggestions for *all* to consider and discuss, the group worked out a plan that led to an economical but enjoyable experience for all.

Group discussions are valuable not only as an aid in reaching decisions but also as an interesting means of becoming better informed on a particular subject. One person could, of course, study the subject by himself. But gathering information and arriving at thoughtful opinions about a subject takes a great deal of time and effort. Often it is more efficient for a group of people who are interested in the same subject to share the work. By pooling ideas and information, all members of the group can become better informed on the subject in a short time.

CHOOSING

A SUBJECT

Almost any subject of special interest or concern to the majority of a group would be a good subject for discussion. Usually the best discussions stem from subjects about which the members hold differing views. For example, a group of television fans would probably have an exciting exchange of ideas and opinions on "Which TV programs should win national awards for excellence?" But they would have little to discuss if they chose the subject "What are the FCC rules governing telecasting?" Once the various rules were stated and explained, what more could be said?

Choosing an interesting subject is not in itself a guarantee of a successful discussion, however. It is what the members of the group *say* about the subject that determines how interesting and exciting the discussion is. And what each member says depends on the thinking he has done about the subject *before* the discussion.

THE IMPORTANCE

OF PREPARATION

Taking part in a group discussion is somewhat like playing in your school band. Your band might choose some very interesting new numbers to play at its next concert. How well the numbers

would be played, however, would depend on the individual members. Suppose that each member decided he need not do much practicing. Suppose that each decided he could play his part well enough if he just played it through once or twice before the concert. This lack of practice would not prevent the band members from giving the concert, but it would make a difference in the kind of concert they gave. It would not be half so enjoyable and satisfying as it would have been if each player had spent more time preparing for it.

Adequate preparation is just as important for group discussions. Let's suppose, for example, that your class has decided to hold a discussion on "What are a student's responsibilities to his school?" This subject, you think, should prove quite interesting—and not very difficult. Since you have been a student for years, it should be easy for you to find something to say. It is so easy, in fact, that in only two minutes of your study-hall time you think of three things to say:

A student should attend school regularly.
He should obey the school rules.
He should be courteous to teachers and other students.

You could stop here, of course. But if you do stop at this point, you will be no better prepared for the discussion than the band members were for the concert.

Ideas that come so quickly to mind as these three are likely to be obvious ones. Being obvious, they will probably have occurred to most of the other members of the class. And if most of the class comes prepared to say the same three things—and nothing more— the discussion will hardly be worth holding. There will be so few ideas and opinions expressed that you will learn little you did not know before.

If, on the other hand, you realize that the first few ideas that come to mind are merely a start, you will go on to do some real thinking about the subject. Slowly perhaps, but surely, you will think of other, less obvious ideas, some of which will not occur to anyone else in the group. What is more, if you are willing to think, you will arrive at some clear-cut opinions about the ideas and will be able to give good reasons for having these opinions. When you reach this point, you will know that you are well prepared. If everyone else is as well prepared, you will have a lively and satisfying discussion. In the exchange of specific, clear-cut ideas, each of you will gain a better understanding of your classmates' views. Moreover, you may even be persuaded to change some of your own views about the subject.

Most of the ideas you will bring to a discussion of a subject like "What are a student's responsibilities to his school?" will be ideas drawn from your own experience and observation. You have been attending school for years; you have had countless experiences that have made you aware of things a student should do and those he should not do. You might start your thinking, then, by recalling some of these experiences. Begin by considering what you do during a school day.

Since the first thing you do is come to school, the first ideas that occur to you will probably have to do with a student's responsibility to attend school. Certainly this is an important topic to consider. Ask yourself what you know about the topic. A number of points and questions will occur to you, and in deciding how to answer the questions, you will arrive at certain opinions about this topic and perhaps others.

Suppose that the first point that comes to your mind is something you learned long ago: A student is obliged by law to attend school until he reaches a certain age (sixteen, seventeen, or eighteen—depending on the state). From this, your mind will move quickly from one point to another: Is attending school strictly a personal responsibility of the student? Or is it up to the law to see to his attendance? Does irregular attendance by one student affect other students? What effect does irregular attendance have on a student's class work? The principal certainly thinks it has an effect— a bad one. Remember the day you tried to skip school and got caught? The principal surely had a great deal to say then about a student's responsibility to attend school. Even though you did not agree with him at the time of the incident, you had gradually come to realize that he was right.

You broke a rule the day you tried to skip. What about school rules? Is a student responsible for obeying them? What if he doesn't know all the rules? Is it his responsibility to find out what they are? Or is it up to the school authorities to make sure the rules are known by all? What about the time you were reprimanded for taking a book from Harold's locker? You didn't know that was against the rules. Harold had given you his permission. Does a student have to obey rules when, as far as he can see, he will do no harm by breaking them? Couldn't a rule apply in one case and not in another? Does a student have to obey rules even when he thinks they are silly or unfair? What would happen if students obeyed only those rules that they approved of?

While you are thinking over the subject in this way, you will find that your thoughts do not always come in an orderly fashion, neatly grouped according to topics. One minute, for example, you may be thinking about the school's traffic rules. The word *traffic* reminds you of the traffic jam after the last basketball game, and the next minute you find yourself thinking about the importance of supporting school games.

Unless you find some way to keep track of your ideas, you are likely to forget many of them. One of the best ways is to take notes as you go. Whenever you think of a general topic—say "School attendance" or "School rules"—jot it down. Leave a blank space under each topic. Then when an idea or a thought-provoking question that has to do with one of these topics occurs to you, list it in the proper space. Be brief; the notes are to be a memory help, not a full report. When you finish, your notes may look something like these:

1. *School attendance*
   Student owes it to himself and to the school to attend regularly. (Quote principal and Spanish teacher on why irregular attendance of some is bad for everyone.)
   Should we have compulsory education?

2. *School rules*
   Up to students to learn rules; information always available. (Remember the principal's comments on this point.)
   Students should learn reasons behind rules before condemning them as silly or unfair. (Explain reason for locker rule; ask about study-hall pass rule and others.)
   How can responsible students go about changing what seems to them a poor rule?
   Shouldn't students have a part in making rules? (Explain way in which this might be done.)

3. *Class work*
   Student owes it to school as well as to himself to study; his duty as a citizen. (Disagree with student in math class who said, "What difference does it make to other kids if I don't study? Isn't that my problem?")
   Every student responsible for taking active part in discussions, class projects, etc. (Quote Mr. Klein, history teacher.)
   Is preventing cheating the responsibility of all students? Why do students cheat?

4. *Conduct*

Students owe courtesy to classmates, teachers, guests of school. (Accidents in corridors due to lack of courtesy; poor conduct of some at last assembly embarrassing to the school.)

The conduct of students outside school may affect the whole student body. (Friday-night dances were discontinued last year because of student rowdiness in town after a dance. Tell why this action was justified.)

5. *School activities*

Unreasonable to expect all students to support *all* games, plays, concerts, charity drives, etc. (Lack of time, money.)

Should students feel obligated to join school clubs or go out for athletics? (Quote Miss Weber on effects of joining too many clubs; tell of other outside interests students may prefer which are as valuable as clubs or athletics.)

Is student ever justified in letting work on club activities cut into his study time?

You can readily see how useful such notes will be when you come to the discussion. Chances are that the discussion itself will not move from point to point in the same order your notes do. But that does not matter. Whatever order is followed, you will have something interesting to say or ask about most of the topics that are brought up.

HOLDING THE DISCUSSION

To make sure that everyone has a fair chance to express his views, the leader chosen to guide the discussion decides who should "have the floor." When you want to enter the discussion, you raise your hand and wait for the leader to "recognize" you by calling your name or nodding in your direction. Since everyone's comments are needed, you must be careful not to talk too often or too long.

What you say is, of course, most important. But to be helpful to the other members, you should give some attention to how you say it. Speak loudly enough so that all can hear you and clearly enough so that all can understand you. Since you will have several opportunities to speak, limit your remarks each time to the point being discussed at the moment.

You will also help by making it clear when you are stating a fact and when you are expressing an opinion. And be sure you give reasons for holding the opinions you do so that the other members can judge their value.

Talking is only part of your job, however. Listening is equally important. By listening carefully, you can avoid repeating what has been said. By listening thoughtfully, you can learn new facts and ideas. And by listening critically, you can compare the differing opinions and reach a better understanding of the question. You may even find that you want to change your own point of view.

Ask questions about any points you do not understand. Feel free to object to statements you think are wrong. But, above all, be tactful and courteous. Arguments and hurt feelings prevent a free exchange of ideas, which, after all, is the purpose of your discussion.

Leading the discussion. As leader of the discussion, your job is similar to a railroad engineer's. You start the discussion, guide it to its destination, and bring it to a stop.

You prepare for the discussion by thinking over the subject in the same way the members do. But instead of noting your ideas on the subject, make a list of questions on various topics that you think should be covered during the discussion. Word the questions so that they cannot be answered by a simple *yes* or *no*.

To begin the discussion, you give a short introduction stating the subject and briefly explaining the purpose of the discussion. Then you start the members talking, usually by asking a question.

To be sure that the discussion will get to its destination, you must keep it moving. See that everyone has a chance to speak, but that no one takes more than his fair share of the time. Do not let the members stay too long on any one point, or there will not be enough time to cover all the topics that should be discussed. If the talk lags, start it going again by using one of the questions you noted in your preparation. And make sure that the discussion stays on the right track. If a member does get sidetracked, tactfully draw him back to the point under discussion.

When the subject has been thoroughly discussed, or when only a few minutes remain, you close the discussion by summarizing the main points that have been made. You will find it easier to make your summary if you jot down a few notes during the discussion.

EXERCISE (1) Bring to class a list of three subjects that you think your classmates would enjoy discussing. Make sure that the subjects are of the type that most of the class will be familiar with through personal experience and observation.

The class is to consider the suggested subjects and make a list of the ten the members like best. (This list should be kept on file to refer to throughout the year when group discussions are assigned.)

· The following subjects have proved interesting to many groups. Perhaps they will suggest subjects for your list.

1 Are grades a reliable indication of a person's ability?
2 Should our school have a literary magazine?
3 Should we try to "keep up with the Joneses"?
4 Is it ever safe to judge a person by first appearances?
5 Should all students be required to learn a modern foreign language?
6 Should a person be frank at all times and in all situations?
7 Is a person really judged by his language?
8 Is the study of poetry a waste of time?

EXERCISE (2) The class is to hold an informal group discussion on one of the subjects chosen in Exercise 1. (The date for the discussion should be set a few days in advance so that everyone will have time enough to think over the subject and prepare notes.) Besides preparing questions on various topics to stimulate the discussion, whoever is chosen as leader should work out a few sentences of introduction.

GETTING MATERIAL

FROM OTHER SOURCES

Most of the facts, ideas, and opinions you need to discuss a question like "What are a student's responsibilities to his school?" you can draw from your own personal experience. Your many years of attending school have made you, in a way, an "expert" on this subject. Similarly, a group of educators who had spent years studying spelling problems could depend on their own past experience and observation for the information they would need to discuss "Would a phonetic alphabet solve common spelling problems?"

But suppose you are to take part in a discussion of the question "Are TV crime programs contributing to juvenile delinquency?" In preparing for this discussion, you could not depend entirely on your own personal experience—what you have seen, done, heard, and read in the past—to provide you with all the facts and ideas you would need. To get enough information to discuss the question intelligently, you would have to go outside your own experience.

There are two ways to get facts, ideas, and opinions about an unfamiliar subject. The first way is to read books and articles about it. The second way is to talk with people who have had experience with it, people whose work and training have made them experts on the subject. Let's see how Joe Crandall drew both on his personal experience and on these two ways of getting information as he was preparing for a discussion on "How reliable are proverbs as guides?"

To start his preparation, Joe decided that he should list a number of specific proverbs to talk about. But when he began making a list, he found he could think of only four. And realizing that most of the class would probably think of the same four, he went to the library to look for others.

He found a few listed in the short article "Proverb" in the *World Book Encyclopedia*. And when, as suggested in that article, he looked up "Poor Richard's Almanac" and "Don Quixote," he found a few more. Still not satisfied, he turned to books of quotations. Both Stevenson's *Home Book of Quotations* and Bartlett's *Familiar Quotations* had sections listing proverbs. He also discovered on the reference shelf a book devoted entirely to this subject—Davidoff's *A World Treasury of Proverbs*. From these various sources he chose eleven proverbs to add to his list.

Next Joe went through the list slowly, trying to determine how reliable the proverbs were. As he read "Better late than never," he was reminded of the time he had handed in a history report two days late and had received no credit for it. And he remembered reading several newspaper accounts of people who had died because rescue teams or medicines had been late in arriving. Even these few cases, then, indicated to him that the advice given by the proverb could not always be relied upon.

On the other hand, after mulling over a number of past experiences, he could think of no instance in which "Two heads are better than one" would not be a reliable guide. In fact, it had usually been a pretty useful guide for him. Whenever Bill Fisher and he thought through a difficult algebra problem together, they could figure out the solution.

When he came to "Clothes make the man," Joe grinned. The sloppiest dresser he knew was not only the most popular boy in school, but also one of the smartest and most capable. Evidently his fellow students did not consider this proverb a very reliable guide.

But the older people he knew seemed to be guided by it. His mother, for example, was always fussing about his appearance and that of his brothers. He remembered the time she had insisted that Bob get all dressed up to apply for a job as a delivery boy. Did employers really judge applicants by their appearance, as his mother had said? Would an employer's experience show that a careless dresser was a careless worker? Did the fact that a person's clothes and general appearance were attractive and neat indicate that he would be a good, dependable worker?

To find the answers, Joe realized that he would have to ask someone with experience in hiring people—someone like Mr. Blake, the personnel manager at the telephone company. In fact, why not ask Mr. Blake himself? Mr. Blake's opinion, based on facts he had observed for many years, would be well worth reporting to the class.

The next proverb on Joe's list had always puzzled him. It was one his Aunt Beth often quoted: "Early to bed and early to rise makes a man healthy, wealthy, and wise." Did she really believe that if he went to bed early and got up early he would never be sick, would make a lot of money, and would be an honor student? The only way to find out was to ask her, so he stopped at her house after school.

Aunt Beth explained that this proverb, like most proverbs, should not be taken literally—that is, word by word, and each word in its usual meaning. It is not intended to mean a specific promise that a man who goes to bed at sunset and rises at dawn will automatically become a perfect physical specimen, a capitalist, and a brilliant scholar, as its *literal* meaning would lead a person to believe. Instead, it is intended to suggest that a man who gets the proper amount of rest is likely to stay in good health. As a result, he will be able to do his work well, which usually means advancement and increased income. And, feeling rested and well, he will probably be far more alert and observant—therefore "wiser"—than he would be if he were tired or ill from lack of rest. The proverb, understood in this way, did seem to Joe to be a reliable guide.

Aunt Beth's explanation helped Joe with the next proverb on his list: "Now that I have a sheep and a cow, everybody bids me good morrow." At first, the proverb had seemed ridiculous to him. Now he began to see that the *sheep* and the *cow* were not meant literally; they were intended as symbols for riches or valuables. The "real" meaning of the proverb was that as soon as a person acquires wealth, everyone tries to make friends with him.

Was this proverb reliable as a guide? Joe himself had never owned anything valuable. But he clearly remembered what had happened when Ted Brady, one of the seniors, got his new red convertible. Within a week everyone was Ted's "friend"—or wanted to be. In this case, at least, the proverb was true.

As Joe continued through his list, he met a new problem. He had thought of several experiences which seemed to prove that "Where there's smoke, there's fire" is a sensible, useful guide. But then he came to "Never judge by appearances." This proverb, too, seemed to him a sensible, useful guide; yet it said just the opposite of the other. How could two proverbs that give conflicting advice both be reliable guides?

Once during an examination, Joe had seen the boy across the aisle quickly stuff a piece of paper into his pocket. Should Joe have been guided by "Where there's smoke, there's fire" and assumed the boy was cheating? Or should he have relied on "Never judge by appearances" and assumed the boy was innocent, at least until he knew what was on the paper?

Actually the boy had not been cheating. So, in his case, "Never judge by appearances" would have been the better guide to follow. But in many similar cases, as Joe knew, the other proverb would have proved a useful guide.

Perhaps, Joe decided, the reason we have pairs of conflicting proverbs is that in certain situations a choice must be made. Whenever there is a pair of contradictory proverbs that apply to a situation, both must be considered. A person cannot rely exclusively on one as a guide, or he may do the wrong thing.

Joe got helpful facts, ideas, and opinions by talking with two people—his Aunt Beth and Mr. Blake, the personnel manager. Talking with a person for the purpose of getting information is usually called *interviewing*. Interviewing someone you know quite well, like Joe's Aunt Beth, is simple. You generally get the information that you want by asking a few questions in the course of an everyday conversation. But when you interview someone who is extremely busy or someone you do not know personally, like Mr. Blake, you are less informal.

First of all you should telephone or write to the person to ask for an interview and explain why you want it. If he agrees, set a time convenient for him. Then, to save time and to make sure you will get the information you want, prepare some specific questions.

On the day of the interview, arrive promptly and quickly get down to business. You should aim to get the other person talking freely without doing much talking yourself. But when you do not understand a comment or when an answer is not complete enough, ask a question or two to clear the matter up.

The more courteous you are, of course, the more successful your interview will be. If the person does not know the answer to a question or seems reluctant to talk about a particular point, shift the talk to another matter. Take notes, but keep most of your attention on the person you are interviewing. If you wish to quote him directly, ask his permission.

When you have the information you need, thank the person and leave promptly. As soon as you can after the interview, review your notes. Add to them any points that you did not jot down and might forget.

PRACTICE IN GROUP DISCUSSION

Each of the two following exercises suggests a subject that your class will find interesting to discuss. Each subject is one for which the members of the class will need to do some reading and interviewing to get facts, ideas, and opinions.

To help you prepare for the discussions, carefully read and consider the topics and questions that are given after each subject. These questions and topics do not cover *all* the phases of the subject. But they will suggest to you the sort of information and ideas needed to make the discussion lively, interesting, and worth while. They will also suggest to the leader the kind of questions he should prepare to keep the discussion moving.

In setting the date for each discussion, remember that everyone will need several days' time for interviewing and reading.

EXERCISE 3 The class is to hold an informal discussion on "How reliable are proverbs as guides?" The topics and questions following the subject are to help you prepare for the discussion. (They need not be discussed in the order shown.)

Subject: How reliable are proverbs as guides?

Topic A: *Understanding the "real" meaning of proverbs*
Why is it important to know that most proverbs are not intended to be taken literally? How does the literal meaning of particular proverbs on your list differ from the intended "real" meaning? For example, does "A stitch in time saves nine" have to do only with mending done with needle and thread? Or is the word *stitch* a symbol for other things? Could this proverb be applied to other things besides mending—to soil conservation, for instance?

Topic B: *Understanding the value of conflicting proverbs*
What proverbs on your list give contradictory advice? Does the fact that two proverbs contradict each other prove they are useless as guides? If not, in what way are they useful? Can you tell of any experiences that illustrate the importance of considering both proverbs of a conflicting pair before making a decision?

Topic C: *Considering the reliability of proverbs*
Which proverbs on your list do you think are reliable guides? Which do you think are not reliable? What experiences in your life or in the lives of others can you tell to show why you reached these opinions?

EXERCISE 4 Prepare to take part in an informal class discussion of the following question.

Subject: Should every high-school student have a part-time job?

Topic A: *Advantages of a part-time job*
According to students who work, what are the advantages of part-time jobs? Have adults who worked during their school days found the experience helpful in later life? In what ways? In what ways do teachers think students can benefit by working after school?

Topic B: *Disadvantages of a part-time job*
According to students who work, what are the disadvantages of part-time jobs? What disadvantages do parents and teachers see in part-time jobs for students?

Topic C: *Who should work part time*
Should a student's grades have anything to do with determining whether he should work or not? Should only those who need money for *necessary* expenses be allowed to work while in school? Should boys who go out for varsity athletics work? What does the coach or a letterman think about part-time jobs for varsity players? Should the decision be left to the individual student?

EXERCISE 5 The class is to choose for discussion a subject of special interest to the group, a subject for which the class will need to find information through reading or interviewing. When the subject has been chosen, it should be explored briefly in class so that all members will get an idea of the sort of topics that should be covered in the discussion. Each member of the class is to prepare to contribute facts, ideas, and opinions about at least two of the topics.

CHAPTER 4

INCREASING

YOUR

VOCABULARY

No one has ever been able to figure out a simple, foolproof formula for success, though many people have tried. One reason is, of course, that "success" means different things to different people. To some, it means making a great deal of money; to others, it means getting an important post in business or politics, or winning honors in sports, or becoming well known in society.

A second reason is that what helps one person to gain success may not help another. Mr. A, for example, may become successful because of years of hard work and study; Mr. B, because of a great natural talent; and Mr. C, because of a combination of luck and ability. So, as you can see, it is really impossible to name the exact ingredients that will guarantee success to everyone.

However, some years ago research scientists at the Human Engineering Laboratories, who under the direction of Johnson O'Connor spent a great deal of time studying this question, came up with an interesting discovery. They found that the one thing that more often than any other accompanies success is a **large vocabulary.**

This does not mean, of course, that every person with a large vocabulary is sure to win success. But since it shows that a large vocabulary is typical of successful people, it means that knowing the exact meanings of words is an important element in success.

To understand clearly how all this concerns you, you will have to know a bit more of what the scientists found in their studies. For one thing, they discovered that vocabulary is, as a rule, acquired rather early in life—*before* success in the business or professional world is won, not after. It is not too early, then, for you to start enlarging your vocabulary this very year.

Even more encouraging, the scientists discovered that a person's vocabulary *can be increased through conscious effort.* You do not have to have a special talent or aptitude for language to acquire a large vocabulary, as many people think. Anyone who is willing to make the effort can train himself to learn more words. What is more, the additional words you learn this year will bring you an almost immediate reward. The Laboratory experiments show that the increased vocabulary you gain by making a conscious effort will be followed by a general improvement in all school subjects the next year.

This chapter deals with words. You will learn not only how words get their meanings, but also how you learn what words mean and how you can set about adding words to your vocabulary.

Why is learning more words so important? You have already been given two practical reasons: (1) a large vocabulary is an important element in success, and (2) an increase in vocabulary will bring you better grades in all your subjects. But the most important of all reasons is this: The more words you know, the more interesting a person you are likely to be. The larger your vocabulary, the easier it will be for you to understand the thoughts of others and to make your own thoughts clear to them.

Without words, in fact, thinking would be impossible. (You can have moods or feelings without the words to tell of them—but not thoughts.) If you doubt this, try to think of something—some fact or idea—without using any words. Can you do it? Of course not. To think about anything, you have to give it a name. And to name it, you have to use words: *Jane, the dent in the fender, the winning touchdown, our best player, the effect of the heat on the metal.* So you see, your *thinking* and *vocabulary* are all tied up together. Here is a chance to improve both.

HOW DO WORDS

GET THEIR MEANINGS?

In order to talk about anything—a person, a place, an object, an action, a feeling—you have to have words that stand for these things. If the people you talk to are to understand what you say, the words you use must have the same meaning for them as they have for you. Otherwise, it would be impossible to communicate.

The people who use a language, in other words, have to be in agreement about what the words in the language mean. It does not matter just what any particular word means—as long as the users agree about its meaning. If, for example, we were all to agree that the sound "dog" stands for a furry, four-legged animal that meows, and that the sound "cat" stands for a hairy, four-legged animal that barks, we would have no more trouble talking about cats and dogs than we do now. But if only half of us agreed and the other half did not, we would have endless arguments (perhaps come to blows) about whether Rin Tin Tin is a cat or a dog. And if this lack of agreement spread to other words, speaking would be a waste of time; no one would understand what anyone else was talking about.

How do words get their meanings? We—the people who use them—give them their meanings. To understand this last sentence clearly, let's see how a new word comes into the language and acquires meaning.

Whenever something new appears in the world—a new product, or invention, or discovery—a name must be provided for it. In 1928, for example, Sir Alexander Fleming discovered a powerful drug for destroying certain bacteria. To tell the medical world about this useful new drug, he had to give it a name. He called it *penicillin*. When the word first appeared in newspapers, in magazines, and over the radio, people in general recognized it as a word, of course. But it had no more meaning for them than the words in an old Greek manuscript would have had. The word, being new, had not yet taken on meaning for them.

In time, however, people learned that all the doctors and reporters and broadcasters who used this new word *penicillin* were using it to stand for a new product—a powerful antibiotic substance useful in treating and preventing certain infections. The new word, you see, was beginning to have meaning. Gradually people in general began using the word in the same way as they had heard it and seen it used. *Through use*, then, the word acquired meaning, a meaning recognized and agreed on by all.

The way *penicillin* got its meaning is the same way all the other words in our language got their meanings. The *users* of words give words their meanings—not the dictionary, as many persons mistakenly think. The word "sun" means what it does because English-speaking people use it to stand for "the heavenly body around which the earth and planets revolve." The word "villain" no longer means "a boorish or clownish person from the country," as it once did. Now its meaning is "a wicked character in a novel or play"—since that is what it stands for to the people who use the word today. Words mean whatever people in general agree they will mean.

EXERCISE (1) Be ready to answer the following questions in class.

1 Would Abraham Lincoln have found the following words in his dictionary: *radar, nuclear fission, jeep*? Explain your answer.

2 Ask your grandfathers and grandmothers if they remember a time when any of the following words did not exist: *garage, sundae, duplex, supermarket, nylon, bazooka, racketeer, juke box, G-man, kibitzer, studio couch.* Urge them to recall their experiences when they first became aware of these words and

their meanings. Be ready to report their experiences to the class and to discuss them.

3 Many new words in our language are words made from the initial letter or letters of other words; for example, *WAC* (from Women's Army Corps), *loran* (from *long range navigation*), *Nabisco* (from *National Biscuit Company*). How many other examples can you think of?

4 Many of the words in the English vocabulary were coined from the names of people who were closely connected with a product, invention, method, treatment, or idea. We have, for example, *pasteurize* (from Louis *Pasteur*), *volt* (from Alessandro *Volta*), *zeppelin* (from Count von *Zeppelin*), and *poinsettia* (from Joel R. *Poinsett*). See how many other examples you can find.

5 English has borrowed a number of words from other languages —words that took on meaning for speakers of English as they became familiar with the things the words stood for. Examples are *kimono* (Japanese), *pretzel* (German), and *pronto* (Spanish). How many other examples can you think of? Perhaps your parents will have some suggestions.

HOW DO WE LEARN

THE MEANINGS OF WORDS?

An exchange student from France or Germany or Italy might have to resort to a dictionary to learn the meaning of such words as *cheeseburger, pole vault, peanut butter, hailstones, shortstop, popcorn, football,* and *traffic jam.* You never would. You learned what words like these mean without having to turn to a dictionary. You might not be able to give a concise definition of the words (such as you'd find in a dictionary), but you still know the meanings of these words and many others that you have never taken the time to look up.

Almost all of the words you know, in fact, you have learned without a dictionary. How? *Through experience*, the best source for finding out meanings.

There are two kinds of experience through which you learn the meanings of words. First, you may have a direct experience with the *thing* the word stands for. For example, there must have been a time in your life when you did not know the meaning of the words "ice-cream cone." But your first experience with this treat quickly taught you. Very probably someone handed you a cone at the same

time that he said the words "ice-cream cone," and you learned their meaning immediately. You connected the words with the object they stood for.

Let's look at a few more examples. You probably learned the meaning of "sour" by hearing someone say the word as you made a face when biting into a green apple or sipping some lime juice. Most of you learned the meaning of "foul ball" not from a dictionary, but by hearing the other players on your team yell the words when they saw that the ball you hit was going to land outside the base lines.

Experiences like these gave you a first-hand knowledge of the meanings of the words. No other way of learning words gives you as clear an idea of their meanings as having direct experiences with the things or the actions that the words stand for. Once you have cooked a piece of beef by browning it in fat and then simmering it in a covered pan (which your mother explained was "braising"), you know exactly what "to braise" means. And if in general-science class you heat water in a flask and let the steam condense as it passes through a glass tube (which your teacher explains is "distilling"), you will surely learn what "to distill" means.

But there are hundreds of words whose meanings you have learned without seeing or feeling or tasting or doing the things that the words stand for. Each of these words you have learned through another sort of experience—by hearing or seeing the word used in such a way that you can gradually figure out its meaning. Let's see how this works. We'll start by assuming that the word *martinet* is a new word to you; you have no idea what it means. One day on the bus you overhear the woman behind you say to her friend:

> "Thank goodness, our new office manager, Mr. Biggs, is not the *martinet* Mrs. Allen was. The typists and file clerks can at least talk to one another for a few minutes without having the boss scowl at us for not tending to business."

Although you do not know as yet exactly what *martinet* means, these sentences do give you a clue. Evidently a *martinet* is an unpleasant person who goes out of his way to see to it that the people under him are spending every minute on the job.

Some time later, in a story you are reading, you run across the word again:

> Captain Brady was a *martinet*—no doubt about it. He had become one soon after he had arrived at the post and found the men acting as if regulations were rules to be read and then forgotten. He soon put a stop to this.

And a day or two later the word crops up a third time, in a letter an angry citizen has sent to the editor of your local paper:

> The lack of equipment at the school I visited was bad, but the lack of discipline was worse. Something should be done. As a rule I don't approve of hiring a *martinet* as principal, but that school could surely use one—for a while at least.

By now the meaning of the word has become quite clear to you. From the way the word was used in these various places, you are fairly certain that a *martinet* is "a person who insists on maintaining very strict discipline." The **context**—the sentences in which the word was used (and the sentences following and preceding them) —gave you the clues that you needed.

The only drawback to learning word meanings from context is that it takes a great deal of time. You may have to see some words in dozens of different contexts before their meanings become clear. Often you can afford to wait this long; you can understand pretty much of what you hear or read without knowing the exact meaning of a particular word. For example, it did not matter especially whether you knew exactly what *martinet* meant when you overheard the woman on the bus. You could still get the gist of what she said.

But sometimes you cannot afford to wait. In order to understand the meaning of certain sentences, you have to know the exact meaning of an unfamiliar word. Suppose, for instance, that in an exercise in a social-studies class you were asked to answer the following question:

> What are two important facts that *extenuate* the crime committed by Mr. X?

Chances are that you do not know the meaning of *extenuate* (unless you are an avid reader of detective novels and are therefore familiar with the phrase "extenuating circumstances"). So unless you looked up the word *extenuate* in a dictionary and found that it means "to excuse in part" or "to lessen the seriousness of a crime by serving as an excuse," you could not possibly answer the question, because you could not understand it. A dictionary is a most valuable aid in learning the meaning of words when the context gives no clue to the meaning.

EXERCISE (2) Divide a sheet of paper into three columns. In the first column, write the words (from the following list) whose meanings you learned from direct experience with the things the words stand for. In the second column, list the words whose meanings you have learned through context clues—from hearing or reading the words in use. In the third column, list the words whose meanings you learned by looking up the words in a dictionary.

Be ready to tell the class what the experiences were that made the meanings of the words in your first column vividly clear. (The experience may be one you have actually had or one that you have seen someone else have in real life, in a movie, or on TV.)

1	slippery	9	kerosene	17	a rattlesnake
2	an iceberg	10	quicksand	18	to untangle
3	a canyon	11	an eagle	19	a submarine
4	a magnet	12	a farm	20	embarrassment
5	a whale	13	a blizzard	21	a dill pickle
6	a swarm	14	to sift flour	22	a tepee
7	dynamite	15	sticky	23	to waltz
8	rancid	16	a tourniquet	24	a mango

EXERCISE 3 Suppose you were asked to teach a foreigner the meaning of the words in the following list. Since he knows very little English, telling him the dictionary definitions of the words will not be of much help; you have to rely on other methods, using as few words as possible. What object or objects could you show him or what experiences could you provide for him to help him get a clear idea of what the words mean?

1	red	6	traffic jam	11	sweet
2	furniture	7	to lisp	12	to poach eggs
3	opaque	8	circular	13	equal
4	silverware	9	damp	14	addition
5	to pour	10	fraction	15	to startle

EXERCISE 4 The groups of sentences in which the italicized words are used should give you a fairly clear idea of what the words mean. Study the sentences carefully and be ready to tell the class what you think each italicized word means and what clues in the sentences led you to decide on this meaning.

If there is disagreement about the meaning of any of the words, your teacher will call on some student to check its meaning in a dictionary.

1.
  a) Many writers begin their letters with apologies for having *procrastinated* so long in writing.
  b) If you *procrastinate* much longer in getting our hotel reservations, we might as well decide to spend our vacation here at home.
  c) Every Saturday he decided to put off spading for another week, *procrastinating* until too late in the season.

2 a) Doubtless Aunt Jane meant well; but to her nephew, who wanted to work out his own problems, she often seemed unbearably *officious*.

b) How *officious* that wealthy cousin of the Andersons' was to rent them a beach cottage next to his own without even inquiring about their summer plans.

c) I wish that new bookkeeper would learn to mind his own business; one *officious* person in the office is bad enough, but two are too much.

3 a) Many living things that cannot defend themselves have various *stratagems* that succeed in fooling the enemy. Opossums, for example, often pretend to be dead when they are cornered by larger animals. Some insects use this same *stratagem*. Other insects escape notice by looking like the leaves, twigs, bark, or flowers they live on.

b) "John knows perfectly well that this family can't afford to send me to Europe for a year," Martha said to her mother. "And I do wish," she added, "that you wouldn't talk to him about all these imaginary rich men who want to marry me." But in spite of Martha's protests, Mrs. Slater used clumsy *stratagems* like these whenever John came to the house.

4 a) Mr. Danvers worked night and day making speeches, serving on committees, and calling on influential citizens. In fact, he seemed truly *indefatigable* in his efforts to convince the town of the need for a new vocational school.

b) All members of the club will have to pitch in and help. Remember that even as *indefatigable* a worker as Mr. Smithson cannot manage this whole project by himself.

5 a) Don't fool yourself that Carter is *altruistic*. His large contribution to the Children's Home, his work on the Civic Reform Committee, and his interest in 4-H activities are all based on a selfish motive—to win votes for himself in the senatorial election.

b) If we could get a group of *altruistic* businessmen interested in our problems, they would find a way to get us a recreation center.

6 a) O. Henry's short stories are full of the *local color* of New York City in the early 1900's—the ferryboats on the North River; the hardships of tenement life; and the glitter, roar, and commotion of Manhattan.

b) *The Adventures of Huckleberry Finn* is full of realistic episodes about the lives of people along the Mississippi River. Published in 1884, this book helps establish Mark Twain as one of our greatest *local colorists*.

Perhaps there are people who have actually increased their vocabularies by using one of the "learn-a-word-a-day" plans that are advertised in many newspapers and magazines. But for most people these plans do not work too well. For one thing, many of the words suggested in the lists to be learned are not particularly useful —words like *glabrous* (meaning "without hair or down; smooth"), and *divagate* (meaning "to wander; stray"), and *integument* ("a natural outer covering, like the skin or shell of an animal").

These are not words you can use in ordinary conversation and expect your listeners to understand. Nor are they words you will run across often in most of the reading that you do. And unless you frequently use or hear or read a word, it will do you no good to learn its meaning; within a few weeks you will have forgotten it.

There are other ways of adding to your stock of words, ways that will bring much better results. We know these ways will work because they are the ways by which you have already learned the many words you know—most of which you learned without realizing you were increasing your vocabulary. What are these ways?

93

DO NEW THINGS

Those of you who know the meanings of the words *serve, lob, ace, deuce,* and *advantage* learned them naturally and easily through playing tennis. The boys in your class who know the meaning of *mortise, tenon, lathe, planer,* and *auger* learned them without trying, through working with wood in a shop at home or at school. The girls who helped their mothers cook and sew had two rewards. Not only did they produce some good meals and attractive dresses, but they also added words like *sauté, marinate, au gratin, tension discs, piping,* and *pinking* to their vocabularies.

The easiest way to increase your vocabulary is to do new things, to have new experiences. Think of the words you could add by becoming interested in photography, in chemistry, in fashion design, in a part-time job at a printing shop, in sailing, in a trip through a local factory—yes, even in collecting stamps. Once you have learned the words, you must use them, in conversations with friends and in the writing you do. Once you have used them, they become a real part of your vocabulary.

EXERCISE 5 Recall the experiences you have had through acquiring a new hobby or taking part in a new sport or activity (learning to type, for example). Bring to class two or three words that anyone who became interested in this hobby, sport, or activity would quickly learn without having to make a special effort. Be ready to explain to the class what the words mean. Make your explanations as clear as possible with simple sketches, diagrams, or demonstrations.

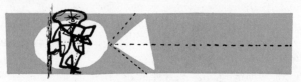

READ MORE

Most people have little chance to travel widely or to have a wide variety of experiences. But anyone can read books, magazines, and newspapers. Reading about a rodeo may not be as exciting as attending one, but it's the next best thing. And in reading about it, you can add to your vocabulary a number of words like *bulldogging*, *corral*, *lariat*, *hoolihan*, *dogfall*, and *honda*. This is true of almost everything that happens anywhere in the world. You may not be able to do all the things you would like to do, but you can read about them. In doing so, you too will have a double reward. Your reading will give you not only new experiences—new facts, new ideas—but also the new words to use in talking about them.

EXERCISE 6 Browse through a recent copy of a magazine like *Reader's Digest*, *Holiday*, *Ladies' Home Journal*, *Popular Mechanics*, *Field and Stream*, *The Saturday Evening Post*, *The Farm Quarterly*, *Practical English*, *Harper's*, or *Time* to find an article on a subject in which you are particularly interested. Read the article carefully and be ready to give the class a brief oral report on what you learn.

In your report, use at least three words that were new to you before you read the article. Before giving your report, write these words on the blackboard. Any class member who does not understand what the words mean after hearing your talk may ask you to explain their meanings. Be ready to do so.

LEARN HOW TO USE CONTEXT CLUES

As you saw on page 90, the context in which an unfamiliar word is used often provides clues to its meaning. Because this is true, you have been able to learn the meaning of a great many words without making a special effort to learn them. You can see, then,

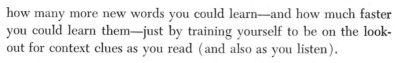

how many more new words you could learn—and how much faster you could learn them—just by training yourself to be on the lookout for context clues as you read (and also as you listen).

Direct clues. If you watch, you will find that many writers and speakers (especially good ones who keep their readers and listeners in mind) provide many clues to help you. Sometimes they give a direct clue right after the unfamiliar word. The word "format," for example, might be new to you before you read the following sentence with its direct clue. But if you take the trouble to connect the clue to the new word, you will surely learn what it means.

> Together the editor and the book designer decide on the **format**—*the shape, size, binding, type, paper, and general make-up of the book.*

Notice how the italicized direct clue in the following sentence explains the meaning of the boldfaced word:

> Before the men could start on the bridge foundations, they had to construct a **cofferdam,** *a watertight enclosure built in the lake and pumped dry.*

Examples as clues. Often the examples given by a writer (or speaker) will give you a fair idea of the meaning of a new word:

> What humor there was in Mr. Elder's talk was purely unintentional, consisting mainly of **malapropisms.** Several times, for example, he spoke of "resting on his morals" instead of "resting on his laurels," and he constantly said "incredulous results" when he certainly meant "incredible results."

The two examples given in the second sentence show clearly that a *malapropism* is a "ridiculous misuse of words caused by the similarity in sound." The writer of the sentences has given you a new word; it is up to you to add it to your vocabulary. This is a word your friends will enjoy.

Contrasts as clues. The clues provided by the context are not always as direct and obvious as the ones you have seen. Sometimes the clue lies in the contrast between two parts of a sentence:

> Since David had always been so energetic and tireless, his **lassitude** in these past few weeks worried his mother.

Since the contrast between David's usual energetic behavior and his recent behavior was the cause of his mother's worry, you can figure out that *lassitude* must mean "lack of energy; a feeling of weariness or of being tired."

Notice the contrast suggested between the two parts of the sentence in this next example:

> Although Mr. Fielder did not have the time to study all the details carefully, a **cursory** reading of the report showed him that Stevens had done an excellent job.

From the contrast, you realize that *cursory* must mean the opposite of slow and careful—in other words, "hasty; superficial; without paying attention to details."

Comparisons as clues. Often a comparison will make clear to you the meaning of a new word, once you train yourself to be on the alert for such a clue. Notice this example:

> As a rule the watchman at Noyes Stadium was as **irascible** as Scrooge on an especially trying day.

Since the watchman was like Scrooge (whom you know from your reading or from seeing him on TV at Christmas time), you can safely assume that *irascible* must mean "cranky; irritable; easily made angry."

Taking advantage of similar clues in the reading and listening you do will help you add many new words to your vocabulary. Make your reading and listening serve two purposes—to give you information and to teach you new words. And to make the new words a real part of your vocabulary, use them in your own speech and writing as often as you can.

EXERCISE (7) Suppose your younger brother (or sister) came to you puzzled about the meaning of the italicized words in the following sentences. Be ready to explain in class what context clues you could point out to him that would reveal the meaning of each word.

1 Though you have never known Marshall to make a mistake in these matters, you must realize that he, like the rest of us, is not *infallible*. This time he may be wrong.
2 Jerry was as *gullible* as the immigrant who let a swindler talk him into buying the Brooklyn Bridge for one hundred dollars.
3 *Ichthyology* next claimed Martin's attention, and for weeks his interest in this branch of zoology kept him busy visiting the Shedd Aquarium.
4 Since Alvin usually did everything his older brothers ordered him to do, I did not expect him to *demur* when they told him to lend Terry his golf clubs.
5 The leading actor's *understudy*, whose job it is to substitute for the star when necessary, is paid a regular salary.

6 The two teams then had a contest to see which could list the most *blends*. Philip Norton started them off by suggesting such words as "snoopervise" (made by telescoping "snoop" and "supervise"), "smog" ("smoke" blended with "fog"), and "brunch" ("breakfast" plus "lunch").

7 The reporters had learned to expect harsh, stinging sarcasm from Editor Weil, but on this occasion his comments were more *caustic* than ever.

8 The Turners were not just poor; they were *destitute*, barely managing to exist on the scraps of food Mrs. Turner brought home from the hotel.

9 His muscles are as *flaccid* as a jellyfish. [How is *flaccid* pronounced?]

10 "I know Mrs. Swift thinks of her son as high-spirited rather than *refractory*," said the principal to the guidance teacher. "But I must disagree. The old mule we had on the farm was easier to manage than Bill Swift is."

EXERCISE 8 Write five sentences in which you use any five of the ten words whose meaning you learned in the preceding exercise. Try to write sentences that contain clues to the meaning of the words. Read and compare the sentences in class.

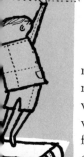

LEARN TO USE THE DICTIONARY EFFECTIVELY

As you saw on page 90, there are times when the context does not provide clues to the meaning of an unfamiliar word, and you must turn to a dictionary for help. There will be many times, too, when you have to turn to a dictionary for help with the meaning of words that you *thought* you knew. For example, you are surely familiar with the word *pedestrian*; you have used it and read it often enough. But what if you met this sentence in a book review:

Paths to Glory, Enoch Davidson's latest literary effort, is a **pedestrian** novel, if ever I have seen one.

The context gives you no help in figuring out the meaning of *pedestrian* in this sentence, but it does give you another sort of help. It shows you, at least, that *pedestrian* is not being used here in its ordinary meaning, the one you know so well. When context clues fail, turn to a dictionary for the meaning that fits. There you will find that the writer of this sentence was using *pedestrian* to mean "dull; slow; without imagination."

A word of warning: Sometimes the context may be deceiving; it may fool you into thinking that a certain word means something it really does not mean. Look at this sentence, for example:

> Corbett had lived in this **noisome** slum for only two weeks, but he would never forget the screaming voices, the angry quarreling, and the fighting that made slum life so miserable.

From the context (and perhaps from the sound and spelling of the word), you would very likely gather that *noisome* means "extremely noisy; filled with the din of fighting and quarreling." But checking in a dictionary would show you that *noisome* has nothing to do with noise. Its most common meaning is "disgusting; smelling bad."

Since context clues may fool you, it is best not to use a new word in your own speech and writing without first being sure of its meaning. There are two ways to make sure: (1) Wait until you see the word several times in different contexts. From these different contexts you can gradually figure out the right meaning of the new word and can learn how to use it correctly. (2) If you do not have time to wait, look up the word in a dictionary to check its meaning.

Unless you know how to use a dictionary easily and quickly, you will not turn to it for help as often as you should. But once you learn how to make efficient use of a dictionary, you will come to consider it one of the most valuable tools you can have. Chapter 7 (page 152) will show you many ways in which a dictionary can help you answer questions that come up in your speaking, writing, and reading. It will also show you a number of ways to improve your skill in finding these answers quickly.

EXERCISE 9 The meaning given in brackets after each of the numbered words in boldface type is its most common meaning, one that you probably know well. But when you read each sentence, you can tell by the context that the italicized word is not intended to have that common meaning. On a sheet of paper, write the meaning of each italicized word as it is used in the sentence. You may be able to figure out the intended meaning from the context. If not, you will have to refer to a dictionary to find the meaning that fits.

1 **become** ["come to be; grow to be"]
It does not *become* Martha to talk so flippantly to her parents.
2 **aggravate** ["annoy; exasperate"]
Rubbing his frostbitten hands with snow *aggravated* the pain, so we stopped.
3 **exhaust** ["tire very much"]
Weapons of the Bronze Age, Price's second book, *exhausts* the subject; you won't need to use any other reference.

4   **couch** ["thing made to sleep or rest on"]
    Mrs. Jones, as usual, *couched* her thoughts in flowery words.
5   **gesture** ["movement of hands, arms, or any part of body"]
    Norton realized that Ann's elaborate apology was merely a *gesture*; she was not at all sorry.
6   **carriage** ["vehicle that moves on wheels"]
    Her graceful *carriage* made her stand out from all the other girls at the party.
7   **collect** ["bring or come together"]
    After this outburst of temper, Jerry *collected* himself and answered their questions calmly.
8   **rat** ["a long-tailed rodent like a mouse but larger"]
    Aunt Jo still wore a *rat* in her hair, as she had back in 1915.
9   **intelligence** ["ability to learn and know; mind"]
    It was Wood's job to pass this *intelligence* on to the major.
10 **compass** ["an instrument for showing directions"]
    He worked hard but was unable to *compass* his goal.
11 **pirate** ["one who attacks and robs ships unlawfully"]
    Mr. Anders had dishonestly made a fortune by *pirating* short stories he ran across in his European travels.
12 **frequent** ["occurring often or every little while"]
    Jim's parents, on the other hand, *frequent* the theater.
13 **moment** ["a very short space of time"]
    Mr. Crawley was a disappointment to those who were concerned about the problems. He talked entertainingly for an hour but said nothing of *moment*.
14 **cracker** ["a thin, crisp biscuit"]
    Joe thought back to those days in the ramshackle Georgia cabin and felt a little proud of his *cracker* background.
15 **majority** ["greater part; more than half"]
    Until her stepson reaches his *majority*, she is in charge of his money.
16 **embrace** ["clasp or hold in the arms; hug"]
    The canine family *embraces* dogs, foxes, and wolves.
17 **exact** ["strictly correct; accurate; precise"]
    Doing the research will *exact* a great amount of time and skill.
18 **competence** ["ability; fitness"]
    The *competence* left him by his grandfather made it possible for Roderick to quit a job whenever he liked.
19 **homely** ["not good-looking; ugly; plain"]
    Although Dr. Grimes was handsome, brilliant, and wealthy, he was the most simple, *homely* person we knew.
20 **grateful** ["feeling gratitude; thankful"]
    "Oh, a cup of hot tea is always *grateful* on a cold day," he said.

WORDS

WORDS

WORDS...

A good vocabulary, as you saw in Chapter 4,
is best developed as a by-product of such interests as
travel, hobbies, sports, the arts, school clubs,
part-time jobs, and reading. At the same time you are
enjoying these activities, you can easily
be learning many of the words associated with them.

Of course, your vocabulary will never grow
if you just wait passively for new words to make
themselves a part of your speech and understanding.
Some effort and interest on your part are also necessary.

While you engage in activities that appeal to
you, you should first of all be aware
that a part of each new experience is the new
words it will make available to you.

Next, you must take advantage of every opportunity
to learn such words. Make a mental note when
you hear them, and then use them yourself on each appropriate
occasion until their use becomes natural and habitual.

If you are receptive to the special words you meet with
every different activity and interest, you will find
yourself with a richer vocabulary, increased ability to
express yourself well, and deepened understanding
in all the language experiences of your life.

You may not remember when words like *scrimmage* and *touchdown* entered your vocabulary. But you probably learned them while watching a football game or learning to play the game yourself. You learned them automatically as part of a direct experience with football.

101

Although you have been riding in cars all your life and have often heard words that refer to the parts of an automobile and their functions, such words probably have little or no meaning to you. But if you become a car enthusiast and get interested in tinkering with an automobile—even a jalopy—words like *carburetor, distributor, muffler, differential, transmission, acceleration,* and *choke* will become a meaningful part of your vocabulary.

Make way for a landslide of
new words whenever you become active
in a new sport. If it's skiing,
your first few days on the slopes should yield
at least *herringbone* and *schuss*—the
straight-down-the-hill thrill. Later you'll
learn *slalom*—what the expert in
the picture is doing as he prepares to
make a *Christie*, or *Christiania*, turn.

Margaret Durrance from Rapho-Guillumette

Or, at another time
of year, your new sport
may be sailing; and
in learning how to handle
a sailboat, you can
also enrich your vocabulary
with such words as *boom*,
jib, *tack*, *sheets*, and *spinnaker*.
Even if actually learning to
sail isn't a possibility for
you now, you can acquire
a nautical vocabulary—and
have an exciting reading
experience at the same time—
from such books as Dana's
Two Years Before the Mast.

Fred Lyon from Rapho-Guillumette

Everyone knows the words *oak* and *moss*. But alert travelers in the deep South observe different varieties of these common plants and learn new words for them. In the picture you see a *live oak* tree hung with curtains of *Spanish moss* on a plantation in Louisiana.

In traveling through the great Southwest, you may see *yuccas, mesquite, buttes, coulees, mesas, arroyos,* and *joshua trees.* If you are interested in broadening your knowledge as well as your vocabulary, you'll ask and learn the names of things you see— and so have another whole new category of words at your disposal.

One kind of travel you have not yet had the opportunity to enjoy, but have had many chances to read about, is travel into outer space. Reading about the exciting experiments scientists are carrying on in preparation for man's first trip into space will add such terms as *count down, blast off, astronaut, orbit, satellite,* and *galaxy* to your vocabulary.

Music offers a variety of pleasures from singing in the high-school glee club or your church choir to playing an instrument "just for fun" to engaging, like the men in the picture, in the specialized artistry of a string trio. Taking part in any one of these activities will give you the opportunity to make your own many musical terms such as *baritone, cantata, crescendo,* and *a cappella.*

Peskin—Free Lance Photographers Guild

Soon after you entered high school,
you probably saw your first track meet.
You may not have known then the
names for all the events you saw; but
if you were interested in track,
you easily learned such terms as *pole vault,*
shot-put, *hurdles*, and *relay*. And if
you should decide to take up tennis, whether
or not you become as skilled a player
as the girl in the picture, words like
backhand, *serve*, and *lob* will quickly
become a part of your active vocabulary.

From Shostal

"Now swing your partners," calls the leader as the couples enjoy the old-fashioned fun of taking part in a square dance. Many of his calls would surely be meaningless to you at your first square-dancing party, and you might fall all over your own feet while trying to follow the lead of more experienced dancers. But in two or three such sessions, you would easily learn words like *allemande, corner, sashay,* and *promenade* so that you too could respond to the various calls and move gracefully through all the steps of the dance.

Peskin—Free Lance Photographers Guild

Ballet is a difficult kind of dancing that requires years of training and a high degree of skill, a skill few people can achieve. But anyone who enjoys watching the performances of expert dancers can add to his pleasure—as well as to his vocabulary—by learning to recognize the *glissades, pirouettes, arabesques,* and other steps the dancers execute.

Commonwealth of Puerto Rico
Economic Development Administration

Have you as yet had any experience with skin diving? If you are a good swimmer, this interesting, comparatively new underwater activity may soon become a source of thrills and fascination for you. It can also be a gateway to some valuable additions to your vocabulary, such as *frogmen, snorkel, spearfishing, flippers,* and *aqualung.*

107

From the floor of the sea to the tops of the mountains . . . there is no end to the opportunities for adventure in today's world. But whether you actually peer into the depths of a *crevasse* yourself or merely read about such hazards in books like Herzog's *Annapurna,* an interest in mountain climbing will give you vividly and easily the meanings of this and other words like *fissure, couloir,* and *crampons.*

A chess enthusiast enjoys not only the
pleasure of pitting his wits against his opponent's,
but also the pleasure of frequently meeting—
in the books, newspapers, and magazines he reads—
such terms as *checkmate, gambit,* and
pawn. To a chess player, a sentence like "The
ambassador-level talks seem to have reached
a stalemate" is immediately and vividly clear.

Once you become a skillful horseback rider,
you too can experience the excitement of riding
through rocks and fording streams. And
while you are enjoying the fun of learning to
ride, you will also be adding to your
vocabulary *canter, post, pommel, bay, roan,*
quarter horse, and many other terms of horsemanship.

A much less strenuous activity, but one that
will also contribute to your vocabulary, is gardening.
Anyone who takes care of his own garden,
perhaps as a 4-H Club project, will soon learn such
words as *bulb, perennial, mulch,* and *compost—*
part of the working vocabulary of all gardeners.

CHAPTER 5

USING

THE LIBRARY

Among the many people you know or have heard of, there are quite likely to be two or three who constantly amaze others with the vast extent of their knowledge of a particular subject. You have probably envied some of these "walking encyclopedias" and have wished that you knew as much as they—about sports, for example, or history, or music. How impressive it would be to be able to answer, correctly and without hesitation, such questions as "How many home runs did Babe Ruth hit in his last season with a major-league team?" or "Which opera star played Desdemona in the first presentation of *Othello* at La Scala?"

If you wanted to badly enough, you too could become a "walking encyclopedia" on a particular subject. You could, that is, if you were willing to spend enough time and effort in studying that subject, memorizing minute details and miscellaneous facts about it. However, unless you considered impressing others to be of utmost importance, it would hardly be worth while to spend your time in memorizing minor facts and details about a single subject. It

would be far better to learn fewer but more important facts about a number of subjects. And it would be far more useful to learn *where and how to find information when you need it.*

The library is the great storehouse of information. In the library there are answers to almost any question you might have on any subject, now or in the future. By learning how to make efficient use of the resources of the library, you will learn how to find, easily and quickly, the answers you want. This chapter will help you.

As you work out the exercises, keep in mind the purpose of the chapter—to give you training in finding information. The facts you find will be interesting; many of them you will think worth remembering. However, the important thing is not the facts themselves, but learning where and how to find them. This knowledge will be useful to you not only now while you are in school, but later also, in whatever work you do. Your employer will not expect you to know everything, but he will expect you to know how to find what you don't know.

If there were only fifty or even a hundred books in a library, it would not matter just how those books were arranged on the shelves. They could, in fact, be grouped by size or even by the color of the covers. Anyone wanting a particular book could quickly find it by starting at one end and glancing at all the titles until he came to the right one. But a public or school library of only one hundred books is rare, fortunately. Most libraries have thousands of volumes, books dealing with a great many different subjects. Without an efficient system of arranging the books on the shelves, finding information on a particular subject would be difficult enough to discourage most people from using the library.

At first thought, arranging all the books alphabetically by title or author might seem to be a good idea. But that would mean that books about a single subject might be scattered about in twenty or even thirty or more spots in the library. A person looking for information about astronomy, or electronics, or dress designing would like to find all the available books together in one spot. Although an alphabetical arrangement would be convenient for the person who had the job of putting books on the shelves, it would not be very helpful to the *users* of the books. And they are the ones to be considered.

Keeping in mind the users of the library, Melvil Dewey, a librarian, devised a system of arranging books which works so well that it is used in more than 90 per cent of all libraries. It is very likely the system that is used in your school and public libraries.

Nonfiction books. In this system, called the **Dewey Decimal System**, all nonfiction is divided into ten main subject groups or classes, each of which is assigned a number:

000–099   **General Works** (general encyclopedias and periodicals, rare books, etc.)

100–199   **Philosophy** (psychology, ethics, logic, personality, etc.)

200–299   **Religion** (Bible, churches, church history, mythology, etc.)

300–399   **Social Sciences** (economics, law, government, education, etiquette, customs, etc.)

400–499   **Linguistics** (dictionaries and grammars, derivations, etc., of various languages)

500–599   **Pure Science** (mathematics, chemistry, astronomy, physics, etc.)

600–699 **Applied Science** (medicine, engineering, aviation, business, etc.)

700–799 **Arts and Recreation** (sculpture, painting, music, photography, games, sports, etc.)

800–899 **Literature** (novels, plays, essays, poetry, etc., of various countries)

900–999 **History** (geography, collective biography, travel, etc.)

As you can see by referring to the chart, any book that has to do with the general subject of history will be given a number in the 900's (from 900 to 999). Any book that deals with religion will be given a number in the 200's (from 200 to 299). The exact number in any group of hundreds that is assigned to a particular book depends on which phase of the subject it deals with. Each of the main subject groups is divided into ten more specific subgroups. For example, the subgroups in the 300–399 class are:

300	Social Sciences	350	Administration
310	Statistics	360	Social Welfare
320	Political Science	370	Education
330	Economics	380	Commerce
340	Law	390	Customs

Each of the subgroups is, in turn, subdivided by tens:

380	Commerce	386	Inland Waterway Transportation
381	Domestic Trade		
382	International Trade	387	Marine Transportation
383	Postal Communication	388	Highway Transportation
384	Communication	389	Standard Weights and Measures
385	Transportation		

Still more specific subdivisions are made by using decimals. For example:

387.52—books dealing with Trade Routes
387.54—books dealing with Steamship Lines
387.7 —books dealing with Air Transportation
387.73—books dealing with Air Terminals

On the spine of every nonfiction book, the librarian writes the Dewey classification number that shows what subject the book deals with. Once these identifying numbers are on the books, it is easy for the librarian to arrange the books on the shelves. She simply glances at the numbers; they tell her what books belong together and in what order they should appear on the shelves. Grouping the books by subject matter and arranging them in numerical order makes it easy for you to find in one spot all the material available on whatever subject interests you at a particular time.

Fiction. Books of fiction are not usually given a classification number. Instead they are marked **F** and are arranged alphabetically by the last names of the authors. If there are several books by one author, they are arranged alphabetically by the first word of the title (not counting such words as *A, An,* and *The*).

Biographies. Biographies, books dealing with the lives of people, are also handled in a special way. In some libraries "individual" biographies are marked **B**; in others they are given the Dewey number **92**. ("Collective" biographies, books dealing with several lives, are usually marked **920**.) Right under the **B** or the **92** the librarian writes the initial letter of the last name of the person the biography is about. (A biography of Paul Revere, for example, would be marked $\frac{B}{R}$.) Then the books are arranged alphabetically by these initial letters. This puts all books about one person conveniently together in one spot.

Though it is necessary for you to understand how the Dewey System works, it is not necessary to memorize the complete chart of classification numbers. But make it a point to notice the numbers assigned to subjects that are especially interesting to you. Once you know these numbers, you can go directly to the shelves that hold the books you need. (The numbers of the books found in each section of shelves are usually shown on large cards posted above the shelves.)

EXERCISE (1) Most of Sir Winston Churchill's books are about World War II. Since they deal with history, librarians using the Dewey Decimal System classify them in the 900's. The following titles clearly reveal what subject matter the books deal with. List the titles (with their authors) on a sheet of paper. After each, tell which of the main Dewey classification groups it would be assigned to.

1 Boris Sokoloff, *Miracle Drugs*
2 Frank Abbott Magruder, *American Government*
3 May Hill Arbuthnot, *Time for Poetry*
4 Selig Hecht, *Explaining the Atom*
5 William James Durant, *Story of Philosophy*
6 Thor Heyerdahl, *Kon-Tiki; Across the Pacific by Raft*
7 Florence Mary Fitch, *One God; The Ways We Worship Him*
8 Lucile Marshall, *Photography for Teen-agers*

9 Wilfred John Funk, *Word Origins and Their Romantic Stories*
10 *World Book Encyclopedia*
11 Charles Lamb, *Essays of Elia*
12 Mario Andrew Pei, *All About Language*

EXERCISE (2) The following titles do not indicate what subjects the books deal with. After each title is given the Dewey classification number and three possible subjects (in parentheses). By referring to the chart of Dewey class numbers, decide which of the three subjects given after each title is the one the book is about. List your answers on a sheet of paper, numbering them with the numbers of the titles.

1 *Apollo*, Salomon Reinach **709** (Greek mythology, history of art, medicine)
2 *Strike Up the Band!* Alberta Graham **920** (a collection of biographies of band leaders, descriptions of musical instruments, Fourth of July celebrations)
3 *Hog on Ice*, Charles E. Funk **427** (agriculture, transportation, origins of common English expressions)
4 *Bright Design*, Katherine B. Shippen **530.9** (physics, painting, fashions)
5 *How Much and How Many*, Jeanne Bendick **389** (recipes for the modern cook, mathematics, the effect of weights and measures on trade and everyday living)
6 *Magic in a Bottle*, Milton Silverman **615.5** (drugs used in modern medicine, magicians' tricks for the amateur, biography of Houdini)
7 *Hullabaloo*, Richard Chase **796** (advertising as a career, television commercials, singing games and folk dances)
8 *Early Moon*, Carl Sandburg **811** (astronomy, a collection of poems, a study of tides)
9 *Good Ways*, Delight Ansley **290** (a guide to super highways, a manual for home craftsmen, a history of world religions)
10 *The Confident Years*, Van Wyck Brooks **810.9** (Brooks's autobiography, literary criticism, life on the frontier)

THE CARD CATALOGUE

Close to the main entrance of every large department store is an information desk where you can get answers to such questions as "Where are the cashmere sweaters?" and "Where can I have packages gift wrapped?" In a prominent place in every library is a "self-help" information center—the **card catalogue**. Here you can find answers to four important questions:

1) Does the library have a book of a particular title?
2) Does the library have a book by a particular author?
3) Does the library have a book or books on a particular subject?
4) If the library has these books, just where on the shelves are they?

A library catalogue is not a large book, like a Sears Roebuck catalogue. Instead it is a series of cards filed alphabetically in drawers. Each drawer is labeled with letters showing which portion of the alphabet it contains. For example, if the first word on the top line of a card is *Arnold* or *Bacon*, the cards would be filed in a drawer labeled, say, ARM—BAL. But if the first word on the top line is *Bell*, you would have to look for that card in the next drawer, the one labeled BAM—COUN (or some similar groups of letters).

As a rule, the librarian puts in the catalogue at least three cards for every nonfiction book—a title card, an author card, and a subject card. The three cards are alike except for one thing—the top line. On a **title card**, the top line gives the name of the book. On an **author card**, the top line gives the name of the author, last name first. On a **subject card**, the top line gives the subject of the book.

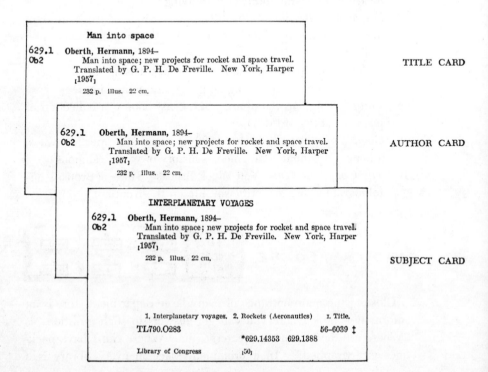

Do you see how important it is to have at least three cards for each book in the library? If a book were listed only by title, you could not find the book unless you knew that title. If a book were listed only by author, you could not find it unless you knew the author's name. And since often you know neither title nor author, but are just trying to find material on a certain subject, it is quite necessary to have books listed by subject.

A book may be listed under more than one subject heading. For example, a book containing the history of basketball may be listed under the subjects SPORTS, ATHLETICS, and BASKETBALL. Therefore, if you do not find a title you need under the first subject you look up, it is a good idea to try a related subject.

Printed catalogue cards of the type shown as samples contain more than just the name of the book and its author, as you can see. They may give such details as the date of the author's birth and death (if he is no longer living), the name of the publisher, the date and place published, whether there are illustrations, and often a summary of the contents.

The call number. In the upper left corner of each card you will find the *call number*—the "address" that tells you where the book is located in the library. The call number usually consists of two parts. The top line (629.1) gives the Dewey classification number. The second line (Ob2) gives the initial letter or letters of the author's last name and the author's number. In small libraries only the initial is given. But in libraries where there are many authors with the same initial, the numbers are included to distinguish one from another.

The call number on the cards matches the one that is written on the spine of the book, making it easy for you to find the book on the shelves. In school libraries it is up to you to get the books you want. In large city libraries the librarians get the books; you merely "call" for the ones you want by giving the call numbers at the desk.

Note: Cards for books of fiction will not usually have a Dewey number, though sometimes **823** is used. Ordinarily the space for the call number is left blank, or the letter **F** is given to show that the book is fiction.

EXERCISE (3) Draw a simple floor plan of your school library, showing the location of the card catalogue, the reference-book shelves, the nonfiction shelves, the fiction shelves, and the shelves or stand for current magazines. Show where the different classes of nonfiction are placed by writing the Dewey numbers (100–199, 200–299, etc.) in the spaces representing the nonfiction shelves.

EXERCISE (4) Copy from the title cards in the card catalogue the names of the authors and the call numbers of at least five of these books.

1 *Strange Animals I Have Known*
2 *When Knights Were Bold*
3 *Introduction to Shakespeare*
4 *Our FBI*
5 *Inventors Behind the Inventor*
6 *United Nations Primer*
7 *Careers for Nurses*
8 *American Songbag*
9 *A Girl Grows Up*
10 *Your Manners Are Showing*

EXERCISE (5) You would probably enjoy reading several of the books in the following list. Refer to the card catalogue to see which of them your library has. List these titles on a sheet of paper. After each, copy from the title card the name of the author and the call number. (If the book is fiction, write "F" after the author.)

1 *When the Stars Come Out*
2 *Mama's Bank Account*
3 *Queens Die Proudly*
4 *Bridle for Pegasus*
5 *King of the Wind*
6 *Spring Comes Riding*
7 *Dogs of Destiny*
8 *Loon Feather*
9 *Boy and His Gun*
10 *Call of the Wild*
11 *Drums Along the Mohawk*
12 *Great Houdini*

EXERCISE (6) Each of the following authors has written at least one book that you might enjoy. Pick five of the authors. From the books your library has by each of these five, choose the one that most attracts your interest. On a sheet of paper, list the names of the five authors, the titles of the books you choose, and their call numbers.

1 Bob Considine
2 Edward Ellsberg
3 Jeanette Eaton
4 Anne Emery
5 John Joseph Floherty
6 Will James
7 Cornelia Meigs
8 Mary O'Hara
9 Howard Pease
10 John R. Tunis

EXERCISE (7) Choose five of the following subjects, the ones that most interest you. Refer to the card catalogue to find what books your library has on these subjects. For each subject, copy on a sheet of paper the title of the book that seems most interesting to you, the name of its author, and its call number.

1 Ballet
2 Birds
3 Etiquette
4 Indians of North America
5 Jet and rocket engines
6 Nurses and nursing
7 Photography
8 Postal service
9 Railroads
10 Stamp collection
11 Television
12 Weather

EXERCISE (8) Some of the following books are biographies; others are books of fiction. Copy the numbers on a sheet of paper and after each write the author of the book. Then write "F" if the book is fiction, "B" if it is biography. The card catalogue will give you the answers.

1 *Beau Geste*
2 *Captain Horatio Hornblower*
3 *Cheaper by the Dozen*
4 *From the Top of the Stairs*
5 *He Heard America Sing*
6 *Invincible Louisa*
7 *Jane Eyre*
8 *Johnny Tremain*
9 *Lantern in Her Hand*
10 *Little Princesses*
11 *Lone Cowboy*
12 *Madame Curie*
13 *Microbe Hunters*
14 *Seventeenth Summer*
15 *Thunderhead*
16 *Circus Doctor*

REFERENCE BOOKS

Almost every day questions about one thing or another come up for which you do not have the answers. Arguments may arise over such matters as who is the world's champion discus thrower, which is the largest river in the world, whether a tarantula's bite is always fatal, whether the great Chicago fire was actually started by Mrs. O'Leary's cow, or what job Lou Gehrig had after retiring from baseball. For a social-studies report, you may need to learn how many students are enrolled in our elementary schools or what the legal voting age is in various states. For an oral report in your English class, you may have to find information about the life of an author or about the theater of Shakespeare's time.

In the **reference** section of your library are books in which you can find answers to questions like these. Since these reference books are in constant demand, they must be used in the library; you are not to take them out of the room. But this is not a hardship, because the books are intended primarily to provide information that can be found quickly and read in a short time.

What sorts of books are found in the reference section? Let's look at the ones you will find most helpful.

Encyclopedias. The Greek words from which our word *encyclopedia* comes mean "a well-rounded education"—a pretty accurate description of what you can get in this type of reference. General encyclopedias contain important and interesting facts about people, places, historical events, inventions, plants, animals, geography, government, art—almost any subject from A to Z that you can name.

119

The articles are listed alphabetically, and letters on the spine of each volume tell which portion of the alphabet is covered.

The articles are written by many people, experts in different fields. Since space is limited, the articles do not include as much information about any one subject as you could find in books devoted to the subject. But for most purposes the articles are more than adequate. They give a general view of the subjects and provide answers to most of the basic questions.

There are several good encyclopedias, some of which are designed especially for high-school students. In your library you will probably find a set of one or all of these:

> *Collier's Encyclopedia*
> *Encyclopedia Americana*
> *Encyclopaedia Britannica*
> *Compton's Pictured Encyclopedia* (especially for high-school use)
> *World Book Encyclopedia* (especially for high-school use)
> *Britannica Junior*

Refer to these whenever you need general information about people, places, and things, and to get background material on subjects that are new to you.

Biographical references. Since encyclopedias have to cover many subjects, they have room for the lives of only the most outstanding men and women of the world and history. But your library has other reference books to give you information about people. For example:

> *Who's Who* (mainly living Englishmen of importance)
> *Who's Who in America* (prominent living Americans)
> *Webster's Biographical Dictionary* (important people of all countries and all times)

Although the articles in these are short, they give an amazing number of facts. If you want more interesting accounts of the lives of outstanding men and women, among the best references to use are:

> *Current Biography* (in monthly pamphlets and annual volumes)
> Kunitz and Haycraft: *Twentieth Century Authors*
> Kunitz and Haycraft: *The Junior Book of Authors* (contemporary authors and illustrators of juvenile literature)

Yearbooks. If you are in search of sports records, award winners, important dates, facts about your state resources and government, school enrollment figures, newspaper circulation figures—statistics of all kinds, in fact—one of these will probably give you the information you want:

> *The World Almanac and Book of Facts* (published yearly)
> *Information Please Almanac* (published yearly)

Here the secret of finding the needed information quickly is to make use of the index. In *The World Almanac* the index appears at the front; in *Information Please,* in its usual place at the back.

Atlases. Often the information you need has to do with geography—the location of a certain city, the area of a particular island, the boundaries of a country in South America or Africa, the course of a river, the extent of a mountain range. You will find the facts you need by referring to one of the atlases in your library. Three that are especially good are:

> *Goode's World Atlas*
> *Rand McNally–Cosmopolitan World Atlas*
> *Hammond's Library World Atlas*

Books of quotations. Who said "Ignorance of the law excuses no man"? What is the rest of the verse that begins "Oh, cakes and friends we should choose with care"? Where can I find an amusing quotation about the fickleness of women?

If you have ever asked questions like these, you should become acquainted with books that have the answers:

> Bartlett's *Familiar Quotations*
> Stevenson's *Home Book of Quotations*

In Bartlett's book the quotations are grouped by their authors. In Stevenson's book, they are grouped by subjects. But both books have, in addition to an index of authors, an index of key words by which you can find a particular quotation.

Using reference books. The descriptions you have read of the different types of reference books can do little more than make you aware of the books that are available. The best way to learn how truly valuable and useful the books are is to use them. The following exercises will give you a clear idea of the sort of information the various books provide. The experience you get in looking for the information will help you gain skill in finding answers by yourself. You will find this much more satisfactory than having to ask other people for help.

EXERCISE 9 Write the answers to eight of the following questions, the eight which interest you most. Give brief but complete answers (not merely a "yes" or "no"). Refer to *Compton's Pictured Encyclopedia, World Book Encyclopedia,* or *Britannica Junior* for the facts you will need.

1 How does the banyan tree differ from other trees?
2 Can cats actually see in the dark, as is commonly believed?
3 What qualifications must a candidate for a position as a special agent for the FBI (Federal Bureau of Investigation) have?
4 How many people are eventually to be honored in the Hall of Fame for great Americans (on the campus of New York University)?
5 Does damaged paper money (a dollar bill with a large section torn off, for example) have any value?
6 How did Oklahoma get its nickname—the "Sooner State"?
7 Does a porcupine defend itself by shooting its quills at an enemy?
8 What were the "seven wonders" of the ancient world?
9 Are our tin cans actually made of tin? Why are "tin cans" good containers for food?
10 What causes an echo?

EXERCISE (10) Refer to the latest volume of *Who's Who in America* or to *Current Biography* (1953, 1954) to find the answers to the following questions.

1 When did Edward R. Murrow first become associated with the Columbia Broadcasting System? What different jobs did he hold for CBS?
2 When and where did Dr. Charles William Mayo get his M.D. degree? Where did he serve his internship?
3 For what dress manufacturing firm has Claire McCardell designed clothes? When did she become a designer for the firm?
4 Clare Boothe Luce, appointed Ambassador to Italy in 1953, is a playwright as well as a diplomat. Name four plays she has written.

EXERCISE (11) Write the answers to five of the following questions. The atlases in your library will give you the help you need.

1 If you were driving from northern to southern Italy, in what order would you come to the following cities—Firenze (Florence), Milano (Milan), Napoli (Naples), Roma (Rome)?
2 Does Bogotá, the capital of Colombia, South America, lie northwest or northeast of Quito, the capital of Ecuador?
3 Which is farthest west—Los Angeles, Sacramento, or Portland?

4 Does Toronto, Canada, lie northeast or southeast of Tacoma, Washington?

5 In what states does Yellowstone National Park lie?

6 What are the five largest islands of the world and what is the area of each?

7 What is the air-line distance between New Orleans and Seattle?

8 What is the nickname and what is the state flower of Arkansas, Maine, Michigan, Missouri, and Tennessee?

9 Illinois is commonly known as a "Northern" state. Which of these "Southern" cities is farther south than Cairo, Illinois: Louisville, Nashville, Richmond, Roanoke, Baltimore?

10 Where and what is the Old Head of Kinsale?

EXERCISE 12 Refer to the most recent volume of *The World Almanac and Book of Facts* or to *Information Please Almanac* for answers to the following questions.

1 Who won the Academy Awards for the best actor and best actress in 1948 and in 1953? In what movies did they play the prize-winning parts?

2 Who holds the record in the Olympic games pole-vault event? What is the record? When was it set? What nation did the man who set the record represent?

3 What is the name of the tallest building in New York, Cleveland, Chicago, and Cincinnati? How many feet tall is each of these buildings? How many stories does each have?

4 What was the total college enrollment (including universities, junior colleges, normal schools) in 1957? Does this figure represent the *actual* fall enrollment or the *estimated* enrollment?

5 Who are the governors of Pennsylvania, Wyoming, and Kentucky? What annual salary does each of these men get?

6 What two organizations shared the Nobel peace prize in 1947?

EXERCISE 13 The expressions enclosed in quotation marks are often heard. Copy the expressions on a sheet of paper. After each, write the name of the person who originated it and the title of the writing in which it first appeared. (Refer to Bartlett's *Familiar Quotations* or Stevenson's *Home Book of Quotations*.)

1 Don't be afraid of Mr. Barnes; "his bark is worse than his bite."

2 I heard him, but what he said was "Greek to me."

3 Just as we started, it began to "rain cats and dogs."

4 Between them sat little Jimmie, as "snug as a bug in a rug."

5 Yes, Mr. Marks generally contributes five dollars, but he is not "a cheerful giver."

EXERCISE (14) Refer to Bartlett's *Familiar Quotations* or Stevenson's *Home Book of Quotations* for help with the following problems.

1 Suppose you are writing a theme about the problems and hardships of commuters. You want an appropriate quotation to use as an introduction. You remember having heard an amusing verse that you are sure would be suitable, if only you could find it. What verse might you use? Who wrote it?

2 Suppose that your class is to have a group discussion about different kinds of advertising and the good and bad points of each. One point you want to bring up is that billboards are ruining the looks of the countryside and spoiling the view for those who love beauty. A book of quotations will give you a verse that you might use to emphasize this point. What is this verse? Who is the author? From what piece of writing does it come?

3 Before the 1948 elections the polls and straw votes all seemed to indicate that Thomas E. Dewey—not Harry S. Truman—would win the presidency. But Truman won. Ever since then many people have had little faith in pre-election polls. These people would agree whole-heartedly with O. Henry's opinion of a *straw vote*. What was his opinion? In which of O. Henry's stories did it appear?

4 At a party you attended you heard a nonsense verse about a *purple cow*. You would like to quote the verse, but you can't remember the exact words. What are they? Who wrote the verse? How did the author feel about the verse? [You will find the answer in the verse following "The Purple Cow."]

5 Where did the proverb "Experience keeps a dear school, but fools will learn in no other" first appear? Who is the author?

FINDING INFORMATION IN MAGAZINES

Things happen fast in this modern age. Before you have mastered the latest step, a new dance becomes the rage. Your doctor hardly finishes learning about a new antibiotic when two or three other newer products to combat disease are written up in the medical journals. Before you can save enough money to buy that new camera you want, an improved, even more miraculous one appears on the market. How can a person keep up with this swift progress? Where can he get the latest, most up-to-date information? The answer is again the library—in the magazines. There you will find information too new to be in books and important material on topics about which books may never be written.

With a card catalogue, finding information in books on a particular subject is no problem. But how about magazine articles? Searching through piles of all available magazines in the hope of finding information on even one topic would be an endless, discouraging job. There is a much easier way—using the *Readers' Guide to Periodical Literature.*

What the card catalogue does for books, the *Readers' Guide* does for magazines. It is an index, printed in book form, to all articles, poems, and stories that have appeared in more than one hundred leading periodicals. (The names of the magazines it indexes are listed at the front of each issue.) The *Guide* has been published since 1900 and is kept so closely up to date that librarians receive a new paper-bound issue every two weeks. These issues are combined, or "cumulated," at regular intervals throughout the year. The cumulated issues, in turn, are combined into one volume covering an entire year. Every two years a hard-bound volume replaces the smaller issues.

Magazine articles are listed alphabetically by subject and author —but *not* by title, except for stories. To find what articles about telephones have appeared in recent magazines, you would turn to the T's for the subject heading TELEPHONE. There you would find a list that looks like this:

TELEPHONE
About telephones: 61,000,000 of them. G. Talese. il N Y Times Mag p29+ S 29 '57
Charts of the week; telephone conversations. Bsns W p61 Ja 4 '58
Do it by telephone with a phone operated switch. T. Diers. il diag Radio & Tv N 58:51–3+ N '57
New vandalproof lighted signs point out public call boxes; New York city. il Am City 72:133 Jl '57
Telephone for the deaf. il Newsweek 50:78 Jl 29 '57
Telephones, people, and machines. J. R. Pierce. Atlan 200:141–3 D '57; Same abr. with title Telephones of tomorrow. Sci Digest 43:8–12 F '58
Telephoning on credit. Good H 145:52 S '57
See also
Emergency communication systems

Amplifying apparatus
Build your own tel-amp. L. Dell. il diags Pop Mech 109:179–82+ Ja '58

Answering service
If Amanda answers, don't hang up. E. Lauter. il Coronet 43:76–7 N '57

History
Telephone history at Smithsonian institution. Hobbies 62:94 Ag '57

Medical applications
Washington's cancer answer. H. Helfer. Coronet 42:125 My '57

A key at the front of the *Guide* explains the abbreviations and symbols used in the entries. The item under the subheading **Amplifying apparatus**, for example, means that the article "Build Your Own Tel-Amp," written by L. Dell, is illustrated and has diagrams. It appeared on pages 179 to 182 (continued on later pages of the magazine) of the January 1958 issue of *Popular Mechanics Magazine*, volume 109.

If you had known the name of the author—Dell—you could have found the same information under the author entry in the D's:

> DELL, Lou
> Build your own tel-amp. Pop Mech 109 :179–
> 82+ Ja '58

You may not find in your school library all articles listed in the *Guide*, since your library may not subscribe to all the magazines the *Guide* indexes and it may not keep back issues of the magazines. However, once you know the issues you want, you may be able to get them at the public library or from friends.

EXERCISE ⑮ The following abbreviations are among those used in *Readers' Guide* entries. Copy the abbreviations on a sheet of paper, and tell what each stands for. Refer to the Key at the front of any volume of *Readers' Guide* for help.

1	Ag.	5	ed	9	Mr	13	abr
2	Ap	6	il	10	por	14	tab
3	cond	7	Ja	11	v	15	rev
4	diag	8	Je	12	+	16	Jl

EXERCISE ⑯ Refer to the list of periodicals given at the front of *Readers' Guide* to find what abbreviations are used for the following magazines. List the abbreviations on a sheet of paper. Be ready to read the names of the magazines from the abbreviations.

1	*Atlantic*	8	*Musical America*
2	*Aviation Week*	9	*National Geographic Magazine*
3	*Better Homes and Gardens*	10	*Popular Science Monthly*
4	*Business Week*	11	*Reader's Digest*
5	*Catholic World*	12	*Saturday Evening Post*
6	*Good Housekeeping*	13	*Scientific American*
7	*Mademoiselle*	14	*Science News Letter*

EXERCISE ⑰ Make an alphabetical list of the magazines indexed in the *Readers' Guide* which your school library receives regularly. Put a check mark (√) after each magazine for which your library keeps back issues.

EXERCISE (18) Make an alphabetical list of the magazines your family receives regularly. Include in your list the dates of any back issues you have of these magazines. Hand your list to a class secretary, who will put an alphabetical compilation of all the lists and subscribers on the board. Make a copy of this final list so that you and your classmates can borrow magazines from one another when you are unable to get them in the library.

EXERCISE (19) Be ready to explain in class what specific information each of the following *Readers' Guide* entries gives.

1 MONEY
Pardon me, I like money. D. Herold. il Coronet 39:114–16 Ap '56

2 PRESIDENT'S daughter; story. See Cousins, M.

3 COUSINS, Margaret (Mary Parrish, pseud)
President's daughter; story. Good H 147: 76–7 S '58

4 ALASKA
Alaska; a star is born. il Sr Schol 73:14–17 S 12 '58
Go north, young man. B. F. Heintzleman. Am For 64:10–11 Ag '58
See also
Aeronautics, Commercial—Alaska
Forests and forestry—Alaska

History
Seward's fortunate folly. F. J. Taylor. Read Digest 73:169–70+ S '58

5 DOGS in police work
Dogs work for man. E. J. Linehan. il Nat Geog Mag 114:190–233 Ag '58

6 SANDS, Thomas Adrian
Storm over Sands. il pors Life 42:92+ Je 3 '57
Teen-age crush. por Time 69:46 My 13 '57

7 DANCING, Cuban
It's new: Gua-pa-cha! D. Byrnes and A. Swanson. il tabs Dance Mag 31:58 S '57

8 PHOTOCOPYING. See Photography—Copying

127

EXERCISE (20) From the subjects listed below, choose the three that interest you most. For each of these three, find in the *Readers' Guide* two recent articles whose titles attract your curiosity. On a sheet of paper, list these titles (and their authors) and tell where they can be found. Look up one of the six articles that you list, and be ready to tell the class whether you found it interesting and why.

1	Acrobats	7	Jazz music
2	Air bases	8	Mars
3	Baby sitters	9	Mountaineering
4	Comets	10	Prize fighting
5	Counterfeits and counterfeiting	11	Skin diving
6	Firearms	12	Women and politics

CHAPTER 6

WRITING

A COMPOSITION

NAR
RA
TION

If Dr. Gallup were to take a poll to determine why some high-school students dislike writing compositions, he would probably find that one of the reasons most frequently given is "I don't have anything interesting to write about." Coming from teen-agers, who spend hour upon hour talking about an endless number of things, this certainly seems a strange reason. If your classmates and friends are interested in *hearing* about your experiences, your ideas, and your opinions, surely they would be interested in *reading* about them.

Actually, you don't have to look very far to find subjects that are interesting. The problem—if there is one—is deciding which of many interesting subjects to write about in a particular composition. Let's think over some of the subjects you might choose.

Tell what happened. Your classmates would enjoy reading about some of the exciting, sad, unusual, or amusing things that have happened to you or that you saw happen. For example, you might tell how you won the fishing contest at Indian Lake or about

the practical joke that cost your brother the leading part in the seventh-grade pageant. As you can see, the incidents you write about need not be any more startling or spectacular than the ones you talk about.

Tell about people and places. Some of the people and places that have impressed you or amused you or aroused strong feelings on your part would also make good subjects for papers. For example, you might write about an arthritic aunt who, although she is in constant pain, is always cheerful; the neighbor you have nicknamed Napoleon because of his short stature and dictatorial manner; or the experimental farm you enjoyed visiting last summer.

Explain how to do something or how something works. Perhaps the most useful sort of paper you might write is an explanation of how to make or do something or how something works. Your hobbies, clubs, and other activities provide a number of subjects for such explanations. If, for example, you frequently go on hunting trips, quite likely you could write an informative paper on how to clean a gun or how to construct a blind.

Of course, you don't always have to rely on personal experience for subjects. Suppose you are curious about how a rotary press works or why volcanoes erupt. You could look up information on the subject and then write a paper reporting *in your own words* what you have learned.

Explain ideas and opinions. Many ideas for another sort of explanatory paper come from the countless talks you and your friends have about personal and social problems, especially those of people your own age. You might, for example, write a paper giving your views on the values of scouting, or pointing out the difficulties of making friends in a new school, or explaining why, in your opinion, boys feel forced to join street gangs. Movies, newspaper and magazine articles, books, and radio and TV programs also supply ideas for papers, such as why you find most science fiction unbelievable, why the life of a counterspy is not for you, or how you came to realize that a physical handicap need not ruin a person's life.

Persuade others. In some papers you might aim to make your ideas about a problem seem so reasonable and convincing that readers will adopt them. For example, suppose that you take a very dim view of the week-night curfew for teen-agers in your town. By showing that the disadvantages of the curfew far outweigh its advantages, you might convince readers that the curfew should be abolished. At times you might even want to urge readers to take action. If, for example, you think it unfair for students to have to pay adult admission prices at movies, you might write a paper urging students to request special rates.

EXERCISE (1) Think over each of the following italicized headings and the example subjects. Then, on a sheet of paper, list each heading and the subjects it suggests to you that you would find interesting to write about. Keep your list of subjects; during the school year you will find it helpful to refer to the list whenever you are assigned papers on subjects of your choice.

1 *Memorable incidents.* [Examples: "Dad Made Me Turn In My Paintbrush," "Searching the Woods for Amy," "How I Got Rock Hudson's Autograph"]

2 *Interesting people.* [Examples: "Our Uninvited Guest," "The Borrower," "Captain Hawkins, Storyteller Extraordinary"]

3 *Interesting places.* [Examples: "Grandmother's Old-fashioned Kitchen," "A Busy Ore Dock at Midnight," "Solitude in a Northwoods Cabin," "Our Living Room After Cub Den Meeting"]

4 *How to make or do something; how something works.* [Examples: "How to Make a Rag Rug," "Scoring a Bowling Game," "Tips for Giving a Good Home Permanent," "How Barometers Indicate Weather Changes"]

5 *Personal problems.* [Examples: "I'm a Reformed Know-it-all," "Making My Allowance Do," "On Being a Foster Child," "When Parents Don't Make Definite Rules"]

6 *Social problems of people my age.* [Examples: "The Dangers of Following the Crowd," "Learning Manners the Hard Way," "Finding Entertainment in a Small Town," "Why Our Elders Do Not Understand Us"]

7 *Ideas and opinions I want to explain or persuade others to believe.* [Examples: "Our School Overemphasizes Sports," "Children's Names Should Be Chosen with Care," "Why I Don't Join Fan Clubs," "If I Could Teach My Sunday-School Class," "Let's Try Pay TV"]

8 *Other subjects I would like to write about.* [Here list subjects of interest to you that do not fit under any of the suggested headings.]

CHOOSING A SUBJECT

FOR A PARTICULAR PAPER

When choosing a subject for a particular composition, make sure you take into consideration how long the paper is to be. Otherwise you may land in trouble by choosing a subject that is too limited. For example, suppose you were to write a paper of 400 words and you chose a subject like "How to Clean a Trout." By the time you had written 250 or 300 words, you would find that you had told all you need to tell to make even the clearest of explanations. To fill up the remaining space, you would have to resort to padding your explanation with unimportant details.

The greater danger, however, is choosing a subject that is too broad. A subject like "The Values of a Newspaper," for instance, would be too broad for a 200-word paper. In order to cover all the phases of the subject—news stories, feature stories, editorials, columns, special sections like sports and society, advertising, and so on —you would have to limit yourself to a sentence or two on each phase. And what could you write in one or two sentences about the value of, say, editorials? It would certainly be nothing specific enough to make your ideas clear, and very little your readers would not have known before reading your theme.

What you should do in such a case is cut the broad subject down to a size you can handle in 200 words. If you limited yourself to writing about one phase of the subject—"The Value of Newspaper Editorials," for example—you would be able to write a clear and convincing paper, one that would give your readers specific information and ideas.

EXERCISE (2) After considering the phases that would have to be covered in writing about each of the following subjects, decide which subjects would be suitable for papers of 100 to 200 words and which are too broad. Be ready to explain your choices and to suggest one way in which each subject you think too broad might be limited.

1 How Manufacturers Advertise Their Products
2 Two TV Commercials That Are Insulting to Viewers
3 Snakes of the West, Their Appearance and Habits
4 How to Treat a Snake Bite
5 What It Feels Like to Make an Emergency Landing
6 The History of Jazz
7 The Value of Crop Rotation
8 Why I Think the View from Twin Peaks Is Exceptional
9 The Man Next Door Reminds Me of Mr. Micawber [in *David Copperfield*, a novel by Charles Dickens]
10 A Poem That Influenced My Life
11 Let's Observe the Rules in the Student Lounge
12 Student Employment
13 Making a Clamshell Ash Tray
14 Budgeting Time—My Major Problem
15 American Poets

EXERCISE (3) The subjects listed below are too broad to be handled in ordinary writing assignments. Choose five of the subjects and limit each of the five to two good ones suitable for themes of 200 to 300 words. For example, the subject "Weather" might suggest "Using a Barometer to Predict Weather" and "My Unsuccessful Attempt to Make Rain." Keep a copy of your suggested subjects; you will need it for Exercises 4 and 11.

Animals	Photography	Money	Farming
Travel	Art	Dancing	Television
Friends	Sports	Automobiles	Baby-sitting
Food	Aviation	Clothes	My Home Town
Music	Clubs	Movies	Camping
Government	Books	My Family	Weather
Religion	Minerals	College	Peacemaking

As you think over your subject and decide how to limit it, the purpose of your composition will gradually begin to take shape in your mind. For example, your purpose in writing a paper stating your views on the values of scouting might be to help others understand why you are so enthusiastic about it. The purpose of a paper telling what happened when you accidentally mixed the tags on several Christmas presents might be simply to entertain your friends. At other times—depending on your subject, of course—you might intend a paper to instruct readers, to persuade them, to defend an idea, or to air a grievance.

Whatever your goal, you must have it clearly in mind. To make sure that you do, put your purpose into words, being as specific as you can. Write it down in a sentence so that you can refer to it as you plan and write your paper.

The following statements of purpose are similar to ones you might write:

> My purpose is to entertain my classmates by telling an incident which made me realize that my dog was training me, and not the other way around.
>
> In my paper I intend to give my cousin Fred directions for teaching a dog three simple tricks.
>
> My purpose is to describe the meetings of the Current Events Club in such a way that the members will see how disorganized the meetings really are and in what ways they might be improved.
>
> My purpose is to persuade the faculty and students of this school that under certain conditions a field trip can be a useful educational experience.
>
> I intend to explain to my classmates three reasons why students who want to go to college cannot wait until the later years of high school to begin planning.

133

Your statement of purpose is not to be a part of your finished composition, of course. Its purpose is to guide you in selecting the material to include. Use it to test each detail. Ask yourself, "Does this bit of information contribute to my goal as I have stated it?" If the detail contributes to your stated goal, you should plan to include the detail in your paper. If it does not, you should discard the detail, no matter how interesting it may be in itself.

For five of the ten limited subjects that you listed in Exercise 3, write a sentence stating the purpose of a composition you might write on that subject. (Indicate in the sentence the reader or readers for whom you intend the composition.) Make your statements of purpose as clear and concise as you can. Keep a copy of your sentences; you will need it for Exercise 6.

PLANNING YOUR COMPOSITION

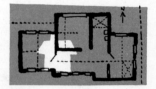

Before an engineer can build a bridge, he must know exactly how he is going to do it and how the finished structure will look. He cannot dig the first hole or pour the first batch of concrete until he has assembled his materials and has drawn up a plan for putting them together.

To construct an effective composition—one that will accomplish its purpose—you must follow the same procedure. Before doing any writing, you must first gather the materials you will need—facts, opinions, examples, illustrations. Then you must work out a plan for presenting these materials so that your subject and purpose will be clear to your readers.

GETTING MATERIAL

From past experience. You can get the material for a great many of your papers from your own past experience. How good the material will be depends in great part on how good an observer you are. If you have trained yourself to observe people, places, and things—to take careful note of the specific details that make you feel as you do about them—you will have plenty of good material to draw from. If, on the other hand, you see people, places, and things *vaguely*—never noticing the specific details that make each of them different from every other—you will have only vague, general impressions to use. Vague, general impressions make pretty flimsy material, as you may have discovered.

Suppose that two students, one observant and the other not, were planning papers on the same subject—a criticism of the Current Events Club in your school. Since both belonged to the club and had attended all the meetings, both could turn to their past experience for material. But what a difference in the material!

The unobservant student would be able to recall nothing but very hazy ideas—the only kind he could have, since he had never really observed what went on. He would know that the meetings were "not so *good* as they used to be," but wouldn't know exactly why. He would remember that "*something* was wrong" with the club programs, but he couldn't explain specifically what it was. He could probably recall that the officers were "not *satisfactory*," but in just what ways, he couldn't say. With material as vague and general as this, the best writer in the class could not produce a good paper.

But what about the other student, the observant one? He would be able to recall specific details about such things as the stifling heat and poor acoustics of the meeting room, the increasingly poor attendance of the members, the many fumbling attempts of the president to maintain order, his ignorance of the simplest parliamentary rules, the various ways in which the members betrayed a lack of interest in the proceedings, and the hastily planned and poorly presented programs. With material of this sort, he could write a most interesting paper.

From other sources. For some papers, of course, what you have learned through personal experience and observation may not be enough. To cover some subjects adequately, you may need to supplement what you already know with material from other sources. Suppose, for example, that you have decided to write a paper to show that owning and caring for a pet teaches people patience and a sense of responsibility. You know that in order to write a convincing paper, you will have to give several examples showing in detail how owners of pets learn from them. But in thinking over what you might tell, you find that the only good example about which you can recall *specific details* is the experience you had teaching your parakeet to talk.

Where can you get more examples? One good source is talking the matter over with friends or relatives who own a dog, cat, turtle, canary, or other pet. Some of these people will surely be able to recall specific instances in which their pets helped them learn patience. Still another good source is reading—books, magazines, newspapers. A book or an article by an experienced dog trainer, for example, will probably contain the sort of material you need.

Whether the material for a particular paper comes from your own experience or is acquired through reading does not matter. What does matter is that you take the time to gather enough material—enough facts, ideas, descriptive details, examples, and incidents—to carry out the purpose of your paper. Once you have gathered this material, you can go on with the next step.

135

EXERCISE (5) Be prepared to tell to what sources—personal experience, others' experience, reading—you would turn to get the necessary material to write a 200- to 300-word composition on each of the following subjects.

   1 My Most Interesting Relative
   2 How to Make Fudge
   3 Some Ways That Animals Protect Themselves
   4 The Ghost I Would Most Like to Meet
   5 Why an Airplane Flies
   6 The Work of the World Health Organization
   7 Christmas Traditions at Our House
   8 A Day I'd Like to Forget
   9 How Bacon Is Cured
  10 Scientific Aids Used in Police Work
  11 How to Avoid the Flu
  12 My Family's Strange Reading Habits
  13 Which Comes First—Success or a Big Vocabulary?
  14 Teen-Age Advice Columns
  15 Everyone Should Learn to Swim

EXERCISE (6) Be prepared to tell to what sources you would turn for material to write each of the papers for which you wrote statements of purpose in Exercise 4.

Give specific sources. If the source for one of the papers is to be an experience, name the specific experience and give a few details. If another source is to be a book or a magazine article, give the title and the name of the author.

ORGANIZING YOUR MATERIAL

How much planning you need to do for a particular paper depends mostly on the sort of paper you are writing and the length it is to be. If you are to write a short paper telling about something you saw happen—for example, a recent incident in the school cafeteria—you surely won't need an elaborate plan. In fact, you can probably do all the planning in your head.

You start by thinking back over the incident, recalling as many details as you can about the place where it happened, the people concerned, and the events that occurred. As specific details come to mind, you decide which you will include and which you will omit because they are not important to your story. You must be careful to include all details that the reader will need to get a clear picture of what happened. But it would be foolish to include details about the weather, for example, or the clothes worn by a particular person —unless such details had some bearing on the point of your story.

Just as important as sorting out the details is deciding where to begin your account. It is usually best, especially when your paper is to be short, not to start too far back—for example, with an explanation of what happened hours before the incident took place. Including more background material than is needed for understanding the incident is likely to lessen the effectiveness of your paper.

Planning the order in which to give narrative details is no problem. In general, the most effective order is the order in which they happened. This is called *chronological*, or *time*, *order*.

A time order is also the best to use in a paper explaining how to make or do something. Unless the steps in your explanation are given in the same order in which they should be done, you will confuse, rather than help your readers. You will probably not need to work out an elaborate plan before writing such a paper, especially if you know your subject well. But jotting down brief notes as you think over the subject will help you make sure (1) that you will give all the steps in the right order and (2) that you will not omit any necessary details.

Subjects that cannot be presented in a time order are a bit harder to plan; in fact, for these you will probably need to prepare a written outline. Let's see what sort of procedure you might follow in working out an outline for a subject of this kind.

Suppose that you have decided to write a paper of some 400 words on student field trips. This is currently a subject of great interest in your community. A group of local businessmen recently approached your school authorities and offered to underwrite student field trips to offices and factories during school hours. Thus far, the school authorities have reached no decision about the offer. But many people—parents, students, teachers, and other interested citizens—have been debating the matter and writing letters to the editor about it. Some see many worth-while advantages in the student field trips; others see little value in them.

After considering all the arguments, pro and con, you have arrived at an opinion of your own. In your paper, you want to persuade the students and faculty of your school to share this opinion—that *under certain conditions* a field trip can be a useful educational experience, one worth the school hours it would take.

Since you know that some of your readers are opposed to the trips and will be hard to persuade, you will have to make your paper especially clear and convincing. To do so, you will have to consider what facts and ideas to use and in what order to present them.

The first step is to think over the subject, recalling all you have heard, read, and thought about it. As soon as an item occurs to you, jot it down on a sheet of paper so that you won't forget it while recalling others. At this stage of the planning, you need not be concerned about the relative importance of the items, the way you phrase them, or the order in which you list them. Your purpose *now* is simply to collect ideas to use in your paper. For example:

1. Direct experience gained on trips can make clear the knowledge acquired in class, can teach what cannot be taught in books.
2. Groups should be kept small to make individual attention possible.
3. Groups usually so large that individual is often unable to see or hear what is going on.
4. Atmosphere of field trip is not one of learning; many students have "we're-on-a-picnic" attitude.
5. Firms often invite students to lunch in company cafeteria.
6. Trips offer a variety of experiences students may not otherwise get.
7. Much experience offered by field trips is of no practical use to students.
8. Trips help indifferent students acquire an interest in school subjects.
9. Make students aware of occupational opportunities.
10. Trips should be carefully selected for practical value to students.
11. Employees of local firms who conduct tours and answer questions are usually so ill-equipped for the job that students merely get confused.
12. Trips should be conducted by employees who are specially trained as guides.
13. Trips give students a better understanding of business and industrial practices and of people involved.
14. Students should be prepared by teachers to understand what they are going to see and do, to understand what benefits they should derive.

As you can see, this is a far from orderly list. Obviously, you cannot present the items in the order in which you have jotted them down. If you did, your readers would have a hard time understanding what you were driving at. Before you can make your ideas clear, you must sort out the items in the list, grouping together those that belong together.

An efficient way to group the ideas is to start with the first item and look down the list for others that are related. For example, since the first item states an argument given in favor of field trips, you will group with it all other items in favor of the trips. By going over the list several times more, you will find that all of the items except one can be grouped under the following three main topics:

1. Arguments given by others in favor of field trips
   Items 1, 6, 8, 9, 13
2. Conditions under which I think the trips would prove valuable
   Items 2, 10, 12, 14
3. Arguments given by others against field trips
   Items 3, 4, 7, 11

Notice that Item 5 ("Firms often invite students to lunch in company cafeteria") is not included in any of these groups. If you consider the item carefully, you will see that though it explains one reason why field trips are attractive to students, it is not a valid argument for or against the *educational* value of the trips. Therefore it should be omitted. Any item that will not help you carry out the main purpose of your paper should be discarded.

The next matter to consider is in what order to cover the main topics. Using the order in which they are now arranged certainly would not result in a very convincing paper. Your purpose is to persuade readers to share your opinion that under certain conditions field trips can be valuable. It would hardly be sensible for you to explain your opinion and then go on to weaken your case by pointing out arguments *against* field trips. It would be better to arrange the main topics in this order:

1. Arguments given by others against field trips
2. Arguments given by others in favor of field trips
3. Conditions under which I think the trips would be valuable

Covering the arguments *against* the trips first will show the readers who are opposed to the trips that you are fully aware of their point of view. Giving the arguments *for* the trips next will acquaint your readers with a number of points they may not have considered. And presenting *your point of view* last will let you end your paper with its most important part—the ideas you want your readers to accept as the best solution to the problem.

Once you have decided on the order of the main topics, you can complete the outline for your paper. The main topics will be the main heads in the outline. Under each main head, you will list as subheads the related items from your list, arranging them in the order you think most effective. Since the items are not of the type that can be presented in a time order, you can use whatever order you prefer. A common practice is to list the subheads in the order of increasing importance. For example:

1. Arguments given by others against field trips
   a. Atmosphere of field trip is not one of learning; many students have "we're-on-a-picnic" attitude.
   b. Groups usually so large that individual is often unable to see or hear what is going on.
   c. Much experience offered by field trips is of no practical use to students.
   d. Employees of local firms who conduct tours and answer questions are usually so ill-equipped for the job that students merely get confused.
2. Arguments given by others in favor of field trips
   a. Trips give students a better understanding of business and industrial practices and of people involved.
   b. Help indifferent students acquire an interest in school subjects.
   c. Make students aware of occupational opportunities.
   d. Offer a variety of experiences students may not otherwise get.
   e. Direct experience gained on trips can make clear the knowledge acquired in class, can teach what cannot be taught in books.
3. Conditions under which I think the trips would be valuable
   a. Trips should be carefully selected for practical value to students.
   b. Groups should be kept small to make individual attention possible.
   c. Trips should be conducted by employees who are specially trained as guides.
   d. Students should be prepared by teachers to understand what they are going to see and do, to understand what benefits they should derive.

With an outline as carefully worked out as this one, you should find it easy to produce a clear and convincing paper. Since your outline will tell you just what main topics and subtopics you need to cover and in what order to cover them effectively, you will be free to concentrate on doing a good job of getting your ideas down on paper. And that is the next step—writing a first draft of your composition.

EXERCISE 7 From each of the following groups of items pick out the one that could be used as a main heading for the group. Write the main heading on a sheet of paper; under it, list the other items as subheads, in the order that seems to you the most effective. Be ready to explain why you think this order is best.

1 Rarely fail; Cheaper in most instances; Advantages of "package" cakes over homemade cakes; Quicker to prepare; Easier to make

2 Carving out the outline; Brushing or rubbing on a thin coat of shellac; Scraping one side of blade for cutting edge; Drawing outline of opener on depressor; Making a letter opener from a tongue depressor; Sanding and smoothing all surfaces and edges

3 Putting money in savings bank; Investing in stocks and bonds; Buying insurance; Ways of saving money; Keeping money in piggy bank

4 Meet latecomer outside; Wander into auction; My unfortunate experience at an auction; Find myself the owner of an ugly umbrella stand; Watch the bidding; Leave, disgusted with myself; Wave fly away from face; Learn later that stand worth $250; Sell latecomer the stand at fifty-cent profit; Horrified when wave taken for bid of two dollars

5 Roman nose; Rather thin; Large gray eyes; Over six feet tall; My brother Tom; Pleasant smile; Small scar on chin; Curly black hair

EXERCISE (8) From each of the following groups of items pick out two that could be used as main headings. Write the main headings on a sheet of paper; under each, list the other items as subheads, in the order that seems to you the most effective. One item in each group does not belong under either main heading. Omit that item.

1 Aardvark; Yacht; Real animals; Centaur; Phoenix; Dinosaur; Mythical animals; Unicorn; Dodo

2 Being overly critical of others; Friendly behavior; Not joining in school and club activities; Choosing friends carefully; Participating in activities of people your own age; Being attentive to others' interests and feelings; Unfriendly behavior; Speaking kindly and generously of others; Ignoring friendly advances of others

3 Necessary training; Hunting dogs; Buying a dog; Breed; Appearance; Taking care of a dog; Correct food; Proper medical attention; Physical condition; Price; Adequate shelter

4 Wind; Ways of preventing soil erosion; Poor farming methods; Reforestation; Flood control; Scientific farming methods; Causes of soil erosion; Construction of windbreaks; Poor lumbering methods; Reclamation of swampland; Heavy rains and bad flooding

5 Allow first coat to dry 24 hours; Wax stained surface; Make table legs even; Putting new finish on table; Scrape off old paint or varnish; Apply paint remover or varnish remover; Apply second coat of stain; Apply first coat of stain; Wash off remains of old paint or varnish and remover; Let dry before sanding to smooth off scrape marks; Allow second coat of stain to dry 48 hours; Removing old finish from table

EXERCISE 9 Each of the following groups contains items that could be used as subtopics for two main topics. Sort out the items into related groups, and list them on a sheet of paper. Above each group write a main heading that tells what the group is about.

1 Admiral; Private; General; Major; Ensign; Commander; Sergeant; Petty officer

2 Thomas Edison; Robert Fulton; Thomas Gainsborough; Guglielmo Marconi; Alfred B. Nobel; Pablo Picasso; Vincent van Gogh; James McNeill Whistler

3 Indian smoke signals; African drum signals; Radio; Telephone; Teletypewriter; Egyptian hieroglyphics; Telegraph; Beacon-fire signals

4 Keeps order at club meetings; Calls most frequently on members who favor his opinions; Makes decisions for club without consulting members; Hurries through business at meetings; Gives all members a chance to express their opinions; Does not follow proper parliamentary procedures; Does not make decisions for club; Sees that all necessary business gets careful consideration

5 TV classes offer learning opportunities for those who cannot attend regular classes; No opportunity for discussion among students; Students cannot easily ask questions of TV teachers; Fewer distractions, since student alone; TV teacher cannot tell when students' interest is flagging; Students learn responsibility because no one checks on their progress; TV classes inexpensive; Students miss out on regular school social activities

EXERCISE 10 Choose one numbered item from each of the following three groups. Suppose that each item is a main topic in a paper you are planning. For each topic supply three or more subtopics, writing them on a sheet of paper.

You may be asked to put one of your main topics and its subtopics on the blackboard. Your classmates will then consider whether you have provided enough subtopics to cover the main topic and whether all of them belong under that topic. Your teacher may also ask you to write a paragraph on one of the main topics you have chosen, using the subtopics you have provided.

A 1 How to make a lamp shade (or anything else)
2 How to play badminton (or any other game)
3 How a transistor radio works (or how anything else works)

B 1 Advertisements are sometimes misleading
2 Some hobbies provide good ways to earn money
3 What bicycle riders can do to help prevent accidents
4 Benefits derived from wide reading
5 Characteristics of a good student (librarian, saleswoman, bus driver, or person in any other occupation)

C 1 Why New Year's resolutions are seldom kept
2 Families should spend a part of their leisure time together
3 I would rather watch an athletic event than take part in it (or just the opposite)
4 A student should (or should not) be allowed to choose the school courses he will take
5 Why I go to church

EXERCISE (11) Look over all the subjects *except narrative subjects* that you listed in Exercises 1 and 3, and think over any subject ideas that have come to mind since. From these subjects, choose one that you know well from personal experience. Limit the subject so that it is suitable for a composition of 200 to 300 words. On a sheet of paper, write down your limited subject and a sentence stating clearly the purpose of the composition. (Indicate in the sentence the reader or readers for whom the composition is intended.) Then plan your paper, following the steps explained in the preceding section.

Your teacher may call on you to copy on the board the list of items you jotted down and then to explain how you grouped the items for your outline. Keep your outline (after it has been checked by your teacher); you will need it for Exercise 16.

WRITING A FIRST DRAFT

Your main concern in writing a first draft should be to get down on paper all the material your reader needs to understand your subject. You should write down your ideas as rapidly as you can, without stopping to improve sentences, check the spelling of words, or correct errors in grammar and punctuation. You are more likely to turn out a paper that sounds natural and that expresses your particular way of thinking if you avoid interrupting your train of thought. And by waiting until your paper is finished—when you can see it as a whole—you will find that you can make improvements and corrections more effectively.

GETTING OFF TO A GOOD START

For short papers it is usually best to go directly into your subject. A good way is to start with some important, interesting, or unusual part—a striking fact, a very brief incident, a thought-provoking statement—something that will stir the reader's interest. You will seldom need more than one or two sentences of introduction. Often they can be made a part of the first paragraph. Here, for example, is how you might begin a short paper explaining why you think the operator of a motor scooter should be required to have a driver's license:

> Last week eight out of twenty traffic accidents in our town involved a motor scooter and a car. All eight of these accidents could probably have been prevented. . . .

For a longer paper you may sometimes need to provide an introductory paragraph of background information. The following paragraph, for example, not only gives the reader the information he needs to understand the paper but also makes clear why it is important to him:

> At the last Student Council meeting it was moved that the students of Elmdale High School adopt a code of dress. The vote on the motion was postponed until the next meeting. During the past few days, upperclassmen have been hotly debating the motion, offering strong reasons for and against its adoption. Few underclassmen have stated their views. Since the decision of the council will affect the entire student body, it is important for us underclassmen to consider the matter carefully and to voice our conclusions so that our council members can report our opinions at the meeting.
>
> Those opposed to the code argue, first of all, that . . .

EXERCISE (12) Look over the beginnings of some of the compositions that you have written so far this year. Choose one beginning that you think is not as effective as it might be and rewrite it in a way that you think would be more likely to catch a reader's attention and get him interested in your subject. Be prepared to read in class both versions of the beginning and to explain what you found ineffective about the first and why you think the second is an improvement. Ask your classmates for their opinions of the beginnings.

PARAGRAPHING

In exposition. In most short papers you will probably devote one paragraph to each main topic that you are going to cover. In other words, if your paper covers three main topics, it will usually consist of three paragraphs (plus, perhaps, an introductory paragraph). But occasionally in a longer paper, if you have quite a few details to give about one main topic, you may want to devote two or more paragraphs to that topic, each covering a subdivision of the topic. [Detailed suggestions to help you in writing effective paragraphs are in Chapter 1, "Writing Good Paragraphs," pages 8–35.]

In narratives. Narrative paragraphs are handled a bit differently. While the details in most expository compositions group themselves neatly around a few main topics or steps, the details in a narrative grow out of one another somewhat like the links in a chain. So in writing a narrative, you will have to rely mostly on your own judgment of when a new paragraph would be helpful to your reader. The usual practice is to begin a new paragraph whenever there is a change from one scene to another, from one time to another, or from one bit of action to another. You also start a new paragraph for each change of speaker. Narrative paragraphs are generally rather short.

145

LINKING YOUR PARAGRAPHS

Your reader should be able to follow your train of thought smoothly from paragraph to paragraph. To avoid any puzzling gaps in thought, you must link your paragraphs together in such a way that he will see how each new paragraph topic is related to the preceding one.

Use direct links. One way to bridge gaps in thought between paragraphs is to use direct links, words like *first, next, as a result, on the other hand.* For example, suppose that you are writing a narrative in which the first bit of action takes place in your back yard.

The second bit of action, for which you begin a new paragraph, takes place at the same time in your kitchen. To indicate to your reader that there is a change of place but not of time, you might begin the first sentence of the new paragraph with this direct link:

> *Meanwhile in the kitchen,* Betty was making enough lemonade for a thirsty battalion. . . .

Or, to take another example, suppose that you are writing a paper giving the advantages and disadvantages of owning a foreign-made car. You have decided that you need *two* paragraphs to cover the topic of disadvantages. To make sure that your reader sees that the second paragraph is a continuation of the topic you introduced in the first, you might begin the second paragraph with this direct link:

> *In addition,* replacing worn-out or broken parts in a foreign-made car can be rather expensive. . . .

Refer to key words or ideas. Another way to link paragraphs together is to refer in the first sentence of a new paragraph to a key word or idea in the preceding one. For example, let's say that you are writing about steamboating on the Mississippi River in the nineteenth century. You have just written a paragraph explaining that river-boat travel was beset by dangers. In the next paragraph you plan to tell about the frequent races between river boats. To link the two paragraphs, you refer to the topic of the first in the beginning sentence of the second:

> *Despite these dangers,* river boats frequently raced one another. . . .

By learning to use paragraph links skillfully, you can make the paragraphs in your papers hang together as naturally as these do:

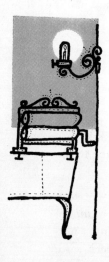

> Everyday life was made easier by a number of other inventions not so often heard about. For many years pipes had been lighted and kitchen fires started by using a clumsy contraption of flint and steel. But after 1836 people began using the newly invented phosphorus match. Housewives welcomed the invention of the apple peeler, the egg beater, and the clothes wringer. Improvements in kitchen stoves and ranges made cooking a much easier task than when it was done in the fireplace. In the cities gas lighting began to replace candles and oil lamps.
>
> Then there were inventions of machines for the factories—machines that enabled the factories to turn out more goods than ever. There was the pin-making machine into which whirred brass wire from a big spool, and out of which poured

pins by the thousands, all with good points and perfect heads. Men thought up improvements in saws for sawmills and machinery for use in furniture factories. Machines were invented to make paper, to shape parts of firearms, to sew shoes.

These are only a few of the thousands of inventions made during this period. There were so many between 1850 and 1860 that one government official in the Patent Office said that soon everything would be invented and the office could be closed. He spoke a little too soon, for after his time came a flood of electrical inventions such as the telephone, radio, television, and radar, and transportation devices like the automobile and the airplane, to say nothing of electric washers, refrigerators, freezers, and countless gadgets.—I. James Quillen and Edward Krug, *Living in Our America.* Copyright © 1956, 1951 by Scott, Foresman and Company, Chicago.

In these example paragraphs, the first sentence of each paragraph indicates a change of topic and links the new paragraph with the preceding one in some way. The first sentence of the second paragraph, for example, makes clear that the writers are still talking about inventions, but that they are moving from inventions for the home to inventions for the factory. The word *Then* helps to prepare the reader for this shift. In the beginning sentence of the third paragraph, the word *These* links this paragraph with the preceding ones by referring to the inventions already named. At the same time the sentence indicates that the topic is turning from the kinds of inventions to the great numbers of them. Although not quite so obviously, the writers have linked their paragraphs in still another way—by repeating the key word *inventions* in the first sentence of each paragraph.

EXERCISE ⟨13⟩ In each of the following numbered pairs, item *a* is the *topic sentence* of one paragraph of a composition. Item *b* suggests the *topic idea* to be developed in the next paragraph. On a sheet of paper, write for the second paragraph of each pair a beginning sentence that would link the two paragraphs together. Be sure that your sentence would lead a reader smoothly from one topic to the next.

1 a) We had a pleasant morning at the National Gallery of Art.
   b) Our visit to Mt. Vernon that afternoon
2 a) Being the youngest in a large family has its disadvantages.
   b) The advantages enjoyed by the youngest child
3 a) Falls account for the majority of fatal home accidents.
   b) Burns and scalds the second most common cause

4 a) From the outside Miss Finch's house looked very cold and forbidding.

   b) The warm, attractive interior of the house

5 a) Each 4-H club carries on a variety of group activities.

   b) Individual project undertaken by each member

6 a) Mildred spent days making careful preparations for her party.

   b) The failure of the party

7 a) A poorly planned wardrobe can be very expensive.

   b) An inexpensive, well-planned wardrobe

8 a) By following a few simple rules, you can take good snapshots of people.

   b) Tips for taking pictures of animals

9 a) A cadet, Dennis Mahan Michie, organized the first football team at West Point.

   b) The long line of noteworthy football players at West Point

10 a) Charlie Brown, the main character in the comic strip *Peanuts*, never fails to arouse my sympathy with his problems.

    b) Lucy, my favorite *Peanuts* character

11 a) In the catch-as-catch-can style of wrestling the emphasis is on prone holds.

    b) The emphasis on standing holds in the Greco-Roman style

12 a) In my experience, a good novel is often as informative as it is entertaining.

    b) *My Ántonia*, a rich study of American pioneer life

ENDING YOUR PAPER

While you rarely need a whole paragraph of conclusion at the end of a short paper, you will generally want some sort of ending to round it off or to serve as a "clincher" to nail down an important point. A sentence or two at the close of the last paragraph is usually all that is needed. For example, after pointing out that the lives of many motor-scooter operators might be saved if they were required to pass driving tests, you might end your last paragraph with these sentences:

> . . . A driver's license costs three dollars. The cost of a life cannot be counted in dollars and cents.

For a longer paper you may sometimes feel that a concluding paragraph is necessary to make sure that you leave your reader with the exact idea or impression you intend. Most often this paragraph should be a brief restatement of your main points in a way that makes clear their importance. For example, if your purpose were to show the usefulness of school grades, you might conclude with this paragraph:

> In these days of crowded classes and understaffed schools, giving a grade seems to be the most efficient way for a teacher to indicate the level of a student's work. For the student, grades are a useful guide in determining whether he is making progress or falling behind and in appraising his ability in different subject fields. But even more important, the grading system prepares a student to face the stiff competition of the social, business, and professional worlds. No matter where he goes or what he does after he leaves school, his performance will constantly be judged, compared, and graded.

EXERCISE (14) Look over the endings of some of the compositions that you have written so far this year. Choose one ending that you think is not so good as it might be. Rewrite the ending in a way that rounds off your paper more effectively and leaves your reader with the idea or impression you intend. Be prepared to read both versions of the ending in class and to explain why you think the second more effective than the first.

CHOOSING A TITLE

The sort of title you choose depends on your subject and purpose. Ordinarily the best title for a paper giving specific information or explaining how to make or do something is one that makes clear what its subject and purpose are. A title like "Why Volcanoes Erupt" or "How to Clean a Shotgun," for example, would tell a reader immediately what information the paper provides.

Occasionally you may want to use a question. For example, although it is a bit long, "Should the School Year Be Lengthened?" is an effective title. It would make most readers—whether they were for or against lengthening the school term or hadn't made up their minds about it—want to read the paper to find out how the *writer* answers the question. But, except for papers on controversial subjects like this, it is a good idea to use question titles sparingly.

For the majority of your papers the most effective title will be a brief phrase or expression that suggests your subject but does not give away all you are going to say about it. The title may be clever or amusing or startling. Or it may be quite simple, like the ones in the second column:

Finders, Weepers	My Reward
I'll Take Vanilla	Behind the Soda Fountain
Moby Dick, Lake Owasco Style	An Unexpected Catch
Rover Took Over	Training My Dog

Since the title of your paper is the first thing that your reader sees, you will want to write it correctly. The usual practice is to capitalize the first and last words of a title, all important words (nouns, pronouns, verbs, adjectives, adverbs), and all prepositions of more than four letters. A title should not be followed by a period, nor should it be put in quotation marks unless it is a direct quotation.

EXERCISE (15) Think over the narrative subjects you listed in Exercises 1 and 3 and any narrative subject ideas that have come to mind since. From these, choose one that would be suitable for a composition of 150 to 300 words. Recall the event you intend to tell about—where it happened, when it happened, who was involved, and exactly what happened. Decide which details you should tell and which you should omit. Get all the details clearly in mind in the order in which they took place. Then write a first draft of your narrative. Keep this first draft; you will be asked to revise it after studying the next section, about revision.

EXERCISE (16) Using the outline you prepared for Exercise 11, write a first draft of the composition you planned. Keep your first draft; you will be asked to revise it after studying the next section.

REVISING YOUR PAPER

In writing your first draft, you give all your attention to providing the material your reader needs. In revising, your main concern should be how clearly and effectively you have expressed your ideas and how easily your paper reads.

A good way to test your paper is to put yourself in your reader's place as you go over it. Will the beginning sentences get the reader interested and make him want to read on? Have you provided enough details to make each phase of your subject clear? Are they all the right details? Or did you unintentionally include one or two minor details that really do not belong and should be eliminated?

Do your paragraphs make clear what topics you are covering? Are your paragraphs linked so that your reader can easily follow your train of thought? Have you used words that express your meaning exactly? Here and there you will perhaps want to substitute a more exact word. How effective is your ending? Will your reader leave your paper with the idea or impression you intend? (If possible, read your paper aloud to someone else or to yourself. Your ear will often catch flaws that your eye may miss.)

You should pay especially careful attention to the matters that you did not give full attention to when writing—grammar, spelling, and punctuation. Have you written complete sentences? Have you shown clearly where each sentence begins and ends? Have you used all the punctuation marks you need? Check carefully to see that you have not used too many exclamation marks or dashes or have not enclosed words in quotation marks unnecessarily. Is there a good reason for every capital letter in your paper? Are there any misspellings? If you are uncertain about the spelling of any word, be sure to look it up.

While errors in grammar, punctuation, or spelling may not prevent a reader from understanding what you have to say, they do make a poor impression. What's more, grammatical and mechanical errors are distracting to a careful reader. And if he has to make many mental corrections as he reads, he certainly will not be able to give all his attention to the most important part of your paper—your ideas.

Making your final draft. When you are satisfied that your paper says what you want it to say, clearly and effectively, copy it neatly with all the changes and additions that you made in revising. (Use black or blue ink, or type.) Then proofread your final draft carefully. Correct clearly and neatly any errors in copying.

151

EXERCISE (17) Carefully read over the first draft of the narrative paper you wrote for Exercise 15. As you read, ask yourself the questions suggested in the preceding section about revising. Make any additions, changes, and corrections on your paper that you think necessary to assure a clear and effective narrative. Then copy your paper neatly, and remember to proofread it accurately before handing it in.

Your teacher may ask that, before making your final draft, you exchange your first draft with a classmate to get whatever suggestions he may have for improving your paper.

EXERCISE (18) Following the directions in the preceding exercise, revise the first draft of the composition you wrote for Exercise 16. Copy your paper neatly, and proofread it carefully before handing it in.

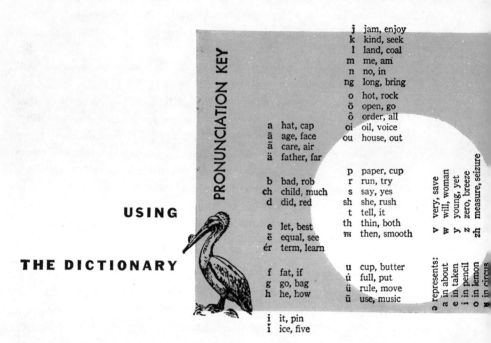

CHAPTER 7

PRONUNCIATION KEY

a	hat, cap	j	jam, enjoy			
ā	age, face	k	kind, seek			
ä	care, air	l	land, coal			
ä	father, far	m	me, am			
		n	no, in			
		ng	long, bring			
b	bad, rob	o	hot, rock			
ch	child, much	ō	open, go			
d	did, red	ô	order, all			
		oi	oil, voice			
		ou	house, out			
e	let, best					
ē	equal, see	p	paper, cup	v	very, save	
ėr	term, learn	r	run, try	w	will, woman	
		s	say, yes	y	young, yet	
f	fat, if	sh	she, rush	z	zero, breeze	
g	go, bag	t	tell, it	zh	measure, seizure	
h	he, how	th	thin, both			
		ᴛʜ	then, smooth			
i	it, pin					
ī	ice, five	u	cup, butter			
		ù	full, put			
		ü	rule, move			
		ū	use, music			

ə represents:
a in about
e in taken
i in pencil
o in lemon
u in circus

USING

THE DICTIONARY

152

To settle an argument about whether a baseball player is "safe" or "out" at home base, everyone turns to the umpire. He rules on all the plays. If he calls a pitched ball a "strike," it *is* a strike, even if to the batter (and to everyone else) it looked like a ball. The opinions of the batter and the others do not count; it is the umpire who decides. What the umpire says goes. He is in a way a dictator—on the baseball diamond at least.

When an argument arises about words—about their meaning, their pronunciation, or their spelling—we turn to a dictionary to settle the matter. The dictionary, in other words, often serves as an umpire. Because it does, many people have the wrong idea about dictionaries. They think that the writers of the dictionaries (like baseball umpires) make the decisions, that the dictionary writers decide what words should mean and how they should be pronounced and spelled.

This is far from the truth. Dictionary makers would be the first to tell you that they do not have the power to rule on words, as a

Pekingese

OLOGY KEY

< from, derived from,
   taken from
? possibly
l. ablative
s. accusative
c. compare
t. neuter
p. past participle
r. present participle
t. past tense
t. ultimately
r. variant

dial. dialect
dim. diminutive
fem. feminine
gen. genitive
lang. language

LANGUAGE ABBREVIATIONS

AF	Anglo-French (= Anglo-Norman, the dialect of French spoken by the Normans in England, esp. 1066-c.1164)
Am.E	American English (word originating in the United States)
Am.Ind.	American Indian
Am.Sp.	American Spanish
E	English
F	French
G	German
Gk.	Greek (from Homer to 300 A.D.)
Gmc.	Germanic (parent language of Gothic, Scandinavian, English, Dutch, German)
HG	High German (speech of Central and Southern Germany)
Hindu.	Hindustani (the commonest language of India)
Ital.	Italian
L	Latin (Classical Latin 200 B.C.-300 A.D.)
LG	Low German (speech of Northern Germany)
LGk.	Late Greek (300-700)
LL	Late Latin (300-700)
M	Middle
ME	Middle English (1100-1500)

par a chut ist (par′ə shüt′ist), *n.* person who uses a parachute; person skilled in making descents with a parachute.

pa rade (pə rād′), *n., v.,* **-rad ed, -rad ing.** —*n.* 1. march for display; procession: *The circus had a parade.* 2. group of people walking for display or pleasure. 3. place where people walk for display or pleasure. 4. a great show or display: *A modest man will not make a parade of his wealth.* 5. a military display or review of troops. 6. place used for the regular parade of troops. —*v.* 1. march through with display: *The performers and animals paraded the streets.* 2. march in procession; walk proudly as if in a parade. 3. make a great show of. 4. come together in military order for review or inspection. 5. assemble (troops) for review. [< F < Sp. *parada*, ult. < L *parare* prepare] —**pa rad′er,** *n.* —**Syn.** *v.* 3. display, flaunt.

Man descending with parachute

square-rigged (skwär′rigd′), *adj.* having the principal sails set at right angles across the masts.
square-rig ger (skwär′rig′ər), *n.* a square-rigged ship.
square root, number that produces a given number when multiplied by itself: *The square root of 16 is 4.*
square sail, a four-sided sail.
square shooter, *Informal.* a fair and honest person.

baseball umpire has to rule on plays. They are not dictators who tell you what words must mean and how they have to be spelled and pronounced. They are merely recorders of facts about words; they make records of the ways that words have been and are being used by people in general.

A dictionary editor, for example, may think it silly to have in our language two different words meaning "easily set on fire"—*flammable* and *inflammable.* His personal opinion is that having both words is likely to lead to confusion. He is sure that many people may think, as he once did, that *inflammable* means just the opposite of *flammable.* So he would like to define *inflammable* as meaning "*not* easily set on fire." Can he do this? He could if he were a dictator of words. But since he is not, he must forget his personal preference, and show in his dictionary that both words are used by people in general to mean the same thing.

How dictionary makers work. Dictionary editors get the facts they give about words from observing the language in use. For example, in working out the definitions, they collect from books and magazines and newspapers hundreds of sentences containing the words they are to define. From these sentences, they determine the various meanings of the words—*as shown by the context*—not from their notions of what the words ought to mean.

By working in this way, they can keep up to date with the changes that constantly take place in our language. For example, suppose that one of the sentences collected for observation was this:

> We turned to Channel 11, but couldn't see the program because of the *snow*.

The context would show clearly that in this sentence the word *snow* does not mean the same as it does in "The men shoveled a path through the snow." In the first sentence, *snow* refers to the flickering mass of white specks that sometimes mars the picture on a TV screen. Since that sentence and many other similar ones show that the word *snow* has acquired a new meaning, the editors will consider adding this meaning in the next edition of their dictionary.

Deciding which words and which meanings to include in a dictionary requires considerable thought on the part of the editors. Most of the old words in our language already have more than one meaning. Not only are many of these old words acquiring new meanings, but many new words are coming into our language— words like *Conelrad, fall-out, Salk vaccine, dynel, Dacron,* and *aureomycin*. There would not be enough space even in a large (unabridged) dictionary to give all the possible information about every word in our language, and in the smaller (abridged) dictionaries there is far less space. So the editors have to choose as wisely as they can just which words and meanings are best to include. Usually the choices made by the editors of standard dictionaries are sound, since they are based on scientific studies of how useful the words will be to the people for whom the particular dictionary is intended. In such teen-age dictionaries as the *Thorndike-Barnhart High School Dictionary, Webster's Students Dictionary,* and *Funk & Wagnalls Standard High School Dictionary,* for example, you will find most of the words and meanings that you will meet in the reading you do. For those few times when your dictionary fails you, you can always turn to the unabridged dictionary in the library.

Now that you have some idea of how the dictionary makers arrive at their definitions and their decisions about what words to include, you can understand why dictionaries may differ—in size, in the words included, in definitions, and so on. In spite of these differences, all of the standard dictionaries are storehouses of valuable information about words and their use.

AND THE DICTIONARY

Having the best tools in the world in your workshop will not help you be a good carpenter if you don't know how to use the tools easily and efficiently. Having a storehouse of facts about words as close to you as your bookshelf will not mean much either, unless you know how to find—easily and quickly—the information you need. Many people who own dictionaries seldom use them because they find it such a chore to locate the facts they want. The reason, sad but true, is usually that they do not know the alphabet.

For such people, looking up the word *squalor* to find its pronunciation would be a long, hard job that could be done only by a time-consuming "trial and error" method. Yet anyone who knew the alphabet could find the word in a matter of seconds. Knowing that *s* comes after *p*, *q*, *r*, but before *t*, *u*, *v*, he could turn quickly to the last third of the dictionary, locate the *s* words, flip the pages rapidly past the words beginning with *sa*, *sc*, *so*, *sp*, until he came to the *sq* words. Surely the speed and ease with which you could find words is worth the time it would take to memorize the alphabet.

For best results, you should learn the alphabet so well that you can give the letters in order without having to think. The exercises will help you.

155

EXERCISE (1) (Only for those who do not know the alphabet.) Spend five minutes reading and repeating to yourself the letters of the alphabet:

a b c d e f g h i j k l m n o p q
r s t u v w x y z

Next, looking away from your book, give as much of the alphabet as you can. Repeat this until you can go straight through all the letters without your book.

Then, working with two classmates, practice increasing your speed at locating words in a dictionary. First take turns asking one another to find a page listing words beginning with different letters. Then have one person name a word which the other two, racing against each other, are to find.

EXERCISE (2) (For the whole class.) The practice this exercise gives in alphabetizing will help you find the words you look up in a dictionary more quickly. Sort the following items into three groups: (1) items usually found in a hardware store, (2) those usually found in a grocery store, and (3) those usually found in a music store. Then list the items in each group on a sheet of paper, arranging them in alphabetical order. There will be twenty items in each of the three lists.

1	tongs	21	cauliflower	41	axes
2	chili	22	humidifiers	42	artichokes
3	fifes	23	prunes	43	piccolos
4	gelatin	24	bugles	44	clarinets
5	nails	25	apricots	45	bassoons
6	cream	26	guitars	46	varnish
7	castanets	27	hatchets	47	chocolate
8	hinges	28	saws	48	anchovies
9	broccoli	29	butter	49	cymbals
10	oboes	30	micrometers	50	hoes
11	apples	31	harrows	51	banjos
12	heaters	32	cherries	52	zithers
13	peas	33	carrots	53	cheese
14	cornets	34	kettledrums	54	harmonicas
15	hammers	35	concertinas	55	buckets
16	caramels	36	harnesses	56	harps
17	cocoa	37	bass drums	57	almonds
18	flutes	38	hobnails	58	bagpipes
19	cellos	39	bolts	59	hampers
20	toasters	40	grapes	60	hacksaws

EXERCISE (3) At the top of each page of your dictionary there are two "guide words" to help you find quickly a word you are looking up. The first guide word (at the left) tells you the first word on the page; the second (at the right) tells you the last word. If you know the alphabet well, you can tell by a quick glance at the guide words whether the word you are looking for is listed on that page. This exercise will give you practice in making efficient use of guide words.

Be ready to tell which of the words in the following numbered groups will be found on a page with the guide words given in brackets at the head of each group. Which of the words will come before that page? Which will come after that page?

1 [insider—installment]
insipid
inclosure
infrared
inspire
instance

2 [frowsy—fulcrum]
frown
fullback
fuchsia
fruitless
fuddle

3   [lunacy—Luxemburg]
    lyceum
    lumpy
    lurch
    lunge
    Luxor
4   [rhythmic—ridge]
    rhythm
    riboflavin
    ricochet
    ridgepole
    rhubarb
5   [submarine—subsidy]
    subscript
    sublime
    subsist
    subtle
    subsidize
6   [beverage—biceps]
    bevatron
    betrothed
    bewail
    bey
    bichloride

THE DICTIONARY ANSWERS

QUESTIONS ABOUT SPELLING

The *easiest* way to find out how a word is spelled is to ask some-one close by—a classmate, a friend, a brother, or a sister. But the *safest* way is to turn to a dictionary; other people may be wrong.

Finding the word you are in doubt about is usually no trouble, since usually you know the first two or three letters. You may not know whether *embarrassed* is spelled with one *r* or two; but since you know that the word begins with *emb,* you can easily locate it and find the answer. Even if the second letter is the one in doubt—should you write *dispair* or *despair?*—you can quickly find out by looking in not more than two spots.

Words like *chronic* (which starts with a *k* sound), *pneumonia* (which starts with an *n* sound), and *pheasant* (which starts with an *f* sound) may be a bit harder to find, since you cannot tell from the pronunciation what the first letters will be. It may take two or three tries before you can find such words. If you find, for ex-ample, that "pheasant" is not listed as "feasant," remember that it may (like *philosophy* and *Philip* and *photo*) begin with *ph.* If you cannot find "gnarled" listed as "narled," remember that it may (like *knave* or *knew* or *knee*) begin with *kn.* When you don't find "knarled," try again. Words like *gnaw* and *gnash* begin with the same *n* sound. This time you do find it—"gnarled."

Compound words. Words that are composed of two or more words (like *black market, blackboard, black-and-blue*) are called *compound words.* Often, although you know how to spell certain compound words, you are not sure whether to write them as sepa-rate words, as one solid word, or with a hyphen. Since there are no simple rules you can learn to guide you in this matter, you must turn to the dictionary if you are in doubt about words like these:

life insurance	lifeguard	life-size
half brother	stepbrother	brother-in-law
show window	showroom	show-off

Dividing words. Sometimes you may be puzzled about where to break a word at the end of a line. For example, you may not have space enough to write all of the word *accommodation* on one line. You know, of course, that you should divide only between syllables. But where do the syllables in this word begin and end? The dictionary will help you; each word listed in boldface type is broken into syllables for you, like this:

ac com mo da tion	ser geant	rec og niz a ble
Wednes day	beau ti ful	en grav ing

The rule is that you can break a word (and insert a hyphen) at the end of any one of its syllables, with these two exceptions:

1) Do not leave a syllable of only one letter at the end of a line:

Write *about*, not *a-bout*. Write *elec-tric*, not *e-lectric*.

2) Do not carry over a syllable of only one or two letters:

Write *pity*, not *pit-y*. Write *In-dian*, not *Indi-an*.

Variant spellings. If a word has two acceptable spellings, both are given in the dictionary. The spelling that the editors have found is more commonly used is indicated in different ways. It may, for example, be given first in the entry: **adviser** or **advisor**, **meager** or **meagre**. Or the more common spelling may be given alone at the beginning of the entry, and the less common one put at the end, introduced by the word *Also:* **maneuver** . . . *Also* **manoeuvre**. In some instances the variant spellings are given as separate entries. For example, both **neighbor** and **neighbour** may be entries. The definition is given after the commoner spelling—*neighbor*; in the other entry there will be only a reference to the commoner spelling.

Since each of the variant spellings listed is correct, you can feel free to use either. Just remember to be consistent. Do not, for example, shift back and forth between *dialog* and *dialogue* or *bronco* and *broncho* in a letter, a theme, or a report.

EXERCISE (**4**) Sort the following words into six groups: words that start with (1) an *f* sound, (2) an *n* sound, (3) an *r* sound, (4) an *s* sound, (5) an *sk* sound, (6) a *k* sound. Label each group. Then study

158

J.J.SMITH
J.J.SMYTH
J.J.SMYTHE

your lists carefully, noticing especially the first two letters that spell the initial sound of each word.

1	gnarled	14	rhinoceros	27	rhythm
2	wrath	15	gnaw	28	swordfish
3	rheumatism	16	squalid	29	knelt
4	phantom	17	pneumatic	30	sculpture
5	knapsack	18	chlorine	31	chord
6	pneumonia	19	wrought	32	sciatica
7	pharmacy	20	censure	33	pheasant
8	gnome	21	schedule	34	rhapsody
9	scepter	22	chiropodist	35	cholera
10	squabble	23	wrench	36	knuckle
11	Philippines	24	scurvy	37	scenario
12	scenic	25	philosophy	38	chronic
13	scorpion	26	scholar	39	physiology

EXERCISE (5) Two of the three spellings given for the following words are correct; the other is wrong. On a sheet of paper, copy the two correct spellings of each word. Circle the spelling that your dictionary shows is the more common (or "preferred") form. Number your answers with the numbers of the groups.

1 colour, collor, color
2 bandanna, banndana, bandana
3 travalogue, travelog, travelogue
4 calcimime, kalsomine, calcimine
5 skilfull, skillful, skilful
6 encyclopaedia, encyclepedia, encyclopedia
7 forebade, forbad, forbade
8 skepticle, skeptical, sceptical
9 kidnaper, kiddnaper, kidnapper
10 gayety, gaity, gaiety

159

EXERCISE (6) Some of the following compound words should be written as two separate words, some as one solid word, and others with a hyphen. Make a list of the words, writing them as you would if you were using them in a report. Then check your spellings in your dictionary. Draw a line through any form that you have wrong, and write the correct form above it.

1	taxpayer	6	byproduct
2	grandopera	7	postmortem
3	loudspeaker	8	cabinetmaker
4	eyewitness	9	fireescape
5	sugarbeet	10	greatgrandmother

Has anything like this ever happened to you? In a magazine story, you run across a new word—*gunwale*. Although you have never heard the word before, the context helps you figure out its meaning: "the upper edge of the side of a ship or boat." That night at dinner when you proudly use the new word, your father and brother laugh heartily. Not having ever heard the word, you naturally pronounced it as it looked—"gun-wale." To your embarrassment, you are told that it should be pronounced "gun'-el" to rhyme with "funnel."

One or two experiences of this kind would teach you that you cannot always depend on the spelling of English words to tell you their pronunciation. Unless you *hear* a new word as well as see it, it is best to look up its pronunciation before you use it in speech.

Everyone knows that a dictionary tells how words are pronounced by respelling the words in specially marked letters. But not everyone knows how to interpret these specially marked letters. Do you? Suppose, for example, that you were using the *Thorndike-Barnhart High School Dictionary*. Would you know that the two dots over the *a* in the pronunciation "mär" show that this word rhymes with *far*, but that the wavy line over the *a* in the pronunciation "mãr" shows that this word rhymes with *fare*? (How are "dãr" and "tär" pronounced?)

Many people have used their dictionaries so often that they have memorized the special marks (called **diacritical** marks) used to show the sounds of the letters. Although knowing the diacritical marks by heart is helpful, it is not absolutely necessary. The marks used in different dictionaries vary slightly. But most dictionaries give a pronunciation key at the bottom of each page to show what sounds the marks represent. By checking with this key, you can easily find how to pronounce the letters, no matter how they are marked. In the key in your dictionary you may find, for example, that "ō" is pronounced like the *o* in *open*, that "ū" is pronounced like the *u* in *use*, and that "ŦH" is pronounced like the *th* in *then*. After you have referred to the key a number of times, you will find yourself learning the marks without having made a special effort.

The pronunciations given in dictionaries tell you not only how the various letters of a word are pronounced, but also which syllable should be accented or stressed. For example:

lu'na tic   tri bu'nal   a'li as

A word of several syllables may be accented on two syllables. The syllable that gets the main stress is marked with a heavy accent mark. The other is given a lighter accent mark to show that it gets less stress. For example:

ra'di a'tor   pre lim'i nar'y   guar'an tee'

Make sure that you notice the accent marks when you look up the pronunciation of a word. The pronunciation of such words as *theater, omnipotent, preferable,* and *incongruous* is not difficult, but it is tricky. Unless you know which syllables to accent, you may not pronounce the words correctly:

the'a ter [Not: the a'ter]
om nip'o tent [Not: om ni po'tent]
pref'er a ble [Not: pre fer'a ble]
in con'gru ous [Not: in con gru'ous]

Many words have more than one accepted pronunciation. Usually the pronunciations most commonly heard throughout the country are listed first. Though any pronunciation recorded in your dictionary is "correct," you will find it a good idea to use the one preferred by the educated people in your community.

EXERCISE 7 This exercise will give you practice in using a pronunciation key to figure out the pronunciation of words from their dictionary respellings. The numbered groups of pronunciations below are taken from the *Thorndike-Barnhart High School Dictionary*. The key that is printed at the end of the exercise contains clue words to tell you how the various letters should be sounded. (The first clue word, for example, shows that an *a* without a diacritical mark is pronounced like the *a* in *hat*; the second shows that "ā" is pronounced like the *a* in *age*.) Be ready to pronounce all the words in the numbered groups correctly in class.

1 pan, pān, pär, păr, stāt, stär, stär, bāt, glär, glad
2 mīt, mit, pīl, pil, grīp, grip, fit, fīt, fīl, fil
3 bet, bēt, lėrn, lēr, lēs, rēd, red, fėrn, met, mēt
4 lōp, lop, lôrd, dōlt, dot, doj, dōnt, dôr, nōt, noch
5 fuj, fūz, fůl, tün, mud, mūl, mūz, mus, půl, prün
6 ə lärm', tō'kən, per'əl, dē'mən, rā'di əm

Key:

hat, āge, cãre, fär; let, ēqual, tėrm; it, īce; hot, ōpen, ôrder; oil, out; cup, půt, rüle, ūse; ch, child; ng, long; th, thin; ŦH, then; zh, measure; ə represents *a* in about, *e* in taken, *i* in pencil, *o* in lemon, *u* in circus.

EXERCISE 8 In brackets at the beginning of each sentence are given the pronunciations of two different words. One of these words could be substituted for the italicized word or words in the sentence. Number your paper from 1 to 18. After each number, write the two words, spelling each correctly. Then circle the one word in each pair that could be used in the sentence. Refer to the key at the end of Exercise 7 if you need help with any of the diacritical marks. Refer to your dictionary if you need help with the spelling or meaning of any word.

1 [pik′chər   pich′ər] My nephew is the *image* of his father.
2 [fėr′nish   fėr′nis] Mr. Evert will *provide* the necessary equipment.
3 [lô′yər   lā′ər] The *attorney* for the defense is confident of an acquittal.
4 [kom′ə   kō′mə] Mrs. Donner lay in a *stupor* for days.
5 [kal′və ri   kav′əl ri] The *troops mounted on horseback* led the charge.
6 [kred′ə bəl   krej′ù ləs] It hardly seems *believable* that he finished his history report so soon.
7 [wėrst   wėrs] Claire is a poor typist, but I am *less good* than she.
8 [prē sēd′id   prə sēd′id] Tim thought a moment and then *went on* with his story.
9 [fėr′lông   fėr′lō] Cassidy was given a *leave of absence*.
10 [en vel′əps   en′və lōps] Soon the fog *conceals* the village.
11 [tə mer′ə ti   tə mid′ə ti] Jean's *shyness* made her seem unfriendly.
12 [fôr′məl i   fôr′mər li] Iran was *once* called Persia.
13 [i lü′zhən   ə lü′zhən] By his skillful use of mirrors, the decorator created a *false impression* of spaciousness.
14 [em′ə nənt   im′ə nənt] The new ambassador soon proved himself a *distinguished* scholar as well as an able diplomat.
15 [prez′ənt   pri zent′] The principal called on Ronald Bates to *give* the awards to the winners.
16 [kon′shəs   kon′shəns] Jim was *aware* of a feeling of hostility between the two interns.
17 [fôrs   färs] He had to use all his *strength* to push the mower through the jumble of weeds.
18 [miz′ər i   mī′zər li] Though wealthy, his aunt was *stingy*.

EXERCISE 9 Read each of the following sentences to yourself, paying special attention to the way you pronounce the word in italics. Then look up the word in your dictionary and copy its pronunciation on a sheet of paper. Put a check mark after each word that you mispronounced. In class, compare your experiences with those of your classmates. Be ready to use each word in a sentence of your own.

1. J. P. Morgan once said that anyone who had to ask the price of a *yacht* couldn't afford to own one.
2. The cap that Elsie had *crocheted* for me was too small.
3. When Mr. Beals *impugned* his honesty, Frank fought back.
4. At the edge of the *chasm*, the men lost their footing.
5. None of these remedies helped him stop his *hiccoughing*.
6. The *blackguard* escaped safely from *Edinburgh* but was caught in Glasgow.
7. In return for his daily ten hours of work he was given one dollar a week, a room in the attic, and his *victuals*.
8. Wilson's partner was also *indicted*, but he was found not guilty.
9. The vocal cords are in the *larynx*.
10. Since the will dated July 3 was not signed, it was *invalid*.

EXERCISE (10) Be ready to read the following sentences aloud, pronouncing and accenting all the italicized words correctly. In some of the sentences the correct pronunciation depends on whether the word is used as a noun or as a verb. Look up in your dictionary any words you are in doubt about.

163

1. So far his *progress* has been slow, but with our new methods he should *progress* faster.
2. In a very short time Roseville's *famous* author had become *infamous*.
3. You can get the whole message in one line if you cross out the *superfluous* words.
4. David asked me to *protest*, but my *protest* was ignored.
5. His mistake is in trying to *compare* two things that are not really *comparable*.
6. Does your favorite newscaster pronounce *modern, southern,* and *western* correctly, or does he end them with "ren"?
7. The *grime* on his arms and hands made the shirt *grimy*.
8. I *suspect* that Michael will be the next *suspect* to be questioned.
9. Though *width* ends with the same sound as "myth," *height* rhymes with "might."
10. I don't *admire* his methods, but the results are *admirable*.

EXERCISE (11) Homonyms [hom'ə nims] are words that are pronounced alike but have different meanings: *plain, plane; great, grate; load, lode; altar, alter.* As far as meaning goes, these words cause no trouble, since the context in which they are used makes clear which is which.

But (usually because of carelessness) the words are often mis-spelled; a person will write *piece*, for example, instead of *peace*.

In each of the sentences in the following pairs, a word—one of two homonyms—has been omitted. The pronunciation in brackets above the sentences will tell you how the missing words are pronounced. List the words that are missing from each pair of sentences, spelling them correctly. Number your answers with the numbers and letters of the sentences.

1 [fãr]
    a) The club held a ———— to raise money for a tape recorder.
    b) After paying his ————, he had only thirteen cents left.

2 [kap′ə təl]
    a) Treason is a ———— crime.
    b) The ———— at Madison is a most impressive building.

3 [sēl′ing]
    a) Hanging from the ———— was an enormous spider web.
    b) After ———— the letter, he put it in the safe.

4 [kôrs]
    a) Aunt Mathilda was shocked at David's ———— manners.
    b) At least half of the students take a ———— in geography.

5 [stā′shən er′i]
    a) You should not use office ———— for personal letters.
    b) We dyed the curtains in the ———— tubs in the basement.

6 [mär′shəl]
    a) Before being elected mayor, Slim Hawks was a United States ————.
    b) ———— music would be more appropriate than dance tunes for a Fourth of July celebration.

7 [prin′sə pəl]
    a) The ———— decided to give the boys one more chance.
    b) Once you understand the ———— by which the machine works, you will know how to repair it.

8 [ə sent′]
    a) Before we proceed with our plans, we must have the ———— of the club members.
    b) For the ———— to the top of Everest, Mallory and Irving decided to use oxygen.

9 [di zėrt′]
    a) His decision to ———— his friends was a grave mistake.
    b) Anyone who is dieting should avoid such a rich ————.

10 [kan′vəs]
    a) Dorothy covered the chair seats with ————.
    b) The boys volunteered to ———— the whole town for orders.

English words are strange. Unless you see or hear them in context (that is, in actual *use* in a phrase or sentence), you cannot be absolutely sure of their intended meaning.

Let's look at a very simple example of just what we mean by this last statement. Suppose that a foreigner reading a newspaper on your bus asked you if you knew the meaning of the verb *crawl*. It is quite likely that you would answer, "Why, of course; it means 'to move slowly along on your hands and knees—like a baby.'"

If you did answer him in this way, chances are that he would be more confused than ever when he turned back to his reading. And you could hardly blame him—if the sentence he was struggling with was something like this:

The sidewalk was crawling with huge black ants.

If *crawl* means what you told him it meant, the sidewalk in the sentence was truly a remarkable one!

This little story has a moral, an important one: *You cannot tell for sure what a word means unless you first see how the word is being used.* If you had seen the sentence about the sidewalk, you could have answered the foreigner's question more helpfully: "*Crawl* may have any one of several meanings, you know. But in your sentence *crawling* means 'swarming with creeping things.'" The way the word was being used in the sentence told you which meaning was intended.

Remembering this story about the crawling sidewalk will help you use the dictionary efficiently to answer questions about word meanings. A dictionary defines thousands of words; and for most of these words, it gives more than one meaning. The best way to find the definition you need is to bring to the dictionary the whole sentence containing the word you are puzzled about. Only then can you easily figure out which of several meanings is the one that fits.

Suppose, for example, that you were puzzled by the word *high* in this sentence from a story you were reading:

The venison was *high*, but since there was no other meat at the camp, the men ate it.

To find out what meaning the writer intended here, you should go quickly through the definitions given for the entry word **high**, discarding all those that do not fit, like "tall," "costly," or "shrill." Soon you will come to one that does fit. It will be something like this:

165

"slightly tainted; strong-scented: *Game is often eaten after it has become high.*"

This definition fits so well, in fact, that it makes clear the meaning of the whole sentence. You had known from the beginning that there was something unpleasant about the venison. Now you know what it was that caused the men to eat it only because there was no other meat available.

Dictionary editors try to make the definitions they give easy to understand by using simple words, words that are "easier" than the terms being defined. But because space is limited, they cannot always avoid using in a definition a word or two whose meaning may not be immediately clear to you. For example, you may look up the word *biconvex* and find it defined as "convex on both sides."

If you know what *convex* means, this definition is clear. If you don't, you will have to look up *convex* and find that it means "curved out, like the outside of a circle or sphere." By putting the two definitions together, you know that *biconvex* means "curved out on both sides." Never let yourself be satisfied with a definition containing an unfamiliar word when you can so easily track down its meaning by turning to another spot in the dictionary.

Make it a point to read carefully any illustrative phrases or sentences that the dictionary gives with the definitions. Seeing a word in an example sentence will help you understand not only what the definition means but also how the word should be used. For instance, in looking up *communicate*, you may find as the first definition: "pass along; transfer." This might suggest that you could use the word in a sentence like this:

I *communicated* from the bus to the subway at State Street.

But reading the example sentence following the definition would show you that when *communicate* has this particular meaning, it should be used in this way:

A stove *communicates* heat to a room.

EXERCISE (12) Look up the italicized word in each of the following sentences. From the various meanings given in your dictionary, choose the one that fits the word as it is used in the sentence. Then rewrite each sentence, using words taken from the dictionary definition in place of the italicized word.

1 In return for these privileges, Captain Lerner gave his *parole* that he would not cross over into the neutral zone.
2 Thirty years ago Uncle Will was considered quite a *blade* by the young ladies of Newton.

3 Mr. Hale could not *steel* his heart against their pleas.
4 Jerry could not *blink* the fact that he had caused the accident.
5 First you will have to *riddle* the sand to remove the pebbles.
6 He was a man of wide reading and *catholic* interests.
7 The new engine will be *proved* at the plant in Seattle.
8 Besides being fined and sentenced to prison, the colonel was *broken* for his part in the transaction.
9 Few people there got the full *import* of his closing remarks.
10 The *legend* at the right gives the names of all the delegates shown in the picture.

EXERCISE (13) The dictionary definitions given for the three boldfaced words below will be clear to you only if you know the meaning of the words in italics. If the words are not familiar, look them up in your dictionary. Then rewrite each definition, substituting simpler, more familiar words for those in italics.

1 **phalanger** [fə lan′jər]: "a small, tree-climbing *marsupial* of the Australian region"
2 **equivocation** [i kwiv′ə kā′shən]: "the use of *equivocal* expressions in order to mislead"
3 **hydrofluoric acid** [hī′drō flü ôr′ik as′id]: "a colorless, *corrosive*, *volatile* liquid used for *etching* glass"

EXERCISE (14) If in your reading you came across the following sentences, you would probably not feel it necessary to stop to look up the italicized words, even though they were new to you. Not knowing the words would not keep you from understanding the gist of what you were reading. But knowing the words would add a great deal of meaning and enjoyment to the stories, as you will see.

Look up each of the italicized words and be ready to identify each person, place, or thing they name.

1 Robert's stories of what had happened on the trip would have made *Ananias* envious.
2 Brooklyn was not the *El Dorado* that the immigrants had been expecting to find.
3 Mrs. Dawes, as usual a slave to *Mrs. Grundy*, disapproved of our going to the tea without hats and gloves.
4 The diary that would have provided the answers was, unfortunately, in *Davy Jones's locker*.
5 Realizing that we were between *Scylla and Charybdis*, Philip left the decision to me.
6 "It was a victory, all right—but a *Pyrrhic victory*," muttered the coach as he thought of the injuries the team had suffered.

7 When Helen walked into their filthy apartment, she realized how Hercules must have felt when he first saw the *Augean stables*.

8 Everyone seemed to be having a good time but Billy; the fear of losing his job was a *Sword of Damocles* over his head.

9 The arrival of these two prospectors started a chain of events that changed the town from *Arcadia* to *Pandemonium*.

10 The children's story led the police to Dave Smiley, the *Fagin* of the gang of pickpockets.

THE DICTIONARY EXPLAINS

THE ORIGIN OF WORDS

Many dictionaries give (in brackets before or after the definitions) the *etymology* of words—a brief account of their origin and development. If you make it a practice to read the etymologies whenever you look up words, you not only will get a clearer understanding of the words themselves, but will also learn a number of interesting facts about our language.

To begin with, you will learn that English words have come from an amazing variety of languages—Latin (*data*), Greek (*azalea*), Chinese (*pekoe*), Hindustani (*bandanna*), Russian (*samovar*), Czech (*robot*), Arabic (*admiral*), Persian (*shawl*), Spanish (*canyon*), Italian (*ballot*), German (*stein*), French (*fiancé*), Hawaiian (*lei*), Norwegian (*ski*), Japanese (*kimono*), and Choctaw (*bayou*), to name only a few.

Through the etymologies you will also learn various ways in which English words have come into being. Hundreds of words, you will find, have been made by combining word elements (prefixes, roots, and suffixes). The noun *tonsillitis*, for example, was derived from the Latin word *tonsillae*, meaning "tonsils," + the suffix *-itis*, meaning "inflammation of"; the noun *decathlon* was derived from *deca-*, meaning "ten," + the Greek word *athlon*, meaning "contest."

You will find that many of our words have come from proper names—from the names of persons or places that are related to the words in some way. The noun *magnolia*, for example, was derived from the name of the French botanist Pierre *Magnol*; the noun *muslin*, from *Mosul*, a city in Iraq where muslin was made. The verb *vulcanize* was derived from *Vulcan*, the Roman god of fire; and *mackintosh* was named after the inventor Charles *Macintosh*.

A number of our words, you will discover, have been made by telescoping or "blending" two other words. The etymology of *chortle,* for instance, shows that it is a blend of *chuckle* and *snort;* the adjective *prissy* came from telescoping *prim* and *sissy.* A slightly different method of word formation—combining the first or first few letters of several words—has produced such words as *radar* (from *radio detecting and ranging*), *jato* (from *jet-assisted take-off*), and WAC (from *Women's Army Corps*).

Since space in a dictionary is at a premium, the etymologies make use of various abbreviations and symbols—for example, *Pg., NL, fr.,* +, and <. A key given in the introductory pages of the dictionary explains the meanings of these.

EXERCISE (15) [In the introductory pages of your dictionary you will find a section explaining how to use the etymologies. Be sure to read this section before doing this exercise.]

Be ready to explain in class the derivation of ten of the following words. If the etymology of a particular word is not given in your student dictionary, refer to an unabridged dictionary.

1	jinrikisha	6	lout	11	ptomaine	16	oligarchy
2	pachyderm	7	obese	12	dessert	17	precocious
3	nasturtium	8	smog	13	namby-pamby	18	rodent
4	chocolate	9	parasol	14	chop suey	19	orang-utan
5	plagiarism	10	WAVES	15	Conelrad	20	isosceles

EXERCISE (16) Each of the following words is derived from a proper name. Look up the words in your student dictionary or in an unabridged dictionary. Be ready to explain in class the connection between the meaning of each word and the name from which it was derived.

1	gerrymander	6	dumdum
2	denim	7	batiste
3	lynch	8	jeremiad
4	maverick	9	Bakelite
5	benedict	10	meander

THE DICTIONARY ANSWERS

QUESTIONS ABOUT WORD FORMS

Should you say "He has drank the milk" or "He has drunk the milk"? Should you write "potatoes" or "potatos"?

Many people do not know that they can easily find the answers to questions like these in a good dictionary. If you are puzzled about the forms of an irregular verb like *wring* or *dive,* the plural of a noun like *mongoose* or *cargo*, or the comparative and superlative forms of an adjective like *gaudy*, simply look up the word. Right after the pronunciation and the abbreviation that tells you what part of speech the word is, you will find the information you need. For example:

> **wring** (ring), *v.*, **wrung** or (*Rare*) **wringed, wring ing.**
> **mon goose** or **mon goos** (mon′güs), *n.*, *pl.* **-goos es.**
> **gaud y** (gôd′i), *adj.*, **gaud i er, gaud i est.**

EXERCISE (17) On a sheet of paper, write the form of the word (in brackets) that should be used in each sentence. Check your answers in your dictionary and correct any that are wrong.

1   [crisis] In each of these _____ Mr. Quarles came to the rescue.
2   [singe] They were _____ the turkeys over a gas flame.
3   [no] "The _____ have it," said the chairman.
4   [swell] In an hour his finger had _____ to twice its normal size.
5   [teaspoonful] Ken stirred three _____ of sugar into his tea.
6   [confer] Mrs. Root is _____ with them now.
7   [picnic] Yesterday we _____ at the beach.
8   [passer-by] Jim sat in the car, watching the many _____.
9   [Chinese] Seven _____ attended the conference.
10 [faux pas] She made several _____ at dinner last evening. [How is the plural form pronounced?]

THE DICTIONARY IS

A MINIATURE ENCYCLOPEDIA

Few people realize that dictionaries contain not only basic information about English words, but also a wealth of fascinating material about people and places and things.

Dictionaries will tell you, for example, such interesting facts as when Amundsen discovered the South Pole, what O. Henry's real name was, how high Mount Rainier is, where to go to kiss the Blarney Stone, and why Chartres is a city no tourist in France should miss.

If you are curious about what an Italian *lira* or a Japanese *sen* is worth, turn to the dictionary. If you do not know what the abbreviations *D.S.M.* or *C.P.A.* stand for, the dictionary will tell you. And if you can't quite imagine what an *anteater*, a *bowline knot*, or a *cuttlefish* looks like, try your dictionary. It will very likely have pictures of things like these.

Browsing through a dictionary whenever you have a spare ten minutes or so will give you an almost endless supply of interesting facts that you can use to inform or amuse your family and friends. Almost everyone that you know, in fact, will enjoy hearing you tell the facts you will learn while doing the next exercise. Try telling them and see.

EXERCISE (18) Answer any twelve of the following questions. You can find the answers by looking up the italicized words in your dictionary. Write the answers on a sheet of paper or be ready to give them orally in class—whichever your teacher asks you to do.

1   Why is a *catbird* so named?
2   How do *crickets* make the chirping sound that you hear on summer evenings?
3   What crime was committed by the *Danaides* and what punishment were they given?
4   What is the difference between a *stalactite* and a *stalagmite*?
5   If you were to earn your living as a boxer, would you prefer the gloves worn today or the *cestus* used in ancient Rome? Explain why.
6   How does an *armadillo* protect itself from attack?
7   What is the difference between a *basinet* and a *bassinet*?
8   Which is the largest island—*Tasmania, Iceland,* or *Ceylon?*
9   What is the usual diet of an *aardvark?* Of an *osprey?* Of a *secretary bird?*
10   What do the items in the following groups have in common?
   a) *dulcimer, psaltery, clavichord*
   b) *banyan, baobab, deodar*
   c) *dingo, whippet, harrier*
   d) *dodo, mastodon, moa*
11   A *sawhorse* is not a horse; *fool's gold* is not gold; a modern *scapegoat* is not a goat. What are they?
12   What is the meaning of the following foreign words: *bête noire, in loco parentis, ad nauseam, ¿quién sabe?, caveat emptor?*
13   What is the meaning of these abbreviations: *Mlle., R.A.F., S.P.C.A., U.S.M.A., R.N., e.g.?*
14   If the following people had appeared on the TV show *What's My Line?* what would the right answers have been?

   a) Samuel Gompers   d) Chester Arthur
   b) Nicolò Amati   e) Fridtjof Nansen
   c) William Cody   f) Clara Barton

171

DICTIONARY

MAKERS

AT WORK

The first dictionary of the English language to become famous and widely used was published in London in 1755. Earlier attempts to list English words and their meanings had been scanty and unsystematic; simply by its thoroughness, this work was the first to deserve the title "dictionary," as we use the word today. Can you guess how many experts it took to compile this dictionary? How many people do you think were needed to read widely enough in the published writings in English—even in the 1750's—to find the words and meanings to include in a dictionary?

Surprisingly, the answer to this question is not "hundreds" nor even "many," but "one." Dr. Samuel Johnson wrote his dictionary in eight years. He also did the reading necessary to find quotations showing how the words he listed had been used. His only help came from six secretaries who copied by hand the quotations he had marked in his reading.

Because Dr. Johnson was an exceptionally able scholar with a prodigious memory for the things he had learned, his dictionary was—for its day—an extraordinary piece of work. No dictionary ever lists *all* the words in a language, but this eighteenth-century *Dictionary of the English Language* came much closer to complete coverage of the words of its time than had any other work; it was, as a result, very useful to the people of that day.

However, it was still a long way from today's dictionaries. The art of dictionary making (we call it *lexicography*, and the men who do the work are *lexicographers*) has developed a great deal in the more than two hundred years since Dr. Johnson's time. Today no one could compile a dictionary from his own reading and knowledge alone. Now lexicographers make use of the studies of men who have devoted their lives to research in language. Today, too, many kinds of experts in different fields help to make a dictionary. Some of these experts are the following:

Etymologists.   They trace and explain in the dictionary the history of words—from what language each came into English or how each was first used.

Phoneticians.   These experts in pronunciation can determine, from their studies, the way or ways most educated people in different parts of the country pronounce a given word.   They advise dictionary editors about what pronunciation, or pronunciations, of that word should be included.

Readers.   As their name implies, they read certain periodicals to discover examples of new words coming into the language or of new meanings and uses for already established words.   Using their findings, a lexicographer can determine when a newly coined term, a word from another language, or a new meaning has become generally used and should be included.

Authorities.   Experts in various specialized fields (such as music and nuclear physics) supply information about words in their particular areas or verify technical data to be used in the dictionary.

The following pages will give you a peek into the offices where the   **173**
Thorndike-Barnhart dictionaries are made.   Here you will see some of the kinds of work needed in the preparation of a dictionary and some of the people who do that work.

Unlike Dr. Johnson, who had to make alone all the decisions concerning his dictionary, a modern lexicographer has the help of many advisers.   Here Clarence L. Barnhart, editor in chief of the Thorndike-Barnhart dictionaries, confers with Dr. Cabell Greet, Professor of English at Columbia University.   An authority on the English language, Dr. Greet is one member of the committee that advises Mr. Barnhart on questions of dictionary policy.

A staff member makes use of a scientifically prepared word list to determine which words should be included in a dictionary designed for high-school students. The list she is using, which is based on a study of words in forty-one different sources, shows how often and in how many of these sources the most common English words have occurred. This information helps her determine which words are most likely to occur in the reading high-school students do. She marks all such words for possible inclusion in the *High School Dictionary*.

Definitions of the
words included in the
dictionary must be
based on the way these words
are used, as you read on
page 154. When dictionary editors
write a definition of a word,
therefore, they make use
of quotations in which that
word occurs. Here a typist copies,
from magazines marked by
readers, examples of uses of
new words and meanings.

The cards on which new usages are copied are then placed in the extensive office file of examples of new words and new meanings.

An editor prepares a definition of the technical term *absorption spectrum*. Opposite is the definition slip she is checking. On it you see the definition, together with the notes and corrections of editors and advisers working on the project.

Physics

C

2 wb

OED OCV O

[The lines

Absorption spectrum.

The dark lines ~~maxima~~ observed with a spectroscope when light passes through a vapor; they correspond to the wavelengths absorbed by the vapor, and are characteristic for different elements. contained in the source.]

from a hot source

hot (cooler running the source ©

indicative of the

λ

00032

This is a letter different from the other type

OK CWB 11/30/59

(work)

[-6]

File

REF+
PM
MTF+

V N JUN19 1956

Another editor refers to the office file of examples
of new words and meanings in order to prepare a definition of
the new word *sputnik*.   You can see on this page
two of the cards he is using.   On the cards are sentences
discovered by readers in which this word has appeared since
its first general use in English in October 1957.
On the cards, too, are editors' comments.

sputniks ; n.

1958 NYkr 3/29 p.43 c.1
Christopher Rand

- The pavilion will have at least
   two sputniks on display, along
   with some live "astronautical"
   dogs that have allegedly been up
   to the stratosphere and back.

CLB — This slip typifies many in file and still
coming in to prove this now very often
EEF generic, lower-case noun   CJL   Make note for
in American use.   ⟨sig⟩   revision
                                      CLB 12/10/58

sputnik ; n.

1958 Econ. 5/24 p.701 c.1

- The Russians used a rocket with a
   thrust of 500,000 pounds to propel
   the latest sputnik.

CLB — Here "Economist" confirming
evidence British use parallels
EEF Amer.   ⟨sig⟩   CJL

An etymologist checks
the library of reference works
on the history of language
to find evidence about the first
use of the medical term
daltonism. On the pink etymology
slip, a question has been addressed
by the editor to two of the
authorities who advise the dictionary
staff. In red you see their replies.

179

45.   E, (R),
                                        T
Daltonism   3

if D   [1841 < F <u>daltonisme</u> < John Dalton [(1766-1844) British
ntered
a biog.] physicist] who first described the condition (which je
        himself had)]

Dr. Fales, Dr. Fowkes — B-W dates this 1844. But
OED citations make clear Prevost proposed
it earlier, at least by '43, when it was
attacked — and evidence of '41. And
presumably Prevost of Geneva wrote in French.

:s
ght.
Fowkes

                                    Yes.   JGK
                                      Fales

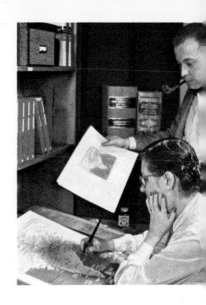

To make clear
the location and relative
size of countries
listed in the dictionary,
maps are often used.
Here an artist and an art
editor confer about
such a map.

To check information about
the pronunciation of a word, Mr. Barnhart
telephones one of the phoneticians
who advise him on such questions.

A great part of Mr. Barnhart's job, and
that of any dictionary editor in chief,
is bringing together the contributions of
the many dictionary editors, the language experts,
the authorities in special fields.   To do
this, Mr. Barnhart keeps in constant touch
with all these people.   Thus he can oversee
the preparation of dictionaries which will be
truly helpful to those for whose use
they are designed.

CHAPTER 8

PRACTICE

IN

ORAL

COMPOSITION

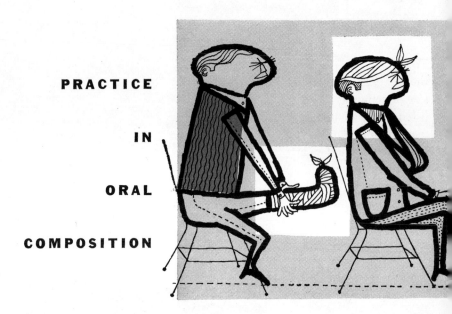

In 1892 an unknown mathematician addressed the American Institute of Electrical Engineers. Charles Proteus Steinmetz was a hunchback. He walked with an awkward limp. He spoke in halting, broken English. Yet when he talked, he captured the complete attention of his audience. For Steinmetz gave the assembled engineers a clear explanation of a mathematical formula which made it possible for them to build efficient generators—something that up to this time they had been unable to do.

Steinmetz's experience is not unusual. If a speaker has something of interest to tell and tells it clearly, his listeners' attention will not long remain on the peculiarities of his appearance and speech. The men Steinmetz spoke to were quite aware of his awkward appearance. And they must have found his foreign accent rather hard to understand, especially at first. But his explanation was so clear and so interesting that his audience soon gave its full attention to what was being said and forgot about the appearance and accent of the man who was saying it.

There is a valuable lesson to be learned from Steinmetz's experience: Your *first* concern as a speaker is to make sure that you have something to say, specific facts and ideas to offer. You must know how to present these facts and ideas in a way that will get and hold the attention of your listeners. This chapter will help you.

GIVING TALKS

During the school year ahead you will be asked to give a number of talks. In your classes, club meetings, and out-of-school activities you will be called on to make announcements, tell personal experiences, report events, make explanations, give directions, and describe people and places. Since your success as a speaker depends greatly on the information you present and the way you present it, you will want to give a good deal of thought to the preparation of each talk you make. The following sections will give you helpful suggestions on how to go about preparing for six of the speech situations you will face most often. You will have opportunities to test the effectiveness of your preparations when you give your talks in class.

MAKING AN ANNOUNCEMENT

In making an announcement, a speaker's main concern is to give as concisely as he can all the details his listeners need to know. For example, consider the announcement Tony Brodda made in assembly:

> The Student Council is sponsoring a square dance in the gym next Friday night from seven to eleven for the benefit of the March of Dimes. The music will be by Sam Slack and his Hill-billies, and Tom Case will do the calling. Tickets, which are fifty cents each, will be on sale daily in the high-school office during noon recess.

Notice that in three sentences Tony's announcement answers all the questions his listeners would ask about the dance: what kind of dance it is, where it is to be held, when, who is giving it, why, who is playing, who is calling, how much tickets are, and when and where they can be bought.

Thinking of all the questions for which your listeners will need answers will tell you what details to include in an announcement. And once you know what details to tell, all you have to do is tell them as briefly and clearly as you can.

Ordinarily, since every detail in an announcement is important, you can present the details in whatever order is most convenient for you to remember. But occasionally, to stimulate interest in what you are announcing, you will want to present first a detail that will immediately get your listeners' attention. Tony, for example, might have used this sentence to arouse interest: "The most popular caller in the state, Tom Case, will be calling at the square dance the Student Council is sponsoring for the benefit of the March of Dimes next Friday night."

At other times you may want to prepare a special closing sentence to stress a point you consider particularly important. To impress his listeners with the reason for the square dance and to encourage attendance, Tony might have added a closing sentence such as this one: "Remember—the five dimes that you pay to dance will help others to walk."

EXERCISE (1) The following numbered events are of the sort you will often be asked to announce. Think over each event carefully and be ready to tell what questions listeners would want answered in an announcement about each.

1 A pep meeting before a basketball game
2 An all-school play
3 A concert to be given by your school orchestra
4 A movie for the benefit of the Red Cross
5 An exhibit of the work done recently in the arts and crafts classes
6 A paper drive for the benefit of the yearbook fund
7 A special edition of the school paper, saluting the school's fiftieth anniversary
8 An essay contest sponsored by the city safety committee
9 A Conservation Club trip to a fish hatchery
10 The student-government elections
11 A lecture by a well-known explorer under the sponsorship of the Key Club
12 An opportunity to inspect a bookmobile making a one-day visit at the public library
13 An exhibit of prize-winning photographs from this year's state high-school photography contest
14 A meeting to discuss forming an art-service club
15 A game day sponsored by the Girls' Athletic Association

EXERCISE (2) You are to choose one of the numbered items in Exercise 1 and make a brief announcement about it. You will, of course, have to make up details in order to answer all the questions your listeners will want answered. Be sure to practice your announcement once or twice before giving it. When giving the announcement, speak slowly and distinctly.

TELLING A PERSONAL EXPERIENCE

A talk about a personal experience is one of the easiest talks to prepare. After all, since you will be telling about something that happened to you or something that you saw happen, getting material to use in your talk is no problem. You have only to relive in your mind the events of the incident, and you will have plenty of details to draw from to use in your talk. Organizing the material is not a difficult problem, either. Simply by presenting the details in the order in which they took place, you can make clear to your listeners exactly what happened that was amusing or exciting or unusual or interesting in some way.

Begin preparing your talk by thinking over the experience. Recall as many specific details as you can. From the details that occur to you, choose the ones that will make the experience vivid and meaningful to your listeners. To make sure that there will be no gaps or backtracking in your story to puzzle your audience, you will find it a good idea to list the details on a sheet of scratch paper. Then read through the list thoughtfully, looking for holes to fill in and checking to see that you have the details in the order of their occurrence.

Since the list serves simply as a check, the items need not be written in complete sentences; key words and phrases are often all you need. Here, for example, is the way your list might look when you have finished:

1. Went to bridal shower at cousin's home with Mother one evening last winter
2. Were an hour late in arriving
3. Had difficulty finding place to park car
4. Finally decided to squeeze in behind Ford on driveway
5. As we came to a stop, saw man carrying fur coat to the Ford
6. Signaled that he wanted to leave
7. Backed up our car, let him out, and took his place
8. Let ourselves in when no one answered doorbell
9. From sounds, could tell party was being held in basement playroom
10. Put coats in hall closet and hurried downstairs
11. Since party in progress, forgot about seeing man
12. When guests prepared to leave, discovered all fur coats and several purses missing
13. Suddenly Mother and I looked at each other and groaned
14. Both realized that after trapping thief in drive, we had let him get away

Remember that it is not necessary to include in your talk every detail that you remember. If a detail is not needed to make clear what happened, do not use it. For example, in telling the incident of the fur-coat theft, it would be unnecessary for you to explain why you and your mother were late for the shower. The explanation would only distract your listeners from the main point of your story.

When you have decided which details you are going to tell and the order in which to tell them, you give some thought to the beginning and ending of your talk. Often your first detail will be enough to arouse interest or curiosity. But sometimes you may want to begin with a brief introductory sentence. Such a sentence should tell just enough to make your listeners want to hear more—for example, "This is one experience I never brag about" or "I used to think that all bridal showers were boringly alike, but I was wrong."

Most of the time you simply end your talk with your last detail. But occasionally, if you think you need a special sentence to finish off satisfactorily, you may add a short statement like "And that's why I wince whenever someone says 'He went thataway.'" Or you may use a question: "Would *you* know a thief when you saw one?" However, if a closing sentence does not come to mind easily, you probably do not need one.

To increase your confidence when you speak, you may want to have some notes in hand. On a card or a small piece of paper, write the beginning sentence you have decided on, then a few key words to remind you of the details you have chosen and their order, and finally your closing sentence, if you have one.

Practicing your talk several times will also give you confidence and at the same time reduce your need for notes. If you have to consult notes very often, they are likely to become a distraction for your listeners.

187

EXERCISE (3) You, like most people, have had a number of interesting experiences. Choose one that you think your classmates would enjoy hearing about and prepare a brief talk telling what happened.

First think of the details you will need to tell and the order in which they occurred. Then practice your talk several times so that you will get all the important details and their order clearly in mind. Time yourself when you practice to be sure that your talk will last no longer than three minutes.

After all the talks have been given, the members of your class will discuss the ones they thought most effective, giving reasons for their choices.

REPORTING A NEWS EVENT

From time to time you will have occasion to report events that you have read about in newspapers. For example, in your science class you may be asked to report on an article concerning an experiment to test the thinking ability of dogs. In a group discussion on traffic safety you might prove a point by telling of a news item about an accident caused by faulty brakes. To entertain a group of friends, you might relate a news story about a night watchman who had outwitted a robber.

Generally, though, you will not want to report the details in the same order that a news story does. The main points of a news story are usually summarized in the first paragraph or two. Then details giving a fuller picture of the event are told in succeeding paragraphs. For example, a news story about the fur theft would probably tell in the first paragraph that a girl and her mother had unwittingly helped a thief escape with several fur coats. In the next paragraph the girl and her mother and perhaps the hostess of the party would be identified. Then the following paragraphs would give details telling exactly what had happened and how the thief had escaped. Since the reader can get the general idea of the story in the first few sentences, he need not read more than a paragraph or two unless he is particularly interested in the event.

The details of news stories are arranged as they are for the convenience of the typical newspaper reader, who does not have time to read the complete account of every event in the paper. When you make a talk reporting an event, however, your listeners usually want to hear all the important details. And you will generally find that your report will be more effective if you tell the details in the order they occurred and do not reveal the main point until the end.

In preparing your report, read the news article about the event you are reporting two or three times to get the details clear in your mind. Then think over the details, arranging them in the order of their occurrence. You may, of course, omit any minor details that you decide will not interest your listeners.

When you have the details in order, you want to consider how to begin your report. If you do not think your first detail will arouse interest, make up a special beginning sentence. The opening sentence of the news story will sometimes give you a clue for a good beginning. Suppose, for example, an article reporting that one of the largest passenger liners in the world had docked for the first time without the aid of tugboats began this way: "American merchant-marine history was made here today." In your report of this event you might use a similar opening sentence, substituting *in New York* for *here* and *Tuesday* for *today*. (Make sure, however, that you do not reveal the outcome of the story in the first sentence.)

EXERCISE 4 Read the following news article carefully to get the details of the story clear in your mind. Prepare to give a short talk reporting the event. In your talk you are to present the details in the order in which they actually occurred.

After two or three reports have been made, the class is to discuss the following questions: Which arrangement of details do you think an audience would find more effective—the time-order arrangement of the oral reports or the order used in the newspaper article? Why do you think so? Why is the order used in the news article better for newspaper readers than a time order would be?

TUGMEN BEAT LAKE STORM TO REACH PORT

While 300 persons waited anxiously at the St. Joseph, Mich., harbor Sunday, two grizzled fishermen, lost in Lake Michigan, fought 60 miles per hour winds and 25 foot high waves in their wooden tug and won.

Warren Richter, 43, and Al Schiele, 62, both of South Haven, Mich., brought their battered 39 foot Venus II, a 15 year old boat, into the harbor at dusk. They were greeted by the cheers of the 300 who waited more than three hours and by Richter's wife, Frances, 42, and one of his daughters, Catherine, 20.

Richter, who has been a lake fisherman "ever since I can remember," kept repeating:

"Two of my brothers were fishermen and they drowned in this lake. All I could think of while we fought it out was that I was gonna be the third."

Tug Icebound 3 Days

Icebound for days in the harbor at South Haven, the tug was freed Saturday by a coast guard icebreaker. Richter and Schiele left there at 9:10 a. m. Sunday for St. Joseph.

"Things went just dandy until about 2 o'clock when we were off Lake Michigan Beach," said Richter.

Forced Out Into Lake

As they neared the beach, five miles north of St. Joseph, they ran into a west wind which had gusts up to 60 miles an hour. The wind tossed up waves 25 feet high.

The rear doors of the tug were splintered by the pounding water, which surged into the boat and reached knee level. Without a radio to appeal for help, the two could only turn out into the lake, hoping to hit calmer water.

Four miles out, they found calmer water, made almost slushy by ice. There the two bailed out the water with buckets "until we ached all over."

Then they started once again for the St. Joseph harbor.

The harbor lies between two piers, and the wind churned the water like a washing machine. Richter tried once, then twice to enter the haven. Fear of the tug's being ground to pieces against the piers made him give up.

"But the third time's the charm, y'know," he said. And it was.

Richter went home to eat. Monday he plans to tackle the lake again.—Chicago *Tribune*.

189

From a newspaper or a news magazine, clip a short article about an event that you think would interest your classmates. Prepare a report of the event. For notes, you may want to use your clipping with key words underlined. Keep in mind, however, that you will probably not want to tell the details in exactly the same order in which they appear in the article. If the order in which you plan to tell the details is very different, you may want to put a few notes on a card.

Be sure to practice your report two or three times before giving it so that you can be certain you will give all the necessary details in the best order.

GIVING DIRECTIONS

You have probably had the experience of receiving directions similar to these: "Go out the main gate and walk straight ahead down Prairie Avenue for eight blocks. Then turn left." Or "Turn right at the next big intersection."

You listened attentively as the directions were given. They seemed quite clear, and you were sure that you understood what they meant. But when you began to follow the directions, you found they were not so clear as they had seemed. After going eight blocks according to the divisions on the right side of Prairie Avenue, you had gone only six blocks according to the divisions on the left side. On which side were you supposed to count the blocks? Or just as you reached a busy four-way stop and were about to turn right, you saw a traffic light about two blocks ahead. Which was the "big intersection"—the one with the four-way stop or the one with the traffic light?

Experiences like these show that making directions clear means more than making them understandable. It means making them so clear that they cannot be misunderstood. If the person giving the directions had said, ". . . walk straight ahead down Prairie Avenue for eight blocks. Then turn left *at Howard Street*" or "Turn right at the next *traffic light*," there would have been no confusion.

When you are asked to give directions, as you often are, make your directions foolproof. Don't, for example, tell a stranger to turn west at a certain corner, unless you first tell him in what direction west is. Or don't tell him to turn west "one block before the Y.M.C.A." if the sign identifying the Y.M.C.A. cannot be seen from the street he is on. And to keep from confusing him, give the steps he must follow in the order in which he should follow them.

You will find it easy to give your directions step by step if, before you begin, you take a few seconds to think the steps through. Consider where you are, where your listener wants to go, whether he is going to walk or go by car or bus, and what exact route he must follow. A little preliminary thought also helps you get the necessary details—the names of streets, the directions to turn, the landmarks to watch for—firmly in mind. Of course, the more familiar the person you are directing is with the area, the less explicit your directions need to be. His inquiry usually gives you a clue to how well he knows the district.

Notice, for example, the carefully thought out directions that Jim Danvig gave a stranger to help him find the Plainview bus stop:

> The Plainview bus stop is on the southeast corner of Third and Main. We are now facing north at the corner of Oak and Sixth. Walk three blocks north on Oak to Third, which is just past the public library, a large stone building. Then, turn left and walk two blocks west on Third to Main. Since there is a traffic light at Third and Main, you can't miss it. The Plainview bus stops directly in front of Schneider's Delicatessen. Remember—*three* blocks north to Third Avenue, then a *left* turn and *two* blocks to Main.

Jim first gave the stranger an idea of where he was. He told him in what direction he was heading and what street he was on. Then, step by step, he told him how to reach the bus stop. Notice, too, that Jim made sure his directions would not be misunderstood. He supplied the names of the important streets, the exact number of blocks to be covered, and so forth. He suggested easily recognizable landmarks—the public library, the traffic light, Schneider's Delicatessen—to help as guides. And finally, he repeated the main points to make them easy for the stranger to remember.

EXERCISE (6) On a slip of paper, write the name of a place within a ten-block radius of your school, such as a park, a store, an office building, or an intersection. Bring the paper to class and drop it in a box that will be placed on your teacher's desk. Each member of the class is to draw a slip from the box and be ready, when called on the following day, to give directions for finding the place as he would give them to a stranger. The starting point for each set of directions is to be your school.

When you are called on, begin by announcing the name of the place you drew from the box. As you talk, the rest of the class is to follow your directions mentally in order to judge whether your directions are as clear and as foolproof as possible.

191

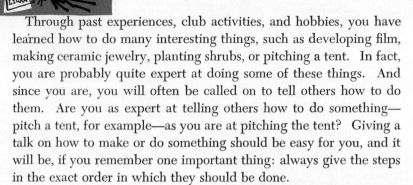

Through past experiences, club activities, and hobbies, you have learned how to do many interesting things, such as developing film, making ceramic jewelry, planting shrubs, or pitching a tent. In fact, you are probably quite expert at doing some of these things. And since you are, you will often be called on to tell others how to do them. Are you as expert at telling others how to do something— pitch a tent, for example—as you are at pitching the tent? Giving a talk on how to make or do something should be easy for you, and it will be, if you remember one important thing: always give the steps in the exact order in which they should be done.

Begin your preparation by thinking through the process you are going to explain. As you recall the steps, jot them down on a piece of paper. Then look over your list to make sure you have included all steps and have arranged them in the right order. For example:

How to Plant a Lilac Bush

1. Unwrap bush and dip roots in mud bath.
2. Dig hole two feet deep and one foot wider each way than the full spread of the roots.
3. Crumble dirt in bottom of hole.
4. Take bush from mud bath and cut off broken or dried roots.
5. Place bush in hole and spread roots apart.
6. Fill hole two-thirds full of dirt, trample dirt down firmly, and water.
7. Fill last third of hole with loose dirt, grading so that water will drain toward trunk of bush.
8. Water thoroughly.

In planning what you are going to say, keep your listeners in mind so that you can tailor your explanation to fit their needs. For example, if you were going to tell a group of boys in your woodworking class how to cut a curved corner with a chisel, you could plan to use such terms as *bevel, bevel side,* and *cutting edge* without explaining them. Knowing that the boys had used chisels before, you could expect that they would understand what parts of the tool you were referring to.

But this would not be true if your audience included girls who were not familiar with woodworking tools. You could not say such things as "hold the bevel side against the wood" and expect them to understand what you meant by *bevel side.* In other words, consider what your listeners already know about the procedure you are explaining and then determine how complete and detailed your directions must be.

Sometimes you can make your explanation clearer and more interesting by actually demonstrating certain steps or showing an object used in the process. For example, the easiest way for you to teach a group how to square dance is to do the steps and turns of the dance as you explain them. And the most effective way to explain the parts of a chisel is to show one, pointing out the differences between the edges.

Sometimes you will find sketches or diagrams helpful in making your meaning clear. For example, to explain what you mean by making diagonal cuts at the corner of a bound buttonhole, you could draw on the board a diagram of a buttonhole and then show exactly where and how the cuts are made. And to make clear where to place the rudders on a model airplane, you could point out the location of the rudders in a sketch of a plane.

EXERCISE (7) You are to give a short talk on how to make or do something. Choose for your subject a process you are quite familiar with and one that is not too complicated, such as how to tie a square knot, how to bandage a sprained ankle, or how to make a tea apron. As you prepare your talk, plan what objects you will show, what diagrams or sketches you will put on the board, or what steps you will demonstrate to make your explanation most clear and interesting. Practice your talk before giving it in class to be sure you will go through the steps smoothly.

193

EXERCISE (8) Every recitation period in each of your various classes offers opportunities for you to put into practice what you have learned about making clear, interesting explanations. In science class, for example, you might be asked to explain an experiment you have worked out; in your driver-education class, you might volunteer to explain the proper techniques for making right and left turns; in your English class, you may be called on to make an explanation at the board of the punctuation of restrictive and nonrestrictive adjective clauses.

For this exercise, you are to prepare an explanatory talk of the sort that you might use in the recitation period in any one of your classes (history, mathematics, etc.). Choose a subject which the class is to study and discuss within the next week or two. Make sure that you understand the subject well enough so that you can make it understandable to the members of your English class. Use the blackboard and whatever objects, charts, or pictures will best help you make a clear explanation.

After you have given your talk in English class, you are to invite your listeners to ask questions about any points you have not made clear. Their questions will indicate what parts of your explanation need to be improved.

TELLING ABOUT PEOPLE

Many of the people you meet—in real life or through magazines, books, radio, television, and movies—make deep impressions on you, either favorable or unfavorable. You enjoy telling others about these people. Yet in talking about them, you often limit your descriptions to such statements as "Gordon is the most ingenious fellow I know" or "Al is the shyest boy I have ever met." Interesting as such comments are, they tell very little about the person himself. They merely tell your opinion of him. It would be far more meaningful to your listeners to be told why you feel as you do. And the best way to tell why is to show the incidents that led you to form your opinion.

To get practice in describing people, you are to give a talk about a real or fictional person. First think over all you know about the person and decide what it is about him that impresses you most. Then recall several incidents you might tell to show how he made this impression on you. On a piece of scratch paper, jot down key words to help you keep the incidents in mind. It is a good idea to include at least one incident in which you can quote the person directly. Hearing his actual words will make him seem more real to your listeners. Suppose, for example, that you have picked as the subject of your talk your cousin Danny—in your opinion, the laziest boy in town. Of the many incidents that you can recall, you decide that the following will be of most interest to your listeners:

1. Lunch incident. [To avoid washing dishes while his mother was out of town for ten days, had same lunch every day—two doughnuts and a quart of milk, which he drank out of the bottle.]
2. Tie incident. [Once bought a tie he didn't like, because to look at a better selection of ties, he would have had to walk up one flight of stairs.]
3. Shoe-polish incident. [Didn't polish his shoes for two weeks recently. Had dropped can of polish behind his bureau and found it too much trouble to get it out until his father insisted.]
4. Summer-job incident. [Had choice of two jobs last summer. Took lower-paying one because it allowed him to sleep fifteen minutes longer each morning. "After all," he explained, "fifteen extra minutes every working day means an extra thirteen and a half hours of sleep for me this summer!"]

Notice that every incident on this list points up only one of Danny's characteristics—his laziness. Since this is the one characteristic you want to impress on your listeners, you do not distract their attention by showing any others in this particular talk.

Although you want your audience to agree with your opinion, you will find that your talk will be most effective if you do not constantly tell them what to think. In telling about the tie incident, for example, instead of actually saying that Danny was "*too lazy*" to walk up a flight of stairs to look at a better selection, it would be more effective to say, "One day Danny had to choose between buying a rather gaudy tie and walking up a flight of stairs to look at a better selection. He bought the gaudy tie." Give your listeners a clear picture of what happened and let them reach their own opinion. If you choose the right incidents to tell, their opinion will match yours.

You will not need an elaborate introduction. You can begin simply by stating your opinion: "My cousin Danny is the laziest boy in town." But since your talk will consist of several separate incidents, you will probably want to think up a special closing sentence to round it off. The talk about Danny might end with a comment like "You can see now why Danny's father calls him 'Perpetual Inertia.'"

EXERCISE 9 Give a short talk about a real or fictional person you are acquainted with, telling three or four incidents to show why he has made a particular impression on you. Practice your talk two or three times, experimenting with different ways of telling each incident to find the most effective way.

EXERCISE 10 REVIEW Each member of the class is to prepare a brief talk (three minutes or less) telling a personal experience, reporting a news event, explaining how to make or do something, or showing why someone has made a particular impression on him.

Before the talks are given in class, each of you is to draw from a box the name of a classmate. Listen especially carefully to the talk given by the classmate whose name you draw.

Then after all the talks have been given, you are to write a brief (one to two paragraphs) criticism of the talk, making clear in what ways you found the speaker's presentation effective and in what ways ineffective. The following questions will help you: What type of talk did the speaker make? Did he give enough specific details to make his ideas clear? Did he use any terms that were puzzling to his listeners? If he used sketches, diagrams, or some other visual aid, were they helpful? Did he present his details in an orderly manner? Was the order easy to follow? Be sure to give reasons and examples to back your opinions.

CHAPTER 9

WRITING

FRIENDLY

LETTERS

Here are just a few of the things that happened to Dan Carter in the course of a week:

1 Alarm didn't go off, so was late for school on Tuesday—the tenth time. Had to appear before Student Council to explain frequent tardiness.

2 Was nominated for president of Science Club but lost the election to best friend Bob. Pleased for Bob but disappointed nevertheless.

3 Ate too many hamburgers and drank too many Cokes at Booster Club picnic. As result, was deathly sick on Thursday night.

4 Found wallet containing $23.65. Owner gave him $3.65 as reward.

5 Got into loud, heated discussion on guided missiles with Ronnie Bates on bus, leading to argument with bus driver. Ended by apologizing to driver for his hot temper.

6   Went shopping for sports jacket; the one he liked best was too expensive. Decided to try to get old paper route back to earn money to supplement allowance.

7   Followed fire engines to scene of fire—the kitchen of small restaurant near school. Impressed by firemen's skill, he thought seriously of future career as a modern fire-fighter.

8   Laughed and yelled himself hoarse at faculty-student game held to raise money for a new trophy case for the first floor.

Now none of these events is especially spectacular or unique; things like these might—and do—happen to anyone. But spectacular or not, these experiences are interesting to others, particularly if described in enough detail to make them come alive.

Dan is quite successful at this. He (like most people) likes to talk about what happened. He doesn't skimp on details. He tells not only what took place, but also what he thought and how he felt about it. Because he does, his friends enjoy listening to him.

But what happens when Dan has a letter to write to an out-of-town friend or relative? Well, he does what many people do—he keeps putting it off as long as possible, mostly because he "can't ever think of anything interesting to write about."

What a poor excuse! He has plenty of interesting things to write about, as you and his family and his friends at home know. Perhaps the real reason is that he doesn't know how to write about these events in an interesting way. Dan, who is so good at *telling* his experiences, writes dull, drab letters that sound like this:

```
                                       374 Fee Lane
                                       Roseville, Kentucky
                                       November 5, 19--


Dear Roy,

     Nothing much has happened around here since you left.
About the only excitement was a fire at Clancy's Hut and
a faculty-student basketball game last Friday.

     I hope you like your new school.  Central is just
the same as usual--teachers still making a big fuss if a
kid is a little late to class.

     The Science Club elected new officers.  By the way,
Bob Anderson and Ronnie Bates, the great arguer, say hello
to you.

     How's your job at the supermarket?  I'm thinking of
getting my paper route again; my money doesn't stretch
far enough these days, even with an extra three bucks I
got last week.

     The gang missed you at the Boosters' picnic.

                                       Your old friend,

                                       Dan
```

The main reason this letter is dull and uninteresting is that it covers too much ground too fast. In spite of the opening sentence, a great deal had happened. But in the letter Dan does little more than list the events: the fire, the faculty game, the club election, and so on. What pleasure can Roy get from reading a list?

Instead of covering so many events so fast, Dan should have picked out two or three (or even just one) to tell about. Then he could tell about them in detail, the way he would do if he had met Roy on the way home from school. He might, for example, start with the faculty game:

Dear Roy,

You should have been here last night. It was a riot! The gym was jam-packed, and the noise was terrific. The funniest thing about it was that the teachers were making more of a racket than the kids. You won't believe it, but some of our most dignified faculty members were pounding on toy drums and banging tin lids together. Before you accuse me of making things up, I'd better explain. This was a game between the faculty men and the regular basketball team to raise money for a new trophy case for the first floor.

I wish you could have seen Mr. Schmitz, the band director. A false nose, glued-on orange whiskers, and a suit stuffed with padding made it almost impossible to recognize him. But that's who it was, all right, leading the faculty cheering section with Miss Jenkins.

Miss J. was wearing one of the girls' pep-squad outfits and as Ronnie Bates, the old expert, said, she looked plenty OK. Her cap kept falling off, but she'd just pick it up, wave it around her head several times, and put it on again. She yelled so hard she could hardly talk in history class today. Notice that I said "hardly"; she could talk well enough to call on me several times. No, I didn't know *all* the answers. It's kind of unreasonable, I think, to expect us to shine in class the day after a big game. Don't you agree?

Mr. Pine—he's the new social-studies teacher—was the star of the faculty team. He's good enough for the varsity, in fact. Mr. Quillan and Doc Brady weren't too bad, either. But Mr. Costello and Mr. Linus really ought to stick to geometry and chemistry. They're much more at home with angles and circles and test tubes than on a gym floor.

The score? Do you have to ask? The *students* won, of course: 63 to 34. That left everybody feeling happy—we were glad because we won, and the faculty was pleased because enough money was raised to buy the new case. I hope we decide to buy a case for the second floor next year; I'd gladly pay another fifty cents to see another shindig like this one.

Even though these paragraphs do not give a play-by-play description of the game, they tell enough to give Roy a fairly clear idea of the excitement and the fun. The references to people he knows will please him. Like everyone else who has moved away from a town, he looks forward to letters containing news of old friends. And the two or three spots in which Dan expresses his opinions and feelings will tickle him particularly; they sound like Dan in person.

Writing good friendly letters, as you can see, takes time and thought, but it is not hard. The main thing to remember is that the person you are writing to wants to hear news of what has been happening to you and to the friends you have in common.

Importance of details. To make the news interesting, you have to give details, just as you would if you were telling the stories. General statements like those in the letter on page 198 do not make interesting reading. In the first place, they mean very little to the person who gets the letter. But worse than that, they are likely to give him the impression that you hurried through the letter, writing it not because you wanted to but because you felt you had to.

Since giving details takes space, you naturally cannot cover every bit of news you have. What items you select to tell about depend on the person you are writing to. For example, if Dan Carter were writing to his friend Cliff Spears, who likes scientific subjects more than sports, he would probably tell Cliff about the fire-fighting devices used at the restaurant fire, his discussion on guided missiles with Ronnie Bates, and the Science Club election. In a letter to his favorite aunt, who has always been interested in his problems, he might tell of his experience before the Student Council, the lesson the picnic taught him about overeating, and the trouble his hot temper caused on the bus. In other words, a person should write about the subjects that he would find himself talking over with his friend if he met him for lunch.

To make your letter truly "friendly," you should not make it exclusively about yourself. Whoever you write to would like to feel that you are interested also in what *he* has been doing. A question or two asking for news of him and his family and a few sentences commenting on something he said in a letter to you will show him that this is a two-way friendship. Besides, one of the surest ways to encourage a reply to your letter is to include a question to be answered.

EXERCISE (1) A. Make a list of things that have happened to you within the past week or two—experiences or events that you have enjoyed talking about with your family and friends.

B. When your list is complete, look over the items carefully and divide them into the following three groups:

1 The things you think would be of special interest to your best friend, who (you will pretend) has moved to another town

2 The things you think would be of special interest to your older brother or sister, who (you will pretend) is away at college

3 The things you think would be of special interest to a favorite teacher, who is now teaching in another state

C. Your teacher may call on volunteers to read their lists in class and to explain why they divided the items as they did. The best way to explain this is to describe each of the persons briefly, telling his special interests, hobbies, likes, and dislikes.

EXERCISE (**2**) Write a letter to one of the persons suggested in Exercise 1. Include in your letter the items you listed as being of special interest to that person. Your teacher may call for volunteers to read their letters to the class. (If your school has an opaque projector, have the letters flashed on the screen.) Members of the class will then be called on to comment on the good points of each letter and perhaps make suggestions showing how it might be improved.

THE PARTS

OF A FRIENDLY LETTER

A friendly letter, as you probably know, generally has five parts: the heading, the salutation, the body, the closing, and the signature. Luckily for letter-writers, the third part—the body, or message—is the only one that takes time and thought. The forms of the other parts are pretty much established by custom. A few minutes spent in examining the forms is all you need:

122 Wilton Avenue
Omaha 3, Nebraska   HEADING
November 14, 19—

Dear Laura,   SALUTATION

. . . .
. . . .
. . . .
. . . .

. . . .   BODY
. . . .
. . . .

. . . .
. . . .
. . . .

Sincerely,   CLOSING
Sue Carter   SIGNATURE

The heading.   The heading in a friendly letter (on stationery without an address printed at the top) usually consists of three lines. The writer's street address is given in the first line; the name of the city, zone number, and state are put in the second. The third line gives the date.

BLOCK STYLE   INDENTED STYLE

2394 Devon Street   *111 Hartman Avenue*
Alton 3, Illinois   *Donner, South Dakota*
July 17, 19—   *March 28, 19—*

Notice that there is no punctuation at the ends of the lines and only two commas inside the lines—one after the zone number or city and one after the day of the month. (Do not use a comma *before* the zone number.) The heading may be written in "block" style, as in the left-hand example, or in "indented" style, as in the right-hand example.

The heading is written in the upper right corner of the page, about an inch or so from the top. Allow yourself enough room so that you can write out in full the name of the state and month and such words as *Street* and *Avenue*.

The salutation.   The salutation is simply a greeting to the person to whom you are writing. Most people use conventional greetings like these:

Dear Tom,   *My dear Miss Wade,*
Dearest Helen,   *Dear Father McKeough,*
My dearest Martha,   *Mother dear,*

But in letters to close friends, you should feel free to use any other short greeting that you think suitable for a particular occasion. For example:

Hi Champ,   *My dear Miss I-Told-You-So,*
Caro Amico,   *Howdy Stranger,*

The salutation in a friendly letter is followed by a comma, and the first word and all nouns are capitalized.

The closing.   The most commonly used closings are such expressions as these:

Sincerely yours,   *Cordially yours,*
Sincerely,   *Cordially,*

In a letter to a relative or a close friend to whom you write often, you may prefer a more personal closing, one that seems especially appropriate for the particular letter. Then you might use one of the following closings or a similar one of your own devising which would fit the message in the letter:

Love,   *Your harassed brother,*
With love,   *Complainingly yours,*
Affectionately yours,   *As always,*

In all of these closings, only the first word is capitalized, and a comma is used at the end.

The signature. In letters to close friends with whom you correspond regularly, just your first name or a nickname will do. Otherwise it is best to give both your first and last names so that there will be no question about which "Jim" or "Robert" or "Kathryn" wrote the letter.

The envelope. Including your return address on the envelope is a wise precaution. Then if the person to whom you are writing has moved or if you have mistakenly given the wrong address, your letter can be returned to you instead of being sent to the Dead Letter Office in Washington. The most convenient place for the return address—and the place recommended by the Post Office Department—is in the upper left corner.

Eric Knudsen
101 Fifth Street
Doyletown, Utah

Mr. Richard Daniels
769 Sheridan Road
Oneida 2
New Jersey

The Post Office Department also recommends using a separate line for the name of the state in the main address, as an aid to postal clerks who have to handle an ever-increasing volume of mail. To prevent possible mistakes, take the time to write out in full the name of the state. A carelessly written "Ia." might be misread and your letter delayed by being first missent to Louisiana (La.) or Pennsylvania (Pa.) or Virginia (Va.) or even to Idaho (Id.).

Use the same style—block or indented—on the envelope as you use in the heading of your letter.

EXERCISE (3) All but two of the following letter parts have one or more errors in form. On a sheet of paper, rewrite each of the incorrect parts as they should be written.

1 2354 Pinecrest Avenue,
    Racine, Wis.,
    Oct. 10, 1960

2 My Dear Mr. Barnes,

3 Yours Truly,

4 Your Loving Son,

5 117 Fifth Street
    Boston, 11, Massachusetts
    February 3, 1959

6 Dear Ralph:—

7 With Love,

8 My Dearest grandpa,

9 Yours sincerely,

10 Rural Route 3
    Clay, Nebraska
    June 6, 1961

11 358 Walnut Street
    October 13, 1960
    Ocean Spray, Florida

12 Dear Mother:

EXERCISE (4) On a sheet of unlined white paper, rule off a space 7¼ by 10¼ inches (to represent a sheet of stationery). In this space, write in ink a "dummy" letter to a friend. For the body of the letter, just draw lines representing three or four short paragraphs. Arrange the five parts of the letter so that they make a pleasing appearance on the sheet. This means having margins on all sides, a straight left-hand margin, and even paragraph indentions.

Be ready to show your dummy letter to your classmates, who are to make suggestions, if necessary, for improving the appearance of the letter.

EXERCISE (5) On sheets of unlined paper, rule off four spaces, each of them the size of an envelope (about 4 by 6 inches). Address each of these "envelopes" to one of the following people. Use your own name and address for the return addresses. Use the block style for three of the envelopes and the indented style for the fourth. Write the addresses in ink—preferably black or blue.

1 miss nora finney   327 sheridan place   lake bluff illinois
2 the reverend joseph bates   1459 laurel drive   clarksburg 2 florida
3 mr and mrs david prockow   33 north erie street   phoenix 7 arizona
4 mr george michaels   rural route 3   milton wisconsin

EXERCISE 6 Everyone in your class owes a friend or relative a letter or has a friend or relative who would welcome a letter. This exercise will give you a chance to pay your debt or please a friend—and get class credit at the same time.

Write your letter on scratch paper first. Then, after you have looked it over carefully and have made all corrections and improvements you can, copy it—in ink—on your personal stationery or on a sheet of plain white paper. Prepare an envelope and enclose the letter.

Your teacher will check through your letter briefly, making sure you have omitted none of the parts. Then she will hand it back to you for mailing.

WRITING INFORMAL NOTES

Informal notes differ from friendly letters in two ways. Notes, as their name suggests, are usually short, while friendly letters are likely to be long. And notes are usually about one thing only, while friendly letters generally cover several items of news.

Since notes are short and are written for a specific purpose—to thank someone for a gift, for example—they are easy to write. There never is the problem of "what should I tell?" You may not know at the start exactly how you want to phrase your message. But since you have a specific message to give, finding the words is not a major problem. Words that make your meaning clear are all you need. A note does not have to be clever or literary or impressive; it just has to be friendly and clear.

The thank-you note. Has anything like this ever happened to you? You spend a great deal of time and thought choosing a gift to send to an out-of-town friend. Weeks pass and you do not hear from him. You start wondering. "Did the package get lost? Should I report the loss to the Post Office? But I can't unless I know for sure that George didn't get it. Perhaps I should write to him and ask. No, he'll think I'm reminding him to thank me. Maybe he didn't like what I sent. Oh, I don't know; I guess I'd better just skip it."

If you have ever been in a predicament like this, you do not have to be convinced of the importance of writing a thank-you note when you have received a gift. The note need not be more than a paragraph long—just a few sentences expressing your appreciation for the sender's kindness. The person who received a note like this, for example, would feel sure that her gift was truly appreciated:

432 Cherry Street
Curtis, Louisiana
March 13, 19—

Dear Aunt Helen,

I know you have always said that you hated show-offs—yet that's just what I have turned out to be. And it's really not my fault. How can you send me such a beautiful watch and expect me to resist showing it off to my friends every chance I get? Seriously, Aunt Helen, it's the loveliest watch I have ever seen. I not only enjoy wearing it; I even like to look at it when it's in the box. I thank you with all my heart for sending me this "beautiful way to tell time."

Affectionately,
Betty Ann

The bread-and-butter letter. Anyone who has been an overnight or weekend guest in the home of a friend unfailingly expresses his thanks at the end of the visit. If he is courteous and really appreciative, he will do more. He will put his appreciation in writing, in a note commonly called a "bread-and-butter letter." A note of thanks after a visit in the home of a school friend is usually addressed to the mother, since she is the person in charge of hospitality.

56 Fourth Street
Jordan, Idaho
August 13, 19—

Dear Mrs. Heinsen,

Mark Twain can have his "Life on the Mississippi," and Jules Verne is welcome to his trip "Around the World in Eighty Days." As for me—I'll take "A Weekend at the Heinsens'." From the time I arrived until the minute I left I thoroughly enjoyed myself. I have you to thank for making me feel so much at home and especially for the superdelicious food. No wonder Bill turned up his nose at the hot dogs and hamburgers we ordered for him at that restaurant near our house!

Will you thank Mr. Heinsen again for driving Bill and me out to Maplecrest and for letting me use his golf clubs. I wish my score had been as good as his clubs.

Sincerely,
Ken Brodda

Other notes. There will be many other occasions for you in the days ahead to write informal notes. A friend or relative in the hospital, for example, would enjoy a short note letting him know he is missed and expressing a wish that he will soon be well. (A note will mean much more to him than a printed get-well card.) From time to time you may hear news of a friend's winning a special prize or award. A note from you congratulating him will double his pleasure at winning the honor. Or suppose that you have, through thoughtlessness or even through no fault of your own, hurt a friend's feelings or caused him some inconvenience. One of the simplest ways to make amends would be to write a note of apology explaining the circumstances that caused the trouble and expressing regret for what happened.

EXERCISE (7) Each item in the following list describes a situation that calls for writing an informal note. Choose two of the situations and write the notes.

Some of the items in the list may suggest to you similar *real* situations for which you might write notes. If so, feel free to change the details so that the notes you write will be "real" notes for you to mail after your teacher has checked them.

1 You promised a friend of yours that you would meet him at the downtown library at seven o'clock on Friday evening and from there you would go to a movie together. On the way to the library, your bus is delayed by a traffic accident. By the time you arrive—at seven forty-five—your friend is gone. The next day you hear that he will "never again" make plans to go anywhere with you. Write a note apologizing for the inconvenience you caused him.

2 You have very much enjoyed a weekend at the summer cottage of a friend you met at camp last year. Write a bread-and-butter note expressing your thanks for the hospitality shown you.

3 One of your friends has been in the hospital for two weeks and will have to stay for two more. Write him (or her) a cheer-up note that will make him smile in spite of his bad luck.

4 The first prize in a photography contest sponsored by the camera shops of your town has been awarded to Jerry Stewart, a young man who lives in a neighboring city. You know Jerry slightly, and you admire him and his work. You had also been a contestant, but your entry won none of the awards. Write a note to Jerry, congratulating him for the honor he won. Try to suggest in your note that he fully deserved the prize.

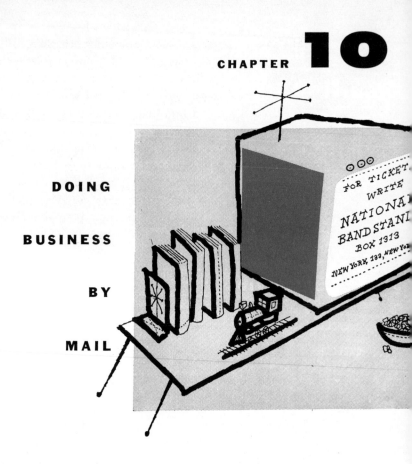

CHAPTER 10

DOING

BUSINESS

BY

MAIL

The Kellys had been living in their new house for five months and were getting quite used to the change. Bob Kelly found that living in the new house was far more pleasant than in the old—except for one thing. In the old house the latest issue of the *TV Guide* was on the table waiting for him every Friday night without fail. Now, since it went first to his old address, where it stayed until someone found the time to forward it to his new address, it was always several days late. As a result, he was missing quite a few good programs.

What an annoyance for Bob! Yet he could easily avoid this annoyance by writing a letter asking the magazine firm to change the address of his subscription. That would cost **him** five cents, less than he was paying for the extra postage due on his magazine each week.

Sam Bruno and Perry Culver spent several weeks planning what they would do during a week's vacation to be spent in New York City. After a great deal of discussion, they agreed on a TV show

that they would most like to see televised. Their week in New York was a great success, except for their disappointment about the television show. They couldn't get in to see it; there were no tickets available when they arrived at the studio. Yet they could easily have avoided this disappointment—if only they had taken the time to write a letter asking for tickets.

Bob, Sam, and Perry are not the only ones who have need for doing business by mail. All of you at some time or other have, or will have, occasions to write business letters—to request samples, travel folders, pamphlets, or price lists, for example; to ask for information; to order items that are not available in local stores; to make arrangements with out-of-town people; or to point out an error that has been made in a shipment of goods. This chapter will give you help in writing letters that will take care of these business problems in an efficient way. A *good* business letter gets things done; your job now is to learn how to make the letters you will write *good* letters.

Most people expect perfect service and efficiency from business firms. Yet many of those same people think nothing of sending business letters hurriedly scrawled off in pencil on a note card or on a scrap of paper torn from a pad. It has never occurred to them, evidently, that a penciled scrawl may be hard or impossible to read and that a small scrap of paper is a nuisance for business firms to handle and file.

Don't handicap your letters from the start. Use plain white paper of the standard size, 8½ by 11 inches. Type the letter if possible; otherwise write it neatly and legibly in ink. Black or blue ink should be used.

The letter should be centered on the page, with side margins of from one to two inches. The size of the top and bottom margins will depend, of course, on the length of the letter. Typewritten letters, unless very short, should be single spaced, with double spacing between the parts of the letter and between paragraphs.

PARTS OF THE BUSINESS LETTER

Business letters sent by individuals usually have six parts. Let us look first at the five parts that will be the same in all the letters you will write.

The heading. Since both the writer's address and the date are essential in transacting the business at hand, these items are placed at the top of the letter, where they can be referred to at a glance. The heading usually consists of three lines:

BLOCK STYLE	INDENTED STYLE
2533 Comstock Street	*59 Hillcrest Avenue*
Dennison 3, Minnesota	*Belmont, Iowa*
March 15, 19—	*November 16, 19—*

In most business letters, the "block" style shown at the left is used, since it saves the writer the trouble of figuring out neat indentions. In your letters, use whichever form you prefer. Just make sure that you use one style consistently in the letter and on the envelope.

The inside address. Since the name and address of the person or firm you are writing to is important for a complete record of the transaction, this information is also placed in an easy-to-find spot, four spaces or so below the heading, starting at the left margin. The inside address usually has three lines:

BLOCK STYLE   INDENTED STYLE

Mr. Laurence Grube   *Johnson Motors*
Rural Route 1, Box 73   *265 Pershing Road*
Horton, New Hampshire   *Waukegan, Illinois*

If the letter is intended for a particular person in a business firm, the inside address will contain an additional line:

Personnel Manager   Mr. John Kells, President
Derwell Kent Company   Root—Blakewell Corporation
1327 Fulton Avenue   130 Main Street
Baltimore 7, Maryland   Edgeworth, California

Notice that in both the heading and the inside address no punctuation is used at the ends of the lines. But commas are used inside the lines, to separate such items as city and state, city zone number and state, route and box numbers, day and year, and person's name and title.

Abbreviations are generally avoided in both the heading and the inside address. However, if the name of a firm—as it appears on its letterhead or in its advertising—contains an abbreviation, use the abbreviation (for example: Time Inc., Polk Bros., Best & Co.).

The salutation. All of the following salutations are commonly used. The one you choose for a particular letter depends on the situation.

To an unknown person: Dear Sir: Dear Madam:
If name is known: Dear Mr. Coe: Dear Miss Ott:
More formal: My dear Mr. Coe: My dear Miss Ott:
To a business firm: Gentlemen: Ladies:

The salutation, which is started at the left margin, two spaces below the inside address, is followed by a colon. Notice that the word *dear* is capitalized only when it is the first word in the greeting.

The closing. The closing is written two spaces below the body of the letter and aligned with the first word in the heading. Appropriate closings in business letters are:

Yours truly, (*to an unknown person or to a firm*)
Very truly yours, (*less formal*)
Sincerely yours, (*more personal*)
Cordially yours, (*more friendly*)
Respectfully yours, (*to a superior*)

Only the first word of the closing is capitalized, and a comma is used at the end.

The signature. In block-style letters the writer's signature is begun directly under the first word of the closing; in the indented style, it is indented a few spaces to the right.

The signature should, of course, always be written by hand, even in a typed letter. Except in typewritten letters in which the writer's name is typed out four spaces below the closing, it is extremely important to write all letters in the signature legibly.

Although the title *Mr.* is never used in a signature, a woman may write *Miss* in parentheses before her name to show how she should be addressed in the answer to her letter:

Yours truly,   Sincerely yours,

Clayton Helms   *(Miss) Leslie Bergen*
Clayton Helms

THE ENVELOPE

The address on the envelope should contain the same items as the inside address in the letter and should be in the same style, block or indented. Begin the address slightly to the left of the center of the envelope, and avoid abbreviations, especially in handwritten addresses.

The Post Office Department recommends putting the names of the city and the state on separate lines, to make the sorting of mail easier for busy clerks. In the return address, which should always be included, a single line is used for the city and state.

```
Charles Newby
1337 Johnson Avenue
Bethesda, Maryland




                    Popular Mechanics Magazine
                    200 East Ontario Street
                    Chicago 11
                    Illinois
```

Folding the letter.   If you are using business letter paper of the standard size and a *long* envelope, first fold the bottom of the sheet up about one third. Then fold the top down to within a half inch of the bottom crease. Holding the folded letter at the top crease, insert it in the envelope.

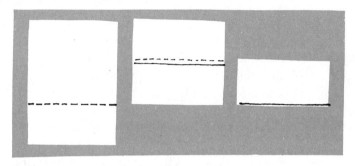

If you are using a *short* envelope, first fold the bottom of the sheet up to within a half inch of the top. Then fold the right-hand edges to the left, and make a crease at a point about one third of the width of the sheet. Next fold the left-hand edges over to within a quarter of an inch of the right-hand crease. Holding the letter by the right-hand crease, insert it in the envelope.

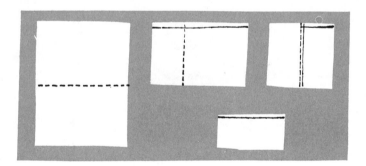

EXERCISE (1) Write out the answers to the following questions.

1 What salutation should be used in a business letter to a firm like Sears Roebuck and Company or United States Steel?

2 What salutation should be used in a letter in which the first line of the inside address is *Circulation Manager?*

3 What salutation should be used in a letter addressed to a dress shop owned by three sisters?

4 Which of these items is correctly punctuated: *San Francisco, 7, California* or *San Francisco 7, California?*

5 Which of these closings is correct: *Very Truly Yours,* or *Very truly yours,?*

EXERCISE (2) Using a sheet of typing paper, prepare a "dummy" business letter. For the body of the letter, draw lines representing three or four short paragraphs. Write out in full the other five parts of the letter, placing them correctly and neatly on the page. The letter is to be sent from your home address to Mr. Edward Selkirk, the sales manager of the Blake and Selkirk Company at 324 Fifth Avenue, New York 16, New York.

EXERCISE (3) Be ready to demonstrate before the class the correct way to fold the dummy letter you prepared for the preceding exercise (1) to fit a long envelope and (2) to fit a short envelope.

EXERCISE (4) On a sheet of paper (turned sideways), rule off two spaces, one the size of a long envelope (4 by 9½ inches) and the other the size of a short envelope (3¾ by 7½ inches). Address these dummy envelopes to the following firms. Use your own name and address for the return addresses.

1 bendix aviation corporation   fisher building   detroit 2 michigan

2 time subscription service   540 north michigan avenue   chicago 11 illinois

214

THE BODY

OF THE LETTER

What should you put in the body of a business letter? The answer can be boiled down to a few words: Include all the information needed to make your message unmistakably clear to the receiver. Anything more is unnecessary; anything less is not enough.

LETTERS OF REQUEST

Requesting samples or circulars. Before you start writing a letter requesting printed matter or samples offered by a business firm, take time to figure out what the receiver of the letter has to know. Suppose, for example, you are writing some company to ask for a booklet you saw advertised in a newspaper or magazine. If you merely ask for "a copy of the booklet your company sends out," you don't give enough information. "Which booklet?" the receiver of the letter will wonder. "We put out dozens of booklets." If you want the right one sent to you, you must identify it clearly, as in this letter:

867 Fremont Avenue
Glendale, Mississippi
March 29, 19—

Bates Novelty Company
753 Windmill Road
Waterloo, Iowa

Gentlemen:

Please send me a copy of your booklet, "Hobbies That Pay Dividends," advertised in the March 19 issue of Arts and Crafts.

I am enclosing fifteen cents in stamps to cover the cost of handling and mailing.

Yours truly,

Robert Clary

EXERCISE 5 Clip from a magazine or newspaper an advertisement offering a catalogue, booklet, or sample that you would like to have. Write a letter on business paper asking for it. (If the advertisement specifies a charge for the material, make sure you tell in your letter that you are enclosing a coin or stamps.) Prepare an envelope for the letter.

In class, exchange letters and clippings with a neighbor. Check first the form of each of the parts of his letter and its envelope. Circle in pencil any errors that you find. Then check the body of the letter. If any necessary details are missing, make a note of them on the bottom of the sheet, and return the letter to the writer.

Unless the indicated corrections are minor ones that can be made without spoiling the appearance of the letter, copy your revised letter before handing it in. When your teacher has checked your letter, she will return it to you for mailing.

Requesting information. Making clear exactly what you want is especially important in writing letters asking for information. And since these requests for information are often written to people who will not profit financially from the correspondence, it is also important that they be phrased courteously. Asking someone to supply you with information is, after all, asking a favor of that person. When favors are asked, politeness is the rule.

A good way to begin such a letter is to explain the reason for your request. Then, as clearly and concisely as possible, ask for the information you want. For example:

```
                              441 Spiral Drive
                              Closter, New Jersey
                              May 5, 19--


Rockefeller Center Guided Tours
Rockefeller Plaza
New York 20, New York

Gentlemen:

     A group of freshman students of Closter High School
is planning a three-day sightseeing trip to New York and
would like, if possible, to include a tour of Rockefeller
Center.  There will be thirty-two students and our two
advisers.

     To help me in making arrangements for the group, I
would appreciate your sending me information about the
following points:

     1. At what time do the tours begin, and how long
        does each tour take?
     2. How many people can join each touring group?
     3. Are there special rates for student groups?

     Would you please send me also a copy of any pamphlets
you have concerning the guided tours.

                              Yours truly,
                              Elsie Campbell
                              Secretary, Freshman Class
```

Since Elsie's request will probably lead to a student tour of the Center, she need not enclose a stamped, self-addressed envelope for the reply, as is usually done when the letter is to someone who will derive no benefit from supplying the information.

EXERCISE 6 Write a letter requesting information. If possible, make it a letter to a real person asking for information that you actually need or are sincerely interested in getting. The following items may suggest situations for which you might write such a letter.

1 As chairman of the program committee of the Camera Club, you may be considering the possibility of inviting a prize-winning photographer from a neighboring city to talk to your club and display his work. You will need answers to a number of questions before final arrangements can be made. What questions should you ask?

216

2 Before you make final plans for a coming summer vacation, you think it a good idea to find out specific information about a resort or dude ranch you have heard friends discussing. What questions should you ask the manager or owner to make sure you will get all the information you should have?

3 Through a magazine advertisement, you have become interested in buying a certain article—for example, a pair of Fiberglas curtains pictured in the ad. The advertisement gives the name of the manufacturing firm, but says nothing about the price, the size, the colors available, or stores that carry the product. None of your local stores sell the curtains. To whom should you write and what questions should you ask if you are really interested in getting the curtains as soon as possible?

4 Your social-studies class has been discussing the possibility of making a trip to a historic spot in your state—the state capitol, for example, the home of a former President, or the site of a famous battle. You have volunteered to get complete information about chartering a bus for the trip. To whom should you write and what questions should you ask so that you can give a full report to the class?

EXERCISE (7) Your teacher will call on several members of the class to read the letters they prepared for Exercise 6. Each of the letters is to be discussed. You will be asked to comment on such points as these:

1 Is the letter clear, concise, and courteous? Are the questions specific or so vague that the receiver would be puzzled about what kind of answer is expected of him?

2 Is the request for information justifiable? Or does the writer ask for information that he could find for himself with a little work, without having to bother a stranger?

3 Is the person to whom the letter is written a person who could be expected to know the answers and would consider supplying the information part of his job?

4 Are the questions reasonable? Or do they ask for information that the receiver would not want to give or could not give without devoting several hours to his reply?

ORDER LETTERS

Most firms that offer merchandise for sale in newspaper and magazine ads have the same sad experience. They receive plenty of orders; there is no question about that. But getting people to give all the information needed to fill the orders satisfactorily seems to be an always-present problem. Even when the advertisements include order slips with spaces in which to write such important details as the color, size, style, model number, and quantity, some orders arrive without all the necessary information. When this happens, a service intended as a convenience to customers turns out to be an inconvenience for both the firm and the buyers.

Often you will want to order articles you have seen advertised which you cannot buy in local stores. Ordering by mail is easy, even when an order blank is not provided. Most order letters need have only three parts:

1 A brief but complete description of the items wanted, including the price
2 Shipping directions, if necessary, stating whether the items are to be shipped by parcel post, express, or freight
3 A statement explaining the method of payment—money order, check, C.O.D., or charge

See how concisely, clearly, and courteously all this information can be given:

```
                                    507 East Daniel Street
                                    Champaign, Illinois
                                    November 17, 19--


Willoughbys
110 West 32nd Street
New York 1, New York

Gentlemen:

     Please send me the following items, selected from
your advertisement in the November issue of Popular
Photography:

     2 Metal slide files, 2 x 2, green, @ $1.69    $ 3.38
     1 Enlarging easel, 11 x 14, white enamel
       base, steel masking bands                     4.95
     2 Mansfield Junior Splicers, for 8 mm and
       16 mm, @ $1.98                                3.96
                                                    12.29
                                    Postage           .75
                                    Total          $13.04

     Will you please send these items by parcel post. I
am enclosing a money order for $13.04 to cover the cost
of the order and the postage.

                                    Yours very truly,

                                    Martha Egan
                                    Martha Egan
```

Before you begin writing an order letter, read the advertisement carefully. It will specifiy what details to include in the order to make sure you will get what you want. It will also tell you whether you should indicate second choices and if you must pay shipping costs. Before sealing your letter in the envelope, read it through once again, pretending that you are the person who is to fill the order. Would you know exactly which items to send—how many, what sizes, what colors, and so on?

EXERCISE 8 Pretend that you have just received a surprise check for $25.00, which the donor insists that you spend on something to be bought by mail. Clip from a newspaper or magazine an advertisement offering something that you would like to order. Write a letter ordering the item or items you choose. Remember that you can spend less than $25.00, but not more. The shipping charges, if any, must come out of that sum.

On the back of the sheet, rule off a space the size of an envelope. In this space, write the address of the firm given in the advertisement and your return address.

EXERCISE 9 Exchange order letters (prepared for Exercise 8) with a neighbor. Hand your neighbor the advertisement also.

Read through his letter carefully. Circle in pencil any errors in form that you find in the heading, inside address, salutation, closing, signature, and envelope addresses. Refer to the advertisement as you check the letter to make sure that the writer has included all necessary details in the body of the letter. If any details are missing, make a note of them at the bottom of the sheet.

When your letter is returned to you, make all the indicated corrections. Copy the letter, if necessary, before handing it in to your teacher.

LETTERS OF COMPLAINT

No one is more anxious to satisfy mail-order customers than the people who run business firms. Yet often for one reason or another something goes wrong. A clerk may make a mistake in filling an order; some items may be damaged in packing or shipping; the firm may not be able to get enough stock to fill all the orders in a reasonable time.

There are two things a person can do when such things happen to his order. First, he can write an angry letter to the firm, expressing his annoyance in sarcastic, insulting words. This kind of letter may be fine for relieving his feelings, but it is not of much help in solving the problem. Often in such letters the writer is so concerned with "telling that fool company off" that he fails to make clear which order he is complaining about and what he wants done about it. And since the person who gets the letter is usually not the person responsible for the mistake, such a letter is not only discourteous but unfair.

A better course of action would be to write a letter clearly describing the situation and courteously explaining the adjustment expected from the company. If the adjustment is reasonable, the firm will be only too glad to make it. The employee who receives the following letter, for example, will not only refund Roberta's money, but will probably write her an apology on behalf of the company for the inconvenience that was caused her.

> 222 Burton Place
> Oak Park, Illinois
> April 19, 19--
>
> Curtis Evans and Company
> 1314 State Street
> Chicago 2, Illinois
>
> Gentlemen:
>
> Last Saturday in your housewares department I bought a Revere stainless steel pan for $5.95 and asked to have it sent to me by parcel post. The salesclerk assured me that the pan, intended as a gift, would arrive by Wednesday of this week at the latest. Since it did not arrive in time, I had to buy another gift in town to substitute for it.
>
> I would appreciate your checking on this order to see whether or not it has been mailed as yet. If it has, I will return it to you when it arrives. If it has not, I would like you to cancel the order. In either case, will you please send me a refund of $6.20, which includes the 25 cents I paid for postage.
>
> Yours truly,
>
> *Roberta Peterson*
> Roberta Peterson

EXERCISE (10) Write one of the letters suggested in the following list, or a "real" letter of complaint, if you have occasion to write one at this time. If your letter is based on one of the situations described below, you are to make up names, addresses, and other details that you will need to make the letter complete. Feel free to change any of the specific details that are given in the described situations if you would like to.

1   A pen and a pencil that you ordered as a gift for your brother have arrived, but the name imprinted on them is spelled *Frances* (with an *e*) instead of *Francis,* as you had specified in your order. Write a letter to the department store explaining the error in the name and courteously asking for the adjustment that you would like made.

2   It is two days before you are to leave on a vacation trip. A raincoat that you had ordered for the trip has not arrived, though you ordered it three weeks ago. Since you cannot count on its arriving in time, you think you had better buy another coat in a local store. Write a letter to the firm from which you had ordered the coat, explaining the situation and asking that the order be canceled and that the money you had sent with the order be refunded.

3   Two of the five articles you ordered from a mail-order firm are unsatisfactory. One is the wrong size; the other, the wrong color. On checking the order blank (which the firm had sent back to you with the merchandise), you find that you had specified the correct size for the first article, but had carelessly forgotten to specify the color for the second article. Write a letter to the firm explaining the errors—one theirs, the other yours— and asking for a satisfactory adjustment.

4   Within the past month you made two shopping trips to a store in a neighboring city and charged several articles to your mother's account. One of the articles, a study lamp for your room, proved unsatisfactory. You mailed it back to the store the day after it arrived and sent a letter asking that the charge be dropped from your mother's account. In her monthly statement from the store, she finds that she is charged for the lamp you had returned. Write a letter explaining the situation and asking for a satisfactory adjustment.

221

EXERCISE 11   In class, exchange complaint letters (prepared for Exercise 10) with a neighbor. Read through his letter thoughtfully, pretending you are the employee in charge of adjusting customers' claims for the firm. On a separate sheet of paper, write a short criticism of the letter, telling (1) its good points and (2) its weak points, together with suggestions for improving them.

   When your letter is returned to you, consider the criticisms carefully. You may want to revise the letter or rewrite it completely before handing it in.

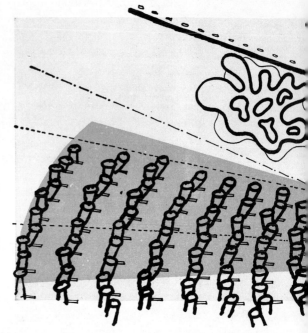

CHAPTER 11

PARLIAMENTARY

PROCEDURE

Purely social clubs have little need of special rules for conducting their meetings. These groups are usually small, and most of their business can be settled through informal discussion. But large clubs with many important matters to take care of need a more formal way of handling their business meetings.

Without formal rules to prevent arguments, a group's meetings soon become disorderly. With no rules to make sure that matters are handled one by one, members are likely to begin discussing several different questions, never reaching a decision about any of them. Then a few aggressive members may step in and make the decisions for the group. Often their decisions turn out to be unacceptable to the majority of the members.

Most of the clubs you will join are likely to follow parliamentary procedure at their meetings. To take an active part in club business and to help make sure that meetings are conducted in an orderly, efficient, and fair manner, you will want to learn the basic parliamentary rules explained in this chapter.

HOLDING A CLUB MEETING

Under parliamentary procedure a club handles its business by means of motions. If you want to bring up a matter for the group's consideration, you first *get the floor* by rising and addressing the *chair*: "Mr. Chairman" or "Mr. President" (*or* "Madam Chairman," "Madam President"). Once the chairman *recognizes* you by nodding or calling your name, you—and only you—have permission to speak. You state your business in the form of a *motion*: "I move that we send the prize-winning photographs from our club contest to the state high-school photography exhibit."

Before your motion (called a *main motion*) can be considered by the group, another member must indicate that he supports your proposal by saying, without rising or being recognized: "I second the motion." The members then discuss your motion and vote on it. If the *majority* (at least one more than half the number voting) are in favor, your proposal will be carried out; if not, no action will be taken. Motions are introduced with the words "I move that . . ." (*not* "I make a motion that . . .").

To make sure that all necessary business is taken care of in the most efficient way, clubs follow a set *order of business*. The following sequence is one that is generally used:

1 Call to order. When it is time for the meeting to begin, the chairman raps for order or stands quietly until he has the members' attention. Then he says: "The meeting will please come to order." From this time on, each member gives his complete attention to the group business.

2 Roll call. If there is any doubt that a *quorum* (the number of members that must be present before the group can do business validly) is present, the chairman asks the secretary to call the roll ("The secretary will call the roll"). Otherwise roll call, which often takes up a great deal of time, is usually omitted.

3 The minutes. One of the secretary's most important duties is to write the *minutes*—a record of all the reports made and business transacted during the meeting. Since questions may arise later about what was reported or decided at a particular meeting, the record must be accurate. To ensure accuracy, most secretaries write the minutes immediately after each meeting, using the notes they have taken during the meeting.

The minutes usually include the following items: the name of the group; the time, date, and place of the meeting; the name of the officer presiding; brief summaries of committee reports and what was done with them; the motions made, the names of those who made and seconded them, and the results of the votes; the time of adjournment; and the secretary's signature.

When the chairman requests the minutes ("The secretary will read the minutes of the last meeting"), the secretary stands and reads them. Here are the minutes of a typical meeting:

> The regular meeting of the Madison High School Camera Club was called to order by the president, Don Barlow, Friday, September 23, at 3:30 p.m. in Room 207. The minutes of the previous meeting were read and approved.
>
> The treasurer reported a balance on hand of $24.13.
>
> The awards committee reported that Mr. Martin Allen, head photographer of the Madison *Herald*; Miss Jane Rosen, adviser of the Madison Junior College Camera Club; and Mr. Henry Phillips, proprietor of the Photo Shop, had agreed to judge the entries in the club's annual contest. The report was filed.

A motion was made by Charles Anton and seconded by Tony Baron that dues be raised from one dollar to two dollars a year. The motion was lost.

It was moved by Barbara Coe and seconded by George West that the president appoint a committee of five to get permission from two or three local business firms to photograph their employees at work on a day to be selected by the committee. The motion was carried. The president appointed James Orr (chairman), Becky Case, Fred Pinno, Jane Gross, and Guy Traskey.

Following a motion by Maxine Laval, the meeting was adjourned at 4:05 p.m.

Respectfully submitted,
Deborah Morgan, Secretary

CHAIRMAN: Are there any corrections or additions? [*Pauses to give members a chance to ask for the floor.*] If not, the minutes stand approved as read.

If a member wants to make a correction or addition, he rises, receives recognition, and states his correction or addition:

GEORGE WEST: The minutes should have read "Allen Martin" instead of "Martin Allen." Allen Martin is the head photographer of the Madison *Herald*.

CHAIRMAN: If there is no objection, the error pointed out by George West will be corrected. Are there any further corrections or additions? [*Pauses.*] If not, the minutes stand approved as corrected.

If no corrections or additions are made, the secretary writes "Approved" and the date below his signature. If a correction is made, he writes "Approved as corrected." After the meeting the president adds his signature.

4 *Treasurer's report.* Since the members of a club should be kept informed of its financial state, at each meeting the treasurer reports briefly the amount of money he has received through dues and other means, the amount he has paid out for expenses, and the balance that remains.

5 *Committee reports.* The chairman first calls for the reports of *standing committees,* those permanent committees established in the bylaws of the club. (See page 236.) A standing committee need not report at every meeting. (Before each meeting the secretary gives the chairman the names of the committees that want to report.) Next, the chairman calls for the reports of *special com-*

mittees. These are temporary committees that are formed to do one special job.

CHAIRMAN: The committee on photographing industry at work will now present its report.

COMMITTEE CHAIRMAN [*stands*]: Mr. Chairman, the committee on photographing industry at work submits the following report. [*Reads report and hands it to the secretary, who places it with the club's records.*]

A committee report may be *adopted, referred back to the committee for further study, filed, or rejected.* If the report contains a recommendation that the group take some action, the committee chairman usually moves that the report be adopted ("I move that this report be adopted"). If the committee chairman makes no such motion, the chairman says: "You have heard the report of the committee. What do you wish to do with it?" Any member may then move to adopt, refer, or file the report. The motion must be seconded before it can be discussed and voted on. If the members vote to adopt the report, they are committed to take whatever action is recommended in the report. When a motion to adopt, refer, or file does not carry, the report is automatically rejected.

A report giving only information is filed, not adopted. If no motion to file the report is made from the floor, the chairman says: "The report will be filed."

6 **Unfinished business.** When all the committee reports have been presented, the chairman asks if there is any *unfinished business*—business that was not completed at a previous meeting.

CHAIRMAN: Unfinished business is now in order. (*or* Is there any unfinished business?)

If there is none, he goes on to new business.

7 **New business.** The chairman announces: "New business is now in order. What is your pleasure?" (*or* "Is there any new business to come before the club?") At this time any member who wants the club to consider a certain matter asks for the floor.

MARY BROWN [*stands*]: Mr. Chairman.

CHAIRMAN: Mary Brown.

MARY: I move that we invite the faculty of Madison High School to submit photographs to be exhibited with the student entries in our annual contest.

FRED LUBINSKI [*without rising or asking recognition*]: I second the motion.

CHAIRMAN:　It has been moved and seconded that we invite. . . . [*Repeats motion.*]　Is there any discussion?

To take part in the discussion (called the *debate*), each member must rise, address the chair, and be recognized before speaking, just as if he were proposing a motion.　If two or more members stand at the same time, the chairman recognizes the one he heard first.　When that speaker is finished, the chairman gives the second person a chance to talk, if he still wants to do so.

In speaking, members keep their remarks impersonal and friendly. A member may criticize another's remarks, but not his personality or motives.　All comments are limited to the motion under discussion. When all the members who ask for the floor have spoken, the chairman repeats the motion and puts it to a vote.　Usually an *oral vote* is taken.

CHAIRMAN:　Is there any further discussion? (*or* Are you ready for the question?)　[*Pauses to give members a chance to ask for the floor.　If no one does, he continues.*]　It has been moved and seconded that. . . .　All those in favor, say *Aye*. [*Pronounced* ī.]

MEMBERS IN FAVOR:　Aye.

CHAIRMAN:　All those opposed, say *No*.

MEMBERS OPPOSED:　No.

CHAIRMAN:　The motion is carried (*or* lost).

To give all members a chance to express their wishes, the chairman always asks for the negative vote, even though he knows that the affirmative vote has carried.　Main motions require a majority to carry.　The chairman does not vote except to make or break a tie.

If the oral vote is close, the chairman may ask for a *show of hands* or a *standing vote*.　If he does not and a member wants a more exact vote, the member rises immediately and says, without waiting for recognition: "Mr. Chairman, I call for a division."　The chairman then asks the members for and against the motion to stand (or raise their hands) in turn, and the secretary counts the votes.　The chairman announces the results: "The vote is 35 for and 31 against.　The motion is carried."

The same procedure is followed for each main motion that is presented for the group's consideration.　Only one main motion may be considered at a time.

8　*Announcements.*　When no more motions are presented, the chairman asks if any member wants to make an announcement. After all the announcements from the floor have been made, the chairman makes his announcements.

9 Adjournment. The chairman next calls for a motion to adjourn the meeting.

CHAIRMAN: If there is no further business, is there a motion to adjourn?

MAXINE LAVAL [*after being recognized*]: I move that we adjourn.

SEVERAL MEMBERS: I second the motion.

The chairman puts the motion to a vote immediately. If it carries, he announces: "The meeting is adjourned." The meeting is not officially adjourned until this announcement is made.

10 The program. Many clubs have a program—a talk, a movie, or some sort of entertainment—after the business part of the meeting has been completed. The chairman of the program committee usually takes charge of this part of the meeting.

MOTIONS

To prevent the members of a club from skipping from one matter to another before some decision is made about the first one, only one main motion may be before the group at one time. But there are other kinds of motions that can be made—even while the group is considering a main motion—to help the club carry on its business efficiently. Four of the most useful are discussed here.

Motion to amend. While a main motion is being discussed, any member may move to amend the motion by adding, dropping, or substituting words. Suppose, for example, that the Camera Club is considering the main motion made by Mary Brown—"that we invite the faculty of Madison High School to submit photographs to be exhibited with the student entries in our annual contest." John Farrell, a member of the arrangements committee, thinks Mary's idea is a good one, but he knows that the exhibit room is not large. So, after getting recognition, he proposes an amendment to Mary's motion.

JOHN: Since the space for the photography exhibit is rather small, and since we always have a great many student entries, all of which must be exhibited, I think we should limit the number of faculty pictures. I move that we amend the motion by striking out the word "photographs" and substituting the words "one photograph each."

FRANK LOPEZ: I second the motion.

John's motion is then discussed and put to a vote. If it carries, the group discusses and votes on the main motion as amended.

Point of order. Suppose that the Camera Club is discussing a main motion to sell picture valentines. During the course of the discussion, one member moves that the club offer to take pictures at the Valentine's Day dance which the Booster Club is giving. When the chairman seems to accept this second motion, Helen Sorensen rises.

HELEN [*without waiting for recognition*]: Mr. Chairman, I rise to a point of order.

CHAIRMAN: State your point of order.

HELEN: The motion just proposed is out of order because there is already a main motion before the group.

CHAIRMAN: Your point of order is well taken. The motion last proposed is out of order. Is there any further discussion on the motion to sell picture valentines?

Notice that a motion of order needs no second or vote; the chairman rules on it immediately.

Motion to refer to a committee. Sometimes you may feel that the vote on a main motion should be postponed until the group has more information on a question. If you think that a special committee could best gather and consider the information needed, you move that such a committee be formed.

MEMBER: Before we vote on this motion, I think we need to know whether the principal will give us permission to sell picture valentines to students and how many valentines we would need to sell in order to make a profit. I move that we refer the question to a special committee of three to be appointed by the president to investigate the matter and report at the next meeting.

After the motion to refer is seconded, it is discussed and put to a vote. If it carries, the president immediately appoints the committee. Further consideration of the main motion is postponed until the committee reports.

Motion to postpone to a certain time. Sometimes a member thinks that the vote on a main motion should be put off until the members have had more time to think it over, especially if he believes that they are acting rather hastily. Or if the proposal is important and barely a quorum is present, perhaps he thinks it only fair to delay action until a time when more members will be there.

MEMBER: I move that we postpone consideration of the motion until the next meeting.

After the motion to postpone is seconded, it is discussed and put to a vote. If it carries, the discussion on the main motion is closed until the time set for further consideration, when it is brought up as unfinished business.

EXERCISE 1 Parliamentary procedure was introduced several hundred years ago in the British Parliament. Since that time many additions and changes have been made to improve the rules, but the purpose of parliamentary procedure has remained the same—to help groups conduct meetings in an orderly, efficient, and fair manner.

In an informal class discussion, consider how each of the following rules helps to produce orderly, efficient, and fair meetings.

1 With few exceptions, a member must be recognized before **he** can speak to the group.
2 A main motion must be seconded before it can be discussed and put to a vote.
3 Only one main motion may be considered at a time.
4 A quorum must be present before a group can do business.
5 The chairman must repeat a main motion twice—before it is discussed and before it is put to a vote.
6 The chairman must always ask for the negative vote.
7 The will of the majority determines the decisions for the group.
8 A member who wishes a more exact vote may call for a division.
9 An amendment to a main motion is voted on before the main motion is put to a vote.
10 A point of order needs no second.

ELECTING OFFICERS

Most clubs find four officers—president, vice-president, secretary, and treasurer—adequate for carrying on business successfully. These officers are usually elected once a year at the time and in the manner specified by the constitution of the club.

The chairman announces the election of officers as the first item of new business. If a nominating committee has been elected or appointed to look over the membership and draw up a list of competent candidates who are willing to accept office, it reports at this time. Then, taking each office in turn, the chairman asks if any member wants to add a name to the committee's list of candidates ("Are there any further nominations for the office of president?").

If there is no nominating committee, the president immediately asks for nominations from the floor, taking each office in turn. Nominations are made in the same way for all offices.

CHAIRMAN: Nominations for the office of president are in order.
TONY BARON [*after being recognized*]: I nominate John Farrell for president.
CHAIRMAN: John Farrell has been nominated. [*As the chairman repeats the nominee's name, either he or the secretary writes it on the blackboard.*]
ERICA MANN [*after being recognized*]: I nominate Connie Meyer.
CHAIRMAN: Connie Meyer has been nominated.
BECKY CASE [*after being recognized*]: I nominate James Orr.
CHAIRMAN: James Orr has been nominated. Are there any further nominations? [*Pauses.*] If not, the nominations for the office of president are closed.

After at least two nominations have been made, any member may move to close the nominations. If the motion is seconded and carried, the chairman declares the nominations closed.

Many clubs elect their officers by *secret ballot*. Often candidates for all offices are nominated before the balloting, and only one ballot is used. The chairman appoints three *tellers* to distribute, collect, and count the ballots. When the votes have been counted, the tellers give the totals to the president, who announces the results. The new president usually takes office as soon as he is elected.

If the electing is done by a standing vote, a show of hands, or a roll-call vote, a vote may be taken on each office as soon as the candidates have been nominated. Unless otherwise specified in the constitution, a majority vote is necessary for election.

Duties of officers. Each officer has specific duties, listed in the bylaws, which the group has a right to expect him to perform if he accepts the nomination. If you are elected *president,* you will be expected to call the meetings to order; announce the business in the order in which it is to come before the group for consideration; recognize members who wish to speak; state motions, put them to vote, and announce the results; and adjourn the group.

If you are the *vice-president,* you preside in the absence of the president and whenever he wants to leave the chair temporarily to take part in the discussion. You may also head a standing committee, if so specified in the bylaws.

As *secretary,* you have a great many duties. You write the minutes of the meetings; keep a file of committee reports and club correspondence; keep an up-to-date list of members and call the roll at

231

meetings; read any papers called for by the group; carry on the official correspondence; hand to the president before each meeting a list of items of unfinished business, of the committees that are to report, and of the announcements to be made. You also preside in the absence of the president and vice-president until a temporary chairman is elected.

Your duties as *treasurer* include collecting dues, holding the funds of the club, paying its bills, and keeping an accurate record of all funds collected and paid out. You make a brief report at each meeting and a complete report once a year. Often organizations that do not collect dues or raise funds omit the office of treasurer.

Duties of committees. *Standing committees* are usually elected by the group or appointed by the president once a year, shortly after the club's officers are elected. The committees' duties are stated in the bylaws. A standing committee is in charge of some job that needs to be done regularly. For example, a program committee may be responsible for putting on a program at each meeting or at certain specified meetings during the year.

A *special committee* (formed to do a particular job) is appointed or elected, depending on the motion that establishes it. Its specific work is outlined either in the motion that establishes it or by the president. When a special committee completes its task, it submits a report and disbands.

To get an idea of how a committee performs its duties, suppose that you are James Orr, the chairman of the special committee on photographing industry at work. Your committee was appointed by the president of the Camera Club to get permission from two or three local business firms to take pictures of their employees at work. Besides getting the permission, you are to make arrangements for the exact date on which the pictures are to be taken.

As chairman, your first duty is to call a committee meeting. When it has come to order, you appoint a secretary or ask the group to elect one. Then, under your direction, the committee discusses what firms should be asked for permission and what date should be suggested for taking the pictures. From a list of local business firms that you have drawn up, the committee members select the five that they think will offer the best subjects for pictures and are most likely to give their permission. They also decide to ask permission to take the pictures on November 11, a day when there is no school. Each member volunteers to get in touch with one business firm, and a date is set for a second meeting at which the members will report.

At the second meeting, the members report that three of the five firms have given permission for the club members to take pictures on November 11. And since each of the three firms has requested that the photographers come in the morning, the committee votes to recommend that the club be divided into three groups, each to be assigned to one firm.

Once the matter is decided, the committee secretary, using the notes taken at the meetings, writes a report to present to the club. A committee report usually includes a statement of what the committee was instructed to do, a brief explanation of how the committee worked, what information was gathered, and whatever recommendations the committee has to make. (Sometimes, especially if the committee was established solely to get information, it will make no recommendations.)

When the report is written, you call a final meeting and have the secretary read the report to get the approval of all members of the committee.

> The committee on photographing industry at work was instructed to get permission from two or three local business firms to photograph their employees at work. The committee was also to arrange the date for this activity.
>
> Each member of the committee got in touch with one company, asking permission to take pictures on November 11, a day on which there is no school. Three companies—the Brewster Chemical Corporation, the Madison Power Company, and the Emonds Engraving Company—gave their permission and requested that the club members come in the morning.
>
> The committee recommends that the club members be divided into three groups and that each group be assigned to take pictures at one of the three firms on the morning of November 11.

If a committee member suggests an addition or a correction and it meets with the approval of the others, it is adopted. Each committee member then signs the report.

A committee holds as many meetings as are necessary to complete its work and meets at whatever time and place are agreeable to the majority of its members. When a regular meeting of the club occurs before the committee has completed its work, the committee chairman reports what has been done so far or simply states that the committee has not completed its work and promises a report for a specific time.

Duties of members. Some students are "joiners"! They join clubs for only one reason—to see how many organizations they can list after their names at graduation. As a result, they belong to so many clubs that they are unable to do their share of the work in any one of them.

As a club member, you have certain responsibilities—the duty of paying dues, for example, and of serving on committees. You also have certain privileges, such as the privilege of joining in and benefiting from club activities. Once you take an active part in club work, you soon find that many of your privileges are also duties—for example, attending meetings, introducing motions, discussing matters up for consideration, voting, making nominations, and running for office.

It is important for you, as a club member, to know your duties and privileges. But it is equally important for you to know that to fulfill your duties and take advantage of your privileges you must limit your memberships to the number of clubs in which you can take an active part.

If you keep your responsibilities as a club member in mind, you won't become a "joiner." Then you'll never feel like the student who wrote this jingle:

> Sing a song of joining
> Every club in school.
> My great love for club work
> Is getting rather cool.
> Motions, votes, committees
> Have put me in a spin.
> Wasn't I a silly soul
> To spread myself so thin?

EXERCISE 2 Write two statements, either true or false, that have to do with parliamentary procedure. [*Example:* The president need not take the negative vote when he knows that the affirmative vote has carried. (False.)] When you are called on in class, read each of your statements and ask a class member to tell whether it is true or false. When all the statements have been read, they will be collected and used by your teacher for a true-false quiz.

EXERCISE 3 Each member of the class will be called on to suggest one subject that he would like a committee of his classmates to investigate. [*Example:* "I suggest that a committee gather the information our class would need to plan a trip to Station XYZ-TV."] Listen carefully to each suggestion, and on a sheet of paper write a list of the ten subjects you are most interested in having investigated. When the lists are collected, your teacher will appoint a secretary to go over them and write on the blackboard a master list of the ten most popular subjects.

EXERCISE (4) The class is to be divided into committees of five or six members each. After choosing a chairman and a secretary, each committee is to decide which of the ten subjects listed on the board (for Exercise 3) it wants to investigate. The committee chairman is to write his name on the blackboard next to that subject. (Only one committee should investigate each subject.) A day should then be set for the presentation of the committees' reports.

After your committee has completed its work, each member is to write a report, which he will read at the final committee meeting. When the members have heard all the reports, they will vote to select one that the committee chairman will read in class. All the reports are to be handed to your teacher.

ORGANIZING A CLUB

Unless your school is very new, most of the clubs that you will join have been established for some time. Still, if you find that you are one of several students who are interested in an activity for which there is no organization, you might want to form a new club—one for amateur radio operators, for example, or an art-service club that would design and make posters and decorations for school dances and programs. How do you go about organizing a club?

The first step is to hold a meeting to which you invite anyone who is interested in being a member. One of the organizers calls the meeting to order and either nominates a *temporary chairman* himself or asks for nominations from the floor. Ordinarily only one person is nominated, and an oral vote is taken immediately. The newly elected chairman then takes the chair and conducts the election of a *temporary secretary.* The temporary chairman and secretary hold office until the club is established and permanent officers are elected.

After the secretary has been chosen, one of the original group gets the floor and explains the purpose of the meeting. He ends his explanation with a motion: "I move that this group form a club to be known as the Madison High School Camera Club, for the purpose of studying and practicing the art of photography." The motion is seconded, debated, and put to a vote.

The next item of business is introduced immediately in the form of a motion that a committee be appointed or elected to draw up a constitution and bylaws for the club. As soon as this motion is passed, the committee is named. The group then votes to adjourn, after setting the time and date for the next meeting.

The constitution and bylaws. A *constitution* is a written statement of the fundamental rules by which an organization is run. It usually includes the name of the organization, its purpose, the qualifications for membership, a list of the officers and the way they are to be elected, the time of regular meetings, the method for calling special meetings, and the method for amending the constitution. The rules are arranged in numbered sections called *articles*. For example:

Article I

The name of this organization shall be the Madison High School Camera Club.

Article II

The purpose of this organization shall be to study and practice the art of photography.

Bylaws are more specific rules for conducting the regular business of the club. They generally provide for such matters as the admission of new members, the payment of dues, the powers and duties of officers, the powers and duties of committees, the *parliamentary authority* (the book that the club will consult when there is a question on parliamentary procedure), the procedure for amending the bylaws, and the number constituting a quorum. (If the bylaws do not stipulate the number, a majority constitutes the quorum.)

Some clubs do not adopt a constitution. Instead, they combine the items usually found in the constitution and bylaws into one document and call it the "bylaws."

At the second meeting of the new club, the chairman of the constitution committee reads both the constitution and the bylaws. The group discusses them section by section, making additions and changes wherever the majority thinks they are necessary. When all the sections have been considered, the group votes to adopt both the constitution and bylaws with whatever additions and changes have been agreed upon.

Next, permanent officers are elected, according to the provisions of the constitution and bylaws. The club is then ready to start conducting business.

EXERCISE 5 The class is to be divided into seven groups. Each group is to choose a chairman and then arrange to present for the class a brief meeting to demonstrate some of the parliamentary procedures you have studied in this chapter. Each group is to be responsible for demonstrating the items in one of the following numbered lists. To ensure a smooth demonstration, the members of each group should get together beforehand to plan and rehearse their meeting.

1 Electing a temporary chairman and secretary for a new club
   Explaining the purpose of the new club
   Making, discussing, and voting on a motion to organize the club
   Making, discussing, and voting on a motion to appoint a committee to draw up a constitution and bylaws
2 Calling a meeting to order
   Reading the minutes
   Correcting and approving the minutes
   Reading the treasurer's report
3 Presenting a committee report
   Making, discussing, and voting on a motion to adopt the report
   Calling for a more exact vote
4 Calling for nominations of officers
   Closing the nominations
   Appointing tellers
   Voting by secret ballot
5 Making a main motion
   Amending the main motion
   Discussing and voting on the amendment
   Discussing and voting on the main motion as amended
6 Making and discussing a main motion
   Rising to a point of order
   Making, discussing, and voting on a motion to refer the main motion to a committee
7 Making and discussing a main motion
   Making, discussing, and voting on a motion to postpone consideration of the main motion to a certain time
   Making and voting on a motion to adjourn

As each group presents its meeting, the rest of the class is to pay careful attention to make sure that the meeting is being conducted according to parliamentary procedure. The class will discuss each demonstration, pointing out any instances where the rules of parliamentary procedure were violated and what happened as a result. Other instances that made clear the value of parliamentary procedure should also be pointed out.

EXERCISE (6) Write the minutes of a typical business meeting of one of the clubs to which you belong. Or, if you prefer, write the minutes of an imaginary meeting. For the latter you may use as many details as you wish from the demonstration meetings presented in Exercise 5. Your teacher may ask you to read your minutes to the class.

CHAPTER 12

PARTS OF

THE SENTENCE

A few years ago Professor Kahane of the University of Illinois woke up one day to find that he had—to his great surprise—made the headlines. He had just finished a study of how people learn language and had written a report of what he had observed. Newspaper reporters, always on the alert for a good story, quickly realized the news value of the report, and within a few weeks papers all over the country carried the story.

The reporters did not give a complete account of the professor's findings; few people would have taken the time to read such an account. Instead they shrewdly based their stories on one of his statements—one that they knew the average person would find interesting, even startling. Here, they said, is a man—and not an ordinary man, mind you, but a language expert—who claims that by the time a child reaches the age of three he has learned all there is to know about the basic ideas of grammar!

It is not hard to imagine people's reactions to this statement and the discussions and arguments it led to. Yet there would have been

no arguments if the news stories had explained clearly what the professor meant.

He did not mean that three-year-olds know the sort of grammar that you study in English class. Kindergarten children cannot name the different parts of speech or describe their various uses in a sentence. They cannot, for example, explain that in the sentence "Johnny hit Tommy" the word *Johnny* is the subject of the verb *hit*, and that *Tommy* is the direct object. Yet they know, somehow, that Johnny, and not Tommy, is the one who did the hitting. They also know, somehow, that Tommy is the one who was hit.

The very fact that they can understand the meaning of such a sentence shows that they understand a basic part of English grammar—the part that "word order" plays in communicating meaning. This is what Professor Kahane meant.

English-speaking people express their ideas, thoughts, and feelings by putting words together in sentences. In these sentences they do not just group words in a hodgepodge order. If they did, they could not make their intended meaning clear to others. Instead, they arrange the words in a certain order, following certain "patterns." For example, the words "Eye Jerry black a has" don't make sense; they have no meaning when spoken in this order. But they do make sense when arranged this way: "Jerry has a black eye." And arranged according to a different sentence pattern, the same words can be turned into a question: "Has Jerry a black eye?"

All speakers of English use the same sentence patterns (there are only a few). They learned the patterns, of course, as you learned them—by hearing and imitating others.

By the time you were three years old, you had heard your parents and friends speak thousands of sentences and, without even realizing it, you had learned not only a great number of words but several of the basic patterns. You could understand the meaning of such a sentence as "The dog bit the man" because your many experiences in hearing sentences had taught you that the order in which the words come gives the key to right understanding. Since the word *dog* came before the word *bit,* you knew the dog was the one that did the biting. Since the word *man* came after the word *bit,* you knew the man was the one who was bitten. Because experience had taught you the connection between word order and meaning, you could easily understand the difference between "The dog bit the man" and "The man bit the dog"—even though exactly the same words are used in both sentences. You, like the three-year-olds in the professor's report, had *unconsciously* learned enough about "grammar" to be able to understand the meaning of sentences—at least sentences of the sort that a child hears and speaks.

Luckily, you did not stop there. As your experiences with language grew, your skill in using language grew, until you finally reached the point where you are now. Most of you have done very well. You have a fairly wide vocabulary, and you can carry on interesting conversations with friends your age and with older people. You can read and understand many books written for adults, and you can effectively discuss a great many subjects. You write many papers and reports, and your writing is much better than it was in grade school. You have come a long way.

But in learning language there is no stopping point. There is no time in a person's life when he can say he has learned all there is to know. There is always more to be learned about how to speak and write effectively. And there are two ways to learn more. The first of these ways you cannot avoid; the second you won't want to avoid.

The first way has already been described: to the end of your life (unless you become a nonreading hermit) you will keep on doing the very same things you did as a child first learning to speak in sentences. You will hear countless numbers of sentences; you will read thousands more. And through observing and imitating what you hear and read, you will gradually become more skillful in your own use of language.

The only thing wrong with this first way of improvement is that it takes too long. Isn't there a short cut, one that will bring results more quickly? Yes, there is—to take advantage of the experience of people who have spent a lifetime observing and studying our language to see what makes it tick. In the grammar chapters of this book, we will pass on to you what these people have discovered about our language and how it can be made to work effectively. By doing so, we will give you a chance to learn quickly what it took them years of study to learn. Why not take advantage of the chance?

A FIRST LOOK AT

SUBJECTS AND PREDICATES

Do you remember that back in the fifth grade, when you first learned how to do long-division problems, you also learned a way to check your answers to make sure they were right? For example, if the problem was to divide 79,345 by 35 and your answer was 2267, you could check by multiplying the answer by 35. If the result was also 79,345, you knew that your answer was right.

How would you like to have an almost foolproof test by which you could check the sentences you write to see that they are true sentences and not just pieces of sentences or two sentences run together?

The test is simple: Just make sure that the group of words you have written as a sentence contains a *subject* and a *verb* and that it makes *complete sense* by itself. This test will work for all sentences with the exception of a few special ones that will be described in a later chapter. It is, then, well worth learning, if for nothing else than to get better grades on the papers you write.

Though the test is simple, we had better warn you that there is a catch in it. You cannot use it successfully unless you know three things: what a "subject" is, what a "verb" is, and what "makes complete sense by itself" means. To find out, you will have to study a number of sentences to see what parts they contain. Only in this way can you be sure what subjects and verbs are—and what "complete sense" means.

We will start with one of the simplest sentence patterns, a very common one that you use every day of your lives when you want to tell someone that some person or thing *did* (or *is doing* or *will do*) some action. You begin, usually, by naming the person or thing:

The lion in the first cage

And then you tell what action the person or thing did:

The lion in the first cage / *growled at the guard.*

Every sentence of this pattern will have these two main parts.

THE "ACTOR" PART	THE "ACTION" PART
Laura	giggled.
The driver of the school bus	swerved to the left.
A heavy gray fog	hung over the roof tops.
The men in the shipping room	argued with the plant manager.

The first of these parts is called the **subject** part; the second is called the **predicate** part. As you can see, both parts are necessary to make a meaningful statement—a sentence. One part alone would not make complete sense by itself.

EXERCISE 1 Some of the following numbered groups of words are complete sentences—that is, they consist of a subject part and a predicate part. Others are just pieces of sentences—that is, they are merely subject parts or predicate parts. On a sheet of paper, write the numbers 1–20. After each number, tell what the word group is by writing "CS" (if a complete sentence), "SP" (if a subject part), or "PP" (if a predicate part).

1 the player on first base
2 hurried out of the store
3 the lawyer for the defense
4 whistles blew
5 sneaked out of the room
6 flags of all colors
7 the wheels skidded
8 the ribbon around the pack of letters
9 hesitated for a minute
10 the heavy wire snapped
11 her brother lied
12 crawled through the basement window
13 angrily complained to the police
14 a second disastrous forest fire
15 every girl there cheered wildly
16 never pried into their affairs
17 the man with the scar swore
18 oily rags in the closet
19 the sheriffs glanced at the names
20 shouted at the top of his lungs

The most important word in the predicate part of a sentence is the *verb.* You will see how true this is if you read the following sentences twice, the second time leaving out the italicized words—the verbs.

> The pennies / *rolled* off the table.
> Jerry / *stumbled* down the stairs.
> The boys / *rushed* to the back of the bus.

Without the verbs, the sentences don't make sense, do they? They name the subjects, but don't tell us anything meaningful about them. The reason they don't is that the "telling" words—the verbs —are missing.

The verb is the word that makes it possible for us to "tell something" about the subject—to "make a statement" about it. Without the verb *rolled,* we cannot tell what the pennies did. Without the verb *stumbled,* we cannot tell what Jerry did. And without the verb *rushed,* we cannot tell what the boys did.

The other words in a predicate are important to the *meaning,* of course. But the verb is essential to the *sentence.* Without it, there would be no sentence; there would just be a group of words.

Being able to recognize verbs is important for two reasons. First, it will help you avoid a common sentence error—the incomplete sentence. Second, it will make your future work easier. Understanding what is taught in many of the later lessons depends in great part on your knowing what verbs are, on being able to recognize them quickly and surely. Here are some clues that will help you:

243

1) Since most verbs express action, look first for a word that tells what action the subject *did* (or *is doing* or *will do*):

> Martha *hopped* over to the desk.
> The cat *pounced* on the terrified mouse.
> The boys *screamed* at the top of their lungs.

You can hardly make mistakes on verbs of this type, since they so clearly express actions—physical actions that you could have seen or heard if you had been around when they occurred.

2) The verbs in some sentences express *mental* rather than physical actions. But notice that these verbs, too, tell what the subject did, even though the action cannot be seen:

> The twins *thought* of a better excuse.
> Jerry *believed* in telling the truth.
> Grandfather *worried* about his hospital bill.

If you think of verbs of this type as expressing actions that take place in the mind, you will have no trouble recognizing them.

3) In some sentences the verb tells not what the subject did, but what happened to the subject:

> The silly girl *was frightened* by a spider.
> Green paint *had been splashed* all over the desk.
> The trip *was planned* weeks ago.

Notice that in these examples, as in the preceding ones, the verb expresses an action, even though it is an action done *to* the subject rather than *by* the subject.[1]

4) The verb may consist of more than one word, as you have just seen. By using one or more "helping verbs" with a main verb, we can express a great number of different meanings that would not be possible if we had to rely only on one-word verbs:

> The baby *is crying* again. [A two-word verb.]
> The dog *may snap* at strangers. [A two-word verb.]
> The janitor *might* not *have left* yet. [A three-word verb.]
> The cast *hasn't been rehearsing* for more than a week. [A three-word verb.]
> Such a lazy person *should* never *have been hired.* [A four-word verb.]
> The police *could* certainly *have been notified* sooner. [A four-word verb.]

In naming the verb in sentences like these, be sure that you give the *whole* verb—and nothing but the verb. It will begin with one of these helping verbs:

> am, is, are, was, were
> do, does, did
> have, has, had, have been, has been, had been
> shall, will, should, would
> can, could, may, might, ought to, must

And it will end with the main verb—the one that tells what the action is. It will not include such words as *not* (or its contraction *n't*), *never*, or *certainly*, which may come between parts of the verb.

EXERCISE (2) Find the verb—the complete verb—in each of the following sentences and write it on a sheet of paper, numbering it with the number of the sentence. (There is only one predicate verb in each

244

---

[1] Verbs that express action done *by* the subject are called "active" verbs. Those that express action done *to* the subject are called "passive" verbs.

sentence.) After each verb, write "A" if the verb tells what the subject did (or is doing, has done, will do, could do, must have done, etc.); write "P" if the verb tells what was done to the subject (or is done, will be done, might be done, etc.).

1 A battered Model T Ford chugged up to the platform.
2 Only three of the letters had been typed by noon.
3 The warehouse next to the glove factory may have been torn down by now.
4 Prentice's best work, a historical novel based on the Revolutionary War, was never published.
5 A long line of tiny white ants streamed across the shelves.
6 Mr. Donner's sister could just as well have left on the earlier train.
7 The directions printed on the package couldn't be read.
8 The people sitting in the next booth glowered at us.
9 The strange little man with the crooked nose was again peering at my newspaper.
10 The families living along the north bank of the river should have been warned of the danger.
11 A second later Lefty Johnson, our heavy-hitting shortstop, sprinted toward home plate.
12 The doorbell in the next apartment is ringing again.
13 The two boys hadn't spoken to each other for weeks.
14 Chief Pontiac's carefully laid plans for a surprise attack on Detroit were betrayed to Major Gladwin.
15 My youngest brother, on the other hand, did not ever complain to Dad.

RECOGNIZING SUBJECTS

Can you explain why the italicized word in each of the following examples is the most important word in the subject part of the sentence?

Two big black *bugs* / scurried out of the crack.
A heavy silver *tray* on the top shelf / crashed to the floor.
The little *boy* with the torn shirt / was snubbed by the others.

The answer to the question is easy: Without the italicized words, the sentences do not make sense; the subject part of the sentence does not do what it should do. Without the word *bugs* or *tray* or *boy*, we wouldn't know *what* scurried out of the crack, *what* crashed to the floor, or *who* was snubbed by the others. Other words in the subject part of each sentence—*big black,* for example, or *heavy silver,* or *with the torn shirt*—add interesting details, but the sentences would still be sentences without them. But the sentences could not get along without the words *bugs* and *tray* and *boy,* since these are the words which name the person or thing that the verb in each sentence tells about. These all-important "naming" words in the subject part of the sentences are called *simple subjects*—or just plain *subjects.*

Two kinds of words are used as subjects of verbs—nouns or pronouns. **Nouns,** as you probably already know, are words that are used as names, as the names of persons, places, or things:

COMMON NOUNS: a *man,* the *city,* his *sword,* our *dog, politics, beauty, friendship, religion*
PROPER NOUNS: *Dwight Eisenhower, Reno, Excalibur, Republican, Democrat, Catholic,* the *Declaration of Independence*

Pronouns are words that we use instead of nouns to refer to persons, places, or things without specifically naming them. Pronouns make it possible for us to indicate what person or thing we mean without having to repeat the name of the person or thing.

NOUNS USED AS SUBJECTS	PRONOUNS USED AS SUBJECTS
Terry stayed at home.	**He** slept for an hour. [*He* refers to Terry; in this sentence *He* "means" Terry.]
The *water* shot out of the tank.	**It** splashed over the walls. [*It* refers to water; in this sentence *It* "means" water.]

Five kinds of pronouns may be used as subjects of sentences:

PERSONAL PRONOUNS: I, you, he, she, it, we, they
POSSESSIVE PRONOUNS: mine, yours, his, hers, its, ours, theirs
INDEFINITE PRONOUNS: all, another, both, each, either, neither, few, many, none, one, others, several, some, someone, etc.
DEMONSTRATIVE PRONOUNS: this, that, these, those
INTERROGATIVE PRONOUNS: who, whose, which, what

Any one of these—plus a verb—may make a complete sentence: *They screamed. Mine was stolen. This won. Some applauded. Others booed. What broke? Who left? Neither moved.*

Finding the subject. Just how should you go about finding the subject of a sentence? Can you find it by reading the first part of the sentence, noticing all the nouns and pronouns, and then choosing the one that seems most important? You can, but chances are that if you use that method you will be wrong more times than you are right. The method works well for only very few sentences. For most sentences the only safe and sure rule is this: *Find the verb first*—then the subject. But see for yourself how important this rule is.

Start by looking at this sentence:

> A complete list of all the women at the reception was printed in the first column on the society page.

Students who do not use the "Find the verb first" rule usually say that *women* is the subject of the sentence. This is the way their thinking goes: "There are three nouns in the first part of the sentence—*list, women,* and *reception.* The most important is *women,* because *women* is what the writer of the sentence is talking about. Therefore *women* is the subject."

The explanation seems sensible, doesn't it? But it is wrong. The subject of a sentence is *not* the person or thing that the writer is talking about—it is the person or thing *that the verb tells about.* As a matter of fact, the writer of the sentence is talking about five things—not only *women,* but a *list,* a *reception,* a *column,* and a *page.* Yet the verb tells about only one thing—the *list.* The list, not the women, was printed in the first column. *List,* then, is the subject.

Remember always to start with the verb. Do this: First ask yourself, "What is the verb?" *Was printed* is. Then ask yourself, "What (or who) was printed?" A *list* was. *List* is the subject of the verb.

EXERCISE (3) Whether a word is a noun or a verb depends on its use in a sentence. Copy the italicized word in each of the following sentences on a sheet of paper. If the word is used as the noun subject of the sentence, write "Subject" after it. If the word is used to tell what action the subject did, write "Verb" after it. In two of the sentences the italicized word is not used either as a noun subject or as a verb. After these words, write "Neither."

1 Loud *cheers* of joy resounded through the hall.
2 News of home usually *cheers* Mrs. Warner.
3 Mr. Hill quite often *comments* on the lack of discipline.
4 Quite often *comments* about his performances anger him.
5 The *paddle* wheel had been damaged.
6 The guide's *paddle* floated out of his reach.
7 The guides *paddle* their canoes skillfully over the rapids.
8 The *camp* at Hill Grove has been put under quarantine.
9 Several of the *camp* chairs were stolen.
10 Gypsies usually *camp* in that clearing.

247

11 My cousins *dream* of owning a sailboat some day.
12 My cousin's *dream* mystified all of us.

EXERCISE (4) Divide a sheet of paper into two columns. In the first column, write the verb in each of the following sentences. (Remember that verbs may consist of more than one word.) In the second column, write the (simple) subject of each sentence. Number your answers with the numbers of the sentences.

1 Those two books should have been returned to the library.
2 The pile of books on John's desk had not been dusted for weeks.
3 A large spotlight is used during the dance numbers.
4 As a rule only one of the spotlights is needed for the dance numbers.
5 The little boy sat down in the middle of the busy corridor.
6 And right in the middle of the busy corridor he sat down!
7 The two women were patiently standing in line.
8 That evening neither of the women would budge from her place in the line.
9 At least a dozen of those circulars have been left on our porch.
10 The fingerprints on the picture frame must have been wiped off.
11 According to the newspaper account both of the casts are scheduled for out-of-town performances.
12 The long list of candidates soon dwindled to three names.
13 Every Wednesday night in April another of the series of concerts will be presented in the auditorium.
14 With such a hungry crew of workmen a pound of butter would disappear in a twinkling.
15 Next week those in the front row of seats will be moved to the last row.

FINDING SUBJECTS OUT OF USUAL ORDER

In all the sentences you have studied so far the subject comes *before* the verb—its usual position. But there may be sentences in which this subject-verb order is not followed. Here are two examples:

Almost out of sight in the far corner of the room sat the actor's new manager.
Never in all his dealings with the two brothers had he ever suspected them of lying.

Can you name the subjects of these sentences? You will run into trouble if you start by looking for the most important noun or pronoun in the first part of each sentence. Begin instead by finding the verbs—the action words. In the first sentence the verb is *sat*. Who sat? The manager did. Then the noun *manager* is the subject, even though it comes *after* the verb. In the second sentence the verb is *had suspected*. Who had suspected? He had. The pronoun *he* is the subject. Notice that it comes between the two parts of the verb.

In sentences that ask questions the subject is quite likely to come between parts of the verb:

Has the chairman of the committee been notified?
Will the boys on the team pay for the broken windows?
Why should the title of the article be changed?

In finding the subject in questions like these, you will find it helpful to begin by changing the questions into statement form:

The chairman of the committee has been notified.
The boys on the team will pay for the broken windows.
The title of the article should be changed (why).

When the questions are in the form of statements, you can hardly mistake the verbs and their subjects:

"Who *has been notified?*" The *chairman* has.
"Who *will pay?*" The *boys* will.
"What *should be changed?*" The *title* should.

In some questions, of course, the subject comes in its usual position—before the verb:

Who **tramped** over the lawn?
What in the world **will happen** next?

Pronoun subjects like the *Who* and *What* in these questions may puzzle you. It is easy to see why these pronouns are puzzling. The reason is that most subjects *name* the person or thing that the verb tells about, but *who* and *what* do not. Since these pronouns are "question-asking" words, they *ask* instead of name. Nevertheless, they serve as subjects of the verbs. To help you understand why, reword the question. Substitute the word *Somebody* for the pronoun *Who* and the word *Something* for the pronoun *What*:

[Who?]
Somebody tramped over the lawn.
[What?]
Something in the world will happen next.

When the questions are reworded in this way, it becomes clear that *Who* [Somebody] is the subject of the verb *tramped* and that *What* [Something] is the subject of the verb *will happen*.

In sentences that give commands the subject is usually not expressed, since everyone clearly understands that the subject is "you" —meaning whoever is being spoken to:

(You) Turn to the right.

The verb here is *Turn*. Who is to turn? *You* are. *(You)* is the subject. [We put parentheses around the word *You* to show that it is the "understood" subject of the sentence.]

EXERCISE (5) Divide a sheet of paper into two columns. In the first column, write the verb (the *whole* verb) in each of the following sentences. In the second, write the subjects of the verbs. Number your answers with the numbers of the sentences.

1 Did the six boys come in one cab?
2 Why has she been tiptoeing around the house all morning?
3 Not until two weeks later did we realize the importance of his words.
4 Martha, who is standing beside Mr. Dale?
5 Why should Kenneth be blamed for Harold's mistakes?
6 Out of the mouths of babes come words of wisdom.
7 What was spilled on the carpet to stain it so?
8 At each of the gates stood a man in uniform.
9 Can't one of the paintings on that wall be used in the first act?
10 Above their heads circled three huge gulls.
11 Look at that silly hat!
12 Down on his head crashed the bucket of paint.
13 For what company does Mr. Larkowski now work?
14 Over the hill, just beyond the lake, he had pitched a tent.
15 In which of Johnson's books has that point been made?

COMPOUND SUBJECTS AND VERBS

The subject of a sentence may be "compound"—that is, it may have more than one part. A compound subject usually consists of two or more nouns or pronouns joined by a connecting word like *and* or *or*:

A *sailboat* and a *cruiser* were lying at anchor in the harbor.
You or *I* should wait here to warn the others.

250

Even though the compound subject of each of these sentences contains two separate nouns or pronouns, it is still considered only *one* subject—not two. Why? Because the two words work together to do *one* job—to name the persons or things the verb in each sentence tells about.

The verb, too, may be compound—that is, two or more separate verbs may be used to tell about one subject:

>Dave **looked** at the pile of dishes and **groaned**.
>She **walked** slowly to the mirror, **peered** at her new hairdo, and **frowned**.
>Mr. Wilson **came** to the meeting, **listened** to all our arguments, but **voted** against the motion.

Sometimes both the subject and the verb are compound:

>*Phil* and *Rob* **dashed** down the porch steps and **ran** for the bus.
>Our winter *coats* and wool *dresses* **were packed** in cartons and **were stored** in the attic.

EXERCISE 6 Divide a sheet of paper into two columns. In the first column, write the subject of each of the following sentences. In the second, write the verb. If the subject or verb is compound, include in your answer the connecting word (*and, or, but*) that joins the parts. Number your answers with the numbers of the sentences.

1   The green balloon whizzed through the air and landed on Miss Wade's desk.
2   The letters to Dorothy and Gene had been written but had never been mailed.
3   For the next week or two Frank and his show-off friend stayed away from the pool.
4   The projector and the tape recorder have been ordered and will be delivered soon.
5   Didn't Larry or his cousin complain about starting so early?
6   Mrs. McCall looked at Jane's ring, smiled approvingly, and then burst into tears.
7   Wednesday or Thursday the office manager and his assistants will move into their new offices.
8   He and one of his friends bought a battered old car, spent a month fixing it, and then sold it to Mr. Wingate.
9   Our Boston terrier and the Andersons' boxer were entered in the dog show.
10 From the small room at the end of the hall came the blare of a trumpet and the wail of a saxophone.
11 Wind, rain, and sleet were predicted for today.

12 Through wind, rain, and sleet the valiant little band struggled on toward the mountains.

13 William Dean Howells was writing novels and was editing the *Atlantic Monthly* at the time.

14 Jack and his bloodhound picked up the child's trail and finally found him huddling under a spruce.

15 Davis was smacked on the shoulder by Hartman's sizzling line drive and retired from the game.

THE DIRECT OBJECT

OF THE VERB

In each of the following sentences the verb—by itself—makes a statement about the subject. When you read each sentence, you know what action the subject did, even if you omit the words in brackets at the end:

Dr. Jones *frowned* [at the patient].
The whistles *blew* [for five minutes].
Larry *stumbled* [over the rug].

But in each of the next group of sentences the verb—by itself— does not make a complete statement about its subject. With the verb alone, the intended meaning of the sentence is not clear. Since the action expressed by the verb is an action that the subject did to some person or thing, the statement is not complete without a word that names the person or thing.

INCOMPLETE STATEMENT	COMPLETE STATEMENT
Mr. Davis examined	Mr. Davis examined the *fingerprints.*
Louise is imitating	Louise is imitating *him.*
Her sister polished	Her sister polished the *silverware.*

A noun or pronoun that follows the verb and tells who or what receives the action expressed by the verb is called the **direct object** of the verb [O]. The noun *fingerprints*, which tells what Mr. Davis examined, is the direct object of the verb *examined*. The pronoun *him*, which tells whom Louise is imitating, is the direct object of the verb *is imitating*. And the noun *silverware*, which tells what her sister polished, is the object of the verb *polished*.

The meaning of the verb determines whether or not an object is needed to complete the statement. For example, when you use the verb *ran* to mean "went swiftly," you do not include a direct object in the sentence:

Helen *ran* to the store.

But when you use *ran* to mean "managed," you add an object to make the statement complete:

Aunt Helen *ran* the **household.**

Here are other examples:

COMPLETE WITHOUT OBJECT	COMPLETE ONLY WITH OBJECT
The ice *had melted* during the night.	The heat *had melted* the **butter**.
The car *turned* at the corner.	I *turned* the **knob**.
Not a person *stirred*.	Ann *stirred* the **batter**.

In the typical English sentence the direct object, if there is **one**, follows the verb: Subject—Verb—Object (S—V—O). But occasionally, for special emphasis, the object is placed first in the sentence, followed by the subject and then the verb:

s—v—o: We can buy the *Cokes* on the way home. [Usual order.]

o—s—v: The *Cokes* we can buy on the way home. [Emphatic.]

No matter where the object comes, you can easily find it by first picking out the verb and the subject. Here the verb is *can buy*, and the subject is *We*. Then ask the question "What (or whom) can we buy?" We can buy the Cokes. The noun *Cokes* is the direct object of the verb.

The object, like the subject and the verb, may be compound:

We carefully packed the *china* and the *glasses* in excelsior.
Did the club elect *Terry* or *Roland*?

"What did we pack?" The *china* and the *glasses*. "Whom did the club elect?" *Terry* or *Roland*.

EXERCISE 7 Divide a sheet of paper into three columns. In the first column, write the subject of each sentence. In the second, write the verb. In the third, write the direct object of the verb. If subject, verb, or object is compound, include in your answer the connecting word that joins the parts. Number your answers with the numbers of the sentences. Five of the sentences do not contain objects.

1 More and more Americans are buying homes of their own.
2 Gail typed and then proofread the report.
3 Penicillin has saved the lives of countless people.

4 The assistant coach will leave Wednesday or Thursday. [Watch out for this one. Does any person or thing receive the action expressed by the verb?]
5 Why didn't you or one of the waiters call the manager?
6 Marilyn's cousin dived off the high board and swam to the rescue.
7 Governor Willis must have forgotten his campaign promises.
8 Half of the group had stopped beside a clear spring and had camped there for the night.
9 The hardest problems I usually leave till last.
10 How can the treasurer explain his stupid mistake?
11 Louise can't even remember the exact title of the book or its author.
12 Why should anyone in his right mind listen to Howard or Ernest?
13 A doctor at the Townsend Clinic bandaged my brother's hand and arm.
14 The personnel manager asked for a copy of the letter.
15 The key to the side door he lost weeks ago.

THE INDIRECT OBJECT

OF THE VERB

When we use a verb like *send* or *buy*, we quite often include in the sentence a noun or pronoun that tells *to whom* something was sent or *for whom* something was bought. For example:

Mr. Martin sent *George* the bill.
Sally bought *him* a red tie.

A noun or pronoun that tells to whom or for whom something is done is called the **indirect object** of the verb [IO]. The indirect object always precedes the direct object:

S   V   IO   O
Who gave **Jimmie** that black *eye*?
Dad built **Spot** a new *house*.
She showed **Laura** and **me** his *picture*. [Compound indirect object.]

EXERCISE (8) Divide a sheet of paper into two columns. In the first column, write the indirect object in each of the following sentences. In the second, write the direct object. (Not all the sentences have indirect objects. Draw short lines in the columns in these spots.) Number your answers with the numbers of the sentences.

1 Who told that pest my middle name?
2 Someone should teach those boys better manners.
3 I will save him a piece of pie.
4 Why didn't you save a piece of pie for him?
5 The movie will give you a clear idea of the work of the underground.
6 Didn't Mr. Matson sell Mike and Phil his golf clubs?
7 No, I brought a hamburger with onions for Tom.
8 She groaned and handed me her report card.
9 I handed the card to her father.
10 The next day the manager bought the new secretary a dictionary and an ink eraser.
11 Then he taught her the alphabet.
12 He fired her the following day.
13 Under no circumstances will Mr. Stemple lend Mr. Sharp **or** his company the money.
14 He told the officers the story from beginning to end.
15 Dad gave Jim, Daisy, and John their fair shares.

THE PREDICATE COMPLEMENT

In all the sentences you have studied so far the verbs were action words—verbs that express either physical or mental action. We use action verbs in our sentences to tell what the subject did or what was done to the subject:

The coach *worried* about the criticism.
Dr. Elson *was hired* that very same day.

But sometimes we do not want to tell what the subject did or what was done to the subject. We just want to describe the subject or to identify it—that is, to explain what it is or was or will be. When this is our purpose, we use verbs like these:

The coach *was* unhappy.
Dr. Elson *is* a top-notch physicist.
Darrell *will be* a junior next year.

As you can see, the verbs *was*, *is*, and *will be* do not express actions. In these sentences the subjects do not "do" anything, and nothing "is done" to them. The verbs serve as **linking** words. The verb *was* links the describing word *unhappy* (an adjective) to the subject *coach*. The verb *is* links the identifying word *physicist* to the subject *Dr. Elson*. And the verb *will be* links the identifying word *junior* to the subject *Darrell*.

Even though these linking verbs do not express action, they are extremely important words. Without them, we could not put *in sentence form* what we want to say about the subjects. Furthermore, without the verbs we would not know what time was meant —the present, the past, or the future. There is a great difference between "Dad is angry," "Dad was angry," and "Dad will be angry." Without the linking verbs we could not make this difference clear.

The word that follows a linking verb and describes or identifies the subject is called a **predicate complement**. (A *complement* is something that "completes." A *predicate* complement, therefore, is a word that completes the predicate.) A linking verb, by itself, cannot make a complete statement about a subject. The intended meaning of the sentence is not clear until a completing word is added.

INCOMPLETE STATEMENT	COMPLETE STATEMENT
Dennis is	Dennis is a *menace*.
The blue pencils are	The blue pencils are *mine*.
Our meals were	Our meals were *expensive*.

Notice that the predicate complement may be a **noun** (*menace*), or a **pronoun** (*mine*), or an **adjective**—a describing word (*expensive*). Whatever it is, it always refers to the subject of the sentence. It either describes the subject or is another name for the subject.

The most common linking verb is the verb *be*. It has several forms, all of which you use constantly: *am, is, are, was, were, will be, shall be, has been, had been, have been,* etc. Other verbs sometimes used as linking verbs are *seem, become, appear, feel, grow, look, turn, taste, smell.* For example:

> The ride *seemed* endless. [That is, it *appeared* **to be** endless.]
> Her brother *became* a hero. [That is, he *turned out* **to be** a hero.]
> He soon *grew* rich. [That is, he *came* **to be** rich.]
> The water *felt* warm. [That is, it *appeared* **to be** warm.]

At first glance, these verbs might seem to you to express action. But if you think about the meaning, you can see that in these sentences the predicate does not tell that the subject acted. Instead it tells that the subject *appeared to be* or *came to be* in a certain condition or state. Contrast the last two example sentences with the following two, in which the verbs *grew* and *felt* do express action:

> Silas *grew* wheat on his farm. [That is, he *raised* wheat.]
> The doctor *felt* Joan's forehead. [That is, he *touched* her forehead.]

In these sentences the verbs are not linking verbs, but action verbs. The words *wheat* and *forehead* are not predicate complements; they are objects of the verbs, since they tell what received the action done by the subjects.

EXERCISE 9 Divide a sheet of paper into three columns. In the first column, list the subjects of the following sentences. In the second, list the verbs. In the third, list the predicate complements. Number your answers with the numbers of the sentences.

1 The swastika was the symbol of the Nazis in Germany.
2 Our next car will be a sedan.
3 The ice seemed solid enough to me.
4 Isn't the clock on the mantel slow? [Begin by changing the question to statement form.]
5 You must not feel bad about the mistake.
6 The Prestons were the only wealthy people in our town.
7 Within a year the starlet had become an important star.
8 Didn't Mrs. Newton's criticism seem unfair to you?
9 That is he on the stage with Mr. Beal.
10 The lions in the front cage were growing restless.
11 Could the mysterious woman in black have been George Trimby's new sister-in-law?
12 *The Rise of Silas Lapham* is Howells's best-known novel.

EXERCISE 10 In one of the sentences in each of the following pairs the verb is an action verb; in the other, it is a linking verb. Divide a sheet of paper into four columns. In the first column, write the subject of each sentence. In the second, write the verb. In the third, write the object of the verb (if there is one). In the fourth, write the predicate complement (if there is one). Number your answers with the numbers and letters of the sentences.

1 a) That silly neighbor of ours grew a mustache.
   b) Finally Rob grew angry at her sarcasm.
2 a) The plums in that basket look ripe.
   b) Why didn't you look behind the door?
3 a) Mother felt the lump on his cheek.
   b) The air felt chilly to me.

4 a) By morning the milk had turned sour.
   b) Someone had turned the picture to the wall.
5 a) The patient in Room 230 hasn't tasted a thing all day.
   b) The butter in my sandwich tasted rancid.
6 a) The pink pills in the blue box smelled strange.
   b) Dave and Ed smelled smoke on the second floor.

EXERCISE 11 REVIEW   On a sheet of paper, indicate whether each of the following statements is true or false by writing "T" or "F" after the number of the statement. After each *F* that you list, explain what change or changes would be necessary to make the statement true. Nine of the statements are false.

1 A group of words that contains a subject and a verb and that makes complete sense by itself is a sentence.

2 The predicate part of a sentence names the person or thing the verb tells about.

3 *May not have seen* and *had never been known* are examples of four-word verbs.

4 In the sentence "The number of traffic accidents at that corner has doubled in the last year," the subject is *accidents.*

5 The word groups "We laughed," "One cracked," and "Neither came" are grammatically complete sentences even though they consist of only two words, a pronoun and a verb.

6 In the question "What are you looking for?" the subject is *What.*

7 The sentence "The owl and the pussy cat went to sea" has *two* subjects.

8 In the sentence "The mayor arrived ten minutes later," the noun *minutes* is not the direct object of the action verb *arrived*, because it does not name the receiver of the action.

9 The normal order of the sentence parts is Subject—Verb (S—V), Subject—Verb—Object (S—V—O), Subject—Verb—Indirect Object—Direct Object (S—V—IO—O), or Subject—Linking Verb—Predicate Complement (S—LV—C).

10 The subject of the sentence "The stamps we can always borrow from Helen" is *stamps,* the first noun in the sentence.

11 The word *is* is a linking verb in "Fred is our best pitcher" and a helping verb in "Fred is raking the lawn."

12 In the sentences "Alice turned green with envy" and "Alice turned to the left," *turned* is a linking verb.

13 In the sentences "Neil gave her the biggest piece" and "Neil gave the biggest piece to Joan," *her* and *Joan* are indirect objects since they tell to whom Neil gave the biggest piece.

14 The action verb in the sentence "Joe was sent to bed without any supper" tells what the subject did.

15 In "The meat had to be thrown out. It had spoiled," the pronoun *It* refers to *meat* and therefore in the sentence really "means" *meat*.

16 Verbs like *is, was, has been, had been,* and *will be* are often used to link a predicate complement to a subject. Besides this, they indicate what time is meant—the present, the past, or the future.

EXERCISE (12) **REVIEW**   Most of the sentences you have studied in this chapter are built on the following sentence patterns:

$$\text{S} \qquad \text{V}$$
SUBJECT—VERB: The dog growled at me.
$$\text{S} \quad \text{V} \quad \text{O}$$
SUBJECT—VERB—OBJECT: The dog bit him.
SUBJECT—VERB—INDIRECT OBJECT—DIRECT OBJECT:
$$\text{S} \qquad \text{V} \quad \text{IO} \qquad \text{O}$$
The dog brought me the shoe.
$$\text{S} \quad \text{LV} \qquad \text{C}$$
SUBJECT—LINKING VERB—COMPLEMENT: The dog was vicious.

Decide which of these patterns is used in the following sentences. On a sheet of paper, write the number of each sentence. After it, write the letters S—V, S—V—O, S—V—IO—O, or S—LV—C to identify the basic pattern of the sentence.

1 Each year his fame grew.
2 The woman in the information booth finally grew impatient.
3 All the men had grown beards for the city's centennial celebration.
4 The girl in the first seat moved closer to the window.
5 The next day Frank offered Sam ten dollars for the bicycle.
6 He moved quickly for a man of his age and size.
7 The boxes had been moved from the showcase.
8 Someone had moved the picture to one side.
9 Early the next morning we started off for Buffalo.
10 In fact, Ed Perkins would not have lent us the money.
11 Slim Higgins is usually quite grouchy during working hours.
12 Her brother Martin had been a test pilot for years.
13 Chicago gave President O'Kelly of Ireland a warm welcome.
14 Who in the world would actually pay twenty dollars for such a ridiculous gadget?
15 At each of the entrances I posted a guard.

CHAPTER **13**

THE WORK

OF MODIFIERS

260

Which is the more important part of a pearl necklace—the pearls themselves or the thread or cord on which they are strung? Asked this question, most people tend to blurt out, "Why, the pearls, naturally." But are they? They are more costly than the cord, of course. But without the cord there would be no necklace; there would be only a handful of pearls. *To be useful as a necklace*, the pearls *need* the cord. In other words, neither part is "more" important; both are necessary.

Now try this question: Which is the more important in each of the following sentences—the italicized words or the words printed in capital letters? The words in capitals, as you know, are the subject noun and the verb—a "naming" word and a "telling" word.

> *Unskilled* WORKERS HAVE *never* BEEN HIRED *here.*
> LARRY CAN *not* DANCE *well.*

Again you have the same problem as with the pearl necklace—and practically the same answer. At first thought, the words in

capitals may seem more important. *Grammatically* they are, of course; without subjects and verbs there would be no sentences. Moreover, the words, by themselves, make sense; they convey meaning: "Workers have been hired" and "Larry can dance." *But to be useful in getting ideas across*, a sentence must convey the meaning the writer intends, not just any meaning. And to convey the meaning intended in these sentences, the italicized words are necessary, as necessary, in fact, as the subject nouns and the predicate verbs are.

The italicized words, which are so important to the meaning, are called **modifiers**. Modifiers, as you can see, are words that "modify"—or affect—the meaning of other words in a sentence. Since we seldom can make our intended meaning clear without these modifying words, modifiers deserve careful study.

In this chapter you will review not only single-word modifiers, *adjectives* and *adverbs*, but also *prepositional phrases*, groups of related words that serve as modifiers.

THE WORK DONE

BY ADJECTIVES

The words you have studied so far have been of two different types, each of which has a specific job to do for us. *Verbs* work as "telling" words; they tell something about the subject of a sentence. *Nouns* (and *pronouns*) work as "naming" words; they name the persons, places, or things we talk about. Now we come to **adjectives**, words that work as modifiers of nouns and pronouns.

Why do we have to have adjective modifiers? We need them because often the nouns (and pronouns) we use do not make our meaning as exact and clear as we want it to be. Take, for example, the noun *chair*. Everyone knows what *chair* means—"a seat for one person." But the word *chair* includes a great variety of "seats for one person"—everything from a chair of the sort you have in your kitchen to the one your dentist has in his office. It includes chairs that are small and those that are large, chairs that cost a great deal and those that are cheap, chairs that are comfortable and those that are not.

Sometimes it is not necessary to specify just which type of chair is meant. If, for example, two visitors walked into your classroom, your teacher might say, "Dick, will you get *chairs* for our guests." In this situation the noun *chairs* by itself is enough. It does not matter much what kind of chairs you get; any kind will do.

But in many other situations the noun alone would not be enough. In order to make all of your intended meaning clear, you would have to describe just which kind of chair you have in mind. You do it by using adjectives:

a *kitchen* chair	the *huge* chair	the *leather* chair
a *wing* chair	a *small* chair	a *comfortable* chair
the *aluminum* chair	the *red* chair	a *rickety* chair
the *antique* chair	a *maple* chair	an *office* chair

Adjectives are used to do more than tell **which kind** of person or thing is meant. They are used to tell also **which one** or **which ones**, **how many** or **how much**.

WHICH ONE(S)	HOW MANY	HOW MUCH
this pencil	*two* fresh eggs	*some* sugar
those cars	*several* books	*no* danger
her error	*no* small pins	*more* time
my raincoat	*few* seats	*little* money
the third act	*all* students	*much* noise

Or they may be used as "question-words," asking which person or thing is meant:

> *Which* doctor did you call?
> *What* books will he need?
> *Whose* coat is that?

Adjectives *usually* come right before the words they modify unless they are used as predicate complements. Then, though they modify the noun or pronoun subject, they follow the verb:

> The concert was *long*. [The predicate adjective modifies *concert*.]
>
> He seemed *lazier* than ever. [Modifies *He*.]

EXERCISE 1 Each of the following sentences contains two or more adjectives. Some precede the words they modify, and some follow the verbs as predicate complements. Divide a sheet of paper into two columns. In the first column, list the adjectives, *one to a line*. In the second column, write the nouns or pronouns modified by the adjectives. (The words *a*, *an*, and *the* are adjectives. But ignore them in this exercise.) Some of the words are modified by more than one adjective. Be sure to list all of these. You should find 44 adjectives in all. Number your answers with the number of the sentences rather than the number of the adjectives.

1 The last person in the line finally became impatient.
2 Does your sister have enough money for the tickets?
3 The tall, dark woman bought four hats.
4 A second-hand car would be cheaper.
5 The city editor is a busy person.
6 The assistant manager was busy, as I had expected.
7 All incorrect answers will count five points against you.
8 To me she seemed kind, patient, and wise.
9 The wide streets, the modern buildings, and the many beautiful parks made a deep impression on Gene.
10 What excuse did his pesky little brother give?
11 The pompous, conceited headwaiter ushered the glamorous actress to a table.
12 Short, fat girls ought not to wear horizontal stripes.
13 The supply of fresh shrimp was low, but the quality was high.
14 Stephen Leacock is famous for his books of humorous essays.
15 Her unfriendly, uncoöperative attitude annoys most people.

EXERCISE 2 The same word may be an adjective, a noun, or a verb, depending on its use in a sentence. Copy the italicized word in each of the following sentences. After each word, write "A" if it is used as an adjective; "N" if it is used as a noun; "V" if it is used as a verb. Number your answers with the numbers of the sentences.

1 The *iron* had become overheated and scorched the collar.
2 Mr. Dowe's gift to the hospital was an *iron* lung.
3 First *iron* the sleeves of the dress.
4 Ted's office is on the *ground* floor.
5 Martha *ground* her heel into the dirt.
6 *Green* is Neil's favorite color.
7 And the *green* grass grew all around, all around.
8 *Answer* keys for the exercises will soon be available.
9 His sister's *answer* was right.
10 His sisters *answer* his fan letters.
11 What a *waste* of time that is!
12 *Waste* not, want not.

EXERCISE 3 On a sheet of paper, list the italicized words in the following sentences, putting each on a separate line. After each word, write "A" if it is used as an adjective, and "P" if it is used as a pronoun. Number your answers with the numbers of the sentences.

1 *Each* member was asked to contribute to the fund.
2 *Each* promised to sell ten tickets.
3 *Which* are you going to send back?
4 *Which* article gives the most accurate account?
5 The prosecuting attorney questioned *both* witnesses.
6 *Both* were hard of hearing.
7 *That* is *my* hamburger!
8 *That* hamburger is *mine*!
9 *These* shoes are too tight.
10 But *those* look too sensible, I'm afraid.
11 *What* does he want?
12 *What* kind of talk is that, young man?

THE WORK DONE

BY ADVERBS

There is a world of difference between "Larry can ski" and "Larry can not ski." The word *not*, which makes the difference, is an *adverb*. There is an important difference between "She walked proudly away" and "She walked meekly away." The words *proudly* and *meekly*, which cause this difference, are *adverbs*.

Adverbs, as you can see, are modifying words—words that affect the meaning of the verb in a sentence. Adverbs add to the meaning of the verb in one of several ways. They may, for example, tell **when** the action expressed by the verb took place:

Harris arrived *yesterday.*
He will call you *later.*
I saw her *recently* at a football game.

Or they may tell **where, how,** or **to what extent:**

WHERE: Turn *south* at the next corner.
              Jane looked *back* and waved.
              The man fell *forward.*
HOW: The doctor worked *swiftly.*
              Drive *carefully* and get there *safely.*
              She *haltingly* told her story.
TO WHAT EXTENT: Bill *seldom* watches TV programs.
                       He moved *slightly* to the left.
                       They have *often* visited us.

Though most adverbs modify verbs, they may be used also **to** modify adjectives or other adverbs:

That hat is *hardly* suitable for the party. [Modifies the adjective *suitable.*]
An *extremely* loud explosion followed. [Modifies the adjective *loud.*]
The sheriff *very* quickly agreed. [Modifies the adverb *quickly.*]
He returned *rather* soon. [Modifies the adverb *soon.*]

Notice that these adverbs that modify adjectives or other adverbs tell *how much* or *how little* is meant. How suitable is the hat? *Hardly* suitable. How loud was the explosion? *Extremely* loud. How quickly did the sheriff agree? *Very* quickly. How soon did he return? *Rather* soon.

A word of warning: The same word may be used as either an adjective or an adverb:

ADJECTIVE: He reserved a seat on the *early* plane. [Modifies the noun *plane.*]
ADVERB: Call me *early* in the evening. [Modifies the verb *Call.*]

ADJECTIVE: *Most* women are careful drivers. [Modifies the noun *women.*]
ADVERB: She is the *most* careful driver I know. [Modifies the adjective *careful.*]

265

The only sure way to determine whether a word is an adjective or an adverb is to see what work the word does in the sentence. If it affects the meaning of a noun or pronoun, it is an **adjective**. If it affects the meaning of a verb, an adjective, or an adverb, it is an **adverb**.

EXERCISE (4) Copy the italicized word in each of the following sentences on a sheet of paper. After each word, write "Adv." if it is used as an adverb, and "Adj." if it is used as an adjective.

1 Frank enjoys *most* novels.
2 Surely you can type *much* better than that.
3 Please step *back* and make room for a few more people.
4 His experiences were *most* unusual.
5 The catcher dusted off *home* plate.
6 General Wainwright desperately needed *more* men at Corregidor.
7 None of us had *much* money.
8 From that day on, she proofread her work *more* carefully.
9 The *back* seat of the car was loaded with books.
10 Run *home*, Sandy.
11 In fact, Helen Brenner and my cousin Margot not only look alike but think *alike*.

12 A return to the ways of our ancestors is not *likely*.

EXERCISE (5) Each of the following sentences contains two or more adverbs (36 in all). Divide a sheet of paper into two columns. In the first column, list the adverbs. In the second, tell what word each adverb modifies. Number your answers with the numbers of the sentences.

1 Now the students in her class speak Spanish fluently.
2 Should we leave earlier tonight?
3 Uncle Ralph almost always pays his bills promptly.
4 Slowly and cautiously they groped their way through the dark cave.
5 Usually Mr. Ames takes a much earlier train.
6 The new boy was not very friendly. [Be careful.]
7 Ken himself put them there and then blamed Clayton.
8 She can type rather fast for a beginner.
9 Too many cooks do not necessarily spoil the soup.
10 Laura is happy and is doing extremely well in her work.
11 The frisky puppies again rushed higgledy-piggledy toward their feeding tray.
12 I had never seen appetites so unashamedly voracious.

13 They hardly ever complain.
14 Hold on tight and do not look down.
15 Ralph will check the figures more carefully tomorrow.

THE WORK

OF PREPOSITIONAL PHRASES

The modifiers you have studied so far have been one-word modifiers: a *yellow* car, a *tiny* spot; sang *loudly*, tried *desperately*. Now we come to another kind of modifier, one that does exactly the same sort of work as adjectives and adverbs do. But this modifier is *not* a single-word modifier; it consists of two or more words that work together as a single unit. To understand clearly what this means, compare the italicized words in the following pairs of sentences:

ONE-WORD MODIFIER	PHRASE MODIFIER
She has an *iron* will.	She has a will *of iron.*
He called on the *Mexican* delegates.	He called on the delegates *from Mexico.*
Ted answered him *scornfully*.	Ted answered him *with scorn.*

As you can see, the words *of iron* together modify the noun *will* in the same way that the adjective *iron* does; both modifiers tell what kind of will she has. The words *from Mexico* tell which delegates he called on, just as the adjective *Mexican* does. And the two words *with scorn* work as a single unit to tell how Ted answered, just as the adverb *scornfully* does.

These groups of related words like *of iron, from Mexico,* and *with scorn,* which work together as a single unit to modify nouns, pronouns, or verbs, are called **prepositional phrases.** All such phrases have at least two parts. The first part is a *preposition*—a word like *of, from, with, on, for,* or *under.* The second part is a *noun* or *pronoun.* This noun or pronoun may be modified by an adjective.

[1]   [2]
The box **on** *the kitchen table* is Dave's.

[1] [2]
It contains a present **for** *him.*

The purpose of the preposition is to show how the noun or pronoun that follows it (called the *object of the preposition*) is related to some other word in the sentence. In the first example, the preposition *on* shows the relationship that exists between the noun *table*

267

and the noun *box*. The preposition shows that this particular box was *on* the table, not *under* or *near* or *beside* or *behind* the table. In the second example, the preposition *for* shows the connection between the pronoun *him* and the noun *present*. This particular present was *for* him, not *from* him. Notice that the prepositional phrases in these sentences are used as adjectives, telling *which box* and *what kind of present* are meant. Such prepositional phrases are called **adjective phrases**, since they do the work of adjectives.

In many sentences the preposition shows the relationship between its object and the verb:

> John ran *to the grocery store.*
> Ted will call Sam *after the movie.*

In the first example, the preposition shows that John ran *to* the store, not *from* or *past* the store. In the second example, the preposition shows that Ted will call Sam *after* the movie, not *before* or *during* the movie. Notice that the prepositional phrases in these sentences are used as adverb modifiers of the verbs, telling *where* and *when*. Such prepositional phrases are called **adverb phrases**, since they do the work of adverbs.

Though a number of words (for example, *down, past, through, behind, before, up, under, above, over*) may be used as either adverbs or prepositions, you should find it easy to tell these uses apart. A preposition always has an object; an adverb never does:

ADVERB: I had spoken to him *before.*
PREPOSITION: I had spoken to him *before* the **meeting.**

ADVERB: He walked *past* but didn't stop.
PREPOSITION: He walked *past* the **post office.**

Remember that an adverb, by itself, is a modifying word. A preposition, by itself, is not. It is the whole phrase—the preposition plus its object—that modifies.

EXERCISE (**6**) Be ready to tell whether the italicized prepositional phrase in each of the following sentences is used as an adjective phrase or as an adverb phrase—and to explain how you arrived at your answer.

1   Esther wouldn't walk *under the ladder.*
2   Most of the packages *under the tree* are Tommy's.
3   The man *behind Nora and me* was smoking an evil-smelling cigar. [Notice that the object of a preposition may be *compound—Nora and me*.]
4   In honor of the occasion, little Suzie had scrubbed *behind her ears*, in fact.

5 Now my uncle walks *without a limp.*

6 Any camera *with a red tag* is reduced 20 per cent.

7 The ten days *before the party* seemed endless to Joan.

8 The spots *on the carpet* never did come out.

9 *Behind each chair* stood a sour-looking waitress.

10 I will call you *after the rehearsal.*

11 The airport installed a 130-foot jet-blast deflector fence as a protection *from the torrid blast* of the engines.

12 I would move the picture *above the mantel* to the den.

EXERCISE 7 Each of the following sentences contains two prepositional phrases. Divide a sheet of paper into three columns. In the first column, write the prepositional phrases, putting each on a separate line. Underline the object of each preposition. In the second column, write the word each phrase modifies. In the third column, write "Adj." if the phrase is used as an adjective to modify a noun or pronoun, or "Adv." if the phrase is used as an adverb to modify a verb. Number your answers with the numbers of the sentences.

1 A motorcycle with a sidecar was parked in the alley.

2 Anyone without a ticket was sent to the office.

3 During the first act Darrel sat between Frank and me.

4 Two reporters from the *Daily News* sneaked past the guards.

5 Toward evening the mournful wail of the foghorn seemed even louder.

6 Lucy hid the toys behind the sofa and swept the dirt under the rug.

7 The two boys tiptoed quietly up the stairs and into Phil's room.

8 Someone had scattered a box of thumbtacks over the stage floor.

9 The ranch houses along the river road beyond the Parker estate have been sold.

10 Dad had stepped on the gas pedal by mistake.

11 The man at the desk scowled at us.

12 The store across the street does not open until noon.

EXERCISE 8 Copy the italicized word in each of the following sentences on a sheet of paper. After each word, write "Prep." if it is used as a preposition, or "Adv." if it is used as an adverb. Number your answers.

1 We looked *around* but saw no one we knew.

2 Frank tied a sweat shirt *around* his neck.

3 Why don't you sit *up* in your chair?

4 The squirrels scrambled *up* one side and down the other.

5 *Down* the street he walked, muttering to himself.
6 Do sit *down* and be quiet for a few minutes.
7 The boys jumped *off*, yelling at the top of their lungs.
8 Turn the water *off* first.
9 Who turned *off* the lights? [Compare with sentence 8 before you answer.]
10 Dave fell *off* the ladder and broke his wrist.
11 Harold looked *on* for a while and then left.
12 His career came to an abrupt end when he missed a turn *on* the narrow, winding road.

EXERCISE (9) *REVIEW* Along the left margin of a sheet of paper, list the numbers 1 to 10. After each number, write the letter of the item that correctly completes each of the following statements.

1 *Adjectives* are words used to modify (a) nouns (b) nouns or pronouns (c) verbs, adjectives, or adverbs.
2 *Adverbs* are words used to modify (a) adjectives (b) verbs, adjectives, or other adverbs (c) nouns or pronouns.
3 In the sentence "Mother felt bad on hearing about the accident," the word *bad* is (a) an adverb modifying the verb *felt* (b) a predicate adjective modifying the subject *Mother* (c) part of the verb *felt bad*.

4 In the sentence "Which hat did you choose?" the word *Which* is (a) a pronoun used as the subject of *did choose* (b) a pronoun modifying the noun *hat* (c) an adjective modifying the noun *hat*.
5 In the sentence "The new Ford is an unusually good car," the word *good* is (a) an adjective used as a predicate complement to modify the subject *Ford* (b) an adjective modifying the predicate complement *car* (c) an adverb modifying the linking verb *is*.
6 In the sentence "George is practicing his music lesson," the word *is* is (a) a helping verb (b) a linking verb.
7 In the sentence "He tucked the photograph under the blotter," the word *under* is (a) an adverb modifying the verb *tucked* (b) a preposition modifying the noun *photograph* (c) a preposition showing the relationship between the noun *blotter* and the verb *tucked*.
8 In the sentence "We pulled down the curtain," the noun *curtain* is (a) the object of the preposition *down* (b) the object of the verb *pulled*.
9 In the sentence "This is an off season for grapefruit," the word *off* is used as (a) an adverb (b) a preposition (c) an adjective.

10 In the sentence "Stand beside Kenneth and her," the object of the preposition *beside* is (a) *Kenneth* (b) *her* (c) compound— *Kenneth* and *her.*

EXERCISE (10) REVIEW On a sheet of paper, copy the italicized words and prepositional phrases in the following sentences, listing each on a separate line. After each word or phrase tell (1) whether it is used as an adjective or adverb modifier and (2) what word it modifies, underlining the word. Number your answers with the numbers of the sentences.

1 *Yesterday* he stepped too close to the edge and fell *over.*
2 Tom answered all *their* questions *without the slightest hesitation.*
3 The tadpole *soon* became an *ugly* frog.
4 The man *in the green car* got out and walked *toward us.*
5 Sam got the *only* piece of cake *with thick frosting.*
6 He seemed *rather cowardly* to me. [Is *seemed* an action verb here?]
7 His experiences *in Africa* are described *in the third chapter.*
8 *Your* work looks *easier* than mine.
9 *Now* hold *up* your right hand.
10 *On the corner* of each page he pasted a *large* yellow label.

EXERCISE (11) REVIEW Find in a newspaper or magazine a paragraph which you think is especially effective because of the adjectives the writer has used. Copy the paragraph or clip it and paste it on a sheet of paper. Underline all adjectives except *a, an,* and *the.*

In class, exchange papers with a classmate. Read his paragraph and check the words he has underlined. At the bottom of the sheet list any adjectives he has missed or any words that he has incorrectly underlined. Then sign your name and return the paper to the owner for corrections.

Your teacher may have one or more paragraphs copied on the board to use for a review quiz in identifying adjective modifiers.

EXERCISE (12) REVIEW Select five words that may be used either as adverbs or as prepositions (for example, *in, down, above,* and so on). Then write five pairs of sentences, using in each pair one of the words you have selected—first as an adverb, then as a preposition. Underline the words. Be ready to read your sentences in class.

Example: Dr. Greenleaf is not in today. [Adverb.]
            Is anyone in the doctor's office? [Preposition.]

CHAPTER 14

WRITING

EFFECTIVE

SIMPLE

SENTENCES

In this chapter you will learn a number of tricks for improving the sentences you write. You will be surprised at how simple the tricks are; you will be even more surprised at how well they work. Once you see how easy it is to turn dull, childish sentences into interesting, adult-sounding sentences that are easy and pleasant to read, you will want to make use of these tricks in all the written work you do. The improvement that results will please you—as well as your readers.

As you go through the chapter, you should keep in mind that it deals only with **simple sentences**, sentences which have just *one* subject-verb combination. However, you will find that simple sentences—when they are written in a way that not only communicates your ideas clearly, but also shows how those ideas are related to one another—can be extremely effective. What is more, once you have learned how to improve your written sentences in the various ways explained here, you will find that your spoken sentences will tend to improve.

THE WORK OF APPOSITIVES

In a story about a sea voyage, you might well run across a sentence like this:

To stop up the cracks in the ship, they used oakum.

If you know what oakum is, this sentence would have real meaning for you. You would have a clear mental image of what the sailors did to stop up the cracks. But suppose you don't know what oakum is. Then you would come away from the sentence without really understanding what the writer had said.

There are two ways in which the writer could have helped the many readers who would be puzzled by the word *oakum*. First, he could have added a sentence of explanation:

To stop up the cracks in the ship, they used oakum. *Oakum is a loose, stringy fiber made by taking old ropes apart.*

But if he were a good writer, he would hate to interrupt his story to detour off into a whole sentence explaining what a word means. Luckily, he could provide the necessary information in another way —by tucking it in right after the word *oakum*:

> To stop up the cracks in the ship, they used oakum—*a loose, stringy fiber made by taking old ropes apart.*

In this sentence the needed explanation is neatly supplied as an *appositive*. An **appositive** is a noun or pronoun (often modified by other words) that is set alongside another noun or pronoun to explain it or to add to its meaning.

Appositives are nothing new to you; you use them constantly in your conversations, and you find them used frequently in what you read. They usually follow the words they explain, though they may not always come immediately after them:

> Excalibur, *King Arthur's* **sword**, was given to him by the Lady of the Lake.
>
> The original Siamese twins, **Chang** *and* **Eng**, lived sixty-three years.
>
> He interviewed one member of the staff, *the sports* **editor**.

274

Sometimes, for special emphasis, the appositive is put at the end of the sentence, though the word it explains comes at the beginning:

> One of the members voted against the motion—**Ed Hill**.

Since an appositive with its modifiers (an "appositive phrase") is used merely to provide extra information, it is not an essential part of the sentence and should be set off by commas. Two commas are needed, one before the appositive phrase and one after, unless the appositive comes at the end of the sentence. Then, of course, one comma serves to set off the phrase.

> Roy Leyden, *her* **cousin** *from Kansas,* is taking Sue to the dance. [Two commas needed.]
>
> I got there just too late to see Perry Como, *my favorite* **singer**. [Only one comma.]

If the appositive phrase itself contains commas or if special emphasis is wanted for the appositive, dashes are commonly used instead of commas:

> Three of the boys—*Gordon, Philip, and Donald*—won honorable mention awards. [Two dashes needed.]
>
> The thief turned out to be Mr. Sweazy—*the president of the firm!* [Only one dash.]

EXERCISE 1 Each of the following sentences contains an appositive. Divide a sheet of paper into two columns. In the first column, list each appositive phrase (the appositive plus its modifiers). Underline the appositive noun in each phrase. In the second column, list the words that are explained by the appositives. Number your answers with the numbers of the sentences.

1 Unfortunately, Steve Durkee, our best pitcher, had a sore wrist.
2 The Colossus of Rhodes, a huge statue of Apollo, was considered one of the seven wonders of the ancient world.
3 Many people confuse President Andrew Jackson with "Stonewall" Jackson, a Confederate general.
4 Worst of all, Gordon lost his watch, a graduation present from his father.
5 One thing made him extremely unpopular—his terrible temper.
6 After the broadcast we met Fahey Flynn, Dad's favorite news commentator.
7 Milt Caniff, the creator of the Steve Canyon comic strip, was once a newspaper reporter.
8 The cockpit covers were made of Plexiglas—a light, transparent plastic substance.
9 Last night three guests—an elephant trainer, a sword swallower, and a woman sheriff—stumped the panelists.
10 Dave's share of the profits, thirteen cents, just paid for his bus ride home.
11 The new branch office will be in Juneau, the capital of Alaska.
12 With these two magic words, *open sesame,* the door flew open.

USING APPOSITIVES

TO IMPROVE SENTENCES

The following sentences, taken from the first draft of a newspaper story about a local art contest, would probably make the editor frown. Can you explain why?

> Arthur Kurtz was asked to judge the paintings and award the prizes. He is the curator of the Davis Art Museum in Crestville.

Grammatically, there is nothing wrong with the sentences: each is complete; each is clear. Nothing is wrong with the facts, either; they are accurate and there are plenty of them. The only thing wrong is the way the facts are presented.

First, the writer has taken a whole sentence—the second—to explain a name (*Arthur Kurtz*) used in the first sentence. By using a whole sentence, he makes the explanation seem as important as the details given in the first sentence, even though it is really less important. Second, the explanation comes a bit late. It belongs earlier, in the spot where the reader will first need it—right after the name *Arthur Kurtz*. By using an appositive for his explanation, the writer could supply the necessary information in a more efficient, less wordy way:

> Arthur Kurtz, *the* **curator** *of the Davis Art Museum in Crestville,* was asked to judge the paintings and award the prizes.

In revising the first drafts of papers you write, be on the lookout for any sentence that merely explains a word used in a preceding sentence. By changing the explanatory sentence to an appositive phrase, you can combine the two sentences into a more effective single sentence. It is easy to do: Just drop the subject and verb of the explanatory sentence and then insert the appositive after the word it explains.

TWO SENTENCES	ONE EFFECTIVE SENTENCE
William Henry Herndon encouraged Lincoln's political career. *Herndon was Lincoln's law partner in Springfield.*	William Henry Herndon, *Lincoln's law partner in Springfield,* encouraged his political career.
That very afternoon Leadville Johnny Brown went prospecting again and discovered "The Little Johnny." *It was one of the richest gold mines in Colorado history.*	That very afternoon Leadville Johnny Brown went prospecting again and discovered "The Little Johnny," *one of the richest gold mines in Colorado history.*

EXERCISE (2) Combine the two sentences in each of the following pairs into one effective sentence, using an appositive phrase in place of the explanatory sentence. (In two of the pairs you will find that the explanatory sentence comes first.) Write your revised sentences on a sheet of paper, setting off the appositive phrases by commas.

1 The most valuable clue was found by a neighbor of ours. It was a brown cotton glove.
2 Edward Jenner introduced vaccination as a protection against smallpox. He was an English physician.

3   Her agent thought her real name was too theatrical to be used. It was Dawn O'Day.

4   In Venice we had ravioli for lunch and polenta for dinner. Polenta is a porridge made of corn meal.

5   My cousin Leonard's allowance seemed a princely fortune to me. It was five dollars a week.

6   Nathan Hale was a captain in the Revolutionary War. Hale volunteered to serve as a spy among the British forces stationed on Long Island.

7   Two of the committee members did most of the work. They were Randy Moore and Lars Neilsen.

8   Judson's third book brought him fame and several offers from Hollywood producers. It was a novel based on his experiences as a stagehand.

9   Dromedaries are the one-humped camels of Arabia. They are trained for fast running.

10 The program committee asked Gerald Frisbie to speak at the February meeting of the Camera Club. Frisbie is a professional photographer.

USING COMPOUND VERBS

TO IMPROVE SENTENCES

The more inexperienced a writer is, the more likely he is to write sentences of this sort:

> Uncle Ben jumped up from his chair. He tucked his brief case under his arm. He stalked out of the room without another word.

> Furniture polishes containing silicone protect the finish. They are easy to apply.

> A careful driver signals his turns. He comes to a full stop at arterial signs.

> Circuit breakers are more expensive to install than fuses. They give better protection.

The sentences in each of these groups are interesting enough, but they sound a bit childish, rather like the sentences in a reader for first-graders. The reason they sound this way is that the writer has used a separate sentence for each idea—as if he thought his readers could not handle more than one idea at a time.

Notice that the sentences in each group are about the same person or thing. Since they are, they would be easy to combine into one sentence. Simply use a *compound verb*, joining its parts with a conjunction like *and* or *but*:

> Uncle Ben *jumped* up from his chair, *tucked* his brief case under his arm, and *stalked* out of the room without another word.
>
> Furniture polishes containing silicone *protect* the finish and *are* easy to apply.
>
> A careful driver *signals* his turns and *comes* to a full stop at arterial signs.
>
> Circuit breakers *are* more expensive to install than fuses but *give* better protection.

With the compound verbs the sentences not only sound more adult, but are actually easier to read than the original chopped-up versions.

In revising your papers, try this trick of using a compound verb to combine two or three sentences that have subjects referring to the same person or thing. The improvement in your writing will be well worth the few minutes it will take you to find and combine the sentences. Exercise 3 will show you how easy it is to do.

EXERCISE (3) Combine the sentences in each of the following numbered groups into one sentence by using a compound verb. Write the revised sentences on a sheet of paper, underlining the parts of the compound verbs. If the compound verb consists of three parts, use commas to separate the parts, as in the revised example sentence about Uncle Ben.

1 The sailors had been exposed to cholera. They had to be quarantined.

2 The bus driver saw the dog dart across the road. He slammed on his brakes.

3 Dad's cigar had rolled off the ash tray. It had burned a long scar on the new table.

4 Dino stepped into the office. He looked sheepishly at Mr. Thomas. He fearfully handed him Miss Hale's note.

5 The four children lined up at the gate. They waited for Grandpa to give them the signal to start.

6 The rolling-mill men were angry about this second delay. They promised to stay at their jobs for three more days. [Use *but* instead of *and* to join the parts of the compound verb.]

7 The elevator boy heartily disliked Mrs. Cranshaw. He did everything possible to annoy her.

8 The blouses were made of nylon. They should not have been pressed with a hot iron.

9 The ring slipped out of Gordon's hand. It rolled across the floor of the barn. It disappeared from sight in a large crack.
10 David worked as fast as possible. He finished only twenty-five of the thirty problems. [Use *but* instead of *and*.]

RECOGNIZING PARTICIPLES

The word *light* is often used as a noun: "The *light* grew dim," "Turn off the *light*." But that does not mean that *light* is always a noun. If it is used to modify a noun, as in "a *light* rain," then we call it an adjective. If it is used to modify an adjective, as in "the *light* blue ribbon," then we call it an adverb. If it is used to assert action, as in "The girls *light* the candles," then we call it a verb.

The preceding paragraph is intended to remind you of a very important fact—that what a word is depends on what kind of work it does in a sentence. Keeping this fact in mind will help you understand what *participles* are.

Start by looking at the following example sentences. You know that the italicized word in each of these sentences is *part of the verb*, because together with a helping verb it tells what action the subject did:

279

> Jim's voice was *trembling* with rage.
> The nurse had *bandaged* Larry's arm.

But these same verb forms, *trembling* and *bandaged*, can also be used in another way—as adjectives to modify nouns (or pronouns):

> We pretended not to notice Jim's *trembling* voice. [Describes *voice*.]
> At first I did not see his *bandaged* arm. [Describes *arm*.]

When verb forms are used as adjectives, they are called **participles**. There are two kinds of participles: active and passive. **Active participles** are easy to recognize; they always end in *ing*:

> the *grinning* boy [Which boy? The boy who is grinning.]
> the *burning* building [Which building? The one that is burning.]
> a *frightening* noise [What kind of noise? A noise that is frightening.]

As you can see, an active participle is a "verbal" adjective that describes by suggesting that the word it modifies is performing a certain action. The boy is grinning; the building is burning; the noise is frightening.

Passive participles may have various forms: *deserted, drowned, driven, stolen, sung, spilt, burnt.* The most common endings are *ed, en,* and *t*:

> a *trusted* friend [What kind of friend? One that is trusted.]
>
> a *broken* hinge [What kind of hinge? One that has been broken.]
>
> the *lost* mittens [Which mittens? Those that had been lost.]

Passive participles, as these examples show, describe by suggesting that the modified word is receiving or has received an action.

Though active and passive participles are forms of verbs, they do the work of adjectives, not the work of verbs. They do not make statements about the subjects of sentences, as verbs do. Instead, they modify nouns or pronouns. But since participles are formed from verbs, they do keep some of the characteristics that verbs have. Like a verb, a participle may have an object or a complement or may be modified by an adverb or an adverb phrase. The participle, together with these related words, forms a **participial phrase** that is used as an adjective to modify a noun or pronoun:

> Tim snapped a picture of Laura *holding the baby.* [The whole phrase modifies *Laura; baby* is the object of the participle *holding.*]
>
> *Being a bully,* Dave took full advantage of his authority. [The whole phrase modifies *Dave; bully* is the predicate complement after the participle *Being.*]
>
> The car *parked in the alley* is Uncle Ben's. [The whole phrase modifies *car; in the alley* is an adverb phrase modifying the participle *parked.*]
>
> Kenneth just sat there, *grinning foolishly.* [The whole phrase modifies *Kenneth; foolishly* is an adverb modifying the participle *grinning.*]

Notice that a participial phrase may come before or after the word it modifies or may even be separated from it by other words, as in the fourth example sentence.

Participles, like verbs, may consist of more than one word:

> **Having slept** *on the train,* Ted felt quite rested. [Active participle.]
>
> **Having been warned** *about the high prices,* Helen ordered only a sandwich and a cup of coffee. [Passive participle.]

We use participles of two or three words when we want to show that the action suggested by the participle was completed *before* the time of the action expressed by the verb. Ted had slept *before* he felt rested. Helen had been warned about the high prices *before* she ordered her skimpy lunch.

EXERCISE (4) Divide a sheet of paper into two columns. In the first column, list the italicized words in the following sentences, each on a separate line. In the second column, write "Participle" if the word is used as an adjective modifier; write "Verb" if it is used as the verb or part of the verb in the sentence. Number your answers with the numbers of the sentences.

1 The two boys were *shivering* with cold.
2 The two boys, *shivering* with fright, dashed out of the house.
3 Dad was *staring* at the *dented* fender, *muttering* to himself.
4 The man *driving* the bus had an *amazing* sense of humor.
5 Gary was *sitting* in the living room, *watching* a TV program.
6 The woman *sitting* in the back booth heard a *terrifying* noise.
7 *Terrified* by the noise, she ran to the policeman *standing* on the corner.
8 The faucet, *repaired* just the week before, was *leaking* again.
9 Jerry is *wearing* that *torn* shirt today.
10 Sam was *tiptoeing* up the stairs, *holding* his shoes in one hand.

281

EXERCISE (5) Find the participial phrase in each of the following sentences and copy it on a sheet of paper. In parentheses after each phrase, write the noun or pronoun the phrase modifies.

1 The two women sitting in front of us talked during the whole performance.
2 The announcement posted on the first-floor bulletin board attracted his attention.
3 The delegates representing Brazil could speak Portuguese, French, and English.
4 The thieves had been interested only in the safe containing the bonds.
5 Having agreed to the terms, he couldn't complain about the payments.
6 The young man coughed loudly several times, hoping to attract the waiter's attention.
7 Impressed by his glib talk, Mrs. Downs subscribed to two magazines.
8 The director paced back and forth, barking directions at stagehands and actors.

9 Having grown accustomed to his bad temper, Miss Tyler paid no attention to his latest outburst.

10 Hearing footsteps in the hall, the boys ducked into the broom closet nearby.

USING PARTICIPIAL PHRASES

TO IMPROVE SENTENCES

Participial phrases, like appositives, are useful in combining sentences. Suppose, for example, that in the first draft of a paper you had written sentences like these:

> The cab driver heard the ambulance siren. He quickly pulled over to the curb.
> The man on crutches was embarrassed by their staring. He left the lobby and went up to his room.

As you can see, the first sentence in each of these pairs gives the reason for what happens in the second. The reason the cab driver pulled over to the curb was that he heard the siren. The reason the man left the lobby was that he was embarrassed. In other words, the ideas expressed in the two sentences of each group are so closely related in meaning that they really belong together instead of in separate sentences. By using a participial phrase to give the reason, you could easily combine the two ideas into one effective sentence:

> *Hearing the ambulance siren,* the cab driver quickly pulled over to the curb.
> *Embarrassed by their staring,* the man on crutches left the lobby and went up to his room.

These revised single sentences are not better because they are longer, but because they clearly show the relationship between the ideas.

Here are other groups of sentences that could be improved:

> An elderly man stopped me at the door and asked to see my ticket. He was wearing a convention badge.
> The leading article was full of wild accusations and vague threats. It was written by a former member of the police department.

Though the ideas expressed in the two sentences of each group are related, they are obviously not of equal importance. The second sentence in each group merely gives an explanatory detail about a person or thing mentioned in the first sentence. By expressing this detail in a participial phrase, you can make the important idea stand out more clearly, as it should:

> An elderly man *wearing a convention badge* stopped me at the door and asked to see my ticket.
> The leading article, *written by a former member of the police department*, was full of wild accusations and vague threats.

EXERCISE (6) Combine each of the following pairs of sentences by using a participial phrase in place of the less important sentence. Write your revised sentences on a sheet of paper, underlining the participial phrases.

Punctuation note: A participial phrase that begins a sentence should be set off by a comma. The comma shows the reader where the phrase ends and the main part of the sentence begins. Though participial phrases that come at the end or in the middle of sentences are not always set off by commas, all the phrases used in this exercise are of the type (nonrestrictive) that should be set off.

1 The manager was angered by their refusal to coöperate. He ordered them to leave the bowling alley.
2 The committee members finally left the office at five-thirty. They were still arguing about which orchestra to get for the dance. [Put the participial phrase at the end of your revised sentence.]
3 Mr. Payton was impressed by the samples of Jean's work. He offered her a job in the advertising department.
4 Mrs. Hill handed David's report card to her husband. She was beaming with pride.
5 Jerry read several articles about gardening. He wanted to make a good impression on Martha's father.
6 Trainer Fred Alispaw fought with the crazed elephant for an hour. He was armed only with an elephant hook.
7 Lieutenant Colonel Travis suspected a trick. He ordered his full force of men to stay on duty.
8 The rotted log creaked under Dixon's weight and then gave way. It toppled him over into the swirling water. [Put the phrase at the end.]
9 Mrs. Kranz was accustomed to the peace and quiet of a small farm. She found life in Chicago hard on her nerves. [Put the phrase after the subject.]
10 The Taj Mahal is considered the most beautiful mausoleum in the world. It was built by Shah Jehan for his favorite wife.

A pair of eyeglasses without lenses would be rather ridiculous; without the lenses the glasses could not do the job they were intended to do. Using a participial phrase in a sentence without including a word for the phrase to modify is just as ridiculous, since without this word you cannot convey the meaning intended. For example, look at these sentences:

> Running through the alley in the dark, a garbage pail tripped her.
>
> Even bundled up in heavy storm coats, the cabin was too cold for comfort.

As a reader, you naturally assume that a participial phrase at the beginning of a sentence will modify the closest noun or pronoun—the subject of the sentence. So these sentences seem to say that the garbage pail was running through the alley and that the cabin was bundled up in storm coats—not at all the meaning the writers intended. The writers could easily make the intended meaning clear by supplying the right words for the "dangling" phrases to modify, making the words the subjects by rephrasing the sentences:

> Running through the alley in the dark, **she** tripped over a garbage pail.
>
> Even bundled up in heavy storm coats, the **boys** found the cabin too cold for comfort.

Now the participial phrases are no longer dangling, since they have the *right* words to attach themselves to.

EXERCISE 7 Correct the dangling participles in the following sentences. Change the wording and supply other words where necessary, but do not change the basic meaning of the sentences.

1 Being in a hurry to get to his appointment on time, the letter was completely forgotten.
2 Having finished her report, the reference books were no longer needed.
3 Being the youngest in our family, my parents spoiled me.
4 Feeling in a bad mood, his silly remarks annoyed Dorothy.
5 Grasping the steering wheel firmly, the dangerous climb up the winding roads started.
6 Scrambling over the fence, Jerry's glasses were broken.
7 Discouraged by this series of setbacks, the project was abandoned by the engineers.

8 Hiking up the mountain trails, our problems were soon forgotten, as a matter of fact.

9 Having spent all her allowance, the money for the concert ticket had to be borrowed from Roy.

10 Finally convinced of his dishonesty, the clerk was fired by the manager that very afternoon.

11 Having lived in London for several years, the cockney dialect was quite familiar to Fred.

12 Knowing very little French, their conversation baffled me.

USING ACTIVE AND PASSIVE VERBS

When a verb expresses an action that is done *by* the subject of the sentence, the verb is called **active**:

> Miss Shaw *corrected* the algebra tests. [*Miss Shaw*, the subject, is the doer of the action.]
>
> The hot grease *had blistered* his right arm. [*Grease*, the subject, is the doer of the action.]

When a verb expresses an action that is done *to* the subject of the sentence, the verb is called **passive**:

> The algebra tests *were corrected* by Miss Shaw. [*Tests*, the subject, is the receiver of the action done by Miss Shaw.]
>
> His right arm *had been blistered* by the hot grease. [*Arm*, the subject, is the receiver of the action.]

Passive verbs generally consist of a form of the verb *be* plus the past participle: *is baked, are being watched, was written, were taken, has been eaten, had been taught, should have been kept, will be stolen.*

Both kinds of verbs—active and passive—are useful. The trick is knowing when it is best to use each kind. If, for example, you think the receiver of the action is far more important than the doer, you can call attention to the receiver by using a passive verb. Notice the difference between these two sentences:

ACTIVE VERB: The frost *damaged* thousands of orange trees. [The emphasis is on the doer of the action—the frost.]

PASSIVE VERB: Thousands of orange trees *were damaged* by the frost. [The emphasis is on the receiver of the action—the thousands of trees.]

Or suppose the doer of the action is unimportant, unknown, or obvious. By using a passive verb, you can express your meaning effectively without even mentioning the doer of the action:

> All residents of the bay area *should be warned* of the danger. [The doer is unimportant.]
>
> A copy of the test questions *had been stolen.* [The person or persons who stole the copy are not known.]
>
> George *was expelled* from school last week. [It is obvious that he was expelled by the head of the school.]

Sometimes it might be tactless or embarrassing to mention the doer of the action. For example:

> Mr. Turner had made a rather costly error in the estimate.

It would be kinder to Mr. Turner to omit his name. A passive verb would make it possible:

> A rather costly error *had been made* in the estimate.

Except for the kinds of sentences you have just seen, active verbs are usually better than passive. Using passive verbs where there is no good reason for them tends to make sentences sound unnaturally stiff and awkward. Do you ever write sentences that sound as wordy and artificial as these?

> The Channel 5 newscast is watched every evening right after supper by my mother and father.
>
> Several post cards to our friends were written by us while waiting at Union Station for our train.
>
> The French test was worried about for two weeks by Jerry.

Such awkward sentences are easily improved. All you have to do is to make the doer of the action the subject of an active verb:

> Every evening right after supper my mother and father *watch* the Channel 5 newscast.
>
> We *wrote* several post cards to our friends while waiting at Union Station for our train.
>
> Jerry *worried* about the French test for two weeks.

EXERCISE (8) Improve the following awkward sentences by using active verbs instead of passive. Write your revised sentences on a sheet of paper, underlining the active verbs.

1 The boat was quickly rowed to the opposite shore by the guide.
2 An attempt to tidy up her room before Aunt Martha's visit had been made by my sister Eileen.

3   A hamburger and a piece of lemon pie were next eaten by the truck driver.
4   *Moby Dick* and *The Sea Wolf* were read during spring vacation by several of the boys.
5   The noise in the upstairs apartment was constantly complained about by the tenants.

EXERCISE (9) In each of the following sentences the doer of the action (the subject) is too unimportant or obvious to be mentioned or should not be mentioned for reasons of tact. Improve each sentence by using a passive verb and omitting mention of the doer. When you write your revised sentences, underline the passive verbs.

1   Grandmother had added the figures in the first two columns wrong.
2   Messengers will deliver all merchandise bought during the sale the day after the purchase.
3   The members elected Clifton president of the Student Council in his junior year.
4   Mrs. Barnes sent Mr. Johnson's letter to Mr. Jolson by mistake.
5   Some unknown thief or thieves robbed the Milford Bank last Friday night.

VARYING THE SENTENCE PATTERN

FOR EMPHASIS

If it were the fashion for the girls at your school to wear low-heeled shoes, a girl who appeared in high heels would attract special attention. If it were the custom for the men in a large business office to wear four-in-hand ties, everyone would notice the employee who came wearing a bow tie. Anything that differs from the usual stands out. This is true not only in fashions but also in language, as you will see.

Most of the sentences we use are of the same general pattern, with the parts in a fixed order: *subject—verb, subject—verb—object,* or *subject—verb—complement.* We are so used to this order, which we learned by imitation in childhood, that most of us use it without even realizing that we do.

There is nothing wrong with this order, of course; do not get the idea that there is. In fact, it is only because most of our sentences follow this order that we have a chance to provide interesting variety and emphasis in our writing. How? By *occasionally* changing the order of the sentence parts.

Begin with a modifier. One of the easiest ways to break the monotony of a paragraph in which every sentence starts with the subject is to look for modifiers that can be shifted to the beginning of one or two of the sentences. The modifiers should be important, of course, because shifting them from their usual place to the beginning will call special attention to them. Unless they deserve this attention, they will seem out of place in an unusual spot.

USUAL ORDER: Complaints began pouring in *immediately.*
SHIFTED: *Immediately* complaints began pouring in.

USUAL ORDER: The Student Council handles all disciplinary problems *at our school.*
SHIFTED: *At our school* the Student Council handles all disciplinary problems. [The sentence now implies that at other schools this is not true.]

USUAL ORDER: Dad finally gave his permission, *hoping to end the argument.*
SHIFTED: *Hoping to end the argument,* Dad finally gave his permission.

Notice how well you can emphasize a contrast between two sentences by shifting important modifiers to the beginning:

USUAL ORDER: Mr. Zwicker was an arrogant, domineering slave driver *at the plant.* He was just a meek, henpecked husband *at home.*
SHIFTED: *At the plant* Mr. Zwicker was an arrogant, domineering slave driver. *At home* he was just a meek, henpecked husband.

USUAL ORDER: Mr. Sweeney was a brilliant orator in Mother's opinion. He seemed quite stupid *to me.*
SHIFTED: Mr. Sweeney was a brilliant orator in Mother's opinion. *To me* he seemed quite stupid.

Put the noun before its adjectives. Since adjectives usually precede the nouns they modify, shifting them to a position after their nouns is another effective way to gain emphasis and to vary the sentence pattern.

USUAL ORDER: His *low, hesitant* voice made a deep impression on the students.
SHIFTED: His voice, *low and hesitant*, made a deep impression on the students.

USUAL ORDER: A *small but beautiful* ivory box was Nancy's choice.
SHIFTED: An ivory box, *small but beautiful,* was Nancy's choice.

Put the verb before the subject.   Shifting a modifier from its usual position is not the only way to gain emphasis and variety in your sentences.   The main parts of a sentence, also, can be shifted about.   For example, notice these sentences, in which the subject comes before the verb, as it does in most statements:

> The *farmer* and the hired *man*, sputtering with rage, **rushed** out.
> The ugliest *woman* ever seen in Madrid **stood** in the center of the stage.

Suppose each of these sentences was important in a story you were writing—so important that you wanted it to stand out in a dramatic way.   You could easily highlight each of the sentences by "inverting" the order of the parts, putting the verb before the subject:

> Out **rushed** the *farmer* and the hired *man*, sputtering with rage.
> In the center of the stage **stood** the ugliest *woman* ever seen in Madrid.

Now, since the sentence pattern is different from the usual pattern, the sentences will get special attention from the reader.

Begin with the predicate complement.   The usual place for a predicate complement is after the linking verb.   Ordinarily that is where you should put it:

> Mr. Leonard had never been a *coward*.
> And they were very *grateful* for our help.

But if you feel that the complement is of special importance, you may want to emphasize it for the reader.   You can do so by shifting it to the beginning of the sentence, preceding the subject:

> A *coward* Mr. Leonard had never been.   [He might have been a liar or a thief.]
> And very *grateful* were they for our help.

Begin with the object of the verb.   If you are sure that the object of the verb in an occasional sentence deserves emphasis, it too can be moved out of its usual spot to the beginning.   Compare the following pairs of sentences to see what a different effect you can produce by shifting the object:

> s—v—o: We carefully packed the crystal *goblets* in excelsior.
> o—s—v: The crystal *goblets* we carefully packed in excelsior.

> s—v—o: No one could explain the *reason* for this outburst.
> o—s—v: The *reason* for this outburst no one could explain.

And see how clearly the contrast between two sentences stands out when the object comes first in one or both of the sentences:

Our counselor didn't mind noise or practical jokes. *Dishonesty,* however, he would not tolerate.

All the easy *jobs* Norman and Sam did by themselves. The hard *work* they left for the rest of us.

Remember that all these ways for gaining emphasis by varying the sentence pattern should be used sparingly—and only when the emphasis is important to the meaning. Used too often or without good reason, they will tend to make your writing sound artificial and stilted.

EXERCISE 10 Rewrite each of the following sentences, changing the pattern in a way that will give special emphasis to the part of the sentence specified in brackets.

1 Mr. Ellery had never heard such outrageous demands before. [Object of the verb.]

2 All hope of saving the trapped men was lost by morning. [The second prepositional phrase.]

3 My brother kept most of the prize money for himself. [Object of the verb.]

4 Very few families owned automobiles in those days. [The prepositional phrase.]

5 Mike kept that job for only three months. [Object of the verb.]

6 A great clinic rose from these humble beginnings. [Invert the sentence to give dramatic emphasis to the idea of humble beginnings.]

7 Jamison will never be a first-rate novelist. [The predicate complement.]

8 His relaxed, friendly manner helped me get through the interview. [The adjective modifiers of the subject.]

9 He stopped suddenly and looked back over his shoulder. [The adverb modifying *stopped.*]

10 The credit for this wonderful achievement belongs to a citizen of our great state. [Invert the sentence to give dramatic emphasis to the "citizen of our great state."]

EXERCISE 11 Rewrite one or both of the sentences in each of the following pairs, changing the word order in a way that will emphasize the contrast between the sentences.

1 Walter saved two of the stories for the February issue of *Hi-Lights.* He threw the rest into the wastebasket.

2 Mr. Hansen was pleasant, easygoing, and rather silly at scout meetings. He was stern and serious in chemistry class.
3 Giving pep talks in assembly was a pleasure for Alice. It was sheer torture for Paul.
4 Most of the reviews of the new Broadway play praised the plot. They severely criticized the acting.
5 Dan put his own gym clothes back in our locker. He left mine on a bench in the shower room.

EXERCISE (12) REVIEW   Rewrite the following sentences, making the changes suggested in brackets at the end of each.

1 John Paul Jones was an American naval officer in the Revolutionary War. He was born in Scotland. [Combine into one sentence by changing the first sentence to an appositive.]
2 The *Daily News* photographer fought his way through the crowd. He ducked under the rope. Then he darted into the warehouse. [Combine the three sentences by using a compound verb.]
3 Suddenly the guide stopped talking and looked upward. He was searching the horizon for clouds. [Combine by changing the second sentence to a participial phrase.]
4 Hurrying to answer the doorbell, the vase was knocked off the table. [Correct the dangling participle by supplying a subject that it can sensibly modify.]
5 The children behaved like angels for the first hour or so. They were unmanageable by the end of the day. [Change the word order in a way that will emphasize the contrast between the two sentences.]
6 A furious wind lashed at them. It swung their packs back and forth on their shoulders. It numbed their hands. [Combine by changing the second and third sentences to participial phrases joined by *and.*]
7 The committee should have provided enough rooms to accommodate all the delegates. [Rewrite in a more tactful way, using a passive verb to avoid mentioning the doer of the action.]
8 The costumes were made by the sewing classes. They were designed for the operetta by Miss Albright. [Combine by changing the second sentence to a participial phrase.]
9 Grandfather approved of our watching variety shows and quiz programs. He despised crime stories. [Change the word order in the second sentence to emphasize the contrast.]
10 The first two chapters were read by Alvin in fifth-period study hall. [Rewrite to avoid the awkward passive verb.]

CHAPTER 15

COMBINING

IDEAS

IN COMPLEX

SENTENCES

292

By now most of you have learned to be suspicious of advertisements that promise to teach the customer how to play a musical instrument in a few easy lessons. The lessons may be helpful; they may even be *easy*—but unless the learner is willing to work hard at practicing, he will never become a skillful player.

In this chapter you will learn two more tricks for combining ideas into effective sentences—*complex* sentences, this time. In several short and quite easy lessons you will see, first, what subordinate clauses are and, second, when and how to use them to make your exact meaning clear. But these lessons, like those in the advertisements, can just teach you the way. How skillful you become in writing good sentences depends on your willingness to practice what you learn.

The exercises in this chapter will give you some practice in combining ideas in complex sentences. But the exercises are only a beginning. To become truly proficient, you must keep on practicing —in your own writing.

THE SUBORDINATE CLAUSE

Suppose that you are telling a story in which a delayed telegram plays an important part. In telling the story, you might use any one of the following sentences:

Mr. Norton's telegram arrived *later.*
Mr. Norton's telegram arrived *in the afternoon.*
Mr. Norton's telegram arrived *after Dad had left for the airport with Andy.*

As you can see, the italicized items in the sentences all do the same kind of work. All are adverb modifiers; each modifies the predicate verb in its sentence by telling *when* the telegram from Mr. Norton arrived.

In the first sentence the modifier is a single word—the adverb *later.* In the second, it is a group of words—a prepositional phrase.

In the third, the modifier is also a group of words, but of a different kind. This kind of word group has a subject and a verb of its own:

$$\text{after Dad had left for the airport with Andy}$$

But (and this is important!) though the group of words has a subject and a verb, it is not a sentence. By itself it does not make sense. It is only a part of a sentence—a part which does the same sort of work that the single word *later* does in the first example sentence.

A group of words that contains a subject and a verb and that does the work of a single word in a sentence is called a subordinate clause.

In this chapter you will learn about two kinds of subordinate clauses: **adverb clauses**, which do the work of adverbs, and **adjective clauses**, which do the work of adjectives. These are the clauses you will find most useful in improving your sentences.

THE WORK DONE

BY ADVERB CLAUSES

294

Most adverb clauses modify verbs. They are extremely useful modifiers, since they make it possible for us to tell such important facts as *where, when, how, for what reason,* or *for what purpose* an action is done:

> I put the presents *where Mike won't find them.* [Tells *where* I *put* the presents.]
> Kenneth left the committee meeting *before Alice arrived.* [Tells *when* Kenneth *left.*]
> He looked *as if he were pleased.* [Tells *how* he *looked.*]
> Norris won *because the farmers voted for him.* [Tells the *reason* why he *won.*]
> She left early *so that she could avoid the heavy traffic.* [Tells her *purpose* in leaving early.]

By using an adverb clause, we can also make clear *under what condition* the main statement is true:

> *If Jerry drives his car,* they can ride with him. [Tells the *condition* under which they *can ride* with him.]
> Dan will come *unless he has to work.* [Tells the *condition* under which Dan *will come.*]

And by using an adverb clause beginning with *though* or *although*, we can make it clear that the main statement is true *in spite of* the idea expressed in the clause:

> *Although he smiled politely,* he was angry.
> Dr. Evans was still in his office, *though it was quite late.*

Subordinating conjunctions. Adverb clauses begin with subordinating conjunctions—words like *when, after, before, until, since, as soon as, because, so that, as if, where, wherever, though, unless.* These words are important because they are the words that make it possible for us to show the relationship between the clause and the verb in the main statement. See what different relationships you can show by changing the subordinating conjunction:

> Jane will call you **if** *he comes.*
> **When** *he comes,* Jane will call you.
> Jane will call you **after** *he comes.*
> **Before** *he comes,* Jane will call you.
> Jane will call you **unless** *he comes.*

In all of these sentences the clause modifies the verb *will call.* Notice that an adverb clause may—like an adverb—come before or after the verb it modifies.

EXERCISE (1) Divide a sheet of paper into two columns. In the first column, write the adverb clause in each of the following sentences. Draw one line under the subject of each clause and two lines under the verb. Circle the subordinating conjunction. In the second column, write the verb the clause modifies. Number your answers.

1 While she was scolding me, two other boys ran across the lawn.
2 Tim hated Mrs. Grimes because she had laughed at him.
3 Joe acts cocky whenever Louise is around.
4 Unless the delegates can agree on a compromise, the conference will end in failure.
5 Even Alvis, their boxer, looked as if he had lost his last friend.
6 When she came back from Atlanta, Cleo had a new hairdo and a Southern accent.
7 If you buy a giant-size box of Brighto, you will get a free sponge.
8 Look before you leap.
9 Most of the animals in the Children's Zoo wander wherever they please.
10 Though she was only in her teens, Maureen had already written a successful novel.

USING ADVERB CLAUSES

TO IMPROVE SENTENCES

If you are an avid reader of detective novels, you probably enjoy being mystified by the authors. The more baffling an author can make his story, the more you enjoy it. But being baffled by a writer who deliberately sets out to be mysterious is one thing; being baffled by a writer who hasn't taken the pains to make his intended meaning clear is quite another.

A good writer does all he can to make it easy for readers to see how his ideas are related. He does not leave it up to the readers to figure out the relationship; he makes it so clear that it cannot be misunderstood. Let's look at a simple example to illustrate this point.

Suppose you had written the following sentences in the first draft of a paper:

> Mr. Paxton liked his job with Atlas Engineers. He had to spend most of his time in mining camps.

You have two ideas here, both expressed clearly. But you haven't made the connection between the ideas clear to the reader. You can make it clear by changing one of the sentences to an adverb clause beginning with a conjunction that shows how the two ideas are related. Did you mean that Mr. Paxton liked his job in spite of having to live in mining camps? You can show this meaning by using the conjunction *although* or *though*:

> *Although he had to spend most of his time in mining camps,* Mr. Paxton liked his job with Atlas Engineers.

If you meant that his having to live in mining camps was the reason for his liking his job, you can show this by using *because* or *since*:

> Mr. Paxton liked his job with Atlas Engineers *because he had to spend most of his time in mining camps.*

Or did you mean that his liking his job (and wanting to keep it) was the cause of his having to live in mining camps? If so, turn the first sentence into an adverb clause and use *because* or *since*:

> *Because Mr. Paxton liked his job with Atlas Engineers,* he had to spend most of his time in mining camps.

Each of the three combined sentences is better than the original two-sentence version. The revised sentences are not better because they are longer sentences. They are better because they contain a word that clearly shows how the ideas are related.

When you write, use this trick of combining related ideas into a complex sentence by using an adverb clause beginning with a conjunction that shows how the ideas are related. Your sentences will not only sound more adult; they will *be* more adult. Children do not often see the relationships between ideas. Adults do—and in their speech and writing they make these relationships clear to their listeners and readers.

EXERCISE (2) Combine each of the following groups of sentences by expressing one of the ideas in an adverb clause. You will use one of the following conjunctions in each of your combined sentences to show how the ideas are related: *after, although, as soon as, because, just as, since, so that, though, when, while.*

Punctuation note: A comma should be used after an adverb clause that begins a sentence, to show the reader where the adverb clause ends and the main part of the sentence begins.

1 The men wore thick woolen socks and heavy boots. Their feet were badly frostbitten before the end of the climb.
2 The paint Dad used was too thick. The kitchen walls are streaked.
3 Miss Larson turned to write the list of spelling demons on the board. Ken slipped the note to Larry.
4 You will find it a good idea to keep all your canceled checks. You will have proof of payment in case the question comes up.
5 I saw the horrified look on Dad's face. I knew immediately he'd never give me permission to quit school.
6 Jim was putting the flask back on the flame. The tube broke off and fell to the floor, scattering bits of glass in all directions.
7 The Hartford High debating team is sure to win. It has far and away the best coach of any school in the state.
8 Dictators demand unquestioning obedience and blind loyalty from everyone. They do little to deserve such rewards.
9 Mr. Cornwall noticed a misspelled word in the first paragraph. He was just signing his name to the letter.
10 The councilmen heard Mayor Tooley's reasons for firing the clerk. They commended his action.
11 Arthur hid the bulky package far back in one corner of the closet. His younger brothers kept watch for him at the top of the stairs.
12 Carol and Mary Ellen went home. Margaret Ann dashed to the telephone to tell Sue about their plans.

BY ADJECTIVE CLAUSES

An adjective, as you know, is a word that is used to modify a noun or a pronoun. A clause that does the same sort of work in a sentence that an adjective does is an **adjective clause**:

ADJECTIVE: A *tactful* man can avoid arguments.
CLAUSE: A man *who is tactful* can avoid arguments.

ADJECTIVE: The staff needs a *larger* office.
CLAUSE: The staff needs an office *that has room for three desks and two files.*

The italicized clause in the first pair of examples describes *man* just as the adjective *tactful* does. The clause in the second pair describes *office* just as the adjective *larger* does.

Relative pronouns.   Most adjective clauses are easy to recognize, since they usually follow the noun or pronoun they describe and begin with one of five pronouns—*who, whose, whom, which,* or *that*:

They want a clerk **who** *can speak Spanish.*

Ed is the only student in our class **whose** *work shows originality.*

I have never known a person **whom** *I have disliked more.*

Dad is still wearing a suit **which** *he bought twenty years ago.*

Phil has a baseball **that** *Ty Cobb autographed.*

These pronouns that begin the adjective clauses are called **relative pronouns**. Notice that in each example the relative pronoun attaches, or "relates," the clause to the word described by the clause (as shown by the arrows).

A relative pronoun not only "relates" the clause to the modified word, but it also has a use in the clause itself. It may have any of the uses that a noun might have in a sentence. It may, for example, be the subject of the clause, the object of the verb in the clause, or the object of a preposition in the clause:

SUBJECT: Any member **who** *sells ten tickets* will get one free.
OBJECT: Mr. Alfonso is the delegate **whom** *Ted interviewed.*
OBJECT OF PREPOSITION: The company **that** *I wrote to* sent me several samples.

You will find it easy to figure out how the pronoun is used if you follow this procedure. First, separate the adjective clause from the rest of the sentence:

SENTENCE: Any member who sells ten tickets will get one free.
CLAUSE: who sells ten tickets

Second, since the relative pronoun "stands for" the noun the clause modifies, substitute that noun for the relative pronoun:

> member
> ~~who~~ sells ten tickets

Once you have made this substitution, the rest is simple. The verb in the clause is *sells*. If you ask "Who or what sells?" you find that the subject of the verb is *member*. Since *member* is the word you substituted for *who*, you know that in the clause *who* is the subject.

Now follow the same procedure with the next example, first separating the clause from the rest of the sentence:

SENTENCE: Mr. Alfonso is the delegate whom Ted interviewed.
CLAUSE: whom Ted interviewed

Substituting the modified word for the relative pronoun gives you:

> delegate
> ~~whom~~ Ted interviewed

In this, the verb is *interviewed*. *Ted* is the subject of the verb. *Delegate*, the person who receives the action of the verb, is the object. Since *delegate* is a substitute for *whom*, you know that in this clause *whom* is used as the object of the verb.

Relative adverbs. Even though most adjective clauses begin with a relative pronoun, they may also begin with such words as *where*, *when*, *why*, and *after*:

> The shop **where** *we bought the records* is closed. [Modifies the noun *shop*; tells which shop is closed.]
> Do you remember the day **when** *the tornado struck?* [Modifies the noun *day*; tells which day.]
> Is that the reason **why** *he got angry?* [Modifies the noun *reason*.]
> Harry was fired the week **after** *Mr. Cramer resigned*. [Modifies the noun *week*; tells which week.]

And sometimes—particularly in conversation or in writing intended to be rather informal—the introductory pronoun or adverb is not used. In speaking the following sentences, for example, you would quite likely not use the words shown in brackets:

Sally wore the corsage [that] *Bill sent.*
We usually watch the TV programs [which] *Miss Elpers recommends.*
I'll never forget the morning [when] *I wrecked the car.*

EXERCISE 3 Divide a sheet of paper into two columns. In the first column, write the adjective clause in each of the following sentences. Draw one line under the subject of each clause, two lines under the verb, and three lines under the object of the verb (if there is one). In the second column, write the noun the clause modifies. Number your answers.

1 The commercials which I disliked most were Joe's favorites.
2 An anemometer is an instrument that measures the velocity of the wind.
3 That was the dean whose pen you borrowed to sign your name!
4 Sally Clark, whom Miss Norton had appointed chairman, was absent.
5 His parents are looking forward to the day when he graduates from Yale.
6 Don Turner, who directs the Little Theater plays, used to be a radio actor when he lived in Chicago.
7 The kitchen was the only place where Charles could do his work in peace.
8 All the candidates whom the Better Citizens League supported were elected.
9 He knew of only one person to whom he could turn for help—the President. [The preposition *to* is part of the clause.]
10 The sibyls were women prophets that the ancient Greeks and Romans consulted about the future.

USING ADJECTIVE CLAUSES

TO IMPROVE SENTENCES

Have you noticed that no matter how many people appear in an elaborate song-and-dance act in a TV show, the stars are always the center of attention? This does not happen by accident. The director knows that to the audience the stars are the chief attraction in any number. So he does all he can to make them stand out from the others. He has the spotlights focused on them; he has them wear costumes different from everyone else's; and he gives them the center of the stage, putting everyone else more or less in the background.

This is as it should be. The important features *deserve* more emphasis and attention than the less important. A good director sees to it that they get the emphasis they deserve and that the less important features do not distract the attention of the audience from them.

Giving emphasis to what deserves emphasis is as important in writing as it is in directing stage shows. A good writer, like a good director, puts important ideas in the spotlight and does not allow less important details to distract the attention of his readers from the important facts. How does he do this? One way is by making effective use of adjective clauses. Let's look at a few examples.

The following pairs of sentences are typical of those that a beginning writer might write in the first draft of a paper:

> Harriet Beecher Stowe and her husband helped a number of slaves to escape to safety. Her husband shared her hatred of slavery.
>
> Ralph Quentin volunteered to get three trucks to pick up the paper for the city-wide drive. Ralph's father owns a trucking company.
>
> Except for the rainy season, the climate of the Caribbean coast is dry and hot. The rainy season lasts from April to November.
>
> Mr. Palmer ended by telling a long, involved joke. Everyone there had heard the joke dozens of times before.

As you can see, the first sentence in each pair tells an important fact. The second merely gives an explanatory or descriptive detail. Each of the details is interesting enough, but certainly not as important as the fact in the first sentence. By expressing the details in adjective clauses instead of in separate sentences, the writer can push them into the background, where they belong. When he does, the important facts will stand out more clearly:

> Harriet Beecher Stowe and her husband, *who shared her hatred of slavery*, helped a number of slaves to escape to safety.
>
> Ralph Quentin, *whose father owns a trucking company*, volunteered to get three trucks to pick up the paper for the city-wide drive.
>
> Except for the rainy season, *which lasts from April to November*, the climate of the Caribbean coast is dry and hot.
>
> Mr. Palmer ended by telling a long, involved joke *which everyone there had heard dozens of times before*.

In each of the example sentences we have just covered, it is easy to see which of the two ideas is more important and should get the emphasis. But suppose you had these two ideas to tell:

> Hoover Dam is as tall as a sixty-story building. It stores the entire flow of the Colorado River for two years.

Only you, as the writer, would know how you wanted your readers to view these facts. If you wanted them to consider the facts equally important, you would use separate sentences, of course. But if the point you wanted to emphasize was the height of this gigantic dam, you should express the second idea in an adjective clause to show that it is of less importance:

> Hoover Dam, *which stores the entire flow of the Colorado River for two years*, is as tall as a sixty-story building.

On the other hand, if you wanted to emphasize the vast amount of water stored by the dam, you should "de-emphasize" the fact about the height by turning it into an adjective clause:

> Hoover Dam, *which is as tall as a sixty-story building*, stores the entire flow of the Colorado River for two years.

As you look over the first-draft sentences in your themes to see if they can be improved, keep your readers in mind. Make it easy for them to see which ideas are of greatest importance by using adjective clauses for the less important, "background" details.

EXERCISE 4 Combine each of the following pairs of sentences into a more effective single sentence by using an adjective clause to express the less important idea. Be ready to read your revised sentences aloud. (The adjective clauses in all revised sentences but 1, 3, 4, and 8 are to be set off.)

1 The clerks sort the envelopes and send them through a canceling machine. This machine postmarks more than five hundred letters a minute.

2 Luckily Dave Perkins was there and stopped the bleeding by applying a tourniquet. Dave teaches a first-aid course at night school.

3 In a showcase along the west wall of the library were twelve silver trophies. McKinley Junior High teams had won these trophies over the past fifteen years.

4 Six months later we found the lost insurance policies in an old suitcase. Mother had stored the suitcase away in the attic and forgotten it.

5   The toastmaster kept the audience laughing for two hours. His voice reminded me of Art Linkletter's. [Use *whose*.]

6   The Interstate Commerce Commission was created to regulate commerce between the States. It consists of eleven people appointed by the President.

7   Ironically, Richard III reigned over England for only two years. He had stopped at nothing to gain the throne.

8   Before the end of the week three of the reference books had disappeared. Miss Martin had put the books on the reserve shelf for our history class.

9   Without thinking, the banquet chairman had seated Mrs. Givens right next to Mr. Townsend. Mr. Townsend had opposed Mayor Givens in the last election.

10 On the way back to the Loop we stopped at the Museum of Science and Industry. Colleen Moore's famous doll house was on display at the museum. [Use *where*.]

AVOIDING MISPLACED ADJECTIVE CLAUSES

An adjective clause should come right after the word it modifies —or as close to that word as possible. In some sentences it is not possible to put the clause immediately after the modified word:

> The producer of the play, *who was an old friend of my father's,* gave us two tickets.

Yet even though the clause follows the noun *play* rather than the noun *producer,* which it describes, the meaning of this sentence is clear. You know that it was the *producer,* not the *play,* who was an old friend. The relative pronoun *who*—which always refers to a person—is a sure sign that the clause describes a person and not a thing.

But sometimes placing an adjective clause too far away from the word it is intended to modify may cause the sentence to have a ridiculous meaning. For example:

> The ski poles belong to his next-door neighbor *that you saw strapped on the top of his car.*
> Friday afternoon the three boys are to report to the superintendent and Judge Davis *who admitted stealing the football tickets.*

The first of these sentences would make a reader chuckle at the thought of the ridiculous plight of the poor neighbor. The second would, on first reading, make him wonder what this world was coming to—what with a superintendent and a judge admitting a petty theft. The reader can, of course, figure out the meaning that was intended. But a careful writer does not leave it up to his readers to juggle the parts of his sentences about until they make sense. He puts the modifying clauses where they belong:

> The ski poles *that you saw strapped on the top of his car* belong to his next-door neighbor.
> Friday afternoon the three boys *who admitted stealing the football tickets* are to report to the superintendent and Judge Davis.

EXERCISE (5) Rewrite each of the following sentences, putting the adjective clause where it will clearly modify the word it was intended to modify.

Punctuation note: None of the adjective clauses in your revised sentences should be set off by commas. All are "restrictive" clauses.

1 The house in Evanston has a large recreation room that the Wilsons bought at such a bargain price.
2 Bob sadly reported that he must have thrown the newspaper clippings into the garbage can which I had borrowed from our school librarian.
3 The reporter asked the player to pose with the Homecoming Queen who had made the winning touchdown.
4 Dad finally let Mother give the gray suit to a neighbor that was too big for him.
5 The little German boy quickly made friends with the janitor whom the Andersons had adopted after their return from Europe last year.

WHAT A COMPLEX SENTENCE IS

What is the difference between the following sentences?

I dislike giggly girls.

I dislike girls who giggle.

As far as meaning goes, there is really no difference between the sentences. But grammatically there is a difference. The first sentence has only one subject and verb combination—*I dislike.* The second has two. One is in the main part (or main *clause*) of the sentence—*I dislike.* The other is in the subordinate clause—*who giggle.*

A sentence that has only one subject and verb is called a **simple sentence.** A sentence that has in it a subordinate clause is called a **complex sentence.**

In a simple sentence the subject or the verb—or both—may be *compound:*

SUBJECT: *Dad* and *Mother* groaned at the news.
VERB: Nora **smiled** sweetly but **shook** her head.
BOTH: *Ted* and *Ned* quickly **stood** up and **bowed.**

A complex sentence may have more than one subordinate clause:

> *Although she complained,* she paid for the window *that Leo had broken.*
>
> We don't want members *who attend the club parties* but *who never show up at the meetings.*

Knowing the difference between a simple sentence and a complex sentence is *in itself* of little importance. What is important is that you make effective use of both kinds of sentences in your speech and writing. If you make a constant effort to combine ideas in the ways you have learned in this chapter and the preceding one, your skill in expressing your ideas clearly, exactly, and interestingly will grow.

305

EXERCISE (6) **REVIEW** Divide a sheet of paper into three columns. In the first column, copy each of the italicized groups of words in the following sentences. In the second column, identify the kind of word group by writing "Phrase" or "Clause." In the third column, write "Adj." if the word group is used as an adjective modifier, or "Adv." if it is used as an adverb modifier. Number your answers with the numbers of the sentences.

1 The day *after he had turned in his report* Terry was called to the office.
2 Terry felt better *after he talked with Mr. Tice.*
3 *After this embarrassing experience* Terry resolved to do his own work.
4 They pitched their tents in a spot *where an overhanging ledge would protect them from the wind.* [What kind of spot?]
5 You should have put the box of matches *where the baby couldn't reach it.*

6　The person *who checks the time for the tests* should have a watch *with a second hand.*

7　Don will never forget the day *when he met President Eisenhower.*

8　*Before she left,* she tucked her report card *under the blotter.*

9　Any passenger *whose baggage was damaged* should file a report *before November 5.*

10　The money *he spent for repairs* would have bought a new house.

11　*Although we have invited him many times,* Harry has never returned to Coral Point *since that summer.*

12　*Since it was late,* David decided to wait until the next morning to tell Greg about the watch *he had found.*

EXERCISE (7)　REVIEW　On a sheet of paper, indicate whether each of the following statements is true or false by writing "T" or "F" after the number of the statement. Be ready to explain in class *why* the statements you labeled *F* are false.

1　The word group "Because copper is a good conductor of heat" is a sentence, since it has a subject (*copper*) and a verb (*is*).

2　Subordinating conjunctions like *because, when,* and *after* are extremely useful words because they can help us show the relationship which exists between two ideas.

3　Most adverb clauses modify adjectives or adverbs.

4　In the sentence "The week *after we moved to our new house* Dad was transferred," the italicized words are an adjective clause modifying the noun *week.*

5　An adverb clause may come before or after the verb it modifies.

6　In the sentence "The book to which he referred was *Moby Dick*," the relative pronoun *which* is the object of the preposition *to.*

7　In the sentence "Frank was fired *because of his impudence*," the italicized words are an adverb clause telling why Frank was fired.

8　In the sentence "The side that gets the fewest points is the winner," the relative pronoun *that* is the subject of the verb *gets.*

9　In the sentence "I gave the package to the woman who answered the door," the relative pronoun *who* is the object of the preposition *to.*

10　In "We haven't heard from him since," *since* is an adverb. In "We haven't heard from him since last month," *since* is a preposition. In "We haven't heard from him since he left for Nevada," *since* is a subordinating conjunction.

EXERCISE 8 **REVIEW** Rewrite the following sentences, making the changes suggested in brackets at the end of each.

1 The Battle of Bunker Hill was a victory for the British. The courage displayed by the American troops strengthened the morale of our country. [Use an adverb clause to combine the sentences in a way which shows that the second statement was true in spite of the first statement.]

2 Laurence Olivier produced and directed the movie. He played the part of Richard III. [Use an adjective clause to combine the sentences in two ways: (a) to emphasize the part Olivier played, and (b) to emphasize his being the producer and director.]

3 Harold had done most of the work on the posters. He thought it unfair of Miss Evans to give all the credit to Laura. [Use an adverb clause to combine the sentences in a way which shows that the first fact is the reason.]

4 As a rule my cousin Gerald is extremely shy. He acted like a clown at the party. [Use an adjective clause to combine the sentences in a way that emphasizes Gerald's behavior at the party.]

5 As he crossed the street, Mr. Wells saw the little boy talking to a policeman that had thrown the snowball at him. [Rewrite so that the adjective clause clearly modifies the right word.]

6 In his hurry to get to the door first, Jim tripped over a toy elephant. His sister had left the elephant in the middle of the floor. [Use an adjective clause to combine the sentences in a way that gives less emphasis to the explanatory detail.]

7 These locusts travel in large swarms. They destroy nearly all the vegetation in their path. [Use an adjective clause to combine the sentences in a way that emphasizes the destructiveness.]

8 Mrs. Martin was putting her charge plate back into her purse. She noticed that her billfold was gone. [Use an adverb clause to combine the sentences in a way which shows that the first action happened at the same time as the second.]

9 The gray cashmere sweater is still in Field's window that I have been planning to buy. [Rewrite so that the adjective clause clearly modifies the right word.]

10 Stephen Crane wrote one of America's best war novels, *The Red Badge of Courage*. He had never seen a battle at the time. [Use an adverb clause to combine the sentences in a way which shows that the first statement was true in spite of the second statement.]

CHAPTER 16

COMPOUND

SENTENCES

308

In one way this chapter is quite different from the preceding one. The main purpose of the preceding chapter was to urge you to use *more* complex sentences in your writing. In this chapter, the main purpose is to urge you to use *fewer* compound sentences. The reason is not that compound sentences are, in themselves, poor sentences. Not at all. For some purposes, in fact, they are better than complex sentences or simple sentences. But many writers, especially untrained writers, tend to overuse compound sentences, expressing most of their ideas in this sentence pattern. And too much of the same thing—whether compound sentences or fried chicken or your favorite TV show—is likely to make it seem less attractive.

Skillful writers avoid this monotonous sameness in their work; they express their ideas in a variety of sentence forms: simple, complex, and compound. Learning how to determine which of your ideas should be expressed in compound sentences and which should be expressed in other kinds of sentences will help you become more skillful in writing. This chapter will show you how.

WHAT A COMPOUND SENTENCE IS

In grammar, the word *compound* means "consisting of two or more equal parts." Any of the parts of a simple sentence, as you probably remember, may be compound. Notice the italicized examples in the following sentences:

COMPOUND SUBJECT: *Terry* and *Timmy* were quarreling, as usual.
COMPOUND VERB: He *sealed* the envelope and *put* it in the safe.
COMPOUND OBJECT: The man ordered a *doughnut* and *coffee*.
COMPOUND INDIRECT OBJECT: Mr. Tompkins gave *Rob, Larry,* and *me* tickets for the All-Star game.
COMPOUND COMPLEMENT: The coat was *pretty* enough but too *expensive*.

Just as we can make any of the parts of a sentence compound, we can also make a sentence compound. We simply put together two (or more) simple sentences, joining them with a connecting word like *and* or *but*:

SIMPLE SENTENCES: Larry raked the leaves. Joe trimmed the hedge.

COMPOUND SENTENCE: Larry raked the leaves, **and** Joe trimmed the hedge.

SIMPLE SENTENCES: I called the number four times. Nobody answered.

COMPOUND SENTENCE: I called the number four times, **but** nobody answered.

A sentence that consists of two or more simple sentences is called a compound sentence.

Students sometimes confuse a simple sentence containing a compound verb with a compound sentence. Yet it is easy to tell the two apart. Just divide the sentence at the connecting word. If the part *before* this word and the part *after* it each has its own subject and verb, and each makes sense by itself, the sentence is truly a compound sentence. If either of the two parts does not have its own subject and verb, the sentence is not compound but merely a sentence containing a compound part.

COMPOUND SENTENCES

Mr. Snyder was wrong, | and | he admitted it.

Louise had plenty of money, | but | she wouldn't lend me any.

SIMPLE SENTENCES WITH COMPOUND VERBS

Mr. Snyder was wrong | and | admitted it.

Louise had plenty of money | but | wouldn't lend me any.

EXERCISE (1)   Five of the following sentences are compound; five are simple sentences with compound verbs. On a sheet of paper, write the numbers of the five *compound sentences*. After each number, write the subject and the verb of each of the two parts. In parentheses between them, write the connecting word.

1   The description starts on page 4 and ends on page 7.
2   Mrs. Higgins offered me a dollar and Dave fifty cents, but we refused them.
3   Every member must work on a committee or must sell tickets.
4   The description starts on page 4, and it ends on page 7.

5   I explained my idea to the manager and to the supervisor, but they just laughed.
6   Frank knew the combination of Tim's locker and Wayne's, but he couldn't remember his own.
7   In spite of the cold, Mrs. Brown took off her fur coat and used it to cover three children huddled in the lifeboat.
8   Mrs. Pitts must have forgotten her appointment, or she would have been here by now.
9   Dr. Walsh likes to tell jokes but always forgets the punch lines.
10 The golf ball bounced down the porch steps and rolled across the sidewalk into a muddy puddle.

WHEN TO USE

COMPOUND SENTENCES

Joining two simple sentences with a connecting word will always make a compound sentence of them. But it will not always make a *good* compound sentence. If, for example, a writer combines two sentences that are not closely related in meaning, the resulting sentence is likely to sound as ridiculous as these:

> The hero of the play was an American naval officer, and there was standing room only.
> Stephen Foster wrote more than 175 songs, and he died in an accidental fall in a Bowery rooming house.

And if a writer combines ideas that are not equal in importance, the compound sentence is almost sure to seem lopsided, as these are:

> In the last minute of play Alan Ameche made the winning touchdown, and he appeared on Ed Sullivan's show once.
> A huge dog barred my way, and it was standing near the gate.

The lesson taught by these "horrible" examples is plain: Use a compound sentence only to join ideas that (1) are closely related in meaning and (2) are equal in importance.

USING THE RIGHT CONNECTING WORDS

The connecting words that are used to join the parts of a compound sentence are called *coördinating conjunctions* because they join parts of equal importance. (*Coördinate* means "of equal rank.") The conjunctions you will find most useful are **and, but, yet, for, or,** and **so**.

Why should we have so many of these conjunctions? Why can't we get along with just one? If the only purpose of a connecting word was to join two simple sentences, then we could get along with just one—the conjunction *and*. But we use connecting words not only to join two sentences, but also (and more important) to show how the sentences are related to each other. So we need connecting words that show several different relationships. Without them, we could not make our exact meaning clear.

If, for example, you want to show merely that two ideas are equally important parts of a process, an event, or a description, the conjunction *and* is the right one to use:

> Peter sanded the shelves, **and** Clifford varnished them. [Two steps in a process.]
>
> In the last inning Jim Corbett made a home run, **and** Elmville won the game. [Two parts of an event.]
>
> His face and arms were covered with scratches, **and** his shirt hung in tatters. [Two parts of a description.]

But if you want to show a contrast between two ideas, you should not use the conjunction *and*, which merely shows an addition. To show contrast, you should use either *but* or *yet*:

> Yes, Peter sanded the shelves, **but** Clifford varnished them.
>
> Professor Stein's lecture was filled with technical terms, **yet** everyone seemed to enjoy it.

Suppose you want to show that one idea is the reason for or the explanation of the other idea. Then the conjunction *for* is the word to use:

> Gerald had little time to devote to social activities, **for** he was earning his way through school.
>
> There was no lack of servants, **for** labor was cheap then.

To join two ideas in a way that gives a choice between them, you would use *or*:

> Uncle Will drives as slowly as a snail, **or** he speeds along the highway like a racer.
>
> We'll have to hurry, **or** we won't get good seats.

Finally, to show that one idea is the result or consequence of the other, you should use the conjunction *so*:

> The sheriff did not want to alarm Mrs. Burke, **so** he said nothing about the robbery.

A comma is ordinarily used before a conjunction joining the two parts of a compound sentence. The comma makes it easy for a reader to tell where one part ends and the next begins. To see how helpful this comma can be, read the following sentences rapidly, as if you were reading them in a story:

> No one could remember their address but Mary knew their phone number.
> Mr. Elliot left a large tip for the waiters had been unusually efficient.
> After the meeting we met Larry and Sam and David gave them ten tickets to sell.

Without commas, these sentences are a bit baffling. Most readers would have to read them twice—slowly the second time—to understand their meaning. With commas before the conjunctions, a second reading would be unnecessary:

> No one could remember their address, **but** Mary knew their phone number.
> Mr. Elliot left a large tip, **for** the waiters had been unusually efficient.
> After the meeting we met Larry and Sam, **and** David gave them ten tickets to sell.

313

Make your compound sentences easy to read; put a comma before the conjunction.

EXERCISE 2 Read the sentences in each of the following pairs and decide (1) whether they are related in meaning and (2) whether they are equal in importance. If they are, make a compound sentence of them, using *and, but, yet, for, or,* or *so* to show the relationship between them. Write the compound sentences on a sheet of paper, numbering each with the number of the pair. Be sure to use a comma before the conjunction.

1 The captain of the *Titanic* had been warned several times of the iceberg. He paid no attention to the warnings.
2 You had better stand away from the curb. You will get splattered with mud.
3 Ten minutes later the fire chief rang a bell. The students trooped back to their classrooms.
4 Sir Alexander Fleming was born in Scotland. He discovered penicillin in 1928.

5 The recruits had been told about Major Holt's surprise inspections. They always kept the barracks in apple-pie order.

6 Hundreds of families had to go on relief. It was almost impossible to find work during the depression.

7 More than twenty-four million people have visited the National Gallery of Art since its opening. It was a gift to the American people from Andrew Mellon.

8 All the construction workers despised the foreman. No one dared complain about him to Mr. Petrie.

9 In 1826 Cooper wrote *The Last of the Mohicans.* The hero of the novel is Hawkeye, a courageous frontiersman.

10 Bill wanted to quit school after his junior year. His parents insisted on his going back.

COMPOUND SENTENCES

WITHOUT CONJUNCTIONS

Sometimes the relationship between two ideas is so obvious that we don't have to use a word like *but, for,* or *and* to show what it is. When you read the sentences in the following pairs, for example, you can easily understand how the two ideas are related:

A jet plane might get him there on time. A DC-6 never could.
Mabel was fired the very first day. She talked back to the boss.
There were three straight chairs along the wall. All were stacked high with books.

Even without the word *but,* you know that the second sentence in the first pair expresses a contrasting idea. You don't need the word *for* to see that in the second pair the second sentence gives the reason why Mabel was 'fired. In the last pair you know, even without an *and,* that the second sentence gives an equally important part of a two-part description.

When two sentences are as closely related in meaning as the ones in each of these pairs, they can effectively be made into a compound sentence. Since the relationship between the ideas is obvious, no conjunction is necessary. But a semicolon is needed to separate the two parts of the compound sentence:

A jet plane might get him there on time; a DC-6 never could.
Mabel was fired the very first day; she talked back to the boss.
There were three straight chairs along the wall; all were stacked high with books.

The semicolon indicates to the reader that there is a clear and close relationship between the two parts of each sentence.

Sometimes you show how the ideas in two sentences are related by using such words as *nevertheless, otherwise, therefore, then, however, besides,* and *in fact.* For example:

> The rules may seem unfair to you. *Nevertheless,* you will have to obey them.
> Gerald was not a good student. *In fact,* he ranked at the bottom of the class.
> Smooth-Glo paint is quite expensive. It will, *however,* outlast the cheaper brands.

If you want to call the reader's attention to the close relationship between the two sentences in each pair, you can do so easily—by making a compound sentence of them. You will not need a coördinating conjunction, since the words *Nevertheless, In fact,* and *however* show how the ideas are related. But you will need a semicolon (not a comma!) to show the reader where the first part ends and the next one begins:

> The rules may seem unfair to you; nevertheless, you will have to obey them.
> Gerald was not a good student; in fact, he ranked at the bottom of the class.
> Smooth-Glo paint is quite expensive; it will, however, outlast the cheaper brands.

315

EXERCISE (**3**) Read the sentences in each of the following pairs. If they are related in meaning, make a compound sentence of them in one of two ways: (1) by using an appropriate conjunction (*and, but, yet, so*) preceded by a comma, or (2) by using a semicolon. Use the second way only when the relationship between the ideas is obvious without a conjunction. The sentences in two of the pairs are not closely enough related to be combined in a compound sentence.

1 We collected eighty-four books for our Used-Book Fair. Only sixty were sold.
2 Dr. Stern's plane was grounded by bad weather. Otherwise he would have attended the conference.
3 It took us three hours to make a two-hour trip. Uncle Steve was driving.
4 By noon the soreness in Grandfather's arm had become an agonizing pain. He let us call Dr. Kent.
5 I knew that Don had plenty of money with him. Nevertheless I hesitated about asking him for a loan.

6 A number of Mark Twain's novels have been made into movies. His name means "two fathoms deep."
7 We should not condemn the ignorant. We should educate them.
8 Dixon managed to get the rubber life raft inflated. The three men crawled onto it.
9 Ed hated spinach in any form. He ate some to please Mother.
10 Mrs. Lincoln's education was fairly good. In fact, it was far superior to her husband's.
11 No one took Jim's warning seriously. He had cried wolf too many times before.
12 The Pony Express operated between St. Joseph, Missouri, and Sacramento, California. Lincoln's first inaugural address was carried by this mail service.
13 Two months later my father lost his job. We had to give up our house and move back to Grandfather's farm.
14 Mayor Norton had grown up in a slum area. Therefore he clearly understood all the problems.
15 I intended the remark as a joke. Clifford took it seriously.

GETTING RID OF "AND" SENTENCES

No matter how much you enjoy seeing Perry Como or Red Skelton or Lucille Ball, it would be pretty boring to have a steady diet of any one of these stars. Variety is important: in TV programs, in food, in clothes—even in the sentences we use.

A common fault in student writing is the overuse of compound sentences, especially those with *and*. Paragraphs in which almost every idea is hooked to another with *and* are likely to sound monotonous and childish to readers. Such paragraphs can easily be improved by changing some of the "and" sentences to other kinds. The *good* compound sentences should not be changed, of course; but the *poor* ones should be. Take these sentences, for example:

> Walter Reed discovered the cause of yellow fever, and he was an American army surgeon.
> The janitor finally found the missing ladder, and it was propped against the north wall of the heating plant.
> Captain Braddock told the detective to follow the tall, thin woman, and she was punching a time clock near the exit.

In each of these sentences the first part states an important idea, while the second merely gives a less important detail. Since the two ideas in each example are *not* of equal importance, they should not be joined in a compound sentence. A better way to express the ideas is to change the less important detail to an appositive, a participial phrase, or an adjective clause:

> Walter Reed, *an American army surgeon*, discovered the cause of yellow fever. [Appositive.]
> The janitor finally found the missing ladder *propped against the north wall of the heating plant*. [Participial phrase.]
> Captain Braddock told the detective to follow the tall, thin woman *who was punching a time clock near the exit*. [Adjective clause.]

The next two compound sentences are poor because the conjunction *and* does not show exactly how the ideas are related:

> Larry and I left the gym, and the snowdrifts were already waist deep.
> Sheriff Greeley won by a landslide vote, and he had been bitterly opposed by the Committee for Civic Reforms.

By changing one of the parts to an adverb clause beginning with a word that shows the relationship between the two ideas, you can easily improve the sentences:

> **When** *Larry and I left the gym*, the snowdrifts were already waist deep.
> **Although** *he had been bitterly opposed by the Committee for Civic Reforms*, Sheriff Greeley won by a landslide vote.

There is nothing wrong with the following compound sentences; the ideas in each are of equal importance, and the relationship between them is clearly shown by the conjunctions *and* and *but*.

> Marge sprained her ankle, and she had to be carried home.
> Sam had bought two flashlights, but he had forgotten to pack them.

But suppose the sentences appeared in a paragraph containing several other compound sentences, also good ones. You could easily provide a bit of variety by changing these particular sentences to simple sentences with compound verbs (since the subject of each part is the same person):

> Marge sprained her ankle and had to be carried home.
> Sam had bought two flashlights but had forgotten to pack them.

This is just a slight change in pattern, but it will help to relieve the monotony in the paragraph.

Improve each of the following compound sentences by changing one of its parts to the construction suggested in brackets.

1 At five minutes before ten Jerry rushed into the doctor's office, and he was wearing a pair of blue jeans. [Participial phrase.]

2 The most colorful character in the movie *Moby Dick* was Captain Ahab, and his part was played by Gregory Peck. [Adjective clause with *whose*.]

3 The young tenor was flattered by this enthusiastic applause, and he sang an encore. [Participial phrase.]

4 Lem Slocum was the referee at the game with Munster High, and he seemed to have it in for our team. [Appositive.]

5 Uncle Steve's most prized possession was a baseball bat, and Babe Ruth had once used it in a world-series game. [Adjective clause with *that*.]

6 King Louis XI was too stingy to spend a few francs for a new hat, and he spent immense sums to extend French territory in Europe. [Adverb clause with *Although*.]

7 The forsythia shrub is named after William Forsyth, and he was an English botanist. [Appositive.]

8 The castles of the Middle Ages were cold and damp even in summer, and the feudal lords spent as much time as possible outdoors. [Adverb clause with *Since*.]

9 The cord fabric of automobile tires is coated with casein, and it helps to keep the tires from overheating. [Adjective clause with *which*.]

10 The Saint Bernard has a wonderful sense of smell, and it can find persons buried several feet under the snow. [Participial phrase.]

11 Mozart was born in Salzburg, Austria, and his father was musical director for the archbishop there. [Adjective clause with *where*.]

12 The tortilla is a flat cake made of corn meal, and it is the staple food of the Mexican farmer. [Appositive.]

13 At night the San Francisco–Oakland Bay Bridge is lighted by yellow sodium-vapor lights, and these lights improve visibility for driving in fog. [Adjective clause with *that*.]

14 Michelangelo was only thirteen years old, and he was chosen to be a student at the new art school. [Adverb clause with *Although*.]

15 An immensely fat man elbowed his way through the crowd, and he was carrying an ice-cream cone. [Participial phrase.]

16 Gloria noticed a sign on the door, but she didn't bother to read it. [Compound verb.]

REVIEW   Which of the sentences in each of the following pairs is better—*a* or *b*?   Write your answers on a sheet of paper, numbering each.   Be ready to explain the reasons for your choices.

1 a) Dad is strict, but he works hard every day.
   b) Dad is strict, but he is always fair.
2 a) Walking past the post office, I suddenly remembered the letter in my coat pocket.
   b) I walked past the post office, and I suddenly remembered the letter in my coat pocket.
3 a) I would like to buy Dave's microscope, but I can't afford it.
   b) I would like to buy Dave's microscope, and I can't afford it.
4 a) For days he talked of nothing but Madison, where he had spent a week visiting friends.
   b) For days he talked of nothing but Madison, and he had spent a week visiting friends there.
5 a) Helen Keller had been blind and deaf from the age of two, and she graduated from Radcliffe with honors.
   b) Although she had been blind and deaf from the age of two, Helen Keller graduated from Radcliffe with honors.
6 a) The rain suddenly turned to sleet, and Jim had to slow the car down to a crawl.
   b) The rain suddenly turned to sleet, and we were tired from our long drive.
7 a) Davy Crockett, accompanied by twelve other Tennesseans, rode to Bexar to join Travis's small force.
   b) Davy Crockett rode to Bexar to join Travis's small force, and he was accompanied by twelve other Tennesseans.
8 a) Andrew Johnson understood the problems of the small Southern farmer, and he was elected governor.
   b) Because Andrew Johnson understood the problems of the small Southern farmer, he was elected governor.
9 a) Man o' War, considered by many the greatest thoroughbred produced in America, was retired after just two seasons of racing.
   b) Man o' War was retired after just two seasons of racing, and he is considered by many the greatest thoroughbred produced in America.
10 a) On its first run *Tom Thumb* made a thirteen-mile trip in seventy-two minutes, and it was the first steam locomotive built in America.
   b) On its first run *Tom Thumb*, the first steam locomotive built in America, made a thirteen-mile trip in seventy-two minutes.

CHAPTER 17

AVOIDING

SENTENCE

ERRORS

Looks are often deceiving, as you well know. Wearing a police-man's uniform will make a gangster *look like* an officer of the law, but his actions will show that he isn't. Adding a bit of red dye to a gallon of water will make the water *look like* strawberry soda, though a taste will prove that it isn't.

The warning "Looks are often deceiving" applies to sentences also. Beginning a group of words with a capital letter and ending it with a period will make the group *look like* a sentence. But many word groups that student writers begin with a capital and end with a period are really not sentences, even though they may look like them. On closer inspection, some prove to be just parts, or "fragments," of sentences instead of complete sentences that make sense by themselves. For example:

> Without giving Terry a chance to answer. [What happened?]
> Carrying a heavy bag of groceries. [Who was carrying the bag?]
> If you can afford to spend that much. [Then what?]

Others are actually two separate sentences—carelessly run together as one:

> Larry couldn't move his foot was caught.
> Joan was late, she missed the first bus.
> Pat was out of breath, he had run the whole way.

Both of these kinds of "counterfeit" sentences—**fragments** and **run-togethers**—are considered serious errors in writing, and for a very good reason: They are a nuisance to the reader, keeping him from understanding the intended meaning as quickly and easily as he should.

If you are sincerely interested in improving your writing, you will want to avoid these two errors. This chapter will help you. The first step is, of course, learning the difference between real sentences and counterfeit ones. Remember that the outward appearance won't help; you will have to look closely at the words between the capital letter and the period.

SENTENCE FRAGMENTS

A piece broken off from a china plate or cup is a "fragment"; so is a piece of wood chipped off from the trunk of a tree. Then a *sentence fragment*, as you can figure out from its name, is a piece of a sentence—a piece cut off from the sentence to which it belongs and punctuated as a separate sentence. For example:

> Phil ran into the kitchen. *Waving the telegram from Uncle Fred.*

The italicized group of words is written as if it were a sentence; it begins with a capital letter and ends with a period. But is it truly a sentence?

To be a sentence, a group of words (1) must have a *subject* and a *verb*, and (2) must make sense standing alone. The word group "Waving the telegram from Uncle Fred" does not do either of these. It has neither subject nor verb, and it certainly does not make sense by itself. It leaves the reader wondering, "Who was waving the telegram?"

The answer to this question is, of course, that *Phil* was waving the telegram. The group of words is, as you can see, a participial phrase which the writer intended to modify the noun *Phil*. And a modifying phrase—like any adjective—belongs in the sentence containing the word it describes. It should be attached to that sentence, not cut off from it:

> Phil ran into the kitchen, *waving the telegram from Uncle Fred.*

It is hardly likely that any high-school student would cut off an adverb from the end of a sentence and punctuate it as a separate sentence:

> Dan said he would pay for the tickets. *Tomorrow.*

A sentence of a single word is so rare that even if a student had written *tomorrow* as a separate sentence, he would quickly realize that something was wrong and correct it. Yet he might not notice his mistake if he had cut off an adverb clause, because the clause has a subject and verb and looks like a sentence. For example:

> Dan said he would pay for the tickets. *When he gets his allowance.*

Though the italicized clause has a subject and verb, it is not a true sentence, because it does not make sense by itself. It merely tells **when** Dan will pay, just as the adverb *tomorrow* does in the preceding example. It should, therefore, be put in the same sentence as the verb *would pay*:

> Dan said he would pay for the tickets *when he gets his allowance.*

Common types of sentence fragments. As you read the following examples of the sorts of fragments that are common in student writing, make sure you understand clearly why each is not a complete sentence. Ask questions in class about any that may puzzle you.

PREPOSITIONAL PHRASE: Sam left his report card lying on the desk but hid Tom's. *Under the blotter.*

CORRECTED: Sam left his report card lying on the desk but hid Tom's *under the blotter.*

PARTICIPIAL PHRASE: Allan drove around the block three times. *Looking for a parking space.*

CORRECTED: Allan drove around the block three times, *looking for a parking space.*

INFINITIVE PHRASE: Ted has been working after school and on Saturdays. *To earn money for a vacation trip to Cuba.*

CORRECTED: Ted has been working after school and on Saturdays *to earn money for a vacation trip to Cuba.*

323

APPOSITIVE: Frank's partner for the first dance number was Luann Smithers. *The clumsiest girl he had ever known.*

CORRECTED: Frank's partner for the first dance number was Luann Smithers, *the clumsiest girl he had ever known.*

PART OF COMPOUND VERB: Finally Jerry's father, who had been watching the fight, ran up to the boys. *And pulled them apart.*

CORRECTED: Finally Jerry's father, who had been watching the fight, ran up to the boys *and pulled them apart.*

ADJECTIVE CLAUSE: There was nothing for breakfast except a dozen rolls and two or three wieners. *Which were left over from the picnic.*

CORRECTED: There was nothing for breakfast except a dozen rolls and two or three wieners *which were left over from the picnic.*

ADVERB CLAUSE: Joan refused Don's invitation to the football dance. *Because she didn't have a new dress.*

CORRECTED: Joan refused Don's invitation to the football dance *because she didn't have a new dress.*

Most sentence fragments are parts cut off from the ends of sentences to which they belong. But sometimes a writer may cut off a piece from the beginning:

FRAGMENT: *Frightened by his threatening to tell Dad.* I agreed to help him pay for the broken window.

CORRECTED: *Frightened by his threatening to tell Dad,* I agreed to help him pay for the broken window.

FRAGMENT: *If the wood is not thoroughly dry.* The paint is likely to blister and then peel off.

CORRECTED: *If the wood is not thoroughly dry,* the paint is likely to blister and then peel off.

Occasionally you may find a fragment that is not a detached piece of the preceding or following sentence, but is incomplete because some important words are somehow missing. For example:

> Just then the janitor, who had warned us not to use the projector without permission

This is not a complete sentence; it has no main verb to tell what the subject (the *janitor*) did. The writer, because of carelessness or haste in writing or copying, has omitted the one word that would make the sentence complete—though he probably had it in mind. He should get it down on paper:

> Just then the janitor, who had warned us not to use the projector without permission, *appeared.*

The remedy for this sort of error is careful proofreading. Read each sentence slowly, thinking of the meaning you intend your reader to get. Doing so will help you spot places where important words are missing.

EXERCISE (1) Decide which item (*a* or *b*) in each of the following pairs is a complete sentence and which is merely a fragment. On a sheet of paper, write the numbers 1 to 10. After each number, write the letter of the fragment. Be ready to point out the subject and the verb of each complete sentence.

1 a) Dr. Ellis was just preparing to leave his office.
    b) Just as Dr. Ellis was preparing to leave his office.

2 a) An excuse that no one in his right mind would have believed.
    b) Jim's excuse no one in his right mind would have believed.

3 a) That decision cost him his job at Allentown.
    b) A decision that cost him his job at Allentown.

4 a) We invited Dick since he was the only one in our gang with a car.
   b) Since he was the only one in our gang who had a car.

5 a) Which was Dan's reason for denying that he had cheated in the test.
   b) This was Dan's reason for denying that he had cheated.

6 a) Wearing his new suit because he wanted to impress Sue Ann.
   b) Lee wore his new suit, hoping that Sue Ann would be impressed.

7 a) Depending on the results of the poll that is being taken in the Midwest.
   b) What he does next depends on the results of the Midwest poll.

8 a) Pierre L'Enfant, a French engineer, drew up the plans for Washington, D.C.
   b) Pierre L'Enfant, a French engineer and architect, who was greatly esteemed.

9 a) With a shopping bag filled with souvenirs that she had collected on her trip.
   b) She arrived with a shopping bag filled with souvenirs of her trip.

10 a) The truck bounced noisily over the rails and came to a stop at the platform.
   b) And, bouncing noisily over the rails, came to a stop at the loading platform.

EXERCISE 2 Each of the following numbered groups consists of two parts—either two complete sentences or a sentence and a fragment. Study the groups and be ready (1) to point out the fragments, (2) to explain why they are fragments, (3) to tell how to correct them.

1 The man at the next table jumped up in alarm. Upsetting the vase of flowers.

2 The next day we had a substitute who gave us a surprise quiz on the *Atlantic Monthly* article. Which Miss Johnson had assigned on Monday.

3 We felt sure that Christine would get the lead in the operetta. Because she could dance and act as well as sing.

4 The two boys tied the magazines and newspapers into neat bundles. And carried them out to the trailer.

5 It was lucky for Kenneth that his parents decided to go to a movie that evening. Any attempt to sneak out of the house without their catching him would have failed.

6 Although Mr. Lindstrom was impatient and often sarcastic. He was the best teacher I ever had.

7 Clifford practiced his speech at least a dozen times that day. To make sure that he knew exactly what to say.

8 The principal greeted Herman with a smile, shook his hand, and then invited him to sit down. Such an unusual welcome made Herman still more suspicious.

9 Katherine spent the whole morning at the National Gallery of Art. Fascinated by the beauty of the building and the paintings.

10 Screaming at the top of his lungs, the little boy ran to his mother. Who tried her best to calm him.

11 His brother Woodrow, on the other hand, had more serious interests. Such as reading scientific magazines, doing chemistry experiments, and studying books on mathematics.

12 All the delegates from Mercer High were assigned to Room 212. Sitting next to me at the first conference was the very girl I had noticed on the bus.

13 Mother was angry because while she was out doing the shopping, Dad and Uncle Will had eaten all the chicken salad. Which she had prepared for her bridge club.

14 The costumes they wore were made of piña. A fabric made from the fibers of pineapple leaves.

15 It didn't take Timmy long to discover that he could get his own way. By holding his breath whenever he was crossed.

16 Catherine the Great wrote two memoirs. One in her youth, the other in her later years.

17 The men then rounded up the cattle. And began the branding.

18 Richard II seized the property of his banished son Bolingbroke. To get money for the Irish wars.

19 In the trunk she found several Revolutionary War letters. Yellowed and faded with age.

20 I would volunteer for a trip to Mars. Without hesitation.

"OFFBEAT" SENTENCES

On page 322 you were told this: "To be a sentence, a group of words (1) must have a *subject* and a *verb*, and (2) must make sense standing alone." Since the sentence patterns we most commonly use contain subjects and verbs, these two tests work about nine tenths of the time. But English-speaking people occasionally use sentences that do not have a subject or a verb yet are perfectly good sentences. For example:

> The sooner, the better.
> How about a subsidy for farmers?
> What a mess!
> How so?
> "A cup of coffee, please."
> ["Which would you choose?"] "The green one."
> ["When did he call you?"] "At five-thirty."
> ["Who told him?"] "Not I."
> ["What's Mother doing?"] "Ironing your shirt."

As you can see, most of these "offbeat" sentences would be used chiefly in speech, and would appear in writing mainly in reporting conversation.

Notice that though these sentences do not have subjects or verbs, they do make sense standing alone. They are not, like fragments, lopped-off pieces of other sentences. You can use them in your writing (wherever they naturally fit) without hesitation or apology. They are not fragments; they are just as "correct" as, and sometimes more effective than, the more generally used subject-verb sentences.

EXERCISE (3) Be ready to tell whether the second group of words in each of the following numbered items is a sentence fragment or a "complete" sentence (even though it lacks the subject and verb of the typical English sentence).

1 We looked everywhere for the key and finally found it. Under the mat on the back porch.
2 "Where did you put the key?" "Under the mat on the back porch."
3 "All the seats in those two sections are taken already. This way, boys."
4 Tell George to come along too. The more, the merrier.
5 Neil spent the rest of that day and part of the next in his room. Working on his new plane model.
6 The investigation demanded by two of our council members is certainly a good idea. But what about the expense?
7 Mrs. O'Neill suggested that I have an interview with Mr. Peterson. The personnel manager at the canning factory.
8 "No, I don't care for apple pie. A hot fudge sundae, please."
9 "And what had Billy been doing all afternoon?" "Working on his new plane model."
10 Carl had to skip his supper and had to run all the way. To get there in time for the meeting.

A reader who had plenty of time and a strong sense of humor would probably be amused by "sentences" like the following, particularly if he was the type of person that enjoyed solving puzzles of various kinds.

> Captain Spence would not give up the ship meant everything to him.
>
> The third time round, Mr. Abrams couldn't answer the question was on the Boxer Rebellion.
>
> Mrs. Jacobsen was told to see Miss Daniel, the principal, Mr. Rowe was out of town.

But to anyone else, "run-together" sentences like these would be annoying. To the ordinary reader, a capital letter is a signal that he is beginning a new sentence, a sentence that will continue until he reaches a "stop" signal—a period (or question mark or exclamation mark). When, without warning, he finds himself in the middle of a second sentence while he thinks he is still reading the first, he has a right to be annoyed. Instead of reading along smoothly, he has to stop, back up, and puzzle out for himself where one sentence ends and the next begins—a job that the writer should have done for him.

Causes of run-together sentences. What causes a writer to run two sentences together with only a comma between them, or even no separating mark at all?

Usually it is because the two sentences are so closely related in meaning that they seem to belong together. For example, the second sentence may give a reason for the statement made in the first sentence:

RUN-TOGETHER: Lucy enjoyed working for Mr. Fentriss, *he was always pleasant and considerate.*

CORRECTED: Lucy enjoyed working for Mr. Fentriss. He was always pleasant and considerate.

The second sentence may give an important detail about a person or thing mentioned in the first sentence:

RUN-TOGETHER: The history test was long, *it covered the whole semester's work.*

CORRECTED: The history test was long. It covered the whole semester's work.

Or the second sentence may make a statement that contrasts with the statement made in the first sentence:

RUN-TOGETHER: Larry was brilliant and studious, *his brother was scatterbrained and lazy.*

CORRECTED: Larry was brilliant and studious. His brother was scatterbrained and lazy.

When two sentences are not closely connected in meaning, writers seldom run them together. Few high-school students would make a mistake like this:

RUN-TOGETHER: Ronnie flopped down on the cot, a few minutes later he closed his eyes and soon was sound asleep.

CORRECTED: Ronnie flopped down on the cot. A few minutes later he closed his eyes and soon was sound asleep.

But if the second sentence were "He was exhausted," which explains the reason for Ronnie's action, then there is danger of error:

RUN-TOGETHER: Ronnie flopped down on the cot, he was exhausted.

CORRECTED: Ronnie flopped down on the cot. He was exhausted.

Words that need watching. In revising your writing, watch out for any sentence that begins with a pronoun—particularly *he, she, it, they,* or *we.* Since these words usually refer to a noun (or nouns) in the preceding sentence, the ideas in the two sentences are likely to be closely related in meaning. But no matter how closely connected in meaning the ideas are, the sentences themselves are grammatically separate and distinct. They should not be jammed together between one capital letter and one period, or the reader will be confused. Help your readers know where the first sentence ends and the next begins by keeping them separated.

RUN-TOGETHER: The committee bought the 21-inch model, **it** was much cheaper than the 27-inch sets.

TWO SENTENCES: The committee bought the 21-inch model. **It** was much cheaper than the 27-inch sets.

RUN-TOGETHER: All of us were afraid of Mrs. Bellows, **she** had a terrible temper.

TWO SENTENCES: All of us were afraid of Mrs. Bellows. **She** had a terrible temper.

Watch out, also, for words like *then, there, now, therefore, however, in fact, nevertheless,* and *consequently.* Often you use these words at the beginning of a sentence to tell the reader how the ideas in that sentence and in the preceding one are related. But even though the ideas are closely related in meaning, the two sentences should not be written as if they were one. Use a capital letter and a period for each sentence. Or, if you prefer, make a compound sentence of them—but show the two parts clearly by separating them with a semicolon (*not* a comma).

RUN-TOGETHER: For an hour or so Dan obeyed the orders, **then** he balked.

TWO SENTENCES: For an hour or so Dan obeyed the orders. **Then** he balked.

WITH SEMICOLON: For an hour or so Dan obeyed the orders; **then** he balked.

RUN-TOGETHER: Ed was sure that none of the keys would fit, **nevertheless** he tried them all.

TWO SENTENCES: Ed was sure that none of the keys would fit. **Nevertheless** he tried them all.

WITH SEMICOLON: Ed was sure that none of the keys would fit; **nevertheless** he tried them all.

Ways of correcting run-together sentences.   So far you have seen two ways of correcting a run-together sentence:

1) Write it as two separate sentences, using a capital letter and a period for each.
2) Write it as a compound sentence, using a semicolon to show where one part ends and the next begins.

The first way is the easiest, and it is always correct. The second way is preferable when you want to emphasize the close relationship between ideas.

There is also a third way that works in some instances. By using a comma and an appropriate coördinating conjunction—*and*, *but*, or *or*, for example—you can change some run-together sentences to effective compound sentences:

RUN-TOGETHER: At first there was a long pause then everybody began to talk at once.

WITH CONJUNCTION: At first there was a long pause, **and** then everybody began to talk at once.

RUN-TOGETHER: Once it cost a nickel, now we pay a dime.

WITH CONJUNCTION: Once it cost a nickel, **but** now we pay a dime.

RUN-TOGETHER: Do not leave the cellophane on the lamp shade, the material will buckle.

WITH CONJUNCTION: Do not leave the cellophane on the lamp shade, **or** the material will buckle.

Decide which of the following numbered items are run-to-gether sentences and which are correct. Correct each run-together sentence in one of two ways: (1) by dividing it into two separate sentences, or (2) by using a semicolon to make a compound sentence.

You need not copy the whole item. Just write the word preceding and the word following the punctuation mark that you change. Number your answers with the numbers of the items. If a sentence is correct as it stands, write "Correct" after its number.

1 The article on turbojet engines was hard to understand, it contained too many technical words.

2 Dad was quite impressed by the new Ramblers, in fact, he is planning to trade in our car for one.

3 First the voices seemed to be coming from Dan's room, then from the room opposite Dan's.

4 Roland insists the money was on the table when he left, however, he may be mistaken.

5 Werner refused to stop making fun of the products he was advertising, consequently he soon found himself without a sponsor.

6 Willie and I exchanged amused glances, we both knew what Mr. Turner would say next.

7 Don't sit in that chair, it has a broken spring.

8 The noise made by the pneumatic drills was so loud, however, that class discussion was impossible.

9 Edward Everett was considered the greatest orator of the times, therefore he was chosen to be the main speaker at Gettysburg.

10 "German silver" is not really silver, it is a white alloy of zinc, nickel, and copper.

11 Glen knew his chances of winning were slim, nevertheless he did his best.

12 My brother was not stupid, he was just not interested in chemistry.

13 Many women ignore the directions completely, in fact, and then complain when the pressure cooker explodes.

14 Mr. Bonney was worried about his son's illness, otherwise he would have made a better showing in the golf tournament.

15 Neither of the men would give in, each was determined to win.

16 Next we heard a scraping noise, as if someone had bumped against a chair, then all was quiet again.

17 A vine growing over a trellis hides an unattractive view, at the same time it keeps out debris blown by the wind.

331

18 The farmer, too, is a gambler, he can't control the weather.

19 First run cold water through the stained spot, then wash the tablecloth in warm water.

20 American citizens do not need passports for trips to Canada, however, naturalized Americans need proof of citizenship.

EXERCISE (5) Decide which of the following numbered items are run-together sentences and which are correct. Correct each run-together sentence by inserting an appropriate conjunction (*and*, *but*, or *or*) to make a compound sentence.

You need not copy the whole sentence. Just write the word preceding and the word following the conjunction you use. Be sure to include the comma before the conjunction. Number your answers with the numbers of the items. If a sentence is correct as it stands, write "Correct" after its number.

1 At one time El Dorado was a prosperous mining center, now it is a ghost town.

2 Jerry waited until Miss Pierce turned back to the test papers, then he tossed the note to Ann.

3 An *immigrant* is a person who comes into a foreign country to live, an *emigrant* is a person who leaves his own country to settle in another.

4 According to most of these critics, then, David Starrett did not deserve to win the award.

5 Think first, then answer.

6 Don't tell Mother what happened, she'll worry about it.

7 A golf pro can tell you what you are doing wrong, he cannot make a champion out of you.

8 We hurried over to the biology lab, there he was, busy with an experiment.

9 Thirty years ago only 10 per cent of our graduates went on to college, now 87 per cent continue their schooling.

10 When Mr. Henderson leaves, there will be a job open in the sales department.

11 The neighbors came over to cheer Mrs. Andrews, they just made matters worse.

12 Use a slightly damp cloth, not a wet one, the material will shrink.

13 In time of peace the Coast Guard is under the control of the Treasury Department, in time of war it is under the control of the Navy.

14 They used to live in the old Davis mansion, now known as the Courtley Apartments.

332

15 Lloyd can make a short story long, he cannot make a long story short.
16 First sand the floor, then wax it.
17 Andy had planned to come, he couldn't because one of the other checkers at the supermarket was sick.
18 Come early, bring your friends.
19 Act at once when you have spilled an acid, it may damage the material and destroy the color.
20 During the winter the flocks of sheep graze in the lowlands, during the summer they move to the mountain slopes.

EXERCISE ⑥ REVIEW List the numbers 1 to 20 on a sheet of paper. If the group of words is a complete sentence, write "S" after its number. If the word group is a fragment, write "F." If it is a run-together sentence, write "R." Be ready to explain how you arrived at your answers.

1 Because he was working a crossword puzzle as he rode.
2 Frank rode past his stop, he was working a crossword puzzle on the bus.
3 Busy with a crossword puzzle, Frank rode past his bus stop.
4 I was annoyed with Mrs. Crawford, she refused to sign the petition.
5 Mrs. Crawford listened, smiled pleasantly, but refused to sign the petition.
6 Annoyed with Mrs. Crawford, who refused to sign the petition.
7 Because of the dim light, we couldn't read the letter.
8 We couldn't read the letter, the light was too dim.
9 Because the light in the hallway was much too dim to read by.
10 The twins were lazy, they would do anything to avoid work.
11 The twins, who were lazy and hated work of any sort.
12 The twins were lazy and would, therefore, do anything to avoid work.
13 Paying no attention to Aunt Sadie's complaints, they went on with the game.
14 The boys paid no attention to Aunt Sadie, she complained about everything.
15 In spite of Aunt Sadie's complaints, which they had expected.
16 The white brick house where he had lived ten years ago.
17 At a turn of the road he saw the white brick house where he had lived ten years ago.
18 He remembered the house, he had lived there ten years ago.
19 Trailers have trouble getting around the sharp curves.
20 Such sharp curves that trailers can hardly get around them.

CHAPTER **18**

USING

VERBS

334

As far as meaning goes, there is no difference between "She don't care" and "She doesn't care," between "I seen her" and "I saw her," or between "He has went home" and "He has gone home."

Yet you are told that the verb in the first sentence of each pair is "wrong" and the verb in the second is "right." Why? If both verb forms mean the same thing, why aren't they both "right"? Who determines what is the "right" form and what is the "wrong" form? Why should a person learn to use the "right" forms, when the "wrong" ones express the same meaning and are easier for him to say? See if you can figure out the answers from the following.

Suppose a four-year-old neighbor came up to you and said, "Mother *catched* a mouse." You would probably laugh first, and then you would tell him that the "right" word to use is *caught*, not *catched*: "Mother *caught* a mouse."

Why don't you let the little boy say *catched* if that is the word that first comes to his mind? After all, what happened to the mouse is clear, whether he says *caught* or *catched*. Yet you tell him that

caught is the "right" word to use. Suppose he asks you why it is. You could probably tell him the answer: "Because *caught* is the word that educated, grown-up people use. As a rule, only small children like you say *catched*. You can go on saying *catched* if you like; everyone will understand what you mean. But if you do, you will sound childish to grown-up people."

A shorter way of answering would be to say simply, "Because *caught* is right and *catched* is wrong." But the longer answer is better because it explains why *catched* is "wrong." It is not because it is a bad word, or an ugly word, or unclear, but because using it will cause a poor impression.

The same thing is true of the verb forms in "She don't," "I seen," and "He has went." We call them "wrong" not because they are unclear or ugly, but because they are not the forms that educated people use in such sentences. If you use them, therefore, you run the risk of making a poor impression on those who speak good English and expect others to do the same.

The usage of educated people—the way they use words—determines which word forms are "right" and which are "wrong." Since the educated people set the standards for our language, we call the forms they use **standard** and those they do not use **nonstandard**.

Nonstandard forms are no easier to pronounce than the standard; they are no easier to spell. Why then do so many students use nonstandard forms, when they know such forms will cause a poor impression? The reason is not always that they do not know the difference between the two. In a test in English class almost all students can make the right choice between *you was* and *you were* or between *he has did* and *he has done*. Yet after taking the test, some of these same students will go on using nonstandard forms.

It is not ignorance nor stubbornness that causes this; it is the strong force of habit. If you are in the habit of saying "You was" and if you constantly hear others say the same, then "You was" sounds right to you. And when words sound right to you, you use them naturally, without giving them the slightest thought.

Getting rid of the nonstandard forms in your speech—if you use any—takes two steps. First you must find out which nonstandard forms you use and what standard forms you should be using in their place. This chapter will help you with the first step. Second, you must practice saying the standard forms over and over again until *they sound right to you—and the others sound wrong.* The exercises will give you some practice, but not nearly enough. It will be up to you to do the rest.

VERB FORMS

The mistake the four-year-old made when he said "Mother catched a mouse" was really a very logical mistake, one that showed pretty good thinking on his part. He had never had a grammar lesson, yet he had figured out an important grammatical rule. He had noticed that when people talked about things that had occurred in the past, they quite often used words that ended with a *d* sound or a *t* sound (spelled *ed*):

We *played* records.
Larry and I *walked* home.

So when he wanted to tell of something that had happened in the past, he followed the same pattern of adding the sound to the action word *catch*—and ended with *catched*.

The only thing wrong, of course, is that *catch* is one of the verbs whose past tense is not formed in the "regular" way. But the boy was too young and therefore too inexperienced in language to have learned this. He had not heard enough English (or read enough) to understand the difference between *regular* and *irregular* verbs or how to form all the different tenses of each. Let's see what a few more years of hearing and using the language would teach him.

The tenses of verbs. Verbs are double-duty words. We use them not only to express actions, but also to give an idea of the time of the actions. When you hear the sentence "Martha pressed your blue suit," you know not only what the action is, but also when it happened—at some time in the past.

The verb in the sentence "Martha will press your suit" expresses the same action, but the time is different; the action is to happen in the future. How do you know? You know by the *forms* of the verb. The *ed* ending on *pressed* shows that the verb is a past-tense form; the action has already happened. The "helping" word *will* shows that *will press* is a future-tense form; the action has not happened yet.

These are only two of the forms; each of our verbs has many more. There are six tenses. Here are *some* of the different forms each tense may have:

PRESENT: We *drop* our letters in that box.
            A bomb *drops* in a long arc.
            He *is dropping* off to sleep.

PAST TENSES
  PAST: Frank *dropped* us off at the corner.
            She *did drop* her subscription, I'm sure.
  PRESENT PERFECT: Who *has dropped* her gloves?
                     Prices *have dropped* again.
  PAST PERFECT: Someone *had dropped* a hammer.

FUTURE TENSES
  FUTURE: I *will drop* him a hint.
             They *will be dropping* in soon.
  FUTURE PERFECT: By then he *will have dropped*
                    too far behind me to catch up.

Principal parts. You need not memorize the different tense forms shown in the preceding section; you know them all already. But have you noticed that though the forms differ, all are made from what we call the *principal parts* of the verb?

First Principal Part	Second	Third
PRESENT INFINITIVE	PAST TENSE	PAST PARTICIPLE
(to) drop	dropped	dropped

Luckily, most English verbs are **regular** verbs, like *drop*. To form the past tense and the past participle, we add *ed* to the first part:

FIRST PRINCIPAL PART [Infinitive]	SECOND [Past Tense]	THIRD [Past Participle]
(to) mark	marked	marked
(to) stay	stayed	stayed
(to) jump	jumped	jumped

Since all the tenses are formed from these principal parts, the forms of regular verbs will cause you no trouble except perhaps in spelling. *Y* changes to *i* before *ed* is added in verbs like these:

pity	pitied	pitied
worry	worried	worried

The final consonant is doubled before adding *ed* in verbs like these:

refer	referred	referred
mop	mopped	mopped

338

IRREGULAR VERBS

If all English verbs were regular, verb usage would not be the problem it is. It is the **irregular** verbs—those whose principal parts are not formed in the regular way—that cause most of the trouble. Notice these examples:

FIRST PRINCIPAL PART	SECOND	THIRD
do	did	(have) done
see	saw	(have) seen
drink	drank	(have) drunk
go	went	(have) gone
tear	tore	(have) torn
freeze	froze	(have) frozen

Here in a nutshell are two simple clues that will help you avoid mistakes in using these irregular verbs:

1) The forms in the *second* column are always used alone:
   They *did* their best. [Not: They *done*.]
   I *saw* him yesterday. [Not: I *seen*.]
   She *drank* the milk. [Not: She *drunk*.]

2) The forms in the *third* column are always used with helping verbs:

The boys *have gone* already. [Not: *have went.*]
He *has torn* his shirt. [Not: *has tore.*]
His shirt *was torn.* [Not: *was tore.*]
The milk *had frozen.* [Not: *had froze.*]

Notice that to show that the forms in the third column are not to be used alone, we put the helping verb *have* in parentheses before each. If you have trouble with irregular verbs, you will find it a good idea to memorize the forms as they are given here, including the *have* to remind you that the third principal part is always used with a helper. Once you grow used to the sound of **have** *gone*, **have** *torn*, **have** *frozen*, you will automatically shy away from using the wrong forms. Only the "right" forms will sound right to you.

USED WITH HELPERS—Third-column forms
They *have gone* home. [Not: *have went.*]
The picture *had been torn* in half. [Not: *had been tore.*]
The pond *will be frozen* by then. [Not: *will be froze.*]

USED ALONE—Second-column forms
I *did* all the work. [Not: I *done.*]
Ted *saw* us there. [Not: Ted *seen.*]
She *drank* a Coke. [Not: She *drunk.*]

EXERCISE (1) Be ready to read each of the following sentences aloud, using the verb form (in parentheses) that should be used in standard English.

1 We never (*saw, seen*) him again.
2 Their well had (*went, gone*) dry.
3 You (*did, done*) very well in yesterday's test.
4 Jim had (*tore, torn*) his ticket to bits.
5 They had never (*saw, seen*) grapes that big before.
6 Has she (*did, done*) any of the work?
7 We were half (*froze, frozen*) before the end of the game.
8 Have they (*drank, drunk*) all the cocoa?
9 When he (*saw, seen*) his father, Mike (*drank, drunk*) the medicine in one gulp.
10 Nancy (*did, done*) her share of the ironing, but I haven't (*did, done*) mine yet.
11 If you had (*went, gone*) to the meeting, you might have (*saw, seen*) Jerry.
12 After he had (*drank, drunk*) all his lemonade, he (*drank, drunk*) Joan's.

13 A corner had been (*tore, torn*) off before I even (*saw, seen*) the letter.

14 He must have (*did, done*) a poor job, or he wouldn't have (*went, gone*) away without getting his money.

15 When Ken (*seen, saw*) what they had (*did, done*), he laughed.

MORE DRILL ON IRREGULAR VERBS

There is no telling just which verbs are special problems for different students. John Jones, for example, may never make a mistake in using the standard forms of *ring* (*ring, rang, rung*), a verb which always trips Sam Smith. Sam, on the other hand, never has trouble with the forms of *bring* (*bring, brought, brought*). But John, who constantly hears his two best friends using nonstandard forms of *bring*, hardly realizes that he is not speaking standard English when he says "I *brung* Sue a present" and "*Have* you *brung* your history book?"

It is, therefore, up to you to discover for yourself which verb forms you are not using correctly (if any). The following list contains forty irregular verbs commonly used in everyday speech. Test yourself by covering the forms in the second and third columns with a sheet of paper. Before you move the paper down the page (one line at a time), say to yourself the last two principal parts of each verb as you think they should be. Then check the forms on the page.

If you had the forms right, go on to the next verb. If you had them wrong, copy the right forms on a sheet of paper before going on to the next verb. (Keep your list of personal verb demons to use in Exercise 2.)

FIRST PRINCIPAL PART [Infinitive]	SECOND [Past Tense]	THIRD [Past Participle]
beat	beat	(have) beaten
become	became	(have) become
begin	began	(have) begun
break	broke	(have) broken
bring	brought	(have) brought
burst	burst	(have) burst
choose	chose	(have) chosen
come	came	(have) come
do	did	(have) done
drink	drank	(have) drunk

drive	drove	(have) driven
eat	ate	(have) eaten
fall	fell	(have) fallen
fly	flew	(have) flown
forbid	forbade, **forbad**	(have) forbidden
freeze	froze	(have) frozen
get	got	(have) got, gotten
give	gave	(have) given
go	went	(have) gone
grow	grew	(have) grown
hide	hid	(have) hidden, hid
know	knew	(have) known
mistake	mistook	(have) mistaken
ring	rang	(have) rung
run	ran	(have) run
see	saw	(have) seen
shake	shook	(have) shaken
sing	sang (rare: sung)	(have) sung
sink	sank, sunk	(have) sunk
speak	spoke	(have) spoken
spring	sprang, sprung	(have) sprung
steal	stole	(have) stolen
swim	swam	(have) swum
swing	swung	(have) swung
take	took	(have) taken
tear	tore	(have) torn
throw	threw	(have) thrown
wear	wore	(have) worn
wring	wrung	(have) wrung
write	wrote	(have) written

341

EXERCISE 2 For each of the verbs whose principal parts you did not know when you tested yourself, write four sentences. Use the second principal part *alone* in two of the sentences; use the third principal part with a helping verb in the other two sentences. Practice saying the sentences to yourself until the verb forms sound right to you.

EXERCISE 3 Be ready to read each of the following sentences aloud, using the verb form (in parentheses) appropriate in standard English.

1 Only three of the boys (*came, come*) to the meeting last night.
2 Phil (*saw, seen*) the billfold first.
3 "You firemen (*did, done*) me a good turn," he said.
4 Letters should not be (*wrote, written*) in red ink.

5   Both knobs had been (*broke, broken*) off.
6   Gyp (*ran, run*) as fast as she could.
7   Prince could have (*ran, run*) much faster.
8   Now the work must all be (*did, done*) over.
9   The opera was (*sang, sung*) in German.
10 Who had (*took, taken*) the money?
11 Jane was sure I had (*saw, seen*) her.
12 Do you think his finger is (*froze, frozen*)?
13 I couldn't have (*swam, swum*) another stroke.
14 Mrs. Crawley had (*sank, sunk*) to the floor in a faint.
15 The bird must have (*fell, fallen*) from its nest.
16 Have you (*ate, eaten*) all you want?
17 I wish I had (*knew, known*) that before.
18 All of the credit was (*gave, given*) to Mr. Linus.
19 Had the manager (*stole, stolen*) the money?
20 Who (*rang, rung*) the bell?
21 The boy's mother (*began, begun*) to scream.
22 Alice (*swam, swum*) back to shore.
23 Five years later he (*became, become*) president of the firm.
24 Haven't you (*wore, worn*) that coat before?
25 They were (*shook, shaken*) up but not hurt.

342 **EXERCISE 4** Be ready to read each of the following sentences aloud, using the appropriate standard form of the verb in parentheses.

1   The project was (*begin*) in 1953.
2   I'm afraid the new doll will soon be (*break*).
3   She screamed when she (*see*) the snake.
4   The warning bell (*ring*) three minutes ago.
5   Someone else must have (*steal*) the bracelet.
6   You should have (*wear*) a hat.
7   Mark has (*write*) a poem for the occasion.
8   Is Spanish or Portuguese (*speak*) in Brazil?
9   Have they ever (*swim*) in Lily Lake?
10 I must have (*tear*) my sleeve on the nail.
11 Jim (*see*) the movie at the Strand last night.
12 Has anyone (*bring*) any salt?
13 The tardy bell hasn't (*ring*) yet, has it?
14 They were (*give*) to me by a friend.
15 My grandfather had never (*fly*) before.
16 The cast was (*choose*) last night.
17 Nora (*drink*) her milk, but Bob hasn't (*drink*) his.
18 The trees had (*burst*) into bloom overnight.
19 Pat Boone may have (*sing*) earlier on the program.

20 Tom had (*drive*) over with the Larsens.

21 Who (*give*) you permission to leave your study hall?

22 Before aid could arrive, the *Titanic* had (*sink*).

23 Clifford (*swing*) at the ball but missed.

24 How tall he has (*grow*)!

25 They must have (*go*) out the back door.

EXERCISE (5) Be ready to read aloud the following anecdote, using the appropriate standard forms of the verbs in parentheses. (All verbs in the anecdote should be past-tense forms.)

(1) Frank Clark liked to read in the bathtub, although his parents had (*forbid*) him to do so. (2) Late one night, when everyone else had (*go*) to bed, Frank (*choose*) a green-covered book from the bookcase, (*hide*) it under his bathrobe, and (*steal*) down the hall to the bathroom. (3) After getting into a brimming tubful of warm water, he (*begin*) to read the book. (4) To his chagrin, he (*see*) that it was one of his mother's many cookbooks. (5) He had (*mistake*) it for a green-bound copy of *Robinson Crusoe* that he had (*begin*) a month before and hadn't finished. (6) If Frank could have (*eat*) some of the pies or (*drink*) some of the beverages he (*see*) in the pictures, he might have liked it better. (7) But he (*go*) on reading about how a "tbsp." of this and a "tsp." of that should be (*beat*) up in flour and milk.

343

(8) Gradually he (*grow*) very sleepy. (9) Before he (*know*) what was happening, he had (*fall*) asleep and had (*sink*) deeper into the water. (10) He didn't wake up until the water had (*become*) cold and he was half (*freeze*). (11) He had just (*begin*) to turn on the hot water when he (*see*) that his hand was green. (12) So were his feet; in fact, he had (*become*) a rather dark green all over. (13) Frank (*spring*) out of the tub in a hurry.

(14) After he had (*throw*) on his robe, he (*run*) to his mother's room. (15) Mrs. Clark turned on the light, and after she had (*take*) one look at him, said, "For goodness sake, Frank Clark, what have you (*do*) to yourself?"

(16) "Why, nothing; I've just (*take*) a bath," he answered.

(17) "Well, you look as if you had (*fall*) into a vat of green ink," his mother said. (18) Suddenly she (*begin*) to laugh. (19) "I might have (*know*) it!" she said, as she (*run*) out of the room. (20) A minute later she (*come*) back holding a soggy green mass. (21) "My prize cookbook," she groaned. "It was (*give*) to me because I had (*write*) the best slogan for Lite-E-Z yeast."

(22) "I guess it must have (*fall*) into the water after I (*fall*) asleep," Frank explained.

(23) "Perhaps it could be (*run*) through a wringer and dried out again," suggested Mrs. Clark.

(24) "It was too dry before," said Frank. "The driest thing that was ever (*write*)!"

(25) When a week had (*go*) by and he had (*take*) ten more baths, the last trace of green dye from the book cover finally (*come*) off Frank's skin.

TRICKY PAIRS OF VERBS

Many students need special drill on three pairs of verbs—*lay* and *lie*, *set* and *sit*, *raise* and *rise*. This section will show you a fairly easy way to determine which of each pair is the right verb to choose for a particular sentence. Then all you will need is enough practice so that using the right verb will *sound* right—as well as *be* right.

Lay and Lie. The following sentences are alike in two ways. First, each contains a form of the verb *lay*, which means "put or place." Second, in each sentence *someone* or *something* receives the action expressed by the verb:

> I usually *lay* the **baby** on the sofa.
> He *laid* the **check** on the blotter.
> I hope they *aren't laying* their wet **umbrellas** on the bed.
> Someone *had laid* a hot **platter** on the table.
> The **turtle** *had been laid* on its back.

Whenever the sentence tells who or what is placed somewhere, the verb *lay* is used. These are its principal parts:

> **lay   laid   (have) laid**

Now look at these sentences. Each contains a form of the verb *lie*, which means "recline" or "be in a flat position":

> I usually *lie* down for a rest at noon.
> The cat *was lying* in the middle of the floor.
> He *lay* there all afternoon and slept.
> I *have* never *lain* in a lumpier bed.

Whenever the sentence tells that someone or something is (or was) reclining or in a horizontal position, then *lie* is the verb to use. These are its principal parts:

> **lie   lay   (have) lain**

Be sure you remember the important clue that will keep you from confusing these two verbs: If the sentence tells who or what "gets put," use:

lay   laid   (have) laid
[Notice that the last two forms end in *d*.]

Otherwise, use:

lie   lay   (have) lain
[There is no *d* in any of the forms of *lie*.]

Note: In everyday conversation you may often hear *lay* used instead of *lie* in a sentence like "Lay down, Blackie." But this usage is not appropriate in careful speech or in writing, unless you are reporting the exact words of a speaker.

Set and Sit; Raise and Rise.   These two pairs of verbs follow the same pattern as *lay* and *lie*. When a sentence tells who or what "gets" the action, use *set* and *raise*:

set   set   (have) set
Set the **kettle** on the stove.
I *set* **it** there before he came.
The **pie** *had been set* on the window ledge to cool.

raise   raised   (have) raised
Raise the **shade** a few inches.
Norman *raised* his **hand**.
She *had* not *raised* her **voice**.

345 .

Otherwise, use *sit* and *rise*:

sit   sat   (have) sat
We always *sit* in the front row.
He *sat* there without saying a word.
Have you ever *sat* in a box at a theater?

rise   rose   (have) risen
Prices usually *rise* in time of war.
The speaker *rose*, bowed, and then sat down.
A sharp wind *had risen* during the night.

EXERCISE (6) Be ready to read the following sentences aloud, substituting for each blank the appropriate standard form of *lie* (lie, lay, lain, lying) or *lay* (lay, laid, laid, laying).

1   While I weeded, Jack _____ on the grass daydreaming.
2   Why don't you _____ down for a while?
3   Where had she _____ her hat?

4 Tom should _____ something aside for a rainy day.
5 You'll catch cold if you _____ on the beach today.
6 Someone had _____ a wet swimming suit on the new table.
7 She had just _____ down to rest when the phone rang.
8 He couldn't remember where he had _____ the letter.
9 He couldn't remember how long he had _____ there.
10 "Someone has been _____ in my bed," said Baby Bear.
11 The next day the pile of dirty shirts still _____ on the chair.
12 He must have _____ awake all night.
13 Half of the men in the steel mill have been _____ off.
14 Jerry _____ there mumbling until it grew dark.
15 I wonder how long he has been _____ in that spot.
16 Why hasn't she _____ out your clothes?
17 The hardest part of the work still _____ before us, as we knew.
18 There _____ his glasses, right where he had _____ them.

EXERCISE 7 Be ready to read the following sentences aloud, using the appropriate form of the verb (in parentheses).

1 Can't the baby (*set, sit*) up without being held?
2 Be sure to (*raise, rise*) when Mrs. Martin enters.
3 Our chairs aren't fit to be (*set, sat*) in.
4 Are you going to (*lay, lie*) there all day?
5 The yeast will make the dough (*raise, rise*).
6 Prices haven't (*raised, risen*) at Field's Grill, have they?
7 Why don't you (*set, sit*) in a more comfortable chair?
8 They made enough noise to (*raise, rise*) the dead.
9 Who was (*setting, sitting*) next to Carol?
10 The hem should be (*raised, risen*) an inch or so.
11 The chairs had been (*set, sat*) in a circle.
12 The same old vase is still (*setting, sitting*) on the mantel.
13 Believe it or not, the cat was (*laying, lying*) beside Rover.
14 You may (*set, sit*) anywhere you like.
15 On the count of three, (*raise, rise*) on your toes and exhale.
16 I'd rather you'd let me (*set, sit*) and watch you three play.
17 The Blodgetts had (*risen, rose*) at five to get an early start.
18 Let George (*set, sit*) in that chair.

LET ME CALL YOU SWEET-HEART

A SPECIAL DEMON

Let and Leave. The first line of a once-popular song goes: "*Let me call you sweetheart; I'm in love with you.*" Notice the first word of the song. It is *Let*—not *Leave*. The meaning is "*Allow* me to call you sweetheart." If you, like the song writer, get into the habit of using *let* whenever you mean "allow" or "permit," you will have no trouble with the troublesome *let—leave* pair.

Learn the first line of the song. *Let* it remind you that *let* is the right form to use in sentences like these:

> *Let* me help you. [Not: *Leave* me help.]
> Dad *let* Ed drive the car. [Not: Dad *left* Ed drive.]
> He made the mistake of *letting* Jim file the letters. [Not: mistake of *leaving* Jim file.]

When the meaning is not "allow," *leave* is the verb to use:

> I *leave* the house at eight.
> He *left* his suitcase at the station.

You need not worry about using the right form in sentences like these; you will seldom, if ever, make a mistake. But be on your guard against using *leave* when the meaning is "allow." Use *let*, the verb appropriate in standard English.

EXERCISE (**8**) Be ready to read the following sentences aloud, using the verb form (in parentheses) that should be used in standard English.

1 (*Leave, Let*) me go!
2 Uncle Will never (*leaves, lets*) anything annoy him.
3 It is silly for you to (*leave, let*) him interfere.
4 Don't (*leave, let*) your suitcases in the aisle.
5 Will you (*leave, let*) me drive home?
6 Ask her to (*leave, let*) the back door open.
7 Neil has (*left, let*) his coat in the car.
8 Should we (*leave, let*) the heater on while we're gone?
9 Dad must have (*left, let*) Terry go to the movies.
10 He wouldn't (*leave, let*) me pay for my ticket.
11 I'm not in the habit of (*leaving, letting*) my work slide.
12 Don't (*leave, let*) your papers lying on the desk.
13 Don't (*leave, let*) the boys lie on the grass.
14 Why did he (*leave, let*) Frank push him?
15 Someone must have (*left, let*) the lights turned on.

347

TWO MORE PAIRS TO WATCH

Bring and Take. A person who "brings" something to a place and a person who "takes" something to a place both do the same action. Whether you speak of the action as "bringing" or as "taking" depends on the *direction* of the action. If the direction is *toward* the place where the speaker is, the verb *bring* is used in standard English:

Bring me an apple.
He *brought* us two sandwiches apiece.

If the direction is *away from* the speaker, the verb *take* is used:

Take this apple to Nancy.
He *took* the note to the girl in the front office.

Learn and Teach. A person who "gains knowledge" by study or through experience *learns*. A person who "gives knowledge" *teaches*. Users of standard English say:

He *taught* us a new card game. [Not: He *learned* us.]
We *learned* a new card game.

EXERCISE (9) Be ready to read the following sentences aloud, using the appropriate verb to express the intended meaning.

1 "(*Bring, Take*) your purchase to the nearest cashier," said the clerk.
2 We asked Bill to (*learn, teach*) us to run the elevator.
3 (*Bring, Take*) these tomatoes to Mrs. Vinson, but (*bring, take*) back the basket.
4 "Don't forget to (*bring, take*) your pictures to the scout meeting," said his mother before he left the house.
5 Mrs. Kirven (*brought, took*) us all to the movies last night.
6 When you go to Chicago, (*bring, take*) a heavy coat with you.
7 When you come to Chicago, (*bring, take*) a heavy coat.
8 He may know a lot about chemistry, but he hasn't (*learned, taught*) me a thing.

348

WATCH YOUR TIMING

Have you ever overheard snatches of conversation that went something like this?

"Mr. Piper *was* still *waiting* at the bus stop when suddenly a cab *races* across the intersection. Just as he *notices* that nobody *seemed* to be at the wheel, he *hears* a scream."

Most people, overhearing this much, would wonder what had happened next. And many of them (users of standard English) would also wonder why the speaker was "spoiling" his story by using the verb forms he did. Every action he was telling about had happened *in the past*. Then why didn't he stick to past-tense forms of the verbs instead of shifting from past tense to present tense? His story would have been just as interesting and would have sounded better and been easier to follow if he had been consistent:

> "Mr. Piper *was* still *waiting* at the bus stop when suddenly a cab *raced* across the intersection. Just as he *noticed* that nobody *seemed* to be at the wheel, he *heard* a scream."

Shifting from a verb form that shows past time to one that shows present time is especially common in sentences containing more than one verb. Watch out for these.

DON'T SAY—

Before I *had* even *opened* my mouth, she *says,* "You be quiet!"

Dorothy *searched* frantically through her purse and finally *finds* the ticket.

SAY INSTEAD—

Before I *had* even *opened* my mouth, she *said,* "You be quiet!"

Dorothy *searched* frantically through her purse and finally *found* the ticket.

Sometimes there is a good reason for shifting from past tense to present tense in a single sentence. For example:

> Scientists *learned* many years ago that air *is* a mixture of gases.

Since the last part of the sentence states a fact that is always true, regardless of time, it is appropriate to use the present-tense verb *is,* even though the first verb is in the past tense. But remember that unless there is a good reason for shifting tenses, you should keep the time of your verbs consistent.

349

EXERCISE 10 Be ready to read the following sentences aloud, substituting for the blanks the appropriate tense forms.

1 Just as I was reeling that huge pickerel in, the line _____. (*breaks, broke*)

2 Then the man in the brown suit leaned over and _____ something to the usher. (*says, said*)

3 Mr. Minehart had forgotten that metal _____ when it _____ heated. (*expands, expanded*) (*is, was*)

4 Miss Martin made Tom copy his paper in ink and then _____ him a failing grade anyhow. (*gives, gave*)

5 Gloria signed the petition and then handed it to Don, who _____ standing beside the booth. (*is, was*)

Make a point of listening to your friends and neighbors for a day, watching one thing in particular—the way they pronounce *have* in sentences like these:

We would have helped them.

I could have hit him!

Chances are that your friends and neighbors are like everyone else's. Unless they are speaking very slowly or very emphatically, the *have* in these sentences will sound exactly like the *of* in "a pound of butter," "a loaf of bread," or "three of the boys."

This fact explains a common spelling error—that of writing *of* instead of *have*. Though the mistake is understandable, it is still a mistake, one that users of standard English seldom make. Try to avoid it in your writing. Don't write *would of come*, *should of stayed*, or *must of heard*. Write:

They would *have* come. [Or: They *would've* come.]

I should *have* stayed in bed. [Or: I *should've* stayed.]

You must *have* heard him.

If clauses and wishes. The helping verb *would* is used in *if* clauses in sentences like these:

If he *would* only listen, you could convince him.

Jane would come if David *would* invite her.

But when the sentence refers to past time, the word *had*—not *would have* (or *would of*!)—is used after *if*:

If Terry *had listened* to me, he would have saved a dollar. [Not: If Terry *would have listened* to me.]

Jane would have come if David *had invited* her. [Not: if David *would have invited* her.]

The same thing is true of wishes that refer to past time. In standard English, the helping verb *had*, not *would have*, is used:

The twins wish they *had been* there. [Not: wish they *would have been* there.]

Don't you wish you *had thought* of it first? [Not: wish you *would have thought* of it first.]

EXERCISE 11 Be ready to read the following sentences aloud, using the verb forms appropriate in standard English.

1 I wish I (*would have, had*) won.

2 He would be here now if he (*would have, had*) taken a bus.

350

3 If only Jenny (*wouldn't have, hadn't*) tried to carry six jars of pickles at once!

4 We (*might have, might of*) done better if we (*would have, had*) had more encouragement.

5 Now he wishes that he (*would have, had*) sold the motorcycle.

6 If she (*would have, had*) had more patience, she (*could have, could of*) untangled the yarn.

7 The glasses (*would have, would of*) broken if you (*would have, had*) poured the hot coffee into them.

8 I wish Uncle Cliff (*would have, had*) seen me.

EXERCISE (12) REVIEW Each of the following sentences contains one or more verb forms that are not appropriate in standard English. List these verbs on a sheet of paper. (Be sure to write the *complete verb*.) After each, write the form as it should be. Number your answers with the numbers of the sentences.

1 While you fellows were laying around doing nothing, Mr. Armstrong learned us a new football formation.

2 Bring the books back to the library on your way to the movies.

3 He had never swam in such icy water before.

4 The soup would of been delicious if you wouldn't have used so much pepper.

5 She knew George had tore the page, but she says nothing.

6 I wish he would leave me play shortstop in the next game.

7 Don't some cats choose the oddest places to lay down in!

8 If Lucy would have sneezed at that moment, the car would of went off the road.

9 Hasn't he wrote to tell you that we seen him in Pittsburgh?

10 He done the planning himself, but he left me help with the work.

11 Ted run up to the door, rung the bell, and then ducks out of sight.

12 If you had chose the blue sweater, I would have took the pink.

13 What become of Larry Barnes after he come to New York?

14 Her precious canary had flew away.

15 The plaster might not of fell from the ceiling if you would of called a good plumber.

16 The man drunk three cups of coffee, ate six doughnuts, and then walks out without paying.

17 If we would have ran out of gas somewhere near a farmhouse, I could of phoned for help.

18 Hundreds of years ago sailors learned that a magnetic compass did not always point exactly to the North Pole.

351

CHAPTER 19

MAKING VERBS

AGREE WITH

THEIR SUBJECTS

Many students have a strange and completely wrong idea about grammar. They think that grammar "experts" sit in their offices and draw up "rules" or "laws" about how our language must be used. Then they publish these rules in textbooks and get English teachers to see that the rules are obeyed—in much the same way that traffic officers see to it that traffic laws are enforced.

But traffic laws are one thing; grammar rules (or laws) are another. Grammar rules are not laws drawn up by members of a city council or a state legislature to tell users of the language what they must do. Instead, grammar rules are simply statements describing the way language has been and is being used. The experts who write grammar books do not "make up" the rules. They arrive at the rules by observing how educated people use words. Then they report their findings for students to use as guides in speaking and writing.

Let's see for ourselves how a grammar expert works, how he arrives at a grammatical rule. We will start, as he does, by observing

words in use—in sentences. Suppose we begin with these, which are typical of sentences that you might hear educated people say dozens of times a day:

The *page* **is torn** out of the book.	The *pages* **are torn** out of the book.
The *clerk* **has left** already.	The *clerks* **have left** already.
The *doctor* **was** here at noon.	The *doctors* **were** here at noon.

Whoever said the sentences at the left was making a statement about a *single* person or a *single* thing: a *page*, a *clerk*, a *doctor*. Whoever said the sentences at the right was making a statement about more than one person or thing: *pages*, *clerks*, *doctors*. In other words, the subjects of the sentences at the left are **singular** in number; those at the right are **plural** in number.

The next step is to compare the verbs in the two groups of sentences. In doing so, you notice that when the speakers use subjects which are singular in number, they use what are called the "singular" forms of the verbs:

SINGULAR SUBJECT	SINGULAR VERB
page	is torn
clerk	has left
doctor	was

When they use plural subjects, they change the verbs to what are called the "plural" forms:

PLURAL SUBJECT	PLURAL VERB
pages	are torn
clerks	have left
doctors	were

By checking not only three pairs of sentences, but hundreds more like them, you will find that educated people generally follow this same pattern. They "match" a singular verb with a singular subject, a plural verb with a plural subject. Since this is true, you (like the grammar expert) can arrive at this conclusion: In standard English, the subject and the verb match, or "agree," in number. Remember that this is true not because you like the idea that two parts of a sentence should match, but because this is the way educated people speak the language.

Anybody who wants to speak and write standard English, therefore, will observe the rule: *A subject and verb should agree in number.* Much of the time, the rule is no problem; we use the right form of the verb automatically. But there are some kinds of sentences that may trick us into making a wrong choice. Let's look at some of these.

IT'S THE SUBJECT

THAT COUNTS

How would you decide whether to use the singular verb *was tacked* or the plural verb *were tacked* in the following sentence?

A list of lost-and-found articles _____ on the bulletin board.

The boy who wrote the sentence in a theme used the plural verb *were tacked.* This is the way he reasoned: "The word *articles* is plural. I would say *articles were*, not *articles was.* Therefore, *were tacked* must be right."

His reasoning was right, but his answer was wrong. You probably could tell him why. He had picked the *wrong word* for the verb to agree with. The verb is supposed to agree with the *subject* of the sentence, not with a noun in a prepositional phrase. The lost-and-found *articles* had not been tacked on the board; the *list* had been. Since the subject noun *list* is singular, the verb should be singular also:

> A list of lost-and-found articles *was tacked* on the bulletin board.

Watch out for prepositional phrases that come between the subject and the verb. Do not let the noun in the phrase trick you into using the wrong verb form. Ignore the phrase and concentrate on the subject:

> **One** [of the walls] *was painted* green. [Not: *were painted.*]
> The **pictures** [on the cover] *remind* me of Hal. [Not: *reminds.*]
> The **suit** [with the two blouses] *costs* more. [Not: *cost.*]
> The **coats** [with the fur trim] *cost* more. [Not: *costs.*]

Would you use the singular verb *listens* or the plural verb *listen* in the following sentence?

> Helen, like her two brothers, _____ to every broadcast.

Even though it is obvious from this sentence that *three* people hear every broadcast, the "grammatical" subject of the verb in the sentence is *Helen*. (The prepositional phrase *like her two brothers* merely adds an extra detail.) Since the subject itself is singular, the verb should be singular:

> Helen, like her two brothers, *listens* to every broadcast.

Remember it is the subject of the verb that counts, not a word in a phrase beginning with *like, as well as, together with,* or *along with*. The number of the subject determines that of the verb:

> **Gasoline,** [as well as several other fuels,] *is made* from petroleum. [Not: *are made.*]
> The **contestants,** [together with their manager,] *are* to ride with Parker. [Not: *is.*]

A special problem. In some sentences the subject is singular and the predicate complement (which means the same as the subject) is plural. Here too it is the subject that determines what the verb should be, not the predicate complement:

> His greatest **worry** *was* the many unpaid bills.
> The many unpaid **bills** *were* his greatest worry.

EXERCISE (1) Be ready to read each of the following sentences aloud, using the verb form (in parentheses) that agrees with the subject.

1 One of the boys (*is, are*) still missing.
2 His suggestions for improving the service (*was, were*) good.
3 The books on the top shelf of the closet (*belongs, belong*) to Fred Johnson.
4 The money in those two boxes (*belongs, belong*) to her.
5 Mr. Scott, like all his employees, (*works, work*) until five.
6 A large carton of toys and books (*was, were*) shipped.
7 The directions on the package (*tells, tell*) how much to use.
8 The verb, as well as the subject, (*has, have*) to be plural.
9 The tines of that fork (*is, are*) bent.
10 The houses in the new subdivision (*reminds, remind*) me of Florida.
11 One of the fenders (*was, were*) dented.
12 A set of mixing bowls now (*costs, cost*) two dollars.
13 The trees in the back yard (*has, have*) to be sprayed.
14 The hat with the veil and the sequins (*seems, seem*) best.
15 The butter in these sandwiches (*tastes, taste*) rancid.
16 The twins, as well as their brother, (*attends, attend*) Morton School.
17 One of his chief problems (*is, are*) the many interruptions.
18 The safe, along with its contents, (*was, were*) undamaged.
19 Your reasons for dropping out of the club (*surprises, surprise*) me, in fact.
20 His pronunciation of those words (*seems, seem*) wrong.
21 My cousin Mickey, like his father and brothers, (*has, have*) red hair and a terrible temper.
22 Only one of the errors (*was, were*) noticed.

TWO-PART SUBJECTS

Subjects joined by Or or Nor.   Although the subject of the following sentence has *two* parts, it is considered singular. Can you tell why?

Larry or **Bob** *has* the ticket.

In a sentence like this, it is the meaning, not the number of parts that determines whether the subject is singular or plural. Here the word *or* shows that only *one* of the boys has the ticket—perhaps Larry, perhaps Bob. When the parts of a compound subject joined by *or* or *nor* are singular, the subject is considered singular and takes a singular verb:

> **Sue, Eileen**, or **Mary** *is going* to help. [Not all three; just one *is*.]
>
> Neither his **answer** nor **mine** *was* right.

When the parts of the subject are both plural, a plural verb is used:

> **Toys** or **clothes** *were* always *appreciated*.
>
> All **candidates** or their **managers** *are* to report to Mr. Peters at five o'clock sharp.

But when one part is singular and the other is plural, the verb is usually made to agree with the part that is nearer to it:

> A large **lump** of butter or two **tablespoons** of oil *are added* last.
>
> Two **tablespoons** of oil or a large **lump** of butter *is added* last.

Subjects joined by **And.**   Most two-part subjects joined by *and* are plural, since they mean more than one person or thing:

> **Mr. Donner** and his **assistant** *were notified* of the change.
>
> The **stamp** and the **envelope** *are* in the drawer.

But when the parts mean only one person, or are thought of as one thing, they are considered singular and take a singular verb:

> George's best **friend** and next-door **neighbor** *was elected* president. [Just one person is meant.]
>
> When you're really hungry, **bread** and **butter** *tastes* delicious. [Thought of as a combination and hence as one item of food.]

357

EXERCISE (2)   Be ready to read each of the following sentences aloud, using the verb form (in parentheses) that agrees with the subject.

1   Jimmie or the dog (*has, have*) tracked mud on the rug.
2   No person or persons (*is, are*) going to stop him.
3   A series of articles on diets and their effects (*is, are*) to be published.
4   The warm weather or the thought of good times ahead (*has, have*) made Sally recover rapidly.
5   Neither she nor he (*needs, need*) your advice.
6   A little dry sage or a few sprigs of parsley (*improves, improve*) the turkey dressing.
7   A few sprigs of parsley or a little dry sage (*improves, improve*) the turkey dressing.

8   Jack's homework or the care of his hamsters (*keeps, keep*) him busy every day.

9   The carpets and the piano (*has, have*) not been moved in yet.

10 Neither the carpets nor the piano (*has, have*) been moved in yet, unfortunately.

11 Neither the piano nor the carpets (*has, have*) been moved in yet, unfortunately.

12 Macaroni and cheese (*is, are*) the only dish I can make.

13 Now a room and bath at that hotel (*costs, cost*) ten dollars a day during the hunting season.

14 Neither Harlow nor Lester (*was, were*) willing to help.

15 His niece and housekeeper, Barbara Wilkins, (*has, have*) arrived and (*wants, want*) to see you.

16 Philip, Robert, or Clifford (*manages, manage*) the grocery store when Mr. Thomas is out of town; but neither Philip or Robert (*knows, know*) the combination of the safe.

SUBJECTS

THAT FOLLOW THEIR VERBS

In most of our sentences the subject comes before the verb, often directly before it. In such sentences, subject-verb agreement is seldom a problem. We are, for example, so used to hearing and saying "The boy *is* here" and "The boys *are* here" that it would be hard for us to say the wrong forms—"The boy are here" and "The boys is here."

But saying the "wrong" forms is not hard in sentences in which the *verb* comes before the subject. Unless we think ahead, we are likely to start off with a singular verb—and then find that the subject, when it comes, turns out to be plural.

Watch out particularly for sentences beginning with the word *There* or *Here*. As you say "There" or "Here," think ahead to the coming subject. If it is going to be singular, use a singular verb:

There *is* a **run** in your stocking. [Or: *There's* a run.]
There *was* an **article** about him in the paper.
Here *is* your **share** of the prize money. [Or: *Here's* your share.]

But if the subject is going to be plural, use a plural verb:

There *are* several **letters** for you on the table. [Not: *is.*]
There *were* thirteen **shirts** to be ironed. [Not: *was.*]
Here *are* the **snapshots** I promised you. [Not: *is.*]

In questions, too, the verb (or part of it) is likely to come before the subject. Think ahead. Make the verb agree with the coming subject.

SINGULAR

Is **one** of the boys going to drive?
Has your **mother or father** *seen* your report card?

PLURAL

Were there any **sandwiches** left? [Not: *Was.*]
Where *are* the car **keys**? [Not: *is.*]
How *have* **Tom and Ken** *been*? [Not: *has.*]

EXERCISE 3 Be ready to read each of the following sentences aloud, using the verb form (in parentheses) that agrees with the subject.

1 Where (*is, are*) the list of names she gave you?
2 Here (*comes, come*) the mayor and the district attorney.
3 (*Has, Have*) the tenants been warned of the danger?
4 When (*is, are*) your nephew and niece going to arrive?
5 There (*goes, go*) those conceited Lindsay girls.
6 Only in emergencies or during air-raid drills (*is, are*) the use of the sirens permitted.
7 (*There's, There are*) the sheet of instructions for assembling the model.
8 Exactly when on that Wednesday afternoon (*was, were*) they given the telegram?
9 (*Does, Do*) he or his friends want part-time jobs?
10 (*Does, Do*) he and his friends want part-time jobs?
11 There (*was, were*) no errors or erasures in the letter.
12 (*Is, Are*) there a man or two strong boys to help lift this trunk?
13 (*Is, Are*) there two strong boys or a man to help lift this trunk?
14 In Mexico there (*is, are*) a village and a volcano named Paricutín.
15 (*Was, Were*) you and Ed asked to sign the petition?
16 I hope (*there's, there are*) enough chalk and erasers at the board in Room 220.
17 (*Does, Do*) the large carton of odds and ends belong to the Prestons or the Wades?
18 (*Here's, Here are*) some stamps for your collection.
19 (*There's, There are*) a stack of magazines on his desk.
20 (*Isn't, Aren't*) there one of them that would fit Joel?
21 Where (*was, were*) the necklace and bracelet hidden?
22 How much (*does, do*) the coat and hat cost?

THE MEANING

DETERMINES THE NUMBER

You cannot always judge by its appearance whether a subject takes a singular or plural verb. It is the meaning, not the form of the subject, that determines whether it is singular or plural. For example, the nouns *measles*, *mumps*, and *rickets* are plural in form. But since they are singular in meaning (each is the name of a disease), they take singular verbs:

> Mumps *is* generally milder than measles.
> Rickets *is caused* by a lack of vitamin D.

The names of some sciences, like *mathematics*, *economics*, *physics*, and *civics*, are also plural in form but singular in meaning. They, too, take singular verbs:

> Mathematics *includes* arithmetic, algebra, geometry, and calculus.
> Physics *was* Roy's favorite subject.

When a plural noun indicating a period of time or a certain weight, distance, or amount is thought of as a single unit, a singular verb is used:

> Five days *seems* a long time to wait.
> Seven dollars *was* a reasonable price, he thought.
> Three and a half miles *is* too far to walk in this rain.

A title is singular. When the subject of a sentence is the title of a book, poem, article, or painting, a singular verb is used. Even though the title contains plural words, it is the name of a *single* thing.

> "Trees" *was written* by Joyce Kilmer.
> "Fourteen Ways to Succeed" *is* the only article worth reading in the February issue.

Collective nouns. A collective noun is one that names a group of persons or things. For example:

audience	class	family
band	committee	jury
chorus	crew	team
majority	crowd	troop

A collective noun may take a singular or plural verb, depending on the meaning intended. To show that you want the group to be thought of as a single unit, you would use a singular verb, as in the following sentences:

> The audience *was* very attentive at first.
> The decorating committee *has ordered* the flowers.

To show that you are thinking of the individual members making up the group, you would use a plural verb:

> The audience *were straggling* out by twos and threes.
> The committee *are* still *wrangling* about the costumes and scenery.

Each and Every are always singular. Since words like *each, every, either, neither, everyone, anyone, somebody,* and *nobody* have a singular meaning, they take singular verbs—even when they are followed by a phrase containing a plural noun:

> I checked the dishes; each *has* a flaw.
> Each of the jobs *has been assigned.*
> Every house and store on those three blocks *belongs* to him.
> Either of the two *suits* me.
> Neither of the programs *sounds* interesting.
> *Has* anyone in the first two rows *finished?*

Sometimes singular; sometimes plural. Words like *all, half, more, most, some,* and *part* may take either a singular or plural verb. When these words tell *how much* of something is meant, a singular verb is used. When they tell *how many* are meant, a plural verb is used.

> Some of the money *was returned.* [Tells how much.]
> Some of the letters *were returned* also. [Tells how many.]

> Most of the camp *was* quiet. [Tells how much.]
> Most of the campers *were* asleep. [Tells how many.]

None—singular or plural. When the pronoun *none* is used to tell *how much* of something is meant, it takes a singular verb:

> None of the old wallpaper *has been removed* yet.
> *Was* none of his work satisfactory?

Otherwise, the meaning the speaker has in mind determines the number of the verb:

> We have four radios, but none of them *works.* [Singular; speaker means that not a single one works.]
> None of the costumes *fit* her. [Plural; speaker means that not any of them are the right size.]

361

Be ready to read each of the following sentences aloud, using the verb form (in parentheses) that agrees with the subject.

1 *The Searchers* (*was, were*) made into a motion picture.
2 Thirty-two cubic feet of water (*weighs, weigh*) nearly a ton.
3 (*Is, Are*) measles an infectious disease?
4 Neither of the explanations (*seems, seem*) clear.
5 His chief topic of conversation (*was, were*) his vacation plans.
6 His vacation plans (*is, are*) the only thing he talks about.
7 Twenty years (*seems, seem*) a long time to spend at one job.
8 Economics (*deals, deal*) with such matters as wages, prices, tariffs, and taxes.
9 (*Has, Have*) either of the girls told Mike the news?
10 The best part of the play (*was, were*) the first two acts.
11 Neither of the children (*has, have*) the slightest fear of water.
12 Every book and magazine on those shelves (*contains, contain*) vocabulary tests.
13 (*Has, Have*) each of them a pencil and some scratch paper?
14 Everyone in the speech classes (*was, were*) to sell tickets.
15 (*Is, Are*) there more of the chicken sandwiches in the kitchen?
16 Half of this piece with the pecans (*is, are*) enough for me.
17 (*Has, Have*) the committee announced the date of the show?
18 (*Is, Are*) either of those clocks right?
19 At least half of the boys in the club (*is, are*) going.
20 None of the pieces of this jigsaw puzzle (*seems, seem*) to fit together, in fact.

362

TWO SPECIAL USAGE DEMONS

Don't and Doesn't. Very few adults ever say "He do not" or "She do not." They use the singular form of the verb with a singular subject:

He *does* not *like* spinach.
Mary *does* not *know* the answer.

Yet when they use contractions, many of these same people switch to a plural verb.

THEY SAY: He *don't* want any.
The toaster *don't* work right.

THEY SHOULD SAY: He *doesn't* want any.
The toaster *doesn't* work right.

Why do people who never would say "He do not" say "He don't"? They will tell you that "He do not" sounds wrong—but "He don't" sounds right. And they will be telling you the truth. They have said "He don't" so often and have perhaps heard it so often that—*to them*—it does sound right. The only way they can be cured of this nonstandard "he don't" habit is to substitute the standard "he doesn't" habit in its place.

If you have the "he don't" habit, you can start to get rid of it by doing the following exercise. But going through the sentences once in class will not be enough. Take two or three minutes to repeat these same sentences (or others like them) every day until "he doesn't" sounds right to you.

EXERCISE 5 Be ready to read the following sentences aloud, substituting for the blanks the appropriate form—either *don't* or *doesn't*.

1 He _____ like spinach.
2 It _____ matter what they think.
3 The car _____ belong to him.
4 Sharon _____ want to go.
5 _____ her voice sound strange?
6 I know he _____ mind the noise.
7 _____ the flowers make him sneeze?
8 I like algebra, but she _____.
9 Why _____ it ever snow enough for skiing?
10 Frank _____ dance.
11 _____ she feel well?
12 That gadget _____ work anymore.
13 The noon train _____ stop here.
14 She _____ want a job.
15 Why _____ he fight back?

363

Was and Were.   In standard English the verb form *was* is used with singular subjects. The form *were* is used with plural subjects —and with the pronoun *you*, even if it means only one person.

NONSTANDARD: There *was* only four sandwiches left.
STANDARD: There *were* only four sandwiches left.

NONSTANDARD: You *was* invited, *wasn't* you, Jerry?
STANDARD: You *were* invited, *weren't* you, Jerry?

If you have fallen into the habit of saying "You was" instead of "You were," you can best get rid of the habit by repeating "You were" until it sounds right and you can say it without thinking. Start by drilling on sentences like the ones in Exercise 6.

1   You _____ wrong again, _____n't you?
2   They _____ planning to leave tonight.
3   Why _____ you worried about it?
4   _____n't you tired at the end of the game?
5   The two boys _____ hiding behind the hedge.
6   Tom _____ with Les, but you _____n't.
7   When _____ they supposed to arrive?
8   _____ you ever in Cincinnati?
9   Ted and I _____ working; you _____ loafing.
10 How _____ you expected to know the answer?
11 When _____ you notified?
12 Why _____n't you notified sooner?
13 You _____ really surprised, _____n't you?
14 Where _____ the girls sitting?
15 _____ you expecting him to call?

EXERCISE (7)   **REVIEW**   Be ready to read each of the following sentences aloud, using the verb form that agrees with the subject.

1   Peter's closest friend and most interested listener (*was, were*) his barber.
2   The radio or the children generally (*drowns, drown*) out the ring of the telephone.
3   The family in the upstairs flat (*has, have*) decided to move.
4   (*Where's, Where are*) the witch's costume and the wig?
5   Many miles of Australia's southwest coast (*is, are*) treeless.
6   Measles sometimes (*leaves, leave*) serious aftereffects.
7   (*Is, Are*) there some rolls and hot dogs to go with all this mustard?
8   The last number on the program (*was, were*) a few harp selections by Miss Kling.
9   (*There's, There are*) about one hundred mosquitoes and a hornet in our tent.
10 (*Has, Have*) the jury reached a verdict?
11 This pen, together with two refill cartridges, now (*costs, cost*) one dollar.
12 I know Jim (*doesn't, don't*) like creamed spinach.
13 Here (*comes, come*) our tennis champion and mathematical genius, Bob Hill.
14 (*Doesn't, Don't*) he work at Stacy's Grill?
15 You (*was, were*) right, and they (*was, were*) wrong.
16 (*Has, Have*) the librarian or her assistant arrived?

17   (*Was, Were*) you there when Mr. Price walked in?

18   (*Doesn't, Don't*) he play shortstop for the Cards?

19   Every one of those pans (*has, have*) to be scoured.

20   Why (*doesn't, don't*) Sharon answer the phone?

EXERCISE 8   **REVIEW**   Rewrite each of the following sentences, following the directions in brackets and making any other changes needed.

1   One dollar seems a fair price. [Change *One* to *Three*.]

2   All the dishes in that pile have been checked for flaws. [Change *All the* to *Every*.]

3   At least half of the food was wasted. [Change *food* to *sandwiches*.]

4   The manager, as well as his assistant, has agreed to attend. [Make *assistant* plural.]

5   Most of his short stories were highly praised by the critics. [Change *Most of his short stories* to "*Death and Taxes*."]

6   Where was Laura last night? [Insert *and Ken* after *Laura*.]

7   The candidates' names were written on the board. [Start with *A list of*.]

8   A year is a long time to spend on one experiment. [Change *A year* to *Three and a half years*.]

9   There were always five or six boys that refused to coöperate. [Insert *a group of* after *always*.]

10   Has either done what he promised to do? [Insert *Bill or Henry* after *either*.]

11   Neither seems to be worried. [Insert *Bill nor his friends* after *Neither*.]

12   There is, I imagine, another reason why he failed. [Change *another* to *several other*.]

13   Hidden under the blotter was a ten-dollar bill. [Insert *two letters and* before *a ten-dollar bill*.]

14   All sophomores and juniors who want to leave early have to get permission ahead of time. [Change *All* to *Every*.]

15   His only worry is his parents. [Shift *his parents* to the beginning.]

16   Neither wants to accuse the other. [Insert *of them* after *Neither*.]

17   Three one-act plays are to be presented. [Change *Three* to *A series of*.]

18   There goes Mr. Werner. [Add *and his wife*.]

19   All the articles in the September issue deal with school problems. [Change *All* to *Each of*.]

20   Some of the tables were sold. [Change *tables* to *furniture*.]

CHAPTER **20**

USING

PRONOUNS

366

Artists who draw comic strips are faced with a special problem—they don't have very much space in which to tell their stories. An author can use a page or two to describe the way his characters looked and acted in a particular situation. But the comic-strip artist must do this in four small panels, with room for only a few words. As a result, he often has to *suggest* a good many details rather than *tell* them.

One way the artist can do this is through the drawings themselves. For example, when he shows a tough-looking character with bristling whiskers, a scarred cheek, and a cigar hanging from the corner of his mouth, even new readers know that here is the "villain." And he usually makes the heroine look much more attractive and glamorous than her jealous roommate who is trying to steal her fortune or her boy friend.

But the artist does not depend on the drawings alone. He can suggest quite a bit about the various characters by the language he has them use. He has most of the characters speak standard Eng-

lish, the sort of English educated people use. But he has certain other persons say such sentences as these:

> *Me* and *him* was framed.
> They should of went *theirself*.
> I ain't talked to Bill and *she* yet.

As the artist knows, one of the chief ways in which standard and nonstandard English differ is in the use of pronouns and verbs. So merely by putting nonstandard forms of pronouns and verbs into the mouths of these persons, he manages to suggest that they are uneducated—or have not been much affected by the schooling they did have.

In and out of a comic strip, the language a person uses is an important factor in the impression he makes on other people. This is the main reason for including this chapter in your year's work. In this chapter you will review the pronoun forms that are used in standard English and will see how they differ from the nonstandard forms. Your goal (if you haven't already reached it) will be to become so familiar with the standard forms that you will use them constantly and automatically. You might keep in mind that the point of using standard English is not primarily to make a good impression, but to keep from making a poor impression.

PERSONAL PRONOUNS

AS SUBJECTS AND OBJECTS

Him and *me* saw Laura yesterday.
Laura saw *him* and *me* yesterday.

Our language is certainly strange. The italicized pronouns in these two example sentences look and sound exactly alike. Yet we say that *him* and *me* are **nonstandard** in the first sentence and **standard** in the second. How can this be?

The explanation lies in the fact that the words are **personal pronouns**—and in standard English, personal pronouns have different forms appropriate for different purposes:

		USED AS SUBJECTS	USED AS OBJECTS
SINGULAR:		I	me
		you	you
		he	him
		she	her
		it	it
PLURAL:		we	us
		you	you
		they	them

In the first example sentence, the pronouns are intended to be the subject of the verb; they are used to tell who saw Laura. Since the pronouns are the subject, standard English would use the **subject** forms for them:

STANDARD: *He* and *I* saw Laura yesterday. [Not: *Him* and *me*.]

In the second example sentence, the pronouns are the object of the verb; they tell who it was that Laura saw. In standard English, *him* and *me* are the forms used for **objects**:

STANDARD: Laura saw *him* and *me* yesterday. [Not: *he* and *I*.]

Using the standard forms is rarely a problem when one pronoun alone is concerned. The trouble comes when two pronouns or a noun and a pronoun are used together as a compound subject or object. Almost everyone you know, for example, says:

> *He* paid for the tickets. [Subject form.]
> Wally called *her*. [Object form—direct object.]
> Dad gave *him* the money. [Object form—indirect object.]
> Paul came with *me*. [Object form—object of preposition *with*.]

Yet many of these same people will switch to nonstandard forms of these pronouns in sentences like these:

NONSTANDARD: *Him* and *her* paid for the tickets.
NONSTANDARD: Wally called Jack and *she*.
NONSTANDARD: Dad gave Peg and *he* the money.
NONSTANDARD: Paul came with Kay and *I*.

Checking pronoun forms. Watch your sentences for a day or two to see if you have fallen into the habit of using nonstandard forms in compound subjects or objects. To check yourself, try using each pronoun by itself in the sentence. For example, since you would say "*He* paid for the tickets" and "*She* paid for the tickets," you should also say:

> *He and she* paid for the tickets.

Since you would say "Wally called *her*," "Dad gave *him* the money," and "Paul came with *me*," you should also say:

> Wally called *Jack and her*.
> Dad gave *Peg and him* the money.
> Paul came with *Kay and me*.

369

Here is another way to check the pronoun forms you use: If the pronoun comes *before* the verb, one of the subject forms should be used—*I, you, he, she, it, we, they*. If the pronoun comes *after* an action verb or *after* a preposition, one of the object forms should be used—*me, you, him, her, it, us, them*. Test the forms you choose in the exercises by using one of the two checks.

EXERCISE (1) Be ready to read the following sentences aloud, using the pronoun forms (in parentheses) appropriate in standard English.

1 Frank and (*him, he*) caught the most fish.
2 Between you and (*I, me*), I think he's a fraud.
3 You and (*me, I*) had better decide now.
4 Grace invited both Betty and (*I, me*).
5 The Martins and (*us, we*) are going in our car.
6 The waitress brought Glen and (*I, me*) the wrong orders.
7 Mr. Allen drives Tim and (*her, she*) to school on Mondays.

8 Carl looked for Larry and (*she, her*) at the party.
9 The books belong to (*they, them*) and (*we, us*).
10 The man asked David and (*she, her*) several questions.
11 Mrs. Neilsen was worried about you and (*they, them*).
12 Why don't you sit between (*her, she*) and (*I, me*)?
13 Neither (*them, they*) nor (*we, us*) were ready at six.
14 Do you blame Spence and (*me, I*) for leaving?
15 Either (*she, her*) or (*he, him*) broke the cup.

EXERCISE (2) Be ready to read the following sentences aloud, using the pronoun forms (in parentheses) appropriate in standard English.

1 Everyone expected Margaret and (*I, me*) to be nervous.
2 Wasn't it strange for Fred and (*her, she*) to complain?
3 My birthday gift from Gene and (*he, him*) came yesterday.
4 You and (*him, he*) must have just missed each other.
5 Either George or (*she, her*) will meet you at the train.
6 Mike and (*us, we*) are in the same class.
7 Dale should give either you or (*I, me*) a copy of the letter.
8 Wait for Helen and (*he, him*) at the glove counter.
9 My uncle and (*him, he*) own the corner drugstore.
10 The drugstore belongs to my uncle and (*him, he*).
11 Either Peggy or (*she, her*) could play the heroine.
12 Pat and (*he, him*) would come if they had a ride.
13 Dan brought sandwiches for you and (*they, them*).
14 The Hawkeyes and (*us, we*) play next week in Somers.
15 Mr. Grimes let Bob and (*me, I*) use his power mower.

370

PRONOUNS

AS PREDICATE COMPLEMENTS

He is the *boy* with the freckles.
Bob and she were the *cheerleaders*.
They must have been the *ringleaders*.

In these sentences *is*, *were*, and *must have been* are all forms of the linking verb *be*. The italicized nouns that follow these verbs are called *predicate complements*, as you learned in Chapter 12. Notice that each of these complements means the same thing as the subject:

Boy = **He**
Cheerleaders = *Bob and* **she**
Ringleaders = **They**

Since the predicate complements and the subjects mean the same, we can turn them around without changing the meaning:

The boy with the freckles is **he.**
The cheerleaders were *Bob and* **she.**
The ringleaders must have been **they.**

Notice that the same pronoun forms are used *after* the verb *be* as were used when the pronouns were the subjects of the sentences. When pronouns come after an *action* verb, the object forms are used. But when pronouns come after the *linking* verb *be,* the subject forms are generally used in standard English:

I'm sure that the one with the scarf *is* **she.** [Not: *is* **her.**]
Was it **she** who called? [Not: *Was* it **her.**]
It *must be* **he** in the driveway now. [Not: *must be* **him.**]
It *might have been* **they** who broke the window. [Not: *might have been* **them.**]

An important exception: In answer to the question "Who is it?" or "Who's there?" you might, of course, give your name: "Mike" or "It's Joan." But what if you use a pronoun instead? Then should you say "It's *me*" or "It is *I*"?

"It is *I*" is preferred by many careful speakers and writers. But so many educated people use the *me* form in this situation that "It's *me*" has also become an accepted form in standard English, one you need not hesitate to use. Remember, however, that though *It's me* is a standard usage, *It's him, It's her, It's us,* and *It's them* are not.

371

EXERCISE (3) Be ready to read the following sentences aloud, using the pronoun forms (in parentheses) appropriate in standard English.

1   The only ones who complained were George and (*he, him*).
2   Was it (*her, she*) or (*him, he*) who told you?
3   Are you sure you saw Jerry and (*she, her*) at the meeting?
4   It might have been (*him, he*) that you saw.
5   Yes, this is (*she, her*) speaking.
6   He refuses to admit it was (*him, he*).
7   If you were (*they, them*), what would you do?
8   The only ones who failed were Ellen and (*me, I*).
9   I'm supposed to give Clifford and (*she, her*) their tickets.
10 Could that have been (*him, he*) in the red car?
11 It was (*they, them*) who suggested the idea.
12 The one at the desk is (*him, he*).
13 The winners are you two and (*them, they*).
14 Wasn't it (*him, he*) who got the job you wanted?
15 I'm sure it wasn't (*they, them*) with the Clearys.

We boys or Us boys. Which should you say: "The coach drove *us boys* to the train" or "The coach drove *we boys* to the train"? Which should you say: "*We boys* wanted to help" or "*Us boys* wanted to help"?

Deciding whether to use *we* or *us* in sentences like these is easy. Which pronoun form would you use if the word *boys* were not in the sentences? Those are the forms appropriate to use in standard English:

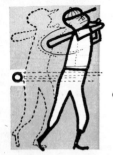

> The coach drove *us* [boys] to the train. [Object of *drove*.]
> *We* [boys] wanted to help. [Subject of *wanted*.]
> She brought gifts for *us* [two]. [Object of preposition *for*.]
> Shouldn't *we* [freshmen] have a meeting? [Subject of *should have*.]

Unneeded pronouns. The following sentences would sound childish to most people. Do you know why?

> Then the batter he swung at the ball but missed.
> My sister she goes to Lincoln School.

Since each of these sentences has a noun subject (*batter* and *sister*), there is no need for the pronouns *he* and *she*. Pronouns are substitute words; they take the place of nouns. Why use them *with* nouns—and run the risk of sounding childish?

Order of pronouns. As a mark of courtesy, it has become a custom among users of standard English to put pronouns that stand for other people *before* pronouns that stand for or include the speaker. When you use a compound subject containing *I* or *we* or a compound object containing *me* or *us*, put these words last:

> *Jean and I* went swimming. [Not: *I and Jean.*]
> *They and we* are neighbors. [Not: *We and they.*]
> No one saw *Sam or me.* [Not: *me or Sam.*]
> It was sent to *you and us.* [Not: *us and you.*]

Them or Those. In standard English the "demonstrative" pronoun *those*—not the personal pronoun *them*—is used to point out which persons or things are meant:

NONSTANDARD: *Them* on the desk are his.
STANDARD: *Those* on the desk are his.

NONSTANDARD: *Them* are the boys she meant.
STANDARD: *Those* are the boys she meant.

EXERCISE (4) Be ready to read the following sentences aloud, using the pronoun forms (in parentheses) appropriate in standard English.

1 After the meeting (*we, us*) girls are going to the movies.
2 (*Them, Those*) are just like the ones Lee bought.
3 Suppose you let (*we, us*) fellows cook the wieners.
4 Why can't (*we, us*) three ride with Bruce?
5 These are all right, but (*those, them*) have flaws.
6 Dad thinks that (*we, us*) men ought to demand our rights.
7 Next week (*we, us*) freshmen are in charge of the program.
8 No, the blue ones are Ed's, and (*those, them*) are yours.
9 Five of (*we, us*) boys can handle the job.
10 Mr. Kranz promised (*we, us*) girls that he'd be at the rehearsal.
11 Do you expect (*we, us*) four to do the work alone?
12 (*Them, Those*) are cheaper, aren't they?

PRONOUNS IN COMPARISONS

If you want to compare the speed with which Jane and Ken can change a tire, you might say:

Jane can change a tire faster than Ken.
Ken cannot change a tire as fast as Jane.

But unless you are naturally inclined to use more words than necessary, you will not expand these sentences to:

Jane can change a tire faster than Ken *can change a tire.*
Ken cannot change a tire as fast as Jane *can change a tire.*

Since the meaning is perfectly clear without the added words *can change a tire*, people seldom bother to say these words. But knowing about these missing "understood" words will help you to decide which form of the pronoun to use in sentences like these:

SUBJECT FORM

Jane can change a tire faster than **he** [*can change a tire*].
Ken cannot change a tire as fast as **she** [*can change a tire*].
Henry told Sue more than **I** [*told her*].

OBJECT FORM

The dress fits you better than [*it fits*] **her.**
Mr. Wells didn't charge Ted as much as [*he charged*] **us.**
Henry told Sue more than [*he told*] **me.**

If you compare the third sentence in the first group with the third sentence in the second group, you will see how important using the "right" form is. Using the "wrong" form would give each sentence a meaning not intended.

Note: In casual conversation you will often hear the object forms (instead of subject forms) in sentences like "He is much taller than *me*" and "I worked harder than *him*." Though these forms are acceptable in informal speech, they are generally avoided in writing and in formal speech.

EXERCISE 5 Be ready to read the following sentences aloud, using the pronoun forms (in parentheses) appropriate in standard written English. Be ready also to tell what the missing "understood" words are that led to your choosing these forms. In two of the sentences either a subject pronoun or an object pronoun could be used. Give both forms for these sentences and be ready to explain the difference in the meaning.

1 Kathleen is a better dancer than (*he, him*).
2 I don't know anyone who works as hard as (*her, she*).
3 Mr. Clancy trusts Laura more than (*I, me*).
4 Though I worked hard to please her, my aunt liked my brother more than (*I, me*).
5 The costume fitted you better than (*he, him*).
6 They can type the letters faster than (*we, us*).
7 It was more fun to tease him than (*her, she*).
8 They didn't make as many first downs as (*us, we*).
9 I disliked Phil as much as (*her, she*).
10 They spent as much money as (*us, we*) for decorations.
11 Since Will is deaf, the noise bothered us more than (*he, him*).
12 Mr. Downs suspected Tom as well as (*we, us*) and watched every move the three of us made.
13 You are just as stubborn as (*him, he*).
14 Isn't he younger than (*she, her*)?
15 We both did the work, so why pay me less than (*her, she*)?

POSSESSIVE FORMS

OF PRONOUNS

An apostrophe and *s* added to a noun is a sign that the noun is possessive—that it shows ownership:

Sharon's coat   the *baby's* toys   a *man's* voice

But to show ownership when pronouns are used, we do not use apostrophes. We merely use the *possessive forms* of the pronouns:

> Nora's hair is lighter than *mine*.
> I saw John's report but not *yours*.
> Those skates are *his*; *hers* are in the hall.
> The dog raised *its* paw. [A pronoun used as an adjective.]
> Ed's share is smaller than *theirs* and *ours*.

Though all of these forms but *mine* end in *s*, remember that they show ownership *without* an apostrophe.

DON'T WRITE—	WRITE INSTEAD—
Is this *her's* or *our's*?	Is this *hers* or *ours*?
Put *your's* with *their's*.	Put *yours* with *theirs*.

Watch the possessive *its* especially when you write. Inserting an apostrophe changes *its* to *it's*—the contraction of *it is*.

DON'T WRITE—	WRITE INSTEAD—
It's wing is broken.	*Its* wing is broken.
It's time to put the canary in *it's* cage.	*It's* time to put the canary in *its* cage.

PRONOUNS ENDING

IN SELF AND SELVES

Study the following list of "self" pronouns, noticing particularly the letters printed in boldface type. Compare these boldfaced forms with the italicized words opposite them.

SINGULAR:	**my**self	*my* father
	yourself	*your* turn
	himself	*his* mistake
	herself	*her* job
	itself	*its* wing
PLURAL:	**our**selves	*our* house
	yourselves	*your* money
	themselves	*their* schemes

These "self" pronouns are another good example of the fact that language is not always logical. Since users of standard English say "*myself*" and "*yourself*" and "*herself*," you would expect that they would also say "*hisself*." But they don't. And since users of standard English say "*ourselves*" and "*yourselves*," you would expect them also to say "*theirselves.*" But they don't. *Hisself* and *their-selves*—though logical—are used only in nonstandard English. Some day perhaps these nonstandard forms will become acceptable. Until they do, you will want to avoid them.

STANDARD: Did Ted hurt *himself*? [Not: *hisself.*]

STANDARD: Tell the boys to help *themselves.* [Not: *theirselves.*]

EXERCISE (6) On a sheet of paper, write the pronoun forms (in parentheses) appropriate in standard English. Number your answers with the numbers of the sentences.

1 (*Its, It's*) too early to give the dog (*its, it's*) food.
2 Isn't the blue nylon sweater (*yours, your's*)?
3 Why should you two blame (*yourself, yourselves*)?
4 Did he do all the work (*hisself, himself*)?
5 (*Our's, Ours*) is a later model than (*their's, theirs*).
6 We had to force (*ourself, ourselves*) to stay awake.
7 They entertained (*theirselves, themselves*) by playing chess.
8 (*Hers, Her's*) was more expensive than (*yours, your's*).
9 (*It's, Its*) paw is hurt, and (*it's, its*) in pain.
10 He made (*himself, hisself*) a ham sandwich.
11 We borrowed (*her's, hers*); (*hi's, his, his'*) didn't fit.
12 Leo could have kicked (*hisself, himself*) for his stupidity.
13 (*It's, Its*) about time you put that back in (*it's, its*) case.
14 They guffawed when they saw (*theirself, themself, themselves*) in the mirror.
15 You men can see for (*yourselves, yourself*) that (*it's, its*) design is excellent.
16 They ate the pie (*themself, themselves, theirselves*).

WHO OR WHOM?

The pronoun *who*, used in questions and in adjective clauses, has different forms, just as personal pronouns do.

SUBJECT FORM: *Who* brought the package?
Do you know the man *who* brought the package?

OBJECT FORM: *Whom* did you call?
I talked to the agent *whom* you called.

POSSESSIVE FORM: *Whose* purse is it?
The girl *whose* purse you found is here.

Formal usage. In formal English (the English educated people use in serious talks or writing for special occasions) the choice between *who* and *whom* depends on how the pronoun is used. When it is used as the subject or the predicate complement of a sentence or clause, *who* is chosen:

> *Who* broke the window? [Subject of *broke.*]
> *Who* was elected president? [Subject of *was elected.*]
> He knew the man *who* was elected. [Subject of *was elected.*]
> *Who* were the winners? [Predicate complement.]

But when the pronoun is used as the object of the verb or of a preposition, *whom* is chosen:

> *Whom* did he recommend? [Object of *did recommend.*]
> Miss Barnes, *whom* he recommended, accepted the job. [Object of *recommended.*]
> To *whom* did they turn for help? [Object of preposition *To.*]
> The people to *whom* they turned for help refused them. [Object of *to.*]

Informal usage. In informal English (the kind used by educated people on everyday occasions) the choice between *who* and *whom* depends on the position of the pronoun. When it comes at the beginning of a sentence, *who* is often used, whether the pronoun is a subject or an object:

> *Who* turned in the alarm? [Subject of *turned.*]
> *Who* did you invite? [Object of *did invite.*]
> *Who* did they turn to for help? [Object of preposition *to.*]

But if the pronoun follows a preposition, *whom* is generally used, just as in formal English:

> *To whom* did they turn for help?
> *From whom* should I order the set?
> The man *from whom* I ordered the set is here.

In sentences like the following, the choice between *who* and *whom* is seldom a problem in informal English. Usually the pronoun is simply omitted or the pronoun *that* is used:

FORMAL: He refused to deal with people *whom* he disliked.
INFORMAL: He refused to deal with people he disliked.
INFORMAL: He refused to deal with people *that* he disliked.

FORMAL: She is the actress for *whom* he wrote the play.
INFORMAL: She is the actress he wrote the play for.
INFORMAL: She is the actress *that* he wrote the play for.

In much of your written work for your classes, you will probably be expected to use the pronoun forms appropriate in formal English. But if you are writing short stories or anecdotes in which you have conversation, you will probably want to use the forms appropriate in informal English. These forms, of course, are appropriate for almost all speaking situations.

EXERCISE 7 Be ready to read the following sentences aloud, substituting for the blanks the pronoun form *who* or *whom*. Use the form that would be appropriate in formal English.

1 _____ was appointed chairman?

2 _____ did she appoint?

3 No one likes the fellow _____ was appointed chairman.

4 For _____ did David work last year?

5 The man for _____ he worked was promoted.

6 Renata Tebaldi, _____ the New York critics praised so highly, was excellent.

7 From _____ did they receive the eviction notice?

8 _____ substituted for _____ during the first half?

9 _____ was expelled besides Larry?

10 The students _____ were expelled are now back in school.

11 Carl Sandburg, _____ we met in Chicago, is to be the speaker.

12 To _____ should we send our entries?

13 The Indians _____ he saw were not wearing war paint.

14 The master of ceremonies, with _____ he had rehearsed, forgot his lines.

15 At the banquet he was seated next to Dr. Martin, _____ he had been avoiding for weeks.

16 Mark, to _____ he passed the ball, fumbled it.

17 Vote for Dave Elliot, _____ understands the farmers' problems.

18 Vote for Dave Elliot, _____ the farmers trust.

19 _____ was chosen to head the new party and by _____ was he chosen?

20 Inspector Zeff, _____ O'Connor interviewed, had little to say.

PRONOUN AGREEMENT

When you use a pronoun as a substitute for a singular noun, the pronoun should be singular also. When you use a pronoun as a substitute for a plural noun, the pronoun should be plural.

These rules seem sensible enough, and most people have no trouble following them. Without the slightest hesitation, they choose the appropriate forms in sentences like these:

> When the *nurse* comes, **she** will bandage Tom's finger. [Singular pronoun to refer to singular noun *nurse*.]
> Before the *nurses* leave, **they** see that **their** patients are comfortable. [Plural pronouns to refer to plural noun *nurses*.]

Yet many of these same people will often use a plural pronoun in a sentence like this, in which the pronoun refers to a singular noun:

> If a *person* asks a stupid question, **they** deserve a stupid answer.

Can you figure out why a speaker does this sort of thing? The reason is simple. The noun *person* in a sentence like this might mean a man or a woman, a boy or a girl. So, thinking of the meaning rather than the form of the pronoun, the speaker chooses the plural *they*, which includes both men and women. He evidently shies away from using the singular pronoun *he* or *she* because of a feeling that *he* would exclude women and *she* would exclude men.

Yet *he* would be the appropriate form to use in the sentence: "If a person asks a stupid question, *he* deserves a stupid answer." The pronoun *he* is singular, as it should be, to match the singular noun *person*. And no one would misunderstand the meaning. In a sentence like this, the *he* refers to either a man or a woman.

379

Indefinite pronouns. The indefinite pronouns *anybody, anyone, everybody, everyone, somebody, someone, nobody, no one, each, either,* and *neither* are singular in number. When you use them as subjects, you always use singular verbs with them:

> Somebody *is coming* up the walk.
> Nobody *has finished* yet.
> Neither *is* worth much.

When pronouns are used to refer to these indefinites, the pronouns should, as a rule, be singular also:

> Somebody has left *his* report on my desk. [*His* is used unless you know that the "somebody" is a girl.]
> Tell everyone to pay *his* dues before *he* leaves.
> Neither of the twins has paid *her* towel fee.

In everyday conversation, a plural pronoun is often used in such sentences, but this form is not appropriate in writing:

SPOKEN: Everyone has paid *their* dues.
WRITTEN: Everyone has paid *his* dues.

Occasionally the indefinite pronoun has a meaning so clearly plural that using a singular pronoun would make the sentence sound silly:

> As soon as everyone got there, *he* started to play bridge.
> Nobody heard the announcement because *he* was intent on *his* work.

There are two ways out of this predicament. In informal English, plural pronouns would be used without hesitation, since the meaning clearly calls for the plural:

> As soon as everyone got there, *they* started to play bridge.
> Nobody heard the announcement because *they* were intent on *their* work.

In formal English, the sentences would be rephrased to avoid the problem:

> As soon as *all the guests* had arrived, *they* started to play bridge.
> Nobody heard the announcement because *everyone* was intent on *his* work.

EXERCISE 8 Be ready to read the following sentences aloud, using the pronoun forms (in parentheses) appropriate in standard written English.

1 Neither of the twins remembered to bring (*her, their*) notebook to class.
2 Has anyone here lost (*their, his*) gloves?
3 Everyone in the sewing class must buy (*her, their*) own material and pattern.
4 Before a person signs (*his, their*) name, (*they, he*) should read the petition.
5 Once a member signs up for the trip, (*they, he*) cannot back out.
6 Neither of the boys heard (*his, their*) name being called.
7 If anyone wants extra copies, (*they, he*) can get them from Miss Finch.
8 I'm sure no one will recognize (*himself, themselves*) in that picture from the *Herald*.
9 Everyone should proofread (*his, their*) paper before handing it to the committee.
10 Each of the girls did all (*they, she*) could to help.
11 It's unfair to judge a person by (*their, his*) looks.
12 Somebody has left (*her, their*) purse and gloves on the table.

13 If a contestant moves (*his, their*) left foot, (*he, they*) will be disqualified immediately.

14 Why not let each of the girls tell (*their, her*) side of the story?

15 If anyone refuses to do (*their, his*) share, (*they, he*) will get no food.

16 Nobody is to park (*their, his*) car in the driveway.

17 A person that never expresses (*their, his*) opinion probably has none.

18 If a student doesn't understand, (*he, they*) should ask questions.

19 Neither Ellen nor Jane had made (*their, her*) own costume for the masquerade party.

20 Has either of the girls weighed (*themselves, herself*) lately to see whether the diet is helping (*them, her*)?

EXERCISE 9 **REVIEW** Each of the following sentences contains one or more pronoun forms not appropriate in standard English. Be ready to read the sentences aloud, substituting standard pronoun forms wherever necessary. Be ready also to explain why you make the changes.

1 Then Bob he came right up to Harley and I.

2 Me and Frank saw the accident.

3 I, my cousin, and Bruce played against Sam and she.

4 For a long time Jerry kept the news to hisself.

5 Anyone who parks their car on that street will be fined.

6 Just between you and I, don't you think he's conceited?

7 Once a person trains theirselves to study, they won't waste their time in study hall.

8 She asked Bob and I the very same question.

9 Most of the students whom were interviewed enjoyed the experience, in fact.

10 It was him who called, not her.

11 Why should us girls work as hard as them?

12 A crew cut suits Ted better than Keith or I.

13 In fact, it wasn't her who complained to Miss Lawrence.

14 He earns more than me, but I save more than him.

15 Mike and him will hurt theirselves with the saw.

16 The last ones, as usual, were Ed and her.

17 Them are the ones you should buy for Tim and she.

18 Why don't you come with Louise and I?

19 He gave we boys a piece of his mind.

20 Sinclair Lewis, to who the Pulitzer Prize was awarded in 1926, declined it.

CHAPTER 21

USING

MODIFIERS

Suppose you saw a carpenter driving a nail with the handle of a screwdriver. Since you know that a hammer is designed to drive nails, and a screwdriver to put in screws, you would wonder why he was using a screwdriver when a hammer would do the work so much better. And you would probably not have a very favorable impression of his skill as a carpenter.

Both adjectives and adverbs are useful tools of language. But, like the hammer and the screwdriver, these modifiers have different uses. When a writer or speaker makes the mistake of using an adjective to do the work of an adverb or of using an adverb to do the work of an adjective, he clearly shows that he lacks skill in using the tools of language.

Perhaps you are not always certain about which modifier you should use in a particular situation. Yet you would like to make a good impression on others; you would like to use language tools like adjective and adverb modifiers correctly and efficiently. If so, this chapter can help you.

ADJECTIVE OR ADVERB?

Which of the two boldfaced words at the right should you use in the following sentences?

Mr. Barnes worked _____.	**steady**	or	**steadily**
Ed takes his job too _____.	**serious**	or	**seriously**
Joe checked the meter _____.	**regular**	or	**regularly**

The boldfaced words in both columns are modifiers. Those in the first column are **adjectives**. Those in the second—with the *ly* ending—are **adverbs**. The way to decide which is the right modifier to use in a sentence is to figure out what work the modifier does. If its work is to modify a noun or a pronoun, the adjective should be used. If its work is to modify a verb, the adverb should be used.

In these sentences the modifiers are being used to tell something about the verb: how Mr. Barnes worked, how Ed takes his job, how often Joe checked the meter. Therefore the *adverbs* are the modifiers to use:

> Mr. Barnes worked **steadily**.
> Ed takes his job too **seriously**.
> Joe checked the meter **regularly**.

Compare the italicized modifiers in the following pairs of sentences. Notice that the forms without *ly* (adjectives) are used to modify nouns and pronouns; the forms with *ly* (adverbs) are used to modify the verb:

Sue has a *neat* appearance.   Sue dresses very *neatly*.

I am *sure* that he needs help.   He *surely* needs help.

Tim's behavior was *bad*.   Tim behaved rather *badly*.

Since an adverb is often formed by adding *ly* to an adjective, many adverbs end in *ly*. Some adverbs, however, have two forms—one ending in *ly* and one that is the same as the adjective:

Walk *slowly*.	Walk *slow*.
Jump *quickly*.	Jump *quick*.
He sang *loudly*.	He sang *loud*.

Since either form of these adverbs is acceptable, the form you use depends on which sounds better in your sentence. The shorter form is more usual in short sentences like commands:

> Drive *slow*.
> When his name was called, Simms rose *slowly* and walked to the front of the room.

A word of warning: Though many adverbs end in *ly*, not all modifiers ending in *ly* are adverbs. Some adjectives also end in *ly*: this *cowardly* act, a *lonely* road, his *friendly* greeting.

EXERCISE (1) Decide whether the italicized modifiers in the following sentences are adjectives or adverbs by figuring out what work the modifiers do in the sentences. Divide a sheet of paper into two columns. In the first column, list the words modified by the italicized modifiers. In the second column, tell whether the modifier is an adjective or adverb. Number your answers with the sentence numbers.

1   He made *quick* work of that.
2   Hide *quick*; he'll see you.
3   The investigators are working *quickly* because the district attorney has demanded *fast* action.
4   Dan is *slow* all right; his favorite saying is "Make haste *slowly*."

5 We heard *loud* cries and ran *fast* to see what was wrong.

6 Does Jim always speak so *loud*?

7 Mrs. Casey treated the children very *kindly* in spite of their bad manners.

8 He was a *kindly* sort of person.

9 Must the radio play so *loudly*? *Kindly* turn the volume down.

10 Is your watch running *slow*, or is my watch *fast*?

EXERCISE (2) Be prepared to read aloud each of the following sentences, choosing the correct modifier—adjective or adverb. Remember that the modifier you choose should depend on the work the word does in the sentence. Be ready to explain your choices.

1 Bob visited our house rather (*frequent, frequently*).

2 Mrs. MacGregor cooked the soup (*special, specially*) for him.

3 I've never seen anyone handle a baby so (*careful, carefully*).

4 The old man needed a shave (*bad, badly*).

5 I know the inspections should be made (*regular, regularly*), but should they be so (*frequent, frequently*)?

6 Several pieces in the set can be bought (*separate, separately*).

7 Don't take what he says so (*serious, seriously*).

8 Jim used to work (*regular, regularly*) at the canning plant.

9 I wonder why they moved so (*sudden, suddenly*).

10 He talked fast and not very (*distinct, distinctly*).

11 Maybe he does play (*bad, badly*), but he couldn't be as (*bad, badly*) as you say.

12 Mrs. Potter was dressed very (*fashionable, fashionably*) as always.

13 Eve shouldn't have talked so (*bold, boldly*) to Mrs. Hill.

14 Amy certainly behaved (*different, differently*) from her sister.

15 Mr. Daly never treated the girls as (*strict, strictly*) as he did the boys.

ADJECTIVE AFTER LINKING VERB

John *tasted* the stew eagerly. [The subject *John* did a physical action—he did the tasting.]

The stew *tasted* delicious to John. [The subject *stew* did not do a physical action—it did not do the tasting.]

The verb in the first sentence is an **action verb**. But the verb in the second sentence—though it looks the same as the one in the first—

is not an action verb. It is a **linking verb**; its job is to link the descriptive adjective *delicious* to the subject noun *stew*, which it modifies.

You have little trouble choosing the correct modifier to tell something about the action verb in sentences like these:

George *looked* **strangely** at Bob.
Mary *felt* her way **carefully**.
The cat *smelled* the fish **suspiciously**.
Jane *tasted* the pumpkin **cautiously**.
The radioman *sounded* the distress signal **steadily**.

You use an adverb to describe the action that is done by the subject.

But sentences like the following—in which the same verbs are used—may be troublesome. Which of the boldfaced modifiers at the right—the adjectives in the first column or the adverbs in the second column—should you use in these sentences?

George *looked* _____ to Bob.	**strange** or	**strangely**
Mary *felt* _____ after hearing the news.	**bad** or	**badly**
The fish *smelled* _____.	**unpleasant** or	**unpleasantly**
The pumpkin *tasted* _____.	**peculiar** or	**peculiarly**
Tim's warning *sounded* _____.	**sinister** or	**sinisterly**

The choice depends, of course, on the work the modifier does in the sentence. The verbs in these sentences are not action verbs; their subjects do not do a physical action. George did not look at anything. Mary did not feel (or touch) anything. The fish did not smell anything. The pumpkin did not taste anything. The warning did not sound anything. The verbs are linking verbs. The missing modifiers are intended to describe the subjects, not to modify the verbs. Therefore, *adjective* modifiers should be used in these sentences:

George *looked* **strange** to Bob.
Mary *felt* **bad** after hearing the news.
The fish *smelled* **unpleasant**.
The pumpkin *tasted* **peculiar**.
Tim's warning *sounded* **sinister**.

EXERCISE 3 Divide a sheet of paper into two columns. In the first column, tell whether the italicized verb in each of the following sentences is a linking verb or an action verb. Then from the pair of modifiers (in parentheses) after each sentence, choose the one—adjective or adverb—that is correct to substitute for the blank in the sentence

386

and write it in the second column. Number your answers with the numbers of the sentences.

1 The grumpy old man *looked* _____ at Carol. (*sour, sourly*)
2 This lemonade *tastes* too _____. (*sour, sourly*)
3 I *felt* _____ about asking Rob to help us. (*timid, timidly*)
4 The puppy *smelled* the bone _____. (*timid, timidly*)
5 When Bill gave his explanation, he *sounded* _____. (*nervous, nervously*)
6 As the patrolman approached the car, Dad *felt* _____ for his driver's license. (*nervous, nervously*)
7 Mr. Cox's refusal *sounded* _____. (*emphatic, emphatically*)
8 Kay certainly *looked* _____ last night. (*angry, angrily*)
9 These apples *smell* _____ from those. (*different, differently*)
10 When Sue realized what trouble she had caused, she *felt* _____. (*bad, badly*)
11 Some of these nuts *taste* _____. (*bitter, bitterly*)
12 Spaniards *sound* the letter *x* _____ from the way we do. (*different, differently*)
13 The tiny sausages *smell* quite _____ while they are being fried. (*unappetizing, unappetizingly*)
14 Several of the committee members *looked* rather _____ when Barton's name was mentioned. (*scornful, scornfully*)
15 If you add a bit of sage, your dressing *will taste* _____. (*delicious, deliciously*)
16 A number of Jordan's answers *sounded* _____. (*scornful, scornfully*)
17 When she heard footsteps behind her in the dark street, Mrs. Prentice *felt* _____. (*uneasy, uneasily*)
18 Although the cake was the first his sister had ever baked, Bruce *tasted* it _____. (*nonchalant, nonchalantly*)
19 A citizens' committee complained to the city manager about the stagnant creek, which *smelled* _____. (*foul, foully*)
20 Hank and Sam *looked* _____ as they entered the principal's office. (*glum, glumly*)

EXERCISE (4) Be prepared to read aloud each of the following sentences, choosing the correct modifier—adjective or adverb. Be ready to explain your choices.

1 The experiment we did today made the laboratory smell (*peculiar, peculiarly*).
2 The native sounded the drum (*steady, steadily*).
3 Nancy's apricot pie didn't taste so (*sour, sourly*) as this one.
4 For years Jack felt (*bitter, bitterly*) about his sudden dismissal.

5 When Carol asked if he thought the plan would work, Tim looked (*doubtful, doubtfully*).

6 Bloodhounds make good trackers because they can smell so (*keen, keenly*).

7 Taste that shrimp (*careful, carefully*). It tastes (*strange, strangely*) to me.

8 I wouldn't have felt so (*bad, badly*) if Ruth hadn't looked so (*suspicious, suspiciously*) at me.

9 Why did Nick look so (*mysterious, mysteriously*) when I asked him where Pete was?

10 No matter what the doctor says, I still think this medicine tastes (*unpleasant, unpleasantly*).

11 Karen was afraid to go into the museum because the guard looked so (*fierce, fiercely*).

12 Every syllable must be sounded (*distinct, distinctly*).

13 The whole staff felt (*sad, sadly*) about his resignation.

14 The sudden clap of thunder sounded (*ominous, ominously*) to the startled picnickers.

15 Aunt Jean's bureau drawers smell (*fragrant, fragrantly*) because she sprinkles lavender sachet in them.

GOOD OR WELL?

Good and *well* are a tricky pair of modifiers, a pair that are often confused. But if you remember that *good* is always an adjective, you will not make the mistake of using it as a modifier of a verb. Use the adjective *good* to modify a noun or pronoun; use the adverb *well* to describe the action of a verb.

ADJECTIVE GOOD	ADVERB WELL
This is a *good* pen. [Describes noun *pen*.]	This pen writes *well*. [Tells how the pen writes.]
The dancer was *good*. [Describes noun *dancer*.]	She danced *well*. [Tells how she danced.]
He felt *good* about passing the test. [Describes pronoun *He*.]	He did *well* on the test. [Tells how he did on the test.]

Note: The word *well* may also be used as an adjective, usually meaning "not ill" or "in good health." But its adjective use seldom causes trouble:

My mother is *well*.   He feels *well*.

Be prepared to read aloud the following sentences, choosing the correct modifier. Be ready to explain your choices.

1 Len's portable radio never has worked (*good, well*).
2 Can Faye ride (*good, well*) enough to stay on that horse?
3 I wish Blaine could hit as (*good, well*) as he pitches.
4 Bill certainly felt (*good, well*) about his promotion.
5 Although he looked pale, Al insisted that he felt (*good, well*).
6 That color looks (*good, well*) on you, and the suit fits you (*good, well*).
7 Dad complained that he hadn't slept (*good, well*) lately.
8 Mrs. Miller's health is as (*good, well*) as can be expected, but she will never be really (*good, well*) again.
9 Jimmy is reliable and works (*good, well*) under pressure.
10 The situation looked (*bad, badly*), but Mr. Harris handled it (*good, well*).
11 Don't feel (*bad, badly*) about missing the third question.
12 Shake the medicine (*good, well*) before pouring it.

COMPARISON

389

The three boys in this picture all have one quality in common— all are "tall." But, as you can see, the three boys are not equally tall. In describing the boys to show how they differ, you would use different forms of the adjective *tall*:

Jack is **tall**.
Ken is **taller** than Jack.
Sam is the **tallest** boy of the three.

These three forms of the adjective *tall* are called "degrees of comparison," since they show to what degree the three boys have the quality of "tallness." The first form (*tall*) is called the **positive degree**; the second form (*taller*) is called the **comparative degree**; the third form (*tallest*) is called the **superlative degree**.

We form the comparative and superlative degrees of adjectives in one of two ways. If the adjective is short—one or two syllables —we add *er* or *est*:

> A 60-watt bulb sheds a *bright* light. [Positive.]
> A 100-watt bulb sheds a *brighter* light than a 60-watt bulb. [Comparative.]
> A 150-watt bulb sheds the *brightest* light of the three. [Superlative.]

If the adjective is long, we use *more* or *most*:

> Jane is *talkative*. [Positive.]
> Betty is *more talkative* than Jane. [Comparative.]
> Donna is the *most talkative* girl in our club. [Superlative.]

For a number of adjectives, either way may be used:

> Stan was *lively*.
> Jack was *livelier* than Stan. **or** Jack was *more lively* than Stan.
> Al was the *liveliest* of the boys. **or** Al was the *most lively* of the boys.

Adverb forms are made in the same two ways:

> Bill worked *fast*.   Bill finished *quickly*.
> Don worked *faster* than Bill.   Don finished *more quickly* than Bill.
> Tom worked *fastest* of all.   Tom finished *most quickly* of all.

The comparisons of some modifiers are irregular. Among the most common are these:

	POSITIVE	COMPARATIVE	SUPERLATIVE
ADJECTIVES:	bad	worse	worst
	far	farther	farthest
	good	better	best
	many	more	most
	little	less	least
ADVERBS:	badly	worse	worst
	far	farther	farthest
	much	more	most
	well	better	best

A word of warning: Though you often have a choice between adding *er* or *est* and using *more* or *most,* you should not use both at the same time:

NONSTANDARD: Norman is *more clumsier* than Charles.
STANDARD: Norman is *clumsier* than Charles.
STANDARD: Norman is *more clumsy* than Charles.

Nor should you add *er* or *more* to irregular comparative forms:

NONSTANDARD: Alice's joke was *worser* than Peggy's.
NONSTANDARD: Alice's joke was *more worse* than Peggy's.
STANDARD: Alice's joke was *worse* than Peggy's.

EXERCISE 6   Be prepared to read aloud the following numbered groups of sentences, substituting for the blanks the correct forms of each of the lettered modifiers. If you think the comparative and superlative degrees of a modifier could be formed in more than one way, be ready to give both ways.

1   (a) tall, (b) bashful, (c) handsome, (d) witty, (e) lively
    My brother David is _____.
    My brother John is _____ than David.
    My brother Martin is the _____ boy in our family.

2   (a) far, (b) awkwardly, (c) fast, (d) slowly, (e) rapidly
    Mary walked _____.
    Helen walked _____ than Mary.
    Ruth walked the _____ of all the girls.

3   (a) delicious, (b) good, (c) soggy, (d) delectable, (e) crumbly
    Mom's spice cake looked _____.
    Her fudge cake looked _____ than her spice cake.
    Her angel food cake looked the _____ of the three.

EXERCISE 7   The comparative and superlative forms of the modifiers used in these sentences are either incorrect or sound awkward. Rewrite the sentences, correcting the incorrect forms and changing the awkward forms to make them more pleasing in sound.

1   Barb says she feels more better today than she did yesterday.
2   Mr. Pendleton is the most jolliest man in our office.
3   David's behavior was the baddest of all.
4   Hank was curiouser about the new neighbors than Jim was.
5   Of the two I think Mr. Beemis is more likelier to win.
6   Franklin was undoubtedly the most oddest of all the Millers.
7   To get a view of the lake, you have to drive more farther on down the road.

8 I've never heard a more noisier car than Bruce's.

9 Tim was voted the most handsomest boy in our class.

10 None of the stories were good, but Harry's was the worse.

Using the comparative degree. In stating a comparison between two persons or things or groups, we generally use the comparative degree of the modifier, not the superlative degree:

> Carol is *neater* than her brother.
> Carol is the *neater* of the two. [Not: the *neatest* of the two.]

> The boys seemed *more enthusiastic* than the girls.
> Which of the two groups seemed *more enthusiastic*? [Not: Which of the two groups seemed *most enthusiastic*?]

> The bracelet was *cheaper* than the earrings.
> Which was *cheaper*—the bracelet or the earrings? [Not: Which was *cheapest* . . .]

Note: In everyday conversation, the superlative degree is sometimes used in making a comparison between two things. But this usage is not considered appropriate in writing or in speech situations that are not informal.

> Use the other knife—it's the *sharpest*. [More formal: it's the *sharper*.]
> Which ride was *most exciting*—the roller coaster or the Loop-o-plane? [More formal: Which ride was *more exciting* . . .]

Making comparisons logical. When you make a comparison, be sure that the two things that are compared in your sentence are the two things you mean to compare. For example, in the following sentence the writer clearly intended to compare the navy and the army:

> In the War of 1812 our navy was more effective than our army.

But notice this sentence:

> At that time England's navy was larger than the United States.

Although the writer obviously intended to compare England's navy with the navy of the United States, he has not actually done this in his sentence. Instead he has compared England's *navy* with the

United States. To make his comparison logical, he must phrase the sentence to show what he meant:

> At that time England's navy was larger than **that** of the United States.

Here is another example in which the writer is making a comparison that he does not really intend:

NOT LOGICAL: Many people believe that the venom of the Gila monster is more deadly than the rattlesnake. [Compares *venom* with a *rattlesnake.*]

LOGICAL: Many people believe that the venom of the Gila monster is more deadly than the rattlesnake's. [Compares the *Gila monster's venom* with the *rattlesnake's venom.*]

Other and Else *in comparisons.* The following sentence makes another kind of illogical comparison. See if you can detect it:

> The center practiced harder than anyone on the basketball team.

In this sentence, the center is being compared with "anyone on the basketball team." But "anyone on the team" includes not only the forwards and the guards, but the center himself as well. Therefore what the sentence really says is:

> The center practiced harder than the forwards, the guards, and the center. .

Now the writer of the sentence certainly did not mean that the center practiced harder than himself—yet that is what his words say. To make his sentence say what he intended it to say, he should have used the word *else*:

> The center practiced harder than anyone **else** on the basketball team.

Whenever you compare persons or things of the same kind, make your comparisons logical by using the word *else* or *other.*

ILLOGICAL: Don is smarter than *any boy* I know.
LOGICAL: Don is smarter than *any other boy* I know.

ILLOGICAL: The comics are more fun than *any part* of the newspaper.
LOGICAL: The comics are more fun than *any other part* of the newspaper.

ILLOGICAL: Melissa was hungrier than *anybody* at the picnic.
LOGICAL: Melissa was hungrier than *anybody else* at the picnic.

393

EXERCISE (8) Be prepared to read aloud each of the following sentences, supplying the comparative or superlative form of the modifier (in parentheses) that would be appropriate to use in writing.

1 Sue is the (*graceful*) of the two girls.
2 Which of the twins is (*friendly*)?
3 I've heard many pointless stories, but that's the (*stupid*) I've ever heard.
4 Serve the (*large*) of the two pies for dessert.
5 Which can run (*fast*)—a camel or an ostrich?
6 Who lives (*far*) from school—Kay or the twins?
7 Which dress looked (*attractive*) on Sally—the velveteen, the jersey, or the tweed?
8 Both the Comets and the Bulldogs have good teams, but the Comets have the (*good*) pitchers.
9 Mike and Ted were arguing about which of them was the (*strong*).
10 Phyllis sings badly, but Art sings even (*badly*).

EXERCISE (9) One sentence in each of the following numbered groups contains an illogical comparison. Be prepared to point out that sentence and to explain why the comparison is illogical.

1 a) The parasol ant is more industrious than any ant.
   b) The parasol ant is more industrious than any other ant.
   c) Parasol ants are more industrious than other ants.
2 a) Rob swims better than anyone else in his scout troop.
   b) Rob swims better than any other boy in his scout troop.
   c) Rob swims better than anyone in his scout troop.
3 a) Although Nevada's area is over a hundred times greater than Rhode Island's, Rhode Island's population is almost five times greater than Nevada's.
   b) Although Nevada's area is greater than Rhode Island, Rhode Island's population is greater than Nevada.
   c) Although Nevada is larger than Rhode Island, Rhode Island's population is greater than Nevada's.
4 a) Recorded history seems to indicate that Egypt's civilization developed faster than China.
   b) Recorded history seems to indicate that Egypt's civilization developed faster than that of China.
   c) Recorded history seems to indicate that Egypt's civilization developed faster than China's.
5 a) His play is more exciting than any other I've ever seen.
   b) His play is more exciting than any I've ever seen.
   c) His play is more exciting than any movie I've ever seen.

6 a) Tracy thinks the articles in *Destiny* are more sensational than *The Jester*.
   b) Tracy thinks the articles in *Destiny* are more sensational than those in *The Jester*.
   c) Tracy thinks the articles in *Destiny* are more sensational than *The Jester's*.

EXERCISE 10 All except two of the following sentences contain illogical comparisons. Rewrite these eight sentences, correcting the illogical comparisons.

1 The palms of the coconut tree are more useful than the date tree.

2 Miami Beach has more hotels for its size than any city in the United States.

3 Walt Disney probably has won more awards than anyone in the movie industry.

4 Henry Adams felt that the invention of the dynamo was more important than any other event in modern history.

5 Although Canada's area is greater than the United States, the population of the United States is over ten times greater than Canada.

6 The whale is larger than any animal that lives on the earth or in its waters.

7 In the United States, coal supplies more power and heat than any source of energy.

8 In the seventeenth century, a British colonist enjoyed greater political freedom than any French or Spanish colonist.

9 Benjamin Franklin deserves more credit than anyone for making Philadelphia the most advanced city in the colonies.

10 This year's tornadoes were more destructive than last year.

395

DOUBLE NEGATIVES

Words like *no, not, none, never, neither, nothing, nowhere,* and *nobody* are called "negative words." We use them to express negative meanings like these:

I had *never* met Sally.
Blake did*n't* say anything to me.

Notice that only one negative word is needed to express a negative meaning. Using two negative words to express one negative meaning—a *double negative*—is an error that users of standard English are careful to avoid.

NONSTANDARD: Shirley *never* did *nothing* to help us.
NONSTANDARD: I did*n't* see *no* stoplight at that corner.

We can correct a double negative in one of two ways:

NONSTANDARD: I do*n't* see *nothing* wrong with that plan.
STANDARD: I do*n't* see **anything** wrong with that plan.
STANDARD: I see *nothing* wrong with that plan.

NONSTANDARD: Bob did*n't* have *no* pencil.
STANDARD: Bob did*n't* have **any** pencil.
STANDARD: Bob had *no* pencil.

Most double negatives are easy to recognize, since most negative words begin with the letter *n*. But words like *hardly* and *scarcely*, which do not begin with *n*, are also negative words:

Jane is *scarcely* ever at home. [That is, she is *almost never* at home.]

I could *hardly* understand him. [That is, I could *almost not* understand him.]

When you use *hardly* or *scarcely* in a sentence, then, make sure that you don't combine it with another negative word:

NONSTANDARD: Hardly *nobody* comes to the games any more.
STANDARD: Hardly *anybody* comes to the games any more.

NONSTANDARD: We could*n't* scarcely see the players from our seats.
STANDARD: We *could* scarcely see the players from our seats.

EXERCISE 11 Be prepared to read aloud each of the following negative statements, choosing the correct word (in parentheses) to complete the sentence.

1 I don't believe it would do (*any, no*) harm to tell Marie.
2 There isn't (*anything, nothing*) you can do.
3 He never tells me anything (*either, neither*).
4 You (*could, couldn't*) hardly expect an answer to your letter so soon.
5 Kay hadn't (*ever, never*) been to a county fair.
6 Bob couldn't find (*either, neither*) of the boys.
7 Betty (*was, wasn't*) scarcely out of the room when Jim came.
8 Cal says it doesn't make (*any, no*) difference to him whether we play golf or tennis.
9 No, that train doesn't go (**anywhere, nowhere**) near Rock Falls.

10 The crate was so heavy that the two men (*could, couldn't*) hardly lift it.

11 As far as we know, he never spoke to (*anybody, nobody*).

12 Ivy wouldn't answer (*any, none*) of our questions.

13 If it hadn't been true, Sam wouldn't (*ever, never*) have told Andy that story.

14 I didn't see (*any, no*) poison ivy, did you?

15 Jo had extra tickets but wouldn't give us (*any, none*).

EXERCISE (12) Rewrite each of the following sentences to eliminate the double negative it contains. If a sentence can be revised in two ways, make both revisions. You should write nine sentences.

1 Jack hasn't done nothing.

2 We left the carnival early because we didn't have no more money.

3 Didn't nobody see the box in the hall?

4 There isn't scarcely enough flour left to make pancakes.

5 Tom wouldn't never have found the present, if you hadn't told him where it was.

SPECIAL MODIFIER PROBLEMS

A or An. Most of us make the choice between *a* and *an* so naturally that we seldom stop to think about what we base our choice on. The choice between *a* and *an* depends on the sound—not the spelling—of the word that follows.

We use *a* before words beginning with a *consonant sound*:

a master of ceremonies	a home	a one-sided game
a D and a B	a union	a European

Notice that although the beginning letters of the words *union, one-sided,* and *European* are vowels, their beginning sounds are consonants sounds.

We use *an* before words beginning with a *vowel sound*:

an apple	an hour	an onlooker
an M.C.	an underclassman	an experience

In these examples, the beginning sounds of all the words are vowel sounds—even though the first letters of *hour* and *M.C.* are consonants.

This kind or These kind. We use the singular adjectives *this* and *that* to modify singular nouns. We use the plural adjectives *these* and *those* to modify plural nouns.

This dog will make an excellent watchdog.	*These dogs* seldom make good pets.
That kind of lock fastens automatically.	We don't recommend using *those kinds.*

We never have trouble using the adjectives correctly in sentences like these.

But we are undecided sometimes whether to use a singular or a plural modifier in sentences like the following, in which the object of the preposition *of* is plural:

(*This, These*) kind of drapes must be dry-cleaned.
Aunt Martha seldom uses (*that, those*) sort of recipes.

Notice that the words to be modified in these sentences—*kind* and *sort*—are singular nouns. It would not be logical, then, for us to use plural adjectives to modify them. We use the singular adjectives *This* and *that* to modify the singular nouns:

This kind of drapes must be dry-cleaned. [Not: *These* kind.]
Aunt Martha seldom uses *that* sort of recipes. [Not: *those* sort.]

The use of a plural adjective to modify a singular noun ("these kind of drapes"; "those sort of recipes") is common in everyday conversation, as you have probably noticed. But until the usage becomes completely acceptable in standard English, you would be wise to avoid it, especially in writing.

Kind of and Sort of. The words *kind of* and *sort of* are often used in everyday conversation as adverb modifiers meaning "nearly; almost; somewhat; rather."

COLLOQUIAL: Travers seemed kind of pleased at the news.
COLLOQUIAL: I sort of expected him to be upset.

This usage, though, is acceptable only in highly informal speech situations. Avoid it in writing, especially in writing that is formal or rather serious.

WRITTEN: Travers seemed *somewhat* pleased at the news.
WRITTEN: I *rather* expected him to be upset.

This here and That there. Users of standard English avoid the expressions *this here* and *that there*. The adjective *this* or *that* alone can do the work of pointing out which person or thing is meant:

NONSTANDARD: *This here* window won't close.
Do you want *these here* books?
STANDARD: *This* window won't close.
Do you want *these* books?

NONSTANDARD: Ask *that there* man which bus we should take.
Who brought *those there* flowers?
STANDARD: Ask *that* man which bus we should take.
Who brought *those* flowers?

Those or Them. We use the adjective *those*, not the pronoun *them*, to point out which persons or things are meant:

NONSTANDARD: *Them* boys don't play on our team.
STANDARD: *Those* boys don't play on our team.

NONSTANDARD: Haven't you found *them* zippers yet?
STANDARD: Haven't you found *those* zippers yet?

NONSTANDARD: He doesn't like *them* kinds.
STANDARD: He doesn't like *those* kinds.

EXERCISE (13) Be ready to read aloud each of the following sentences, choosing the word (in parentheses) that would be appropriate to use in writing.

1 Aunt Ruth usually sends (*this, these*) kind of post cards.
2 John's writing is careless; he never dots (*a, an*) *i* or crosses (*a, an*) *t*.
3 (*This, This here*) letter of recommendation should help you.
4 There is a big demand right now for (*that, those*) sort of books.
5 Casey seemed (*rather, kind of*) embarrassed when the coach asked him to say a few words.
6 Isn't the rule requiring everyone to wear (*a, an*) uniform (*a, an*) unfair one?
7 (*This, These*) kinds of apples aren't good for baking.
8 You seldom see (*that, those*) sort of people at a football game.
9 The Camera Club is (*somewhat, sort of*) disorganized at present, unfortunately.
10 Even after receiving so great (*a, an*) honor, Mr. Britton remained (*a, an*) humble man.
11 Karen explained why (*this, these*) kind of animals can't live in (*that, that there*) climate.
12 Bill never learned to use (*that, those*) sort of tools.

13 Morton seemed (*almost, sort of*) glad to lose the game.

14 (*A, An*) R.N. written after a girl's name usually stands for "registered nurse," while (*a, an*) P.N. means "practical nurse."

15 Have you ever made (*this, these*) sort of decorations before?

EXERCISE 14 **REVIEW** Be prepared to read aloud each of the following sentences, choosing the words (in parentheses) that would be appropriate to use in writing.

1 Jim shouldn't have talked so (*disrespectful, disrespectfully*) to his uncle.

2 Since the last time we had it repaired, our TV set hasn't (*ever, never*) worked (*good, well*).

3 Dave is certainly (*friendlier, more friendlier*) than Bruce.

4 I (*rather, kind of*) expected Jake to know better than to try (*those, them*) tricks on Mr. Brady.

5 Sue felt (*bad, badly*) because the salesman couldn't find a pair of (*this, these*) kind of shoes to fit her.

6 This salad dressing tastes (*odder, more oddly*) than (*that, that there*) one.

7 Even though his promises don't sound as (*good, well*) as Stanley's, Richards is the (*more, most*) popular of the two candidates.

8 I don't want (*any, none*) of (*those, them*) caramels.

9 It's Bert's own fault if he's lost weight and doesn't feel (*good, well*); he never eats (*proper, properly*).

10 Ryan won't (*ever, never*) say (*anything, nothing*) good about the Cubs; he's a Braves fan.

11 If (*this, this here*) boy will stand out of the way, I'll show you how to weld (*those, them*) rods.

12 You won't catch (*any, no*) bus on (*this, this here*) corner; you should be standing on (*that, that there*) one.

13 The melon looked (*delicious, deliciously*), but it tasted (*peculiar, peculiarly*).

14 Are (*those, them*) tools made (*good, well*) enough to stand hard use?

15 When I asked him why he stopped so (*sudden, suddenly*), he couldn't give me (*any, no*) reason.

16 Mrs. Larrabie was dressed even (*gaudier, more gaudily*) than usual.

17 The health commissioner looked (*sad, sadly*) when Dr. Walsh explained how (*bad, badly*) the serum was needed.

18 Sylvia dresses (*neater, more neatly*) than Carol, but of the two Carol is the (*more, most*) stylish.

19   Carstens can't expect (*anybody, nobody*) to take (*that, those*) sort of regulations (*serious, seriously*).

20   Tim dances (*rather, sort of*) (*awkward, awkwardly*), but then he has never had (*any, no*) lessons.

EXERCISE (15) *REVIEW*   Some of the usages in the following sentences are nonstandard; others are not appropriate in writing. Rewrite each of the sentences, correcting the nonstandard usages and revising the inappropriate usages to make the sentences appropriate for standard written English.

1   The school nurse said that Bobby is the most healthiest boy in his class.

2   Baseball is more popular in America than anywhere in the world.

3   When Nan said that the whipped cream didn't taste good, the waiter looked indignantly.

4   Buy the other dress—it's the smartest of the two.

5   The seats at the Palace are more comfortable than the Bijou.

6   Never having faced those sort of problems before, Dan was kind of discouraged.

7   If you stir the pudding good while it's cooking, it won't have no lumps in it.

8   Which of the two clubs had the most successful dance?

9   Mr. Bronson said he could finish them shelves easy before noon.

10   The champion felt badly because he didn't do as good in the race as he had expected.

11   I don't know a more clumsier or more noisier boy than Robert.

12   I sort of doubt that the Emporium sells those kind of awnings.

13   The city editor praised Stacy, saying that he handles his assignments more efficiently than anyone on the newspaper.

14   The first act of the new musical was so bad that I couldn't hardly see how the second could be any worser.

15   Carter certainly couldn't have finished the test no faster than he did; he wrote steady for three hours.

16   I couldn't never understand why Toby liked those kind of television programs so much.

17   Which of them two photographs is most flattering to him?

18   Maybe Max couldn't speak English good, but we never had no trouble understanding him.

19   Why not divide the work equal between Tess and Barbara? Both girls type very neat.

20   Most authorities agree that Sarah Bernhardt had more talent than any actress of her era.

a marshal

Mar.
Dil

CHAPTER **22**

CAPITALS,

PLURALS,

AND

POSSESSIVES

402

The recipe for making fudge seems simple enough, yet very few people can make really good fudge. The directions say you should cook the mixture until it "forms a *soft* ball" when tested in a cup of cold water. These directions sound easy enough for anyone to follow. But there is a catch. You won't have good candy unless you know how to recognize just what degree of softness is "right." In other words, directions are often not so simple as they sound.

This is certainly true of the directions for capitalizing words in sentences. The rule is simple; it sounds easy: **Capitalize all proper nouns and all adjectives formed from proper nouns.** Learning the rule is no problem; anyone can learn it. But again there is a catch. The rule is of little help unless you know how to recognize which words are considered proper nouns and proper adjectives.

Proper nouns. A noun, as you know, is a word used as a name of a person, place, or thing. When the noun is a name that could be applied to any one of a class of persons or things, it is called a *common noun.* When the noun is a name that belongs only to one

a conductor

Leonard Bernstein

a baseball player

Mickey Mantle

particular person, place, or thing, or to a special group of persons or things, it is called a *proper noun*. Proper nouns are capitalized; common nouns are not (unless they begin a sentence).

COMMON NOUNS [*Any one of its class*]	PROPER NOUNS [*A particular one*]
poet	Robert Frost
voters	Republicans
churchgoers	Catholics
city	Atlanta
college	Lake Forest College

Suppose that in a theme about your savings account you wrote the following sentence:

At ten-thirty I went to the *bank*.

Even though you know that the word "bank" in this sentence refers to a particular place (the bank building where you have your account), the word itself could be applied to any bank building in the world. Therefore it is considered a common noun and should not be capitalized.

On the other hand, suppose that you had written this sentence:

At ten-thirty I went to the *First National Bank.*

In this sentence you have used a name that belongs only to one particular bank (in your city, at least). Because "First National Bank" is the special name of one particular building—a name that distinguishes that building from all others of the same type in your city—it is considered a proper noun and is capitalized.

In your writing, be sure to capitalize all nouns that are the special names of—

PEOPLE: Benjamin Franklin, Pearl S. Buck, Casey Stengel

PLACES: Great Britain, Ohio, Will County, Mount Everest, the Orient

ANIMALS: Flicka, Nashua, Fido, Bossie

RACES, TRIBES, LANGUAGES: Negro, Sioux Indians, Arabic, Spanish

CHURCHES AND THEIR MEMBERS: the First Baptist Church, a Catholic, Methodists

DAYS, MONTHS, HOLIDAYS, HOLY DAYS: Saturday, December, Fourth of July, Yom Kippur, Palm Sunday

BUILDINGS: the Museum of Modern Art, the Capitol, the Wrigley Building

ORGANIZATIONS: the Parent-Teacher Association, the Boy Scouts of America

POLITICAL PARTIES AND THEIR MEMBERS: Republicans, Tories, a Democrat

INSTITUTIONS: Fordham University, Wesley Memorial Hospital

HISTORICAL EVENTS, PERIODS, DOCUMENTS: the Korean War, the Stone Age, the Bill of Rights

GOVERNMENT BODIES AND AGENCIES: the Senate, Congress, the Census Bureau

BUSINESS FIRMS: United Aircraft Corporation, Curtis Publishing Company

TRADE NAMES: Kleenex, Rambler, Tide

SHIPS, TRAINS, PLANES: S.S. *North American,* the *Cannonball Express,* the *Spirit of St. Louis*

NAMES REFERRING TO GOD, SACRED FIGURES, THE BIBLE AND ITS PARTS: the Almighty, the Redeemer, the Holy Family, Genesis, the New Testament

Words like *park, river, street, hotel, building, club, high school, freshman, junior, prom,* and *company* are not ordinarily capitalized, since they are names that could be applied to any one of a group of similar things. But when these words are used as part of a proper noun, they should be capitalized:

at the *park*
near the *river*
on our *street*
joined a school *club*
entered *high school*
a party for *freshmen*

at *Glacier National Park*
near the *Ohio River*
on *Market Street*
joined the *Science Club*
entered *York Community High School*
tickets for the *Freshman Frolic*

Note: A number of newspapers and magazines do not capitalize words like *river*, *street*, and *high school* when these words are part of a proper noun (for example, *Illinois river, Houston street, Emerson high school*). But in most other writing, these words are capitalized, and you will be expected to capitalize them in your work.

Proper adjectives. Proper adjectives (adjectives formed from proper nouns) and trade names used as adjectives are capitalized:

a *Norwegian* festival
a *Teutonic* language

Red Cross shoes
Elizabethan England

Notice that the words modified by these adjectives are not capitalized—unless they too are proper nouns, as in the last example.

405

EXERCISE (1) Copy each of the following groups of words, capitalizing all proper nouns and proper adjectives.

1 a ford truck
2 in the hospital
3 an indian dance
4 a nearby lutheran church
5 the set of cannon towels
6 in the old testament
7 at the prudential building
8 on the street opposite the park
9 the freshman team
10 on the s.s. *constitution*
11 the spanish-american war
12 at passavant hospital
13 sent by the knights of columbus
14 near holland avenue
15 from taft high school
16 in the rocky mountains
17 belong to the girl scouts
18 the federal bureau of investigation
19 from the eastman kodak company
20 a walt disney program
21 at st. paul's church
22 four new goodyear tires
23 a portuguese custom
24 a black chrysler sedan
25 a box of lux soap flakes
26 left the high school
27 a bottle of bayer aspirin
28 the house of representatives
29 a mexican red skelton
30 the declaration of independence

Three groups of words seem to cause more than their share of capitalization problems. A close look at these groups should help you avoid errors in your writing.

1 **The points of the compass**—*north, east, southwest, northeast,* etc.—are capitalized only when they are used to name or to refer to geographical regions of a country:

> Many romantic stories are written about the *West*.
> Beef is usually cheaper in the *Southwest* than in the *East*.
> The war raged on in China and in other parts of the *Far East*.
> Dave reads nothing but *Western* stories. [That is, stories about the *West*.]

When these words are used to indicate *direction*, they are not proper nouns and so are not capitalized:

> Go *south* for three miles before turning *west*.
> The wind is from the *north* today.
> The tornado struck the *northeast* part of the state.

2 **School subjects** are not capitalized unless they are names of languages or of specific numbered courses:

> John is taking *English, history, French,* and *chemistry*.
> He spends all his time on *American History I* and *Chemistry II*.
> Did you sign up for *English Literature 2* or *American history*?

3 The names of the **seasons of the year**, strangely enough, are not considered proper nouns (even though each names one particular season). Therefore they are not capitalized:

> We go to Florida in the *winter* and to Maine in the *summer*.
> Our team does not hold *spring* practice.

EXERCISE 2 Decide which words in each of the following sentences should be capitalized. After the number of the sentence, write these words, supplying the necessary capital letters.

1 Neither german nor italian will be taught at our high school this fall.
2 To the north of the spaniards were the utes; to the east, the kiowas; to the south, the apaches; and to the west, the navahos.
3 If we don't go to san diego this winter, we'll go next may.
4 The porcupine mountains along the lake superior shore are the highest point in the great lakes area.

406

5 The house to the north of the school reminded him of his home in the south.

6 Are both the democrats and the republicans holding rallies on labor day?

7 Since you are already taking english composition, social studies, and chemistry, will you be allowed to take both algebra 3 and geometry?

8 The tribes of the northwest produced some of the finest indian art in north america.

9 Why do you prefer a royal typewriter to an underwood?

10 His wife would rather live in the northwest than in the east.

11 Is crest made by procter and gamble or by lever brothers?

12 Be sure to visit independence hall, where the declaration of independence was adopted.

13 One of the best trains on the union pacific railroad is the *city of portland*.

14 Tony, who is an episcopalian, attends holy trinity church.

15 Is that the church next door to good shepherd hospital?

16 In august you are to represent our club at the district meeting of the future farmers of america.

17 After capturing vicksburg, grant struck at the confederate force in northeast mississippi.

18 Toby remarked that if the american generals, gates and schuyler, had lost the battles at saratoga, we might now be talking with british accents.

19 According to legend, the british in boston were attending a play when the americans attacked bunker hill.

20 On march 17 the irish celebrate in honor of st. patrick.

TIPS ON TITLES

Personal titles. Words like *sergeant, colonel, senator, governor, mayor, bishop,* and *professor* are nouns that show a person's rank, office, or profession. And words like *dad, sister, grandmother, uncle,* and *cousin* are nouns that show family relationship. These words are always capitalized when they are used *with a person's name* as part of a proper noun:

Write to **Senator Martin Jacobs.**
Uncle Walter had never met **Bishop Turner.**
He asked **Cousin Sue** to write the letter to **Mayor Clausen.**

And we generally capitalize personal titles when they are used alone in place of a specific person's name:

> Will you vote for the bill, *Senator*?
> We introduced her to *Dad*.

At other times, small letters are used:

> Write to your *senator* and urge him to vote for the bill.
> He gave the money to my *dad*.
> Mr. Andrews, the new *mayor*, was very efficient.

Notice this exception: The title *President*—when used to refer to the President of the United States—is generally capitalized as a special mark of respect:

> Last Wednesday the *President* held a press conference.

Other titles. One general rule covers the capitalization of other titles—the names of books, magazines, newspapers, stories, articles, poems, plays, songs, operas, paintings, movies, and radio and TV programs. In these titles we usually capitalize the first word, the last word, all important words (nouns, pronouns, verbs, adjectives, and adverbs), and prepositions of more than four letters. Notice what words are capitalized in these titles:

This Is My Story	"On the Road to Utopia"
Men Against Death	"They Wouldn't Give Up"
My Eyes Have a Cold Nose	*Adventure in Time and Space*
the Chicago *Daily News*	*Town Meeting of the Air*

EXERCISE (3) Decide which words in each of the following sentences should be capitalized. After the number of the sentence, write these words, supplying the necessary capital letters. Be ready to explain why you capitalized the words you did.

1 Our alderman, harold barker, is supporting mayor wilson's clean-up campaign.
2 Does alderman mooney like superintendent hill's proposal?
3 Be sure to read the article by general john belasco in *harper's*.
4 The professor referred to the article " in a state of siege."
5 His only experience before television cameras was when he appeared on *the author meets the critics*.
6 Was it tom's aunt who wrote the novel *and walk in peace*?
7 A lieutenant told cousin jane that the eastbound train was late.
8 My father is one of the new york *herald tribune*'s most faithful readers.
9 Do you think dad will like this plaid tie, mother?

10 Later captain mason **told** my cousin that he was the author of "it's fun to be boss."

11 It was the district attorney **who** brought the doctor's record to the attention of judge austin.

12 Last tuesday my sister borrowed uncle andy's car to drive grandfather blaine to the station.

13 The grandfather of dr. vannevar bush, the dean of american scientists, was a provincetown whaler.

14 Have you seen the mayor yet, professor?

15 The mayor and governor emerson are in the office with dean lantow.

PLURAL FORMS OF NOUNS

If you can spell the singular form of a noun, you seldom have trouble writing its plural form, since usually all you have to do is add an *s*:

boat—boats	horse—horses	alley—alleys
crowd—crowds	Mr. Butler—the Butlers	toy—toys
ring—rings	Mrs. Smith—the Smiths	monkey—monkeys

But how about nouns whose plural is not formed in the regular way? Is the plural of *gas* written *gases* or *gasses*? Should you write "three *spys*" or "three *spies*"? If your uncle's name is *Rawlings*, are your cousins "the *Rawlings*" or "the *Rawlingses*"? Reviewing several groups of nouns with "irregular" plurals should help you answer such questions.

1 We form the plural of nouns ending in **s, x, z, ch,** and **sh** by adding *es*, pronounced as a separate syllable:

gas—gases	waltz—waltzes	Mr. Adams—the Adamses
glass—glasses	witch—witches	Mr. Metz—the Metzes
fox—foxes	brush—brushes	Mr. Rawlings—the Rawlingses

2 To form the plural of nouns ending in **y preceded by a consonant,** we change the *y* to *i* and add *es*:

spy—spies	party—parties	lady—ladies
ally—allies	baby—babies	penny—pennies

Names of people are exceptions to this rule:

There are three *Nancys* in our class. [Not: *Nancies*.]
The store belongs to the *Kellys*. [Not: *Kellies*.]

EXERCISE (4) On a sheet of paper, write the plurals of the following nouns. Be ready to write the plurals from dictation (of the singulars).

1	boy	11	hoax	21	principle
2	watch	12	Jones	22	association
3	crash	13	wish	23	lady
4	machine	14	verse	24	Hintz
5	Larry	15	absence	25	ally
6	grizzly	16	Higgins	26	necessity
7	typewriter	17	alley	27	branch
8	ray	18	waltz	28	Pickens
9	monarchy	19	family	29	success
10	penny	20	luxury	30	Spenser

3 Nouns ending in **o preceded by a vowel** form their plural regularly. We simply add an *s*:

radio—radios	zoo—zoos	cameo—cameos
studio—studios	igloo—igloos	rodeo—rodeos

But the plural of nouns ending in **o preceded by a consonant** varies. Some add *s*:

solo—solos	cello—cellos	soprano—sopranos
alto—altos	piano—pianos	dynamo—dynamos

410

Others add *es*:

potato—potatoes	echo—echoes	Negro—Negroes
tomato—tomatoes	hero—heroes	torpedo—torpedoes

And still others add either *s* or *es*:

banjo—banjos or banjoes   mosquito—mosquitoes or mosquitos
hobo—hobos or hoboes   tornado—tornadoes or tornados
zero—zeros or zeroes   volcano—volcanoes or volcanos

4 The plural forms of nouns ending in **f and fe** also vary. Some end in *s*:

belief—beliefs	chief—chiefs	safe—safes
sheriff—sheriffs	dwarf—dwarfs	fife—fifes

Others end in *ves*:

life—lives	self—selves	thief—thieves
half—halves	loaf—loaves	wolf—wolves

And still others end in either *s* or *ves*:

scarf—scarfs or scarves	wharf—wharves or wharfs
hoof—hoofs or hooves	staff—staves or staffs

5 Compound words (words made up of two or more other words): When a compound word is written as one solid word, the plural is formed regularly, by adding *s* to the end:

cupful—cupfuls	leftover—leftovers	teacup—teacups
hairdo—hairdos	handful—handfuls	stepson—stepsons

When the parts are written separately or are hyphened, the plurals vary. Usually the principal word is made plural:

looker-on—lookers-on	court-martial—courts-martial
tap-dancer—tap-dancers	major general—major generals
ghost writer—ghost writers	mother-in-law—mothers-in-law

But notice these plurals:

stand-by—stand-bys	two-year-old—two-year-olds
tie-up—tie-ups	do-gooder—do-gooders
drive-in—drive-ins	good-for-nothing—good-for-nothings

EXERCISE (5) On a sheet of paper, write the plural forms of the following words. The words that are starred have two acceptable plurals; give both of these. Look up in your dictionary any forms you are uncertain about. Be ready to write the plurals from dictation (of the singular forms).

411

1	potato	11	passer-by	21	sheriff
2	hoof*	12	solo	22	stand-in
3	wife	13	self	23	mosquito*
4	hero	14	rodeo	24	curio
5	thief	15	scarf*	25	dynamo
6	cargo*	16	studio	26	consul general
7	four-year-old	17	tariff	27	wharf*
8	game of chance	18	piano	28	teen-ager
9	volcano*	19	safe	29	tomato
10	sister-in-law	20	cupful	30	teaspoonful

6 Plurals without s: A small group of nouns form their plural by a change in spelling:

man—men	mouse—mice	child—children
woman—women	louse—lice	ox—oxen
foot—feet	goose—geese	tooth—teeth

7 Foreign language plurals: A number of nouns that we have borrowed from foreign languages have English plural endings. For example:

pizza—pizzas   campus—campuses   ignoramus—ignoramuses

But others of these borrowed words still keep the foreign plural endings. For example:

datum—data (from Latin)   alumnus—alumni (from Latin)
larva—larvae (from Latin)   stimulus—stimuli (from Latin)
crisis—crises (from Greek)   analysis—analyses (from Greek)

And still others have both a foreign plural ending and an English one:

beau—beaus or beaux   bureau—bureaus or bureaux
cactus—cactuses or cacti   formula—formulas or formulae
radius—radii or radiuses   seraph—seraphs or seraphim
index—indexes or indices   bandit—bandits or banditti

The English plurals are preferred in all but formal, literary, or scientific writing (and frequently in these kinds of writing too).

8 The plurals of **letters, numbers, signs, and words** (when they are thought of as things) are generally formed by adding *'s*:

Dot your *i*'s and cross your *t*'s.
Your *4*'s look too much like *+*'s.
Don't use so many *if*'s and *but*'s.

9 A few nouns have the **same form** for both the singular and the plural. For example:

sheep   moose   headquarters
Swiss   Chinese   Japanese

A *deer* came to the brook to drink.
Later several *deer* gathered at the brook.

EXERCISE (6) On a sheet of paper, write the plural forms of the following words. The words that are starred have two acceptable forms; give both of these. Look up in your dictionary any plurals you are uncertain about. Be ready to write the plurals from dictation (of the singular forms).

1 saleswoman	11 oasis	21 seraph*
2 beau*	12 radius*	22 arena
3 *a* [the letter]	13 manservant	23 bureau*
4 louse	14 man-of-war	24 index*
5 alumnus	15 Chinese	25 freshman
6 ox	16 tooth	26 ignoramus
7 mongoose	17 mouse	27 formula*
8 *w* [the letter]	18 *and* [the word]	28 crisis
9 stimulus	19 cactus*	29 analysis
10 larva	20 bandit*	30 + [the sign]

Can you spot the misspelled word in each of the following sentences?

The ladie's hats have been moved to the mezzanine.
The psychiatrist talked to the other patient's later.
Some peoples' complaints were ludicrous.

If you immediately spotted the three mistakes in the sentences and can tell how to correct them, you will hardly need to study this section, except by way of review. But if you did not recognize the incorrect forms—*ladie's*, *patient's*, and *peoples'*—chances are that you make the same sort of mistakes in your writing. Making a special effort to learn and apply the apostrophe rules explained in this section will help you avoid such mistakes in the future.

Possessive forms.   In *speech*, the possessive form of a noun (the form we use to show ownership) always ends with an *s* or a *z* sound. In *writing*, the possessive form always ends with an apostrophe and at least one *s*—though not necessarily in that order:

the bishop's sermon	the dukes' protests
the king's plea	the mice's tails
Mr. White's paper	the Smiths' cottage
Alice's gloves	the men's jobs

413

The only problem, as you can see, is deciding on the right order. Which comes first—the apostrophe or the *s*? The answer is simple: *It depends on who the owner is.* Let's see how this works.

One owner.   If the noun that names the owner is singular, it will very likely be a word that does not end in *s*: the *boy*, the *lady*, a *woman*, my *sister-in-law*. To form the possessive of these nouns, first write the singular form. Then add an apostrophe and an *s*:

the boy	the boy's book
the lady	the lady's smile
a woman	a woman's salary
my sister-in-law	my sister-in-law's cat
the attorney general	the attorney general's report
Mr. Morgan	Mr. Morgan's answer

When the singular form ends in an *s*, an apostrophe alone is sometimes used, especially if the next word begins with an *s*:

Frances	Frances' sister *or* Frances's sister
the hostess	the hostess' suit *or* the hostess's suit

More than one owner. If the noun that names the owner is plural, it will very likely be a word that ends in *s*: the *cats*, the *boys*, the *ladies*, the *Morgans*. To form the possessive of these, first write the plural forms. Then add just an apostrophe:

the cats	the cats' howls
the boys	the boys' mother
the ladies	the ladies' aprons
the Morgans	the Morgans' garage
the Bateses	the Bateses' car

If the plural does not end in *s*, add an apostrophe and then an *s*:

the men	the men's chorus
the women	the women's screams
the children	the children's playground
my sisters-in-law	my sisters-in-law's letters
our alumni	our alumni's contributions
the mice	the mice's squeals

Get into the habit of taking two steps in writing possessive forms. First write the word that tells the owner or owners. The ending of this word will tell you whether you should add an apostrophe and an *s*, or an apostrophe alone.

Here is a simple test you can use to check the possessives you write. Look at the letters to the left of the apostrophe. If the letters spell the name—the complete name—of the owner or owners you are writing about, then the apostrophe is in the right place.

Using this test would quickly show you that these possessive forms are wrong:

Jame's new hat [But the hat belongs to *James*, not to *Jame*.]
the two *babie's* cribs [They belong to two *babies*, not to two *babie*.]
many *peoples'* homes [*People*, not *peoples*, own the homes.]
Mr. *Jone's* ladder [The owner is Mr. *Jones*, not Mr. *Jone*.]

The test will show you that these forms are right:

POSSESSIVES	OWNERS
the two *babies'* cribs	two babies
the *baby's* bonnet	the baby
many *people's* homes	many people
the *Joneses'* property	the Joneses
James's new hat	James

Note: The apostrophe is a sign of possession; it should not be used in a noun unless you intend that noun to show ownership.

People who do not clearly understand this use of the apostrophe sometimes fall into the habit of tucking an apostrophe in any noun that ends in *s*. They write:

> I put the *book's* and *magazine's* on the desk. [Wrong: No ownership is intended.]

They should write:

> I put the *books* and *magazines* on the desk. [Right: No apostrophe is needed in plural form.]

Joint accounts. When we want to show joint ownership by two or more, we make only the last noun possessive:

> *Lindsay and Crouse's* play [One play owned by both Lindsay and Crouse.]
> *Tom, Jim, and Sam's* workshop [The three together own the workshop.]
> the *juniors and seniors'* exhibit [It belongs to both groups.]

Separate accounts. When we want to show separate ownership, we make each noun possessive:

> *Lindsay's and Crouse's* scripts [Each had a script.]
> *Tom's, Jim's, and Sam's* cars [Each of the three had a car.]
> the *juniors' and seniors'* dances [Each group had a dance.]

415

EXERCISE 7 The first item in each of the following groups tells what is owned. The second item names the owner or owners. On a sheet of paper, write the number of each group. After it, write a phrase containing the possessive form of the owner followed by the name of the thing owned. Check each possessive form by making sure that the letters to the left of the apostrophe spell the name of the owner or owners given in the group.

Example: car   the Rosses
            the Rosses' car

1	car his brothers		11	tails the dogs
2	voice her baby		12	sarcasm her father
3	cribs the babies		13	mother the twins
4	convertible Ted Jones		14	advice my doctor
5	locker Tom and Jerry		15	parents both boys
6	report cards Tom and Jerry		16	temper that lady
7	signature his father-in-law		17	dresses the ladies
8	son her neighbors		18	haircuts the men
9	schedules both doctors		19	letter Mr. Wiggins
10	turn my father and mother		20	Ford the Andersons

EXERCISE (8) On a sheet of paper, write the possessive form of each noun in parentheses. Number your answers with the numbers of the word groups.

1 (*Scrooge*) dream
2 Mr. (*Keats*) tie
3 the (*sheep*) tails
4 the (*baby*) eyes
5 the (*spy*) message
6 their (*wives*) cooking
7 the (*mice*) feet
8 the (*thief*) escape
9 his (*sons-in-law*) help
10 the (*deer*) hoof
11 the (*Harrises*) plans
12 the (*jockeys*) saddles
13 the (*babies*) mothers
14 the (*men*) scores
15 his (*children*) books

16 my (*half brothers*) letters
17 the (*editor in chief*) suggestion
18 that (*lady*) package
19 the (*gypsy*) scarf
20 the (*gypsies*) camp
21 the (*mosquitoes*) buzzing
22 the (*members*) complaints
23 the (*attorney general*) speech
24 the (*hero*) return
25 the (*saleswoman*) receipts
26 the (*gentlemen*) agreement
27 the (*actress*) agent
28 the (*policeman*) whistle
29 the (*ladies*) packages
30 that (*teacher*) class

EXERCISE (9) REVIEW Decide which of the words in the following sentences should be capitalized and which need apostrophes to complete their possessive forms. Then after the numbers of the sentences, write these words, supplying the necessary capital letters and apostrophes. You should supply 75 capital letters and 10 apostrophes.

Example: we repaired johns buick on tuesday.
  We, John's, Buick, Tuesday

1 the history of english settlement in america began on a beautiful spring morning in 1607, when captain christopher newports three ships anchored in chesapeake bay.
2 commodore deweys cruisers sailed immediately for manila, the capital of the philippine islands, the last spanish possession in the far east.
3 the war between the virginia settlers and chief powhatans tribes ended in a complete indian defeat.
4 queen annes war is usually considered one phase of the french and indian war.
5 benjamin franklins newspaper, the philadelphia *gazette*, is known to us today as *the saturday evening post*.
6 in 1733 parliament passed the molasses act, restricting new englands trade with the west indies.
7 while general cornwalliss troops stacked their arms, their band played "the world turned upside down."

8 under chief justice marshall the supreme courts position became as powerful as that of congress or of the president.

9 the first public library in the united states was established in philadelphia in robert graces home in pewter platter alley.

10 alfred lunt and lynn fontannes comedy, *the great sebastians*, was produced on television.

EXERCISE 10 **REVIEW** From each group of words in parentheses, choose the correct form and write it after the number of the sentence. Be ready to write the sentences from dictation.

1 Neither of the (*locksmithes, locksmiths, locksmiths'*) was able to repair the lock.

2 Your (*Ms, M's*) and your (*Ws, W's*) look alike.

3 We'll all meet at (*James's, Jameses', Jame's*) house.

4 We'll all meet at the (*James's, Jameses', James'*) house.

5 Can you add (*prefixses, prefixes, prefixs*) to all the words in the list?

6 Kay saw some beautiful (*cameos, cameoes, cameo's, camei*) at Cartier's.

7 The (*sheep dogs, sheep's dog, sheep dog's*) collar was loose.

8 When you finish washing the (*shelfs, shelfes, shelves*), put the linen back.

9 The (*ladys', lady's, ladies, ladies'*) husbands were all invited.

10 Are those last two numbers (*3s, 3's*) or (*5s, 5's*)?

11 What sort of games would you suggest for a (*two-year-olds', two-year-old's*) birthday party?

12 One (*witch's, witchs', witches*) broom was missing.

13 The (*Blighs, Blighes', Blighs'*) farm is about three miles down the road.

14 Is it next to the (*Moss', Mosses', Mosses*) farm?

15 Those (*trophys, trophy's, trophyes, trophies*) belong to Dad.

16 We found two (*oasis, oases, oasises*) marked on the map.

17 Both (*Pat and Mike's, Pat's and Mike's*) shirts were torn.

18 (*Jim and Judy's, Jim's and Judy's*) father arrived at 6 o'clock.

19 (*Jim and Judy's, Jim's and Judy's*) bicycles were stolen.

20 Joe (*Barneses, Barne's, Barnes's*) column appears daily.

21 We searched through that (*boys', boys, boy's*) locker first.

22 Our company lost eight hundred (*man-hours, man-hour's, men-hours*) last week.

23 He is a partner in both his (*sons-in-laws', sons-in-law's*) firms.

24 Joan said that the (*babies, baby's, babies'*) were sound asleep.

25 The (*freshmans', freshmens', freshmen's*) bonfire could be seen for miles.

417

CHAPTER 23

YOU CAN

SPELL WELL

418

If you received an invitation as unconventional as the one shown above, you would probably be safe in guessing that the party your friend was inviting you to would be full of original ideas. You could look forward to having a good time, too, for the unusual and rather amusing spelling used in the invitation would tell you that you should be in the mood for fun.

But what would your uncle think if he received the following note from you thanking him for his hospitality during a recent visit?

Dere Unkl,
I hop I kan cum to see yu agen. I had a wunderfull tyms.

Ur luving nefu,
Fred

Of course your uncle would be glad to know you had enjoyed your stay. He would probably be disappointed, however, to see

U R 2 CUM A TREZUR HUNT 2 NITE AT ATE. Bill

that you hadn't shown him you know how to spell, for in our society accurate spelling is important. We expect people who have an education to be able to spell correctly, just as we expect them to be able to read.

You and your classmates have been studying spelling ever since you started to learn how to read. Some of you, of course, are already very good spellers. Perhaps you can even spell a word like *prestidigitator*, which, by the way, is just a fancy name for *magician*. But many of you still need quite a bit of practice. A few of you may even think you need a prestidigitator to help you master the tricks of spelling, for you have discovered that English spelling is often quite tricky.

But good spellers—like good magicians—do not acquire their skill in a flash of inspiration, without any effort on their part. A good speller is a person who has acquired certain habits, habits that help him spell correctly the words he uses, whether they are familiar, everyday words or new, useful words whose meaning he has just learned. By acquiring these same habits—listed below—you too can improve your spelling.

1 *A good speller pronounces words carefully and accurately.* For example, because he says *ath lete* (not "ath a lete"), *film* (not "fi lum"), and *li brar y* (not "li bar y"), he does not misspell these words.

2 *A good speller makes use of the magic of association.* To help him remember how to spell *truly*, for instance, he links it in his mind with *duly*, which he never misspells. Then *duly* reminds him to write *truly* without an *e*.

3 *A good speller takes mental snapshots of words.* To learn to spell a word like *col umn*, he focuses his attention on the word and gets a clear picture of how it looks so that when he writes *column* he will know that it "looks right."

4 *A good speller knows a few simple spelling rules* which he uses to help him avoid mistakes.

5 *A good speller proofreads his papers carefully* to be sure that he has spelled all the words correctly. He turns to the dictionary to find the spelling of words he is not sure of.

The explanations and exercises in this chapter will help you acquire these habits and make steady progress in becoming a good speller. Like Benjamin Franklin, who set up goals for himself and then checked himself regularly to be sure he was improving, you may want to check your progress. If so, you will find that keeping a spelling notebook is an invaluable aid.

List in this notebook the words whose spelling causes *you* trouble. Include not only the words you habitually misspell in your written work, but also those that you avoid writing because you are not sure of their spelling. Then whenever you have a few minutes of free time, use them to drill on your personal spelling "demons." Do not work on too many words at a time; concentrate on two or three. Once you are sure you have mastered their spelling, check them and move to the next group on your list.

PRONOUNCE WORDS CAREFULLY

If you say "I went *acrost* the street," you are very likely to spell the word *across* incorrectly. Many spelling errors result from careless pronunciation. It is important, then, that you hear every syllable of a word correctly and develop the habit of saying it correctly.

If we write the word *across* in syllables, it looks like this: *a cross*. It is a two-syllable word because it is pronounced as two units. In each unit is a vowel sound (*a, e, i, o, u* are vowels). Here the first syllable is a vowel by itself; the second consists of consonants with a vowel.

EXERCISE (1) The following common words are often misspelled because they are pronounced incorrectly. Pronounce them silently to yourself several times. Then, as a classmate dictates them to you, write the words (without syllable divisions). When you finish, check your words with the list to see that you have spelled them all correctly. Study carefully any words you misspell so that you will be able to spell all the words correctly when your teacher dictates them to you in class.

film (*not* fi lum)   light′ning (*not* light en ing)
qui′et (*not* quite)   hin′drance (*not* hin der ance)
drowned (*not* drown ded)   en′trance (*not* en ter ance)
pos′si bly (*not* pos a bly)   can′di date (*not* ca ni date)
quan′ti ty (*not* quan i ty)   ath let′ics (*not* ath a let ics)
dis as′trous (*not* dis as ter ous)   ath′lete (*not* ath a lete)
re mem′brance (*not* re mem ber ance)

DON'T SHIFT INTO REVERSE

Careful pronunciation will also help you avoid reversing letters, a common type of spelling error. If you write *hunderd* for *hundred*, and *calvary* for *cavalry*, you are misspelling the words by reversing letters. You need to train your ear to hear words correctly.

Here are some more words that are often misspelled through the reversing of letters. Pronounce them to yourself, noticing especially the order of the boldfaced letters.

per haps	mod ern	pre fer	does n't
per form ance	south ern	pref er ence	first
per spire	pat tern	pre scrip tion	trag e dy

EXERCISE (2) Be ready to write these sentences from dictation.

1 His first play was a tragedy, not a comedy.
2 Nora doesn't ever use a pattern.
3 Stoneby expressed a preference for pictures of pretty girls on prescription labels.

4 The cavalry officer perspired profusely to get a perfect performance from the hundred men.

5 Perhaps he would prefer a more modern room with a southern
exposure.

USE SPELLING PRONUNCIATIONS

The usual pronunciation of many words does not give an accurate
clue to their spelling. Notice, for instance, that the unstressed second *o* in the word *sophomore* sounds like the *e* in *taken*, and that
the *t* in *often* is usually not pronounced at all. Unstressed or unpro-
nounced letters are trouble spots for spellers.

To help you remember the spelling of words like these, pronounce
the words *to yourself* as you write them, exaggerating the sound of
the letters that cause trouble. If, when writing the following words,
you stress the sound of the boldfaced letters, you will spell the words
correctly: *soph o more, math e mat ics, bound a ry, gov er nor, of ten.*
And to help you spell these words, pronounce them to yourself in
three syllables: *Wed nes day, ev er y.*

Pronounce to yourself the words in the following list, stressing the
sound of the boldfaced letters to help you remember the spelling.

prob a **bly**	rec og nize	li brar y	which
arc tic	par **li a** ment	sur prise	ac ci den **tal** ly
Con nect i cut	gov ern ment	stretch	in ci den **tal** ly
hand some	lab **o** ra to ry	an swer	re **al** ly
in **ter** est ing	Feb ru ar y	to ward	u su **al** ly

EXERCISE (3) Be ready to write these sentences from dictation.

1 The athletic sophomore drowned in the disastrous flood.

2 When Smith was surprised by a quiet tiger, the hunt ended in
tragedy.

3 Incidentally, we recognize the fact that the mathematics in the
entrance examination is often a hindrance to candidates.

4 The question about the stretch of land which lies along the
boundary will probably be answered in parliament.

5 A quantity of interesting film was accidentally lost on the arctic
trip.

6 Starting in February, Dan will be at a government laboratory in
Connecticut to do research on lightning.

7 Every Wednesday as we walk toward the library, we usually
meet the governor, a most handsome woman.

THE MAGIC

OF ASSOCIATION

One way that you can make association work magic in your spelling is by **grouping similar forms.** For example, to help you remember to write *all right* as two words, link it in your mind with *all wrong* and *all in*, which you never misspell. You have no trouble with *mitten, kitten,* and *bitten,* so let them help you remember the two *t*'s in *written.* And let *nice, rice,* and *spice* remind you to put the *c* in *advice.*

Grouping similar forms in a sentence will also help. Do you have trouble with the word *led*? Then remember the sentence "**Ted led Ned** to the shed." To remind you to put the two *o*'s in *loose,* think of "The **noose** was **loose.**"

Using memory tricks is a second way to make association work magic in your spelling. Do you have trouble remembering the first *e* in *cafeteria*? Let *café* remind you to put the *e* in **cafeteria.** Everyone is polite at court. *Court* will help you remember the spelling of **courtesy** and **courteous.** Reminding yourself that a *critic* **criticizes** and gives **criticism** will help you spell these words correctly. And be sure there is a *bullet* in **bulletin** when you write it.

Have you noticed that there is *sand,* but no *witch,* in **sandwich**? Do you remember to keep the *man* **permanently** in *permanent*? Pa and ma will help you with two other common spelling "demons." Be sure you have *pa* in *separate,* and *ma* in *grammar.*

Recalling that a bookkeeper keeps books will remind you to put both *book* and *keep* in **bookkeeper** and **bookkeeping.** You can spell *extra* and *ordinary*; just put them together and you'll have **extraordinary.**

You won't have trouble with the *ery* in *cemetery,* if you remember that three *e*'s lie in *cemetery.* And you can settle the *c* and *s* problem in *license* by remembering that *c* comes before *s* in the alphabet.

EXERCISE (4) The most valuable associations for you are those *you* make for words you frequently misspell. Make up associations by grouping similar forms or by inventing memory tricks for three words that you often misspell, and be prepared to tell them to the class. (Be sure that the associations you make are simple and easy to remember, or they will not be very helpful.)

EXERCISE (5) Be ready to write these sentences from dictation.

1 Joe's lack of courtesy earned him much criticism.
2 You must pass a written test to get a permanent license.

423

3 Brown's extraordinary bookkeeping led to his arrest.
4 Is it all right to criticize his grammar?
5 To get into the cemetery, Bob had to crawl under a loose board in the fence.
6 My advice is not to order a sandwich in that cafeteria.
7 The bookkeepers received a separate bulletin all right.

ASSOCIATE SIMILAR SOUNDS

Grouping words with similar sounds can help make trouble spots disappear. Pronounce the name *William* to yourself. Did you notice that the second syllable has a *y* sound: "Will-yam"? Other words that have the same *y* sound also have an **ia** as *William* does: *brilliant, familiar, peculiar.*

Now pronounce *villain.* There is no *y* sound in this word, is there? The *i* follows the *a* in the second syllable of *villain.* This same **ai** appears in other words that end with the same sound: *certain, captain, bargain, curtain, mountain.*

All the following words end with the same sound—"zhun":

collision	division	persuasion
decision	occasion	invasion

It is the single *s* before *ion* that gives them this "zh" sound.

Now pronounce these words, each of which ends with the sound "shun":

discussion	profession	concession
omission	succession	admission

It is the two *s*'s before *ion* that gives them this "sh" sound.

EXERCISE (6) On a sheet of paper, write the incomplete words in each of the following sentences, supplying the missing letters. Number your answers with the numbers of the sentences. Be ready to write the sentences from dictation.

1 The capt...n offered the vill...n a pecul...r barg...n.
2 The deci...ion to send the divi...ion into the inva...ion was made later.
3 The omi...ion of an admi...ion fee for children is cert...n to encourage business.
4 The curt...n fell after the hero's profe...ion of undying love.
5 Dad made the conce...ion that on occa...ion Will...m could be rather brill...nt.

6 We had a long discu...ion about the succe...ion of colli...ions on the mount...n.

The *ci* in the words *delicious*, *precious*, and *suspicious* has an "sh" sound. Without the *i* the *c* would sound like *k*: "delikous," "prekous," "suspikous." Notice that the "sh" sound in these words is also spelled with *ci*:

ancient	efficient	beneficial
sufficient	artificial	financial

The *i* after the *g* in the word *religious* gives the *g* a *j* sound. If there were no *i*, the *g* would sound like the *g* in *asparagus*. Keep the *j* sound of the *g* in mind when you spell *religious* and *allegiance* and *contagious*, and you won't omit the *i* after the *g*. "His allegiance to the religious cause was contagious."

Pronounce the word *descend*. Did you notice that the letters *sc* work together to make one sound: "de-send"? Remember the silent partner *c* when you spell the words *science*, *discipline*, and *fascinating*. "The discipline of science can be fascinating."

425

But what happens to the *sc* partnership when an *h* is added? The silent partner *c* joins the *h* to make a *k* sound in words like *school*, *scheme*, and *schedule*. Be sure to include all three members of the company when you spell these words. "He has a new scheme for the school schedule."

You have no trouble spelling words like *action* and *station* in which the *ti* has an "sh" sound. Remember that the "sh" sound in these words is also spelled *ti*:

initial	essential	confidential	patience

EXERCISE (7) Be ready to write these sentences from dictation.

1 Dad is very suspicious of my financial schemes.
2 Jane thought the ancient religious ceremonies fascinating.
3 Patience is essential in science.
4 One contagious disease can be sufficient to upset a school schedule for weeks.
5 Despite its artificial blue coloring the pudding was delicious.
6 Efficient discipline is beneficial to students.
7 Tim was asked to initial the club's oath of allegiance.
8 A confidential report was sent to the governor in February.

When you have had **fun at a costume** party, it is easy to close your eyes afterwards and see your friends exactly as they looked. In fact, if you were asked, you could probably draw quite accurate pictures of them.

You can use this same power of visualizing to help you spell correctly. Just as you took a mental snapshot of your friends, you can focus on a word you want to remember and take a mental snapshot of it. Then only the correct spelling of the word will "look right" to you, because only it will match your mental picture.

Here is the way to use mental snapshots in learning to spell words. First, look at a word carefully and pronounce it by syllables, emphasizing the trouble spot. Second, as you look away and say the word, try to "see" the word as it looks in the book. Next, write the word, pronouncing it to yourself. Then compare the word you wrote with the word in the book to be sure your picture is in focus. Go through these steps at least three times, making sure that you can spell each word correctly before you go on to the next.

Practice taking mental snapshots of the words below, focusing particularly on the boldfaced trouble spots.

426

busi ness	sense	an a **lyze**	**prai** rie
colo nel	con **science**	cam **paign**	res **tau** rant
hy **giene**	con **scious**	bu **reau**	anx ious
mys te ri ous	mar **riage**	meant	ex er **cise**
phys i cal	straight	ser geant	choice
pam **phlet**	strength	ceased	ab sence

EXERCISE (8) Be ready to write these sentences from dictation.

1 The bachelor seemed unusually anxious to avoid marriage.
2 Only the colonel knew what the mysterious message meant.
3 We had no choice but to report the sergeant's absence.
4 The candidate's wife never ceased to be a tower of strength during his campaign.
5 If you'd come straight to the point, you'd make more sense.
6 To quiet his conscience, Parker returned to the restaurant and paid his bill.
7 Was he conscious that the bureau was investigating his business?
8 The cavalry rode straight across the prairie toward the fort.
9 This pamphlet on hygiene analyzes the effects of physical exercise on older people.

Unless you spot the silent letters in words like *aisle, rhythm, knowledge, guarantee,* and *guardian,* you are very likely to misspell these words. As you study new words, be sure to take careful note of any silent letters they contain. Concentrate on the boldfaced silent letters in these words:

debtor	psychology	rhyme
acquaintance	exhaust	almond
acquire	ghost	solemn
adjourn	shepherd	column
characteristic	knew	subtle
chorus	know	mortgage

EXERCISE 9 Be ready to write these sentences from dictation.

1 This poem has neither rhythm nor rhyme.
2 The shepherd surprised us with his knowledge of psychology.
3 Few knew how Drew had acquired his money.
4 Can you guarantee that the ghost will appear?
5 A solemn chorus filed down the aisle between the columns.
6 Don't exhaust the supply of almonds.
7 On such short acquaintance how did you know that he needed a guardian?
8 The villain knew the debtor was unable to pay the mortgage.
9 It is characteristic of Tom to think of a subtle scheme.
10 I know he will adjourn the court until Wednesday.

427

GROUP PICTURES: DOUBLE LETTERS

The double letters in *communicate, commercial, arrange,* and *arrival* are trouble spots. If you concentrate on "seeing" the double letters in these words, you will learn to spell them correctly.

Now study the following words, looking carefully at the double letters:

accept	excellent	appearance
accident	intelligent	approach
account	parallel	opportunity
proceed	immediate	opposite
different	recommend	suppose
exaggerate	choose	necessary

The words *committee, Mississippi,* and *Tennessee* are some of the few words having three sets of double letters. A number of other words have two sets. Concentrate on the two sets of double letters when you visualize these words:

| accommodate | possession | succeed |
| address | embarrass | successful |

EXERCISE (10) Be ready to write these sentences from dictation.

1 The committee recommended an immediate change in commercial communications.
2 I cannot accept Art's account of the accident.
3 Morgan was successful in gaining possession of the land parallel to ours, opposite the Tyler estate.
4 The spy found it necessary to proceed to Tennessee by a different route.
5 Dill's intelligent approach to the problem brought him an excellent raise.
6 By giving an exaggerated account of his rescue, Jane succeeded only in embarrassing Sam.
7 The star did not choose to arrange her schedule to accommodate her fans.
8 I suppose the senator from Mississippi will take this opportunity to make an address.
9 Henry's carelessness about his appearance often embarrassed the other committee members.
10 Tom's arrival gave Jack an excellent excuse for leaving.

428

GROUP PICTURES: SINGLE LETTERS

Use memory clues whenever you can to help you visualize words. For example, let *Sahara* remind you to look for the single *s* in *desert,* a bad place to be *deserted.* The single *r* in *around, arouse,* and *various* is troublesome. Try grouping these words in a sentence: "Revere rode around to arouse the various rebels." Pay special attention to the boldfaced single letters as you study the following words:

imagine	apology	always
imagination	apologize	altogether
across	apiece	already
pastime	operate	almost
until	opinion	although

EXERCISE (11) Write five sentences, using in each sentence at least two of the words you have studied in this section. Your teacher may ask you to dictate your sentences to the class.

STUDYING SIMILAR FORMS

Words with A. In this and the following three lessons you will have an opportunity to practice the spelling habits you have been learning. Each lesson contains groups of words with similar trouble spots. The words in this lesson all have troublesome a's.

You won't overlook the *a* in *realize* if you pronounce the word carefully—*re al ize*. Does the *ary* ending of the word *secretary* cause you difficulty? Then think of "**Mary**, the secret**ary**." Concentrate on the *ar* ending of *particular, calendar*, and *similar* to help you put an *a* before the *r* in these words. "That particul**ar** calend**ar** is simil**ar** to mine."

Let the *a* of *adjective* remind you to put the *al* ending on these three adjectives: *fundamental, personal, practical*. Let a sentence like "**Ann's anger affected Andy**," in which each word begins with *a*, remind you that the verb *affect* starts with *a*. And be sure to keep the *a*'s in *pleasant* and *weather* in mind when you tell about "pleasant weather."

Putting the word *plan* in *explanation* will banish the problem of the first *a*. And the sentence "**Lance** made Ann's acquain**tance** at the **dance**" will help you remember the final *a* in *acquaintance*.

429

EXERCISE (12) Be ready to write these sentences from dictation.

1 On that particular Wednesday the weather was quite pleasant.
2 I did not realize that Amy was so practical.
3 The fact that William gave a similar explanation may affect her decision.
4 It is his personal opinion that a fundamental change in our calendar is necessary.
5 Is his secretary an acquaintance of yours?

Words with E. As you study these words with troublesome e's, be sure to get a clear picture of each word so that only the correct spelling will look right to you.

Bene, a Latin word, means *well*. A *benefactor* is a "well-doer." Be sure to put *bene* in these words: *beneficial, benefit, benediction*.

The word *recede* also comes from a Latin word, meaning "to go back." Let the *cede* of *recede* help you with the spelling of two other words having to do with going—*precede* (to go before) and *intercede* (to go between).

Since you have little trouble spelling the word *petition* correctly, let this word help you with *repetition* and *competition*. Watch for the *ten*, a trouble spot, in *competence*, *sentence*, and *existence*. Put a *den* in *tendency*, and a *dent* in *dependent*, *independent*, and *superintendent*.

Be sure you have a clear picture of the *e*'s in these words:

describe	despise	excellent	whether
description	angel	excellence	effect (noun)
despair	nickel	absence	breathe
destroy	counsel	experience	before

EXERCISE 13 Be ready to write these sentences from dictation.

1 Who preceded Jim as counsel for the committee?
2 Ask for a repetition of his description.
3 The excellence of Tom's work proves his competence.
4 Why did Jane despise Ellen's tendency to be dependent on her mother?
5 Jane was determined to lead an independent existence.
6 The sugar angels cost a nickel.
7 Before we could intercede with the judge, he passed sentence on Smith.
8 I wonder whether he will benefit by his experience.
9 The superintendent's absence had no effect on the competition.
10 Do not breathe a word of my decision to anyone.

Words with I, U, LE. If you pronounce *finite* carefully, you will spell it correctly. Let *finite* help you with the troublesome *i*'s in *definite*, *indefinite*, and *infinite*.

Notice the *gin* ending of *origin*. Watch for the same *gin* in words derived from *origin*: *original*, *originally*, *originate*.

Look carefully at the second syllable of each of these words: *med i cine*, *del i cate*, *pos i tive*. The second syllable of each word is the vowel *i* by itself; concentrate on that *i*.

The first *i* in *divine* and *divide* is a troublemaker; so is the *i* in *disturb* and *disease*. Keep an eye on these *di* words. And here are three words with two troublesome *i*'s to watch: *eligible*, *eliminate*, *privilege*.

Thinking of "U turn" will help you remember the *u* in *turn* and *turning*. Each of these spelling demons also has a *u*: *bury*, *buried*, *minute.* Notice that there are two *u*'s in *murmur, luxury, pursue,* and *pursuit.* But there is only one *u* in *custom, customer,* and *accustomed*; the letter after the *t* is an *o*.

The word *circle* is seldom a problem. Let the **le** ending of *circle* remind you of the *le* ending of *article, particle,* and *angle.*

EXERCISE (14) Be ready to write these sentences from dictation.

1 Can the new medicine definitely eliminate the disease?
2 I am positive the customer was not accustomed to such luxury.
3 Originally they planned to bury the treasure.
4 It is not the custom to divide the money immediately.
5 Whether or not Spike is eligible to play is a delicate question.
6 Henry claimed many privileges under the divine right of kings.
7 Do not disturb Dad while he is turning the steaks.
8 Sam's article certainly had an original angle.
9 In minutes the pursuit planes were in the air.
10 Without a murmur she let me remove the particle from her eye.

Words with O, OU. Don't let a single **o** stand between you and the correct spelling of the words *lose* and *whose.* Linking *forty* and *forth* with *fort* will help you spell these demons. "Forty men went forth to storm the fort." And let *rose, those,* and *hose* remind you of the single *o* in *chose.* "Rose chose those hose."

The *o* in the word *among* has a "u" sound; so does the *o* in *some.* Group these troublemakers with words with similar *o*'s like *monk, come,* and *from.* "Some will come from among the monks."

Concentrate on the *or* ending of *doctor, professor, author, sponsor,* and *humor* to help you remember the *o* before the *r.* "The doctor or the professor will sponsor the author with a sense of humor."

The first *o* in *thorough* is very necessary to do a *thorough* job of spelling this word. Take a second look at *thorough* to notice the **ou.** The same *ou* is found in *though* and *dough.* Have you spotted the silent letters in *thorough, though,* and *dough?*

Four, fourteen, and *fourth* all have to do with *amounts.* Grouping these four words will help you remember the *ou.*

EXERCISE (15) Be ready to write these sentences from dictation.

1 Whose shoes did the doctor lose?
2 The comedian's sponsor did not see any humor in his jokes.
3 One fourth of the amount was divided among the fourteen brothers.
4 Be sure to mix the dough thoroughly.
5 Some forty students came forth to greet the professor.

431

6   Though the author gave only four clues, I knew the butler was guilty.
7   The colonel chose forty men for the special mission.

BEWARE OF WORDS

THAT SOUND ALIKE

Homonyms—words that sound alike, but have different meanings —cause about forty per cent of all spelling errors. As you probably know from experience, the difficulty with homonyms is not that you cannot spell the words correctly, but that their similarity of sound leads you to write the wrong spelling for the meaning you intend. For instance, although you know the difference in spelling and meaning between the homonyms *forth* and *fourth*, their similarity of sound might lead you to write *forth* instead of *fourth* in a sentence like "Tom saved a fourth of his salary."

Always check any homonyms in your writing to be sure that you have written the word that expresses the meaning you intend. To help you distinguish between homonyms and spell them correctly, visualize the words in sentences or phrases that will remind you of their meanings.

Here are some common troublesome homonyms. Look at them carefully and study especially those that you frequently confuse.

hear	You hear with your ear.
here	We looked here, there, and everywhere.
its	The cat washed *its* paws. [Group *his, hers, its.*]
it's	*It's* now or never. [It's = It is.]
	It's been very cold this winter. [It's = It has.]
passed	The band *passed* the reviewing stand. [*Passed* is used only as a verb.]
past	The *past* president just walked *past*.
peace	Peace is the peak of our hopes.
piece	He ate a piece of pie.
their	Take *their* chairs. [Group *your, our,* and *their.*]
there	There is where we found him.
they're	*They're* seldom early. [They're = They are.]
to	I do so want *to* go *to* the show.
too	Noon came *too* soon.
two	We bought two bicycles for the twins.

EXERCISE 16 Choose from each group of homonyms (in parentheses) the word that is correct to use in the sentence and write it on a sheet of paper. Number your answers with the numbers of the sentences. Be ready to write the sentences from dictation.

1 (*Their, There, They're*) share of the cake is (*their, there, they're*) on the table.
2 Do you think it's (*to, too, two*) late (*to, too, two*) hand in my report?
3 Susan didn't (*hear, here*) (*their, there, they're*) call.
4 We plan to buy a (*peace, piece*) of land (*hear, here*).
5 (*Their, There, They're*) constant quarreling disturbed John's (*peace, piece*) of mind.
6 (*To, Too, Two*) new engines were installed (*hear, here*) during the (*passed, past*) year.
7 After Tom (*passed, past*) the library, he turned and walked (*passed, past*) the drugstore.
8 (*Their, There, They're*) not permitted to let the snake out of (*its, it's*) cage.
9 (*Its, It's*) been years since we (*passed, past*) this way.
10 Call me when (*its, it's*) time to leave.

433

FOLLOWING THE RULES

Good spellers are, as a rule, very observant; they notice differences and similarities in words. They notice, for example, that in the word *believe*, the *i* comes before the *e*, but in *receive*, the *e* comes before the *i*. They notice that when *occur* and *refer* have an *ed* at the end, they also have a double *r*: *occurred* and *referred*. They notice that *misspell* and *misstep* have two *s*'s, but *misprint* and *mislead* have just one.

People who are this observant have little need for studying spelling rules; they *observe* the rules without even realizing that they do. But for other people, studying the rules is well worth the effort. The rules are simply guides that direct attention to the ways certain large groups of similar words are spelled. They point out the spelling patterns that help us write correctly many words that we might otherwise misspell.

Remember that learning the exact wording of the rules by heart is not important. But learning what the rules mean so that you can apply them when you write is of great importance if you want to improve your spelling.

Rule out IE-EI problems. Do you ever have trouble deciding whether to write *ie* or *ei* in words like *believe, deceive, weigh,* and *friend*? A two-part general rule will help you spell *ie-ei* words correctly.

Here is the first part of the rule: **Write *i* before *e* when the sound is long *e*.** The long-*e* sound is, of course, the sound of *e* in *see* and *beet*. Notice the long-*e* [ē] sound in these words with *ie*:

achieve	reprieve	chief	shriek
believe	belief	thief	field
grieve	grief	fiend	shield
relieve	relief	priest	wield
retrieve	brief	niece	yield

Notice these four words with *r* after the *ie*: *pier, fierce, pierce,* and *frontier*. You have seen *siege* and *besiege* often in history books. Have you seen the *ie*? And who hasn't read about the World *Series*? Be sure to put the *ie* in *series*.

There are six common exceptions to this rule about *i* before *e*: *seize, inveigle, either, weird, leisure, neither*. If you learn the *ie* rule and these six exceptions, you will spell words with *ie* correctly.

EXERCISE (17) Be ready to write these sentences from dictation.

1 After a brief fight, order was achieved along the frontier.
2 In a series of fierce attacks the army seized the pier.
3 The besieged men had neither rest nor leisure.
4 With relief we saw the chief still wielding his sword.
5 I do not believe the priest will yield.
6 The thief inveigled his niece into stealing a piece of meat.
7 The weird fiend shrieked as the arrow pierced his shield.
8 We were relieved to hear that the siege was over.
9 The governor refused to grant Stone a reprieve.
10 Did either the shortstop or the left fielder score any runs?

EI words. Here is the second part of the *ie-ei* rule: **Write *ei* after *c* or when the sound is not *ē*.** Concentrate on seeing the *ei* after the *c* in these words:

receive	deceive	conceive	perceive
receipt	deceit	conceit	ceiling

"I perceive that you meant to deceive me about the ceiling."

The words *sovereign, foreign, surfeit,* and *counterfeit* do not have a long-*e* sound; therefore they are spelled with *ei*. "The foreign sovereign had a surfeit of counterfeit money in his land."

A number of words spelled with *ei* have a long-*a* sound (like the *a* in *gate*). Notice these *ei* words with a long-*a* sound:

weigh	vein	rein	eighth	reign
sleigh	skein	reindeer	neighbor	veil

Three more *ei* words with a long-*a* sound are *eight, freight*, and *weight*. "Could none of the **eight** tell the **weight** of the freight?"

Still other words spelled with *ei* have a long-*i* sound (like the *i* in *bite*). Note carefully the *ei* in these words:

height	sleight	Fahrenheit	eider

After you have studied the second part of the *ie-ei* rule well, study these seven exceptions to it: *financier, fiery, mischief, friend, sieve, view,* and *handkerchief*. If you learn to visualize the *ie* in these words, they will be no problem to you.

EXERCISE (18) Be ready to write these sentences from dictation.

1 The freight weighed eight tons.
2 We were not deceived when we received the counterfeit bills.
3 The financier's fiery temper caused much mischief.
4 At a tug of the reins the reindeer began to pull the sleigh.
5 My friend is very conceited because of the success of his sleight of hand.
6 Mary demanded a receipt for the skein of yarn, the veil, and the sieve.
7 All during his reign the sovereign viewed his foreign neighbors with alarm.
8 The freezing point on a Fahrenheit thermometer is 32 degrees.
9 On the eighth line he wrote down his height and weight.
10 Neither the eider down nor the handkerchief is mine.

435

IE and EI: *the whole rule.* Can you repeat the entire *ie-ei* rule? Unless you can, it will be no help to you in spelling *ie-ei* words. Here it is all together:

> Write *i* before *e* when the sound is long **e,**
> Except: seize, inveigle, either,
>   weird, leisure, neither.
> Write *ei* after *c* or when the sound is not **ē,**
> Except: financier, fiery, mischief,
>   friend, sieve, view, handkerchief.

EXERCISE (19) On a sheet of paper, write the incomplete words in the following sentences, supplying the missing letters. Number your answers with the numbers of the sentences. Be ready to write these sentences from dictation.

1 Do you bel...ve that he rec...ved the fr...ght?
2 N...ther the s...ve nor the handkerch...f was ever retr...ved.
3 During his br...f r...gn he conc...ved much misch...f.
4 Ed spent his l...sure drawing a w...rd design on the c...ling.
5 We could not inv...gle my fr...nd into v...wing the f...ry scene.
6 ...ther rel...ve the bes...ged city at once, or y'...ld the r...ns of government.
7 Pursue that advice and you'll ach...ve the h...ghts of success.
8 The th...f came to gr...f when the ch...f caught him with the roll of counterf...t money.
9 A for...gn sover...gn conc...ved the idea of s...zing his n...ghbor's throne.
10 The financ...r sh...lded his n...ce from the shr...king f...nd.

Rule out prefix and suffix problems. A **prefix** is an addition put at the *beginning* of a word to change its meaning. If you add the prefix *mis* (which means "wrong") to the word *spell*, you'll have the word *misspell*.

Adding a prefix does not change the spelling of the base word. Notice that no matter what letter the following base words begin with, their spelling is not changed when a prefix is added:

dis + appear = dis**appear**   mis + place = mis**place**
dis + satisfy = dis**satisfy**   mis + sent = mis**sent**
dis + similar = dis**similar**   mis + state = mis**state**
over + look = over**look**   un + usual = un**usual**
over + rule = over**rule**   un + natural = un**natural**
over + ripe = over**ripe**   un + necessary = un**necessary**

A **suffix** is an addition put at the *end* of a word to change its meaning. For instance, by adding the suffix *ful* to the noun *skill*, we form the adjective *skillful*. And by adding the suffix *ly*, we form the adverb *skillfully*. The addition of a suffix sometimes changes the spelling of the base word. Knowing when to change the spelling of base words and when not to will be no problem for you if you learn the general rules about adding suffixes that are explained on the following pages.

Words with silent E. If you pronounce the words *hop* and *hope* to yourself, you will notice that the silent *e* in *hope* gives the *o* a long sound. This *e* is dropped, however, before a suffix like *ing*

436

that begins with a vowel: *hoping.* Because the *i* of *ing* keeps the long sound of the *o* in *hoping,* the *e* is no longer needed.

Words ending in silent *e* drop the *e* before a suffix beginning with a vowel (*a, e, i, o, u*).

desire + able = desirable	mature + ity = maturity
use + ed = used	sense + ible = sensible
write + er = writer	create + or = creator
shine + ing = shining	continue + ous = continuous

A few words are exceptions to this rule. Verbs ending in *oe* (like *hoe*) keep the *e* before *ing: hoeing, tiptoeing, shoeing. Dyeing* and *singeing* keep the *e,* to distinguish them from *dying* and *singing.* And the *e* is retained before the suffixes *able* and *ous* in words like *noticeable, peaceable, serviceable, changeable, manageable,* and *courageous* to keep the *s* sound of the *c* and the *j* sound of the *g.*

EXERCISE 20   This exercise will give you practice in adding suffixes beginning with vowels to words ending in silent *e.* On a sheet of paper, write the following groups of words, adding the suffixes indicated.

1   Add *able* to: love, change, excite, advise, notice.
2   Add *er* to: use, lose, dine, grieve.
3   Add *ing* to: lose, write, come, argue, dine, shine, die, canoe.   **437**
4   Add *ous* to: desire, outrage, grieve, fame, advantage, continue.
5   Add *or* to: narrate, refrigerate.

EXERCISE 21   Be ready to write these sentences from dictation.

1   Losing the game after coming so far was a grievous blow.
2   He is arguing that dyeing the suit will make it more serviceable.
3   If the letter was missent, it will be returned to the writer.
4   In writing about the canoeing trip, the narrator often praised his courageous companions.
5   Jim would seem more sensible if he weren't so changeable.
6   I was hoping that you would make a peaceable settlement.
7   Dad says hoeing is unnecessary if you are willing to overlook the more noticeable weeds.
8   Is it advisable to buy a used refrigerator for the diner?
9   To avoid Sue's continuous scolding, Hank often found it desirable to disappear for a while.
10   He is the famous creator of that lovable character Sam Sadly.
11   John's dissatisfaction went unnoticed.
12   The writer overruled his friend's outrageous plan.

More about words with silent E. So far we have practiced adding only suffixes beginning with vowels. Suppose now that you are adding to the word *hope* the suffix *ful*, which begins with a consonant. Since there is no vowel to take the place of the *e* and keep the long-*o* sound, you do not drop the *e*. You write *hopeful*.

Here, then, is the second rule about adding suffixes: **Words ending in silent *e* usually keep the *e* before a suffix beginning with a consonant.**

peace + ful = peaceful	achieve + ment = achievement
care + less = careless	accurate + ness = accurateness
lone + ly = lonely	nine + ty = ninety
sure + ly = surely	safe + ty = safety

There are five common exceptions to this rule. The following words do not have an *e* before the suffix: *truly, duly, wholly, ninth, argument.*

EXERCISE 22 Divide a sheet of paper into five columns, heading each column with one of these suffixes: *ful, less, ly, ment, ness.* Then add as many of these suffixes as possible to each of the following words, writing each new word in its appropriate column. For instance, for the word *care* you would put *careful* in the *ful* column and *careless* in the *less* column. You should have at least 25 words. (You may want to refer to your dictionary.)

hope	purpose	excite	use
advertise	arrange	nice	scarce
improve	immediate	require	definite
sincere	announce	sure	entire

EXERCISE 23 Be ready to write these sentences from dictation.

1 The building inspector duly noted the scarceness of improvements.
2 I definitely think the arrangements should be made immediately.
3 It was truly an achievement for Max to bring that argument to a peaceful conclusion.
4 By the ninth inning the situation looked hopeless for our team.
5 Accurateness is the first requirement for a good reporter.
6 Tom was so wholly absorbed in his work that he scarcely noticed the excitement in the next room.
7 The ninety lonely men wrote an advertisement asking for pen pals.
8 Surely you don't think I purposely ignored the announcement!

438

9 Do you sincerely believe that your invention is useful?

10 The announcement states that employees on the ninth floor have been entirely too careless about safety measures.

Doubling the final consonant. *Hop* is a one-syllable word which ends in a single consonant—*p*—preceded by a single vowel—*o*. When we add the suffix *ing*, which begins with a vowel, we double the *p*: *hop* + *ing* = *hopping*. If we did not double the *p*, the *i* of *ing* would give the *o* of *hop* a long sound, as it does the *o* in *hoping*. It is important, then, to double the final consonant of words like *hop* before adding a suffix beginning with a vowel.

Words of one syllable ending in a single consonant preceded by a single vowel double the final consonant before suffixes beginning with a vowel.

drop + ed = dropped   grim + est = grimmest
run + ing = running   flat + ish = flattish
ship + er = shipper   rob + ery = robbery

Notice that this rule does not apply to words like *stamp* and *strict*, which end in two consonants, or to words like *keep* and *steal*, which have two vowels preceding the final consonant:

stamped   strictest   keeper   stealing

439

EXERCISE 24 On a sheet of paper, write each of the following words, completing the addition of the suffix. For *dim* + *er*, for instance, you would write *dimmer*. Be ready to explain how you determined the spelling of each word.

1	plan + ing	11	green + ish
2	plane + ed	12	sad + est
3	big + er	13	stop + ed
4	red + ish	14	dine + er
5	cute + est	15	win + er
6	cream + ery	16	tan + ery
7	mop + ing	17	bet + ing
8	pine + ed	18	trim + est
9	stir + ed	19	weld + er
10	pin + ing	20	cut + ing

EXERCISE 25 Be ready to write these sentences from dictation.

1 All the while he was trimming the hedge, Jim kept stealing glances at his new neighbor.

2 Dropping his tools, the welder stamped off toward the office.

3 Why are they painting the shipping department that ugly greenish shade?

4 The diner stopped the waiter and demanded a bigger steak.

5 The lion hardly stirred while the keeper mopped its cage.

6 That reddish building is the tannery, not the creamery.

7 Pinning medals on the winners was one of Mary's duties as queen of the meet.

8 Bob was the saddest boy in town because he wasn't running in the track meet.

9 The thief escaped by hopping the ditch and cutting through the woods.

10 Looking grimmer than usual, the chief said he was sure the robbery had been planned in advance.

More about doubling the final consonant. For words of more than one syllable we add one more requirement for doubling the final consonant—an accent on the last syllable. The word *prefer*, for example, is a two-syllable word that ends in a single consonant —*r*—preceded by a single vowel—*e*—and is accented on the last syllable: *pre fer'*. When we add the suffix *ed*, which begins with a vowel, we double the final *r*: *prefer* + *ed* = *preferred*.

This is the rule covering the many words like *prefer*: **Words of more than one syllable which end in a single consonant preceded by a single vowel and are accented on the last syllable double the final consonant before a suffix beginning with a vowel.**

ad mit' + ance = admittance	pro pel' + er = propeller
con trol' + able = controllable	o mit' + ing = omitting
oc cur' + ence = occurrence	sub mit' + ed = submitted

Words like *ac quit'* also come under this rule because here the *u*, which has a *w* sound, is considered a consonant. If we add a suffix beginning with a vowel, we double the *t*:

 acquitting   acquitted   acquittal   acquittance

Words like *affect* and *descend*, which end in two consonants, and *reveal* and *succeed*, which have two vowels preceding the final consonant, do not come under this rule. Nor can you use this rule for words like *alter* and *develop*, which are not accented on the last syllable.

 affecting   revealing   altered
 descending   succeeded   developed

EXERCISE (26) On a sheet of paper, write each of the following words, completing the addition of the suffix. Be ready to explain why you did or did not double the final consonant before adding the suffix to each word.

1	transfer + ing	11	occur + ed
2	repeat + er	12	rebel + ing
3	regret + able	13	remit + ance
4	equip + ed	14	conceal + ed
5	acquaint + ance	15	acquit + ing
6	commit + ed	16	refer + ed
7	defer + ing	17	desert + er
8	begin + er	18	compel + ing
9	benefit + ed	19	cancel + ed
10	redeem + able	20	control + er

EXERCISE 27 Be ready to write these sentences from dictation.

1 The remittance must be submitted immediately.
2 Ann developed a strong dislike for Ted because of his uncontrollable temper.
3 Kay preferred to forget the regrettable occurrence.
4 The deserter succeeded in getting an acquittal.
5 Deferring to his manager's wishes, the candidate altered the beginning of his speech.
6 The controller admitted that he had committed the crime.
7 Equipping the boat with an extra propeller was a good idea.
8 Stan rebelled at being compelled to pay a quarter for one cup of coffee.

Words with Y. Notice what happens when we add a suffix beginning with a consonant to a word like *happy*. *Happy* ends in *y* preceded by a consonant—*p*. When we add the suffix *ness*, which begins with a consonant, we change the *y* to *i*: *happy* + *ness* = *happiness*. This change from *y* to *i* is usual before suffixes beginning with a consonant:

pretty + ly = prettily   merry + ment = merriment
lonely + ness = loneliness   mercy + less = merciless
pity + ful = pitiful   beauty + fy = beautify

Now suppose we want to add to *lonely* the suffix *est*, which begins with the vowel *e*. Again we would change the *y* to *i*: *lonely* + *est* = *loneliest*. We also change the *y* to *i* before other suffixes beginning with *e*:

pity + ed = pitied   happy + er = happier
dry + ed = dried   busy + er = busier
cry + es = cries   penny + es = pennies

Words ending in *y* preceded by a consonant usually change the *y* to *i* before a suffix beginning with a consonant or the vowel *e*.

But notice what would happen if we changed the *y* to *i* before adding the suffix *ing* to the word *pity*. We would have *pitiing*, a strange-looking word. For this reason we keep the *y* when adding *ing* to verbs ending in *y*:

pity + ing = pitying	carry + ing = carrying
study + ing = studying	hurry + ing = hurrying

EXERCISE (28) On a sheet of paper, write each of the following words, completing the addition of the suffix. Be ready to explain why you did or did not change the *y* to *i* before adding each suffix.

1	try + ed	11	employ + er
2	coy + ly	12	lucky + est
3	worry + er	13	weary + ness
4	easy + ly	14	plenty + ful
5	joy + ful	15	penny + less
6	heavy + er	16	occupy + ing
7	pay + ment	17	satisfy + ed
8	glory + fy	18	greedy + ness
9	busy + ly	19	beauty + ful
10	hurry + ing	20	accompany + ment

EXERCISE (29) Be ready to write these sentences from dictation.

1 Luckily, Jim was busily studying when Dad found him.
2 Mr. Pinch was easily the greediest and the loneliest man in town.
3 My pitiful attempts to beautify the shack caused much merriment among the neighbors.
4 The penniless pianist was worried because he couldn't meet the payments.
5 Mr. Sterns tried to explain why he was dissatisfied with the accompaniment.
6 The prettiest girl of the three was happily occupying the center of attention.
7 A more merciful employer would make sure that the stronger men were carrying the heavier loads.
8 Despite their weariness the men sang merrily as they hurried on.
9 After her uncle gave her the pennies, Debbie dried her tears and smiled prettily at him.
10 The busier Bruce is, the happier he seems to be.

CONTRACTING WORDS CORRECTLY

In informal speech we often use contractions. For example, instead of saying "does not" we say "doesn't." In contracting words, we usually omit one or more letters and indicate the omission in writing by putting an apostrophe where the omission occurs. Notice that in writing *doesn't* we use an apostrophe to indicate the omission of the letter *o*. An apostrophe also indicates the omission of the *o* of *not* in these words:

is not—isn't	was not—wasn't	have not—haven't
are not—aren't	were not—weren't	could not—couldn't
did not—didn't	has not—hasn't	should not—shouldn't

Three contractions with *n't* are formed irregularly. We write *can't* for *can not*, *won't* for *will not*, and *shan't* for *shall not*.

Some other contractions are formed by dropping the first letter or letters of the verb. For example, we contract *I have* to *I've*. Here the apostrophe shows the omission of the letters *ha* of *have*. Notice where the apostrophe is placed indicating the omitted letters in these contractions:

Dan is—Dan's	I will—I'll	they are—they're
here is—here's	you will—you'll	we are—we're
who is—who's	we have—we've	you are—you're
it is—it's	you have—you've	we would—we'd
I am—I'm	I would—I'd	he had—he'd

443

EXERCISE 30 Number a sheet of paper from 1 to 9. Then as your teacher reads the following story, write after the number of each sentence any contractions that might be formed with the verbs in that sentence. You will have fifteen contractions.

(1) I have just read an amazing story that you will never believe could be true. (2) Now do not get me wrong. (3) I did not see the cat it is about and I can not produce any evidence. (4) But the newspaper certainly would not have printed the story if it were not true.

(5) Here is the story. (6) Because their pet kitten was sick, the Jones family decided they would have to drown it. (7) After the kitten was drowned, the children could not resist giving it a funeral. (8) I guess the kitten had not really died, for eight days later a dog dug up the box they had buried it in and the kitten jumped out. (9) Now is that not one of the strangest tales you have ever heard?

CHAPTER **24**

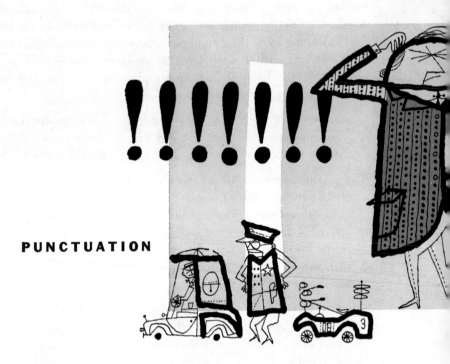

PUNCTUATION

444

Bob Frazer wrote the following sentences in the course of a day. He knew exactly what he meant. Do you?

[In a note to a friend:]
Then your father insisted the officer was absolutely wrong.

[In a report for English class:]
Edgar Lee Masters wrote Lucinda Matlock a short poem about the need for courage in life.

[In an answer to a question in a social-studies test:]
No income taxes must be paid if a person has a gross income of over $600.

[In an article about the Drama Club for the school paper:]
Just a week before the club had decided to present a one-act play in assembly.

Bob, you should have been told, had no use for punctuation marks; he seldom bothered with such things as commas and quota-

tion marks. As a result, the meaning you got from his sentences is very likely quite different from the meaning he had in mind. As a matter of fact, it was the *officer*—not the *father*—who was so outspoken, as the proper punctuation would have shown:

"Then your father," insisted the officer, "was absolutely wrong."

Edgar Lee Masters may have written poems to a girl named Lucinda, but the *Lucinda Matlock* that Bob meant was not a person. Punctuation would have made this point clear:

Edgar Lee Masters wrote "Lucinda Matlock," a short poem about the need for courage in life.

A comma in the third sentence would have added ten points to Bob's test grade. Without this comma, how was the teacher to know that he meant just the opposite of what he said?

No, income taxes must be paid if a person has a gross income of over $600.

And you can't blame the editor of the school paper for refusing to accept Bob's article—with its puzzling lack of punctuation. It took him two or three minutes just to figure out that the fourth sentence was really a sentence, that nothing was missing but a comma:

> Just a week before, the club had decided to present a one-act play in assembly.

Punctuation marks are not just decorations; they are signals that a writer has to use if he wants to make his meaning clear to a reader. If Bob *had spoken* the four sentences, his listeners would have had no trouble understanding what he meant. By pausing after certain words, by changing the tone and pitch of his voice, by emphasizing some words more than others, he would have made his meaning unmistakably clear.

Bob did not realize that *in writing*, punctuation marks are necessary substitutes for the pauses and voice changes that are used in speech. He relied on written words alone to carry his meaning; and written words alone, as you have seen, cannot do the whole job. Punctuation marks are so important to meaning that they deserve careful study. Let's see what the various marks are and how they are used.

446

END MARKS

A sentence may end with a period, a question mark, or an exclamation mark. Your purpose in writing the sentence determines which of these three marks you use. If you want to make a statement or give a command or request, use a period:

> In the jewelry trade, 24-carat gold is pure gold.
> Margaret asked Ellen to feed the guppies.
> He asked me where you live.

> Open the door, please.
> When you have a chance, try skiing in Vermont.

If you want to ask a *direct* question, use a question mark:

> What time is it?
> Why does a boomerang return to the thrower?

If you want to be very emphatic or want to show strong feeling (like anger, joy, horror, disapproval, surprise), use an exclamation mark. This mark may come after single words, groups of words, or complete sentences (including commands):

Help!   Fire!   How silly they sound!
What a fantastic story!   Stand back!

Remember that it is the *purpose* of the sentence—not the form—that determines the mark to use. The following sentences have the form of simple statements. But to show that he intends them to be read as questions, the writer uses question marks:

It was you he saw?
Jerry paid for the tickets?

The next two sentences are phrased in question form for the sake of courtesy. But since the writer intends them as requests, and not as questions for which he wants answers, he uses periods at the end:

Will you please see me before you leave.
Would you please return the questionnaire this week.

EXERCISE (1)   Read the following sentences and decide what punctuation mark should be used at the end of each. If more than one mark might be used for any sentence, be ready to explain when each should be used.

1   How long can a whale stay under water
2   A cornet is easier to play than a trumpet
3   He asked whether a cornet is easier to play than a trumpet
4   How dare you say such things about Uncle Jim
5   What a chump I've been
6   Buoys are the navigator's traffic signs
7   Watch out   A train is coming
8   Will all those in favor of the motion say "Aye"
9   How can you tell the age of a tree
10   Mary asked if I knew how to tell the age of a tree
11   He didn't remember the difference between a meteor and a comet
12   Hurry   You'll miss the bus
13   What a fuss she made
14   Ted won the first prize
15   How stupid his arguments were

EXERCISE (2)   The following paragraph consists of 15 sentences. Read the paragraph and decide where the sentences begin and end. Number a sheet of paper from 1 to 15. After each number, write the first word and the last word of each sentence. Capitalize each first word. Put the appropriate end mark (period, question mark, or exclamation mark) after each last word.

anyone who can walk can ski skiing, like walking, calls for balance but it is a special kind of balance because of the vertical angle of the slope how can you learn this balance you'll need to practice flexing your knees and bending forward no, that won't do at all bend forward much more now do you feel ready to try your skis on a slope first there is something else you must learn there may be a tree or some other obstacle in your path put your weight on your right foot and pivot on your left to circle that tree or obstacle or do you want to turn to the left then put your weight on your left foot and pivot on your right that's the way it isn't hard to ski, is it

PERIODS

WITH ABBREVIATIONS

Abbreviations are useful time savers and space savers—for a writer. But for general readers, many abbreviations may be quite puzzling. For example, do you know offhand what all of these stand for: *r.p.m.*, *jct.*, *ht.*, *Gk.*, *dr.*, *Bp.*, and *mg.*? Since so few readers would recognize such abbreviations, you can understand the reason for this bit of advice: Except for a few commonly used forms, avoid abbreviations in your ordinary writing.

Among the abbreviations that are appropriate to use in the general writing that you do are these. Notice the period at the end of each.

1 Titles and initials: *Mr.* and *Mrs.* George *N.* Pappas
Dr. Ellison   *Dr.* Kenneth *C.* Pratt
St. Margaret   Frank Parker, *Jr.*

Unless these words are used as titles *with* names, they should not be abbreviated:

WRONG: The Dr. will be in this afternoon.
RIGHT: The doctor (or Dr. Richards) will be in this afternoon.

2 Degrees: Joseph B. Nash, *A.M.* (Master of Arts)
Kenneth C. Pratt, *M.D.* (Doctor of Medicine)
Lloyd F. Baxter, *Ph.D.* (Doctor of Philosophy)

3 Expressions of time: 8:45 A.M. (or) 8:45 *a.m.*
27 B.C.   958 A.D.
The program begins at 11:30 *p.m.*
Who was the emperor in 27 B.C.?

Notice that only one period is used when an abbreviation comes at the end of a sentence. But if any other punctuation mark is required by the sentence (such as the question mark in the last example), the mark comes after the period used for the abbreviation.

EXERCISE (3) Rewrite each of the following sentences, placing periods after the abbreviations (and initials) that would be appropriate to use in ordinary writing. Write out the full form of all abbreviations that should not be used in ordinary writing. Add the appropriate end marks.

1 Fred Neal, Jr, lives in the same bldg as our Dr does
2 Is there a plane leaving for Phila, Pa, at 5:45 p m
3 Mrs C L Lewis ordered four lbs of steak and two qts of cream last Mon
4 Dr and Mrs Martin were chaperons at the Jr Prom last Wed night
5 St Joseph is David's patron St
6 The Rocky Mts, which we will see next Oct, extend from Alaska to N Mexico
7 Sue paid fifty cts for three yds of the ribbon at the dime store on Elm St
8 No, 432 Turner Ave is at least three mi from Lincoln Sr H S

COMMAS

IN A SERIES

If no commas were used in the following sentence, would you know how many girls had come?

Mary Louise Joan Carol and Helen came to the party.

Depending on the commas used, three, four, or five girls came:

THREE: Mary Louise, Joan Carol, and Helen came.
FOUR: Mary Louise, Joan, Carol, and Helen came.
FIVE: Mary, Louise, Joan, Carol, and Helen came.

Not every written sentence is so open to misunderstanding as this, of course. But any sentence containing three or more items in a series is easier to read and understand if the items are made to stand out as distinct units. **Commas are therefore used between items in a series to separate them clearly.**

The items may be long or short. They may be words or groups of words:

> *Mosquitoes, hornets,* and *ants* made our lives miserable.
> Will you go *by bus, by plane,* or *by train?*
> Tom *signed the letter, folded it, put it in an envelope,* and *handed it to Mr. Forbes.*

Notice that the number of commas used is *one less* than the number of items. If you have three items, use two commas:

> I saw Ted, Larry, and Ken at the station.

If you have four items, use three commas:

> The boys hid in the garage, behind the hedge, under the porch, and on the roof.

The comma before the conjunction that joins the last two items is sometimes omitted, as you may have noticed in your reading. But most writers prefer this comma because they know that it makes their sentences easier to read. Since anything that helps your readers get your meaning quickly is important, it will be a good idea for you to get into the habit of using this final comma. After all, it takes very little time and effort to put it in.

When all the items of a series are joined by conjunctions, no comma is needed:

> The men clapped *and* cheered *and* whistled for five minutes.
> Dad insists he doesn't ever want to skate *or* ski *or* dance again.

EXERCISE (4) Read the following sentences and decide where commas are needed to separate items in a series. On a sheet of paper, write the number of each sentence. After it, put the commas needed in the sentence and the word preceding each comma. Some sentences do not need commas. Draw a line after the number of these.

Example: Ted had orange juice cereal toast milk and eggs.
juice, cereal, toast, milk,

1 Air conditioning is now common in offices stores and trains.
2 The menu gives you a choice of fried chicken steak or ham.
3 The attendant filled the gas tank and checked the oil and wiped the windshield.
4 Jean Donna Sue and Doris are playing doubles at the court.
5 Mary Ellen Ann and I are looking for a fourth for tennis.

6 We explored the city thoroughly—by car by bus by streetcar and on foot.

7 Marshall Field's has that blouse in pink yellow blue and white.

8 Archie climbed the stairs tiptoed along the corridor and knocked at the door.

9 The restaurant was crowded in spite of the dirt and the poor food and the insolent waiters.

10 The people upstairs complained constantly angrily and noisily.

11 Foods rich in iron are liver molasses egg yolks whole-grain breads and cereals leafy vegetables and dried fruits.

12 A trail of muddy footprints led us across the porch through the front hall and into the kitchen.

COMMAS

IN COMPOUND SENTENCES

What does the following sentence mean to you?

> Uncle Henry left his property to Rita and George and Helen contested the will.

Did George inherit the property too? Or did he and Helen contest the will? As the sentence is written, you cannot be expected to know. But the writer could have helped you and other readers by putting a comma before the *and* connecting the two parts of the compound sentence:

> Uncle Henry left his property to Rita, *and* George and Helen contested the will.
> Uncle Henry left his property to Rita and George, *and* Helen contested the will.

In each of these, the two parts of the sentence are clearly indicated, and you have no trouble understanding the meaning the writer intended. The comma tells you where the first part of the sentence ends; it signals the spot where you would pause if you *said* the sentence to someone.

A comma is ordinarily used to separate the two parts of a compound sentence joined by a conjunction (*and, but, or, nor, for, yet, so*):

> Mrs. Hodd owns the newspaper, **and** her husband is president of the bank.
> The dress can be washed, **but** the belt must be dry-cleaned.
> Write down the address, **or** you'll never remember it.

If the two parts of the sentence are short and there is no possibility of misunderstanding, the comma may be omitted:

Listen and you'll learn.   Mother came and all was well.

Make sure you understand the difference between a compound sentence and a simple sentence with a compound verb. A compound sentence has a subject *and* a verb in each of its parts. A comma is needed to separate the two subject-verb units:

Dad **sanded** the desk, and my *brother* **waxed** it.

A simple sentence with a compound verb has only *one* subject-verb unit, though the verb has two parts. The subject should not be separated from the second part of the compound verb by a comma:

Dad **sanded** the desk and **waxed** it four times.

EXERCISE (5) Read the following sentences and decide where commas are needed to separate the parts of a compound sentence joined by a conjunction. On a sheet of paper, write the number of each sentence. After it, write the comma needed in the sentence and the words that precede and follow it. Some of the sentences do not need a comma. Draw a line after the number of these sentences.

Example: Jane complimented everyone but Martha said nothing.
               everyone, but

1   On the way home we met Nora and Joan and Mike gave them their tickets.
2   You had better not tell Grace or her brothers will worm the secret out of her.
3   Will Staub owed money to everyone in town but Mr. Hill still trusted him.
4   I like English and Spanish isn't too bad.
5   Florence did most of the work for Ellen had a headache.
6   Absent-minded Mr. Lewis turned the corner and the bus almost ran him down.
7   The architect hasn't finished his work yet I am sure you will be pleased.
8   Jerry can't work with gloves on and I can't work without them.
9   Jerry can't work with gloves on and gets blisters without them.
10 Ned tensed his muscles and arched his back but still he couldn't lift the bar.
11 The nurse cleaned a spot on my arm and then inserted the needle.
12 The nurse cleaned a spot on my arm and the doctor inserted the needle.

13 Hazel liked all the toys but the panda was her favorite.
14 We had to run for the bus was just rounding the corner.
15 The trapper stumbled and fell but he got up again and struggled on.

COMMAS

WITH PARENTHETICAL WORDS

Without the italicized words, each of the following examples is still a complete, meaningful sentence. The italicized words are **parenthetical**—that is, they are used simply to add an explanatory comment or an interesting side remark:

> The whole family is coming, *I'm afraid.*
> *To tell the truth,* I really don't like to dive.
> George Danvers, *of course,* found the best blueberry patch.

When you read these sentences aloud, notice how you pause before or after the parenthetical words and how your voice drops. When you write such sentences, you use commas to signal the spots where the pauses occur.

Parenthetical words are set off by commas. One comma is used if the words come at the beginning or at the end of the sentence. Two commas are used if the words come inside the sentence.

Words like *Yes, No, Well, Oh,* and *Why* (used at the beginning of a sentence) and expressions like *doesn't it* and *aren't they* (used at the end) are considered parenthetical and should be set off:

> *Yes,* the prices have gone up. *No,* a flat paint is best.
> *Well,* it won't hurt to try again, *will it?*
> The contest closes on Saturday, *doesn't it?*

Notice what a difference in meaning a comma may make:

No criticism is necessary now.	Well water is cheaper.
No, criticism is necessary now.	Well, water is cheaper.

EXERCISE (6) Read the following sentences and decide where commas are needed to set off parenthetical words. On a sheet of paper, write the number of each sentence. After it, write any commas that are needed and the word preceding each.

1 The summer suits by the way will go on sale next week.
2 Mrs. Martin on the other hand is a good typist.
3 She has been given a raise hasn't she?

4 At any rate try to be on time for the dress rehearsal.
5 It would be foolish however to count on his help now.
6 Dr. Smithson she noticed was sitting next to Mr. Beals.
7 In the first place I'm sure that Norton wants to tell the truth.
8 Jerry at least should have known better.
9 No we have had at least ten complaints this past week.
10 To tell the truth her hat was just plain ugly wasn't it?
11 Oh I expect him to help of course.
12 May I expect arrived after all the work was done didn't she?
13 No nobody in the store had noticed the man in brown as a matter of fact.
14 Mary Swanson for example has perfect pitch.
15 Yes Mr. Allen will have the bill ready for you by Friday in fact.

COMMAS WITH NOUNS OF ADDRESS

AND APPOSITIVES

Nouns of address.   The name or expression you use in a sentence to show to whom you are talking is called a *noun of address*:

> *Dad*, a telegram came for you.
> Is Diane at home, *Mrs. Norton*?
> And now, *you scamp*, tell us what really happened.
> We chose, *ladies and gentlemen*, to appeal to you for the needed funds.

A noun of address is set off from the rest of the sentence by commas.   The commas are needed to warn the reader to keep the set-off words apart from the rest of the sentence.   Without the commas, sentences with nouns of address would be a bit puzzling on first reading.   In fact, leaving the commas out may sometimes make a difference in the meaning.   Notice how the meaning of the fourth example sentence changes when the commas are omitted:

> We chose ladies and gentlemen to appeal to you for the needed funds.

Appositives.   To give additional information about some person or thing we are talking about, we often use *appositives*:

> Mr. Owens, *our neighbor*, is building his own house.
> Norris, *one of their best players*, will graduate next June.

The appositive *our neighbor* explains who Mr. Owens is; the appositive *one of their best players* gives an additional fact about Norris.

This information, interesting and useful as it may be, is not an essential part of the sentences. It is something extra—a "bonus"—that is inserted. **Appositives, therefore, are set off from the other words in the sentence.** Remember that "set off" means using *two* commas, unless the appositive comes at the end of the sentence:

> The Pentagon, *the largest office building in the world,* should be seen from the air to be appreciated.
> The scenes were filmed in Oporto, *the second largest city in Portugal.*

EXERCISE (7) Read each of the following sentences and decide where commas are needed to set off nouns of address and appositives. On a sheet of paper, write the number of each sentence. After it, write any commas that are needed and the word preceding each.

1 Mrs. Cooper understands Thelma and wants to help you.
2 The Quillans' car a blue Rambler was parked behind ours.
3 The first story in the book the one by Damon Runyon was made into a movie.
4 The governor called Senator Daly to invite you to lunch.
5 Prince Rainier married Grace Kelly an American movie star.
6 Ladies and gentlemen I would like to introduce Mrs. Olson the president of the Little Theater Group.
7 Amsterdam the capital of Holland has about forty canals and one hundred islands.
8 They canceled their plane reservations and booked passage on the *Andrea Doria* the pride of the Italian fleet.
9 Did you say sir that you were the last passenger to leave the *Andrea Doria* before it sank?
10 Slim Newton the captain of the team weighed at least two hundred pounds.
11 The special attraction that evening was the Globetrotters an internationally known basketball team.
12 Dad may I present Fred Lietz.

COMMAS

WITH ADDRESSES AND DATES

When you tell someone your complete address—your house number and street, the city, and the state—you pause after each of these three items to make it easy for your listener to understand. When you *write*, you should show the same sort of consideration for your reader. **Use commas to set off the second and all following items in an address:**

> The Carsons have lived at 312 South Spruce Street, Spokane, Washington, since 1955.
>
> Send all entries to Mr. Peter Frenz, 433 East Erie Street, Chicago 11, Illinois.

Notice that if the address comes inside the sentence a comma is used both before *and* after the last item. Notice too that the zone number and the city are considered one item.

The same rule applies to dates that have more than one part. To make it easy for your reader, set off each item after the first:

> Jim will never forget Thursday, July 3, 1958, as long as he lives.

EXERCISE (8) Read the following sentences and decide where commas are needed to set off items in addresses and dates. On a sheet of paper, write the number of each sentence. After it, write any commas that are needed and the item preceding each.

1 Ann lives at 539 80th Street Brooklyn New York.
2 The Porter Paint Company 4234 Boynton Avenue Cincinnati Ohio is sure to have the supplies you need.
3 The Costellos live in Quincy Massachusetts not Quincy Illinois.
4 Wednesday November 14 1956 was an important day for the people of Cramden Utah.
5 Hull House is at 800 South Halsted Street Chicago 7 Illinois.
6 The meeting was held at the Conrad Hilton Hotel in Chicago on March 7 1957.
7 On January 7 1785 Jeffries and Blanchard crossed the English Channel in a hydrogen balloon.
8 The Atomic Age began on the morning of July 16 1945 on a stretch of land some fifty miles from Alamogordo New Mexico.

COMMAS AFTER INTRODUCTORY

CLAUSES AND PHRASES

What do the following words mean to you?

> If you can come early.

Could you tell at first reading that these words are a complete sentence and "make sense" by themselves? Probably not. Yet if the writer had used a comma after the word *can* to keep you from reading *can come* together, the meaning would have been clear to you at once.

>*If you can,* come early.

Each of the following examples, like the one you have just seen, begins with an adverb clause. Without commas to show where these introductory clauses end, you are quite likely to be puzzled the first time you read the sentences.

>Before Mr. Grimes took over the company was in the red.
>Although our team won the game was not very interesting.
>When the clock strikes Dad will be boarding the plane.
>Because Eunice knows how to save her money goes twice as
>   far as mine.

How much easier these sentences would be to read if commas were inserted after *over, won, strikes,* and *save.* For the sake of the reader, then, we have this rule: **An introductory adverb clause is set off from the rest of the sentence by a comma.**

Note: As you may have noticed in the books, magazines, and papers you read, some writers omit this comma, especially if the introductory clause is short. But even a short clause may puzzle the reader. (Remember the first example.) It is best, therefore, to get into the habit of using the comma whether the clause is short or long.

• **457**

Introductory phrases. Participial phrases at the beginning of a sentence are also set off by commas:

>*Keeping time with his foot,* Lester listened to the band.
>*Hoping for a handout,* the tramp told a heart-breaking tale.
>*Blinded by the driving rain,* Kirk didn't notice the two men.

A prepositional phrase at the beginning of a sentence is usually not set off:

>*In winter* the temperature drops to forty below zero.
>*From my seat in the back row* I could hardly hear what he said.

But when there is any chance that a reader will run together two words that do not belong together, a comma should be used. Notice how useful this comma is:

>During the summer time passed quickly.
>During the summer, time passed quickly.

>At our school dances are held after each game.
>At our school, dances are held after each game.

EXERCISE 9 Read the following sentences and decide where commas are needed to set off introductory clauses and phrases. On a sheet of paper, write the number of each sentence. After it, write the needed comma and the word that precedes it. Some sentences do not require a comma. Draw a line after the number of these.

1 Whenever Pearl came to visit Vernon was all attention.
2 If Angelo forgets Vincent will be sure to remind him.
3 Not wanting Dad to hear Tom took off his shoes and tiptoed upstairs.
4 Eaten fast and washed down with milk the food was passable.
5 To Steve Allen seemed the greatest hero of them all.
6 When Sandra returned the purse was still on the desk.
7 Helped by his neighbors Mr. Arnold rebuilt the barn.
8 If Marilyn joins the club will gain a valuable member.
9 If Marilyn joins the club a valuable member will be gained.
10 Waiting for his turn at bat Rudy studied the pitcher's style.
11 Whatever Wilbur offers Sam will outbid him.
12 Before his turn at bat Rudy studied the pitcher's style.
13 Coming the week before this rain would have been a catastrophe.
14 Whenever Uncle Will drove my aunt tried not to show her nervousness.
15 After Mike fell through the ice was declared unsafe for skating.
16 After Mike's disastrous experience the ice was declared unsafe.
17 Lured West by dreams of wealth the Forty-Niners found a hard life awaiting them.
18 Because the new styles were attractive and feminine women rushed to buy them.
19 After the children left the house became unbearably lonely.
20 While Harry was pounding the nail slipped out of my hand and rolled under the bookcase.

COMMAS WITH NONRESTRICTIVE

ADJECTIVE CLAUSES

All of you know about "restricted" parking areas. Between certain signs you are limited to parking only at certain hours. Some adjective clauses, too, are **restrictive**, or limiting. In the following sentence, for example, the italicized clause restricts, or limits, the meaning of the word *Students*:

Students *who dislike math* should not study engineering.

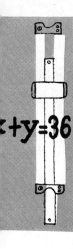

To understand how important the clause is to the meaning, let's look at the sentence without it:

Students should not study engineering.

But the writer did not mean that *all* students should not study engineering; he meant that just certain students should not. He used the adjective clause to tell exactly which students he meant—those "who dislike math." The clause, in other words, is *restrictive*. It limits the meaning of *students* to certain particular ones. Restrictive clauses, because they are essential to the meaning intended, are not set off from the words they modify.

Now look at the italicized clause in the following sentence:

My cousin Steve, *who dislikes math*, wants to be a mechanic.

Here the adjective clause does not tell which particular boy wants to be a mechanic. The words *My cousin Steve* do that. All that the clause does is to give additional information about Steve. Because the clause is not needed to tell who is meant, it can be omitted without changing the essential meaning of the sentence:

My cousin Steve wants to be a mechanic.

Such an adjective clause is called **nonrestrictive**. Like the appositives, which also give additional information but are not an essential part of the sentence, **nonrestrictive adjective clauses are set off from the rest of the sentence by commas.**

Compare the sentences in the following groups. Notice that the clauses that are needed to tell which particular ones are meant are not set off. But the *nonrestrictive* clauses—those that are used merely to give an explanatory detail—are set off. They could be omitted without changing the intended meaning of the rest of the sentence.

It is foolish for you to wear shoes *which are too narrow.*
Jane's new red shoes, *which are too narrow*, make her wince.

No reporter *who did not have a pass* was permitted to enter the laboratory.
A reporter from the *Daily News* and Hal Martin started out together. But the reporter, *who did not have a pass*, was stopped at the gate.

Notice that in the last example the first sentence makes clear which reporter the writer means—the one "from the *Daily News*." The adjective clause in the second sentence, therefore, is not needed to point out the particular person meant. Since it is used merely to give additional information about the reporter, it is set off.

459

Read the following sentences and decide which of the italicized adjective clauses are restrictive, and which are nonrestrictive and should be set off by commas. On a sheet of paper, write the number of each sentence. After it, write any commas that are needed and the word that precedes each.

1 Girls *who pretend to know everything* annoy Jerry.
2 The second feature was **Moby Dick** *which I had already seen.*
3 All members *who miss three consecutive meetings* will be dropped.
4 Mr. Cummings *whose category was ancient history* missed the $16,000 question.
5 Mrs. Martin really became alarmed when she noticed his left wrist *which had swollen to twice its normal size.*
6 There was nothing else to do but wear Dan's new coat *which was much too long.*
7 Uncle Will glared at the boy *who was making the disturbance.*
8 Sue was sitting next to Mr. Till *who was puffing on an evil-smelling cigar.*
9 What is more useless than a fountain pen *that doesn't hold ink?*
10 Unfortunately the message was written in Greek *which nobody in the office had ever studied.*
11 Johnny Evans *who had shown such promise in the minor leagues* was a great disappointment in his first season with the Yankees.
12 No, the John Evans *that she was talking about* is not the John Evans *that you know.*
13 Elmwood *which he hadn't seen for ten years* had changed.
14 People *who like to read* are never lonely or bored.
15 I gave the books to my youngest brother *who likes to read.*
16 On the table she placed a silver jewel box and a wallet. The box *which was badly tarnished* had belonged to her grandmother.
17 She placed the two silver boxes and a wallet on the table. Sally chose the box *that was badly tarnished* and Mary chose the wallet.
18 Mother said I had to wear either my blue nylon sweater or my jacket. I finally decided to wear the sweater *which wasn't as heavy as the jacket.*
19 There were enough ham sandwiches and coffee for everyone there. But the sandwiches *which had been made the day before* were pretty dry.
20 Mr. Mellon interviewed fifteen people. But he found only two men *who seemed qualified for the job.*

COMMAS WITH NONRESTRICTIVE

PARTICIPIAL PHRASES

Participial phrases, like adjective clauses, may be restrictive or nonrestrictive. To understand how these differ, let's start with the italicized phrase in this sentence:

> All delegates *wearing blue badges* were given free tickets to the movie.

As you can see, the phrase is needed to tell which particular delegates are meant. Not all who were there got free tickets—just the ones "wearing blue badges." Since the phrase limits (or restricts) the meaning of *delegates* to certain ones, it is *restrictive*. Because a restrictive phrase is needed to make the intended meaning clear, it is not set off from the rest of the sentence.

Now look at the participial phrase in this sentence:

> Tim and Phil Jenkins, *wearing blue badges*, marched at the head of the parade.

The phrase in this sentence merely adds a descriptive detail about Tim and Phil. Interesting as this detail may be, it is not essential. You could omit it and still know that it was two particular boys who marched at the head of the parade. Since the phrase is not needed to make clear exactly who is meant, it is *nonrestrictive*. **Nonrestrictive participial phrases are set off by commas.**

Remember: Restrictive phrases (necessary to the meaning) are not set off. But to show that nonrestrictive phrases merely give additional details, we fence them off with commas.

> Directions *printed in small type* are usually overlooked. [Necessary.]
> Peter studied the diagrams and then looked at the directions at the bottom of the page. But the directions, *printed in small type*, merely confused him. [Not necessary.]

EXERCISE 11 Read the following sentences and decide which of the italicized phrases are restrictive, and which are nonrestrictive and should be set off by commas. On a sheet of paper, write the number of each sentence. After it, write any commas that are needed and the word preceding each.

1 Harriet's roommate *overhearing their remarks* rushed back to tell Harriet.
2 All members *suspected of disloyalty* were closely watched.

3   Most of the cars *parked in the alley* belong to the tenants.

4   Mr. Lane's battered old jeep *parked dangerously close to a fire hydrant* was the only car in sight.

5   Mrs. Kertz finally decided to use the Wedgwood dishes and the sterling silver her mother had left her. The silver *not used for months* had to be polished, of course.

6   The people *sitting in the back seat* were unharmed.

7   In those days any woman *wearing lipstick* was frowned upon.

8   Two weeks later we examined the two slices of cheese. The slice *wrapped in aluminum foil* was still fresh; the slice *left unwrapped* was as stiff as cardboard.

9   Searching through the cupboard, he found a box of crackers and some Cheddar cheese. The crackers were stale; but the cheese *wrapped in aluminum foil* was quite fresh.

10 Opinions *based on such flimsy evidence* are worthless.

11 Dan *struggling to control himself* answered the man quietly.

12 Icebergs *floating in the shipping lanes* menace navigation.

13 This fat little urchin *isolated from his playmates by the new picket fence* wailed at the top of his voice.

14 It was the man *shouting from the roof* who had caused all the trouble.

462

QUOTATION MARKS

If the person who invented quotation marks could return to life and visit a school library, he would probably be quite amused. He would frequently find his invention being used as a guide by students in search of a "good book" to read. The way these students decide whether a book looks promising is to flip through the pages. If the pages contain a great number of quotation marks, the book passes the test.

The quotation-mark test works pretty well. Quotation marks mean *conversation*. And conversation in a story usually means that the story will be lively and interesting. It will sound "real"—as if the events were actually happening.

If conversation is so important in the stories you read, it is also important in the stories you write. You can make your stories come to life by letting the people in them do their own talking. Don't just report indirectly what the people say; use *direct quotations* whenever you can. This section will show you how to punctuate these quotations.

Punctuating quotations. When you quote the exact words of a speaker, use quotation marks to enclose what he says, as in the following sentences:

"My parakeet can say five words," said Carl proudly.
Carl said proudly, "My parakeet can say five words."
"My parakeet," said Carl proudly, "can say five words."

Study the above examples carefully, noticing these important points:

1) The first word of the direct quotation begins with a capital letter, whether the quotation comes at the beginning of the sentence or at the end. Here is another example:

Nora answered, "He left at least an hour ago."

2) Words used to tell who spoke (like *Carl said, she answered, he asked*) are set off from the direct quotation by commas. The comma always comes *before* the quotation marks. So does the period, when the direct quotation is at the end of the sentence.

"Mr. Martin," replied the clerk, "is out of town."
The clerk replied, "Mr. Martin is out of town."

3) When the direct quotation is given in two parts, *two* sets of quotation marks are used, but only *one* capital letter.

"The blue coat," he explained, "was much too large."

Since the words that follow *he explained* are not *another* direct quotation, but the rest of the quoted sentence, the word *was* begins with a small letter.

Questions and exclamations. The following examples show the punctuation that is used when the direct quotation is a question or an exclamation:

"Are you going with Bob?" Sharon asked Jane.
Sharon asked Jane, "Are you going with Bob?"
"Move out of the way!" yelled the driver.
The driver yelled, "Move out of the way!"

Notice that the question marks and exclamation marks come *before* the final quotation marks, not *after*, because they indicate the nature of the quotation.

Two or more quoted sentences. Suppose that the person you are quoting speaks more than one sentence. How do you handle the punctuation in such cases?

If the quoted sentences come together, only one set of quotation marks is used:

> "We'd better leave. It's getting late," said Clifford.
> Mark said, "That's a strange title. What's the book about?"

But if they do not come together, two sets of quotation marks are needed:

> "I wouldn't complain if I were you," replied Jerry. "You were lucky, as a matter of fact."
> "Don't bother me now," ordered Mr. Higgins. "Can't you see I'm busy?"

Indirect quotations. Remember that quotation marks are used only when you are quoting the exact words said by the speaker. If you merely report what he said in your own words (an "indirect" quotation), quotation marks are not used:

DIRECT: "Do you have a duplicate?" asked George.
INDIRECT: George asked *whether I had a duplicate.*

DIRECT: "I didn't break the window!" Neil insisted.
INDIRECT: Neil insisted *that he hadn't broken the window.*

Quotation marks for titles. The titles of short stories, magazine articles, chapters of books, essays, songs, and short poems are generally enclosed in quotation marks:

> If you like exciting stories, read "The Most Dangerous Game."
> "Something for Nothing" was the only article worth reading.
> He spent an hour memorizing the first stanza of "Old Ironsides."

EXERCISE 12 Some of the following groups of words consist of one sentence; others consist of two. Copy the groups, adding quotation marks and capital letters and all other needed punctuation marks.

1 I don't like sauerkraut Martha explained
2 Martha explained that she didn't like sauerkraut
3 Tom nudged Fred and whispered did you hear a noise
4 Kill the umpire shouted the angry crowd
5 The reference books continued Miss White are not to be taken from the library
6 The woman pointed to the dog and asked does he bite
7 My father voted for Eisenhower both times said Jimmie
8 Don't step on the floor screamed Mother it's just been waxed
9 Why can't I go Mike persisted give me one good reason
10 That's not fair whined Ralph why do you always pick on me
11 Ralph asked why Mr. Bruce always picked on him

12 Rob said that his favorite story was The Second-Rater
13 Who is he what does he want asked the manager
14 Jack called the number twice she said but got no answer
15 The man on the ladder yelled move back this wall might collapse at any minute
16 But fifty million Frenchmen he replied *might* be wrong
17 Talking to Darrell sighed Aunt Alice is like talking to a brick wall he never listens
18 I'm not interested said she we have enough magazines
19 Mrs. Betz said she wasn't interested in buying more magazines
20 She sang White Christmas for an encore

SEMICOLON

When the two parts of a compound sentence are joined by a coördinating conjunction (*and, but, or, so, yet, for*), a comma is used to mark the end of the first part:

The restaurant was crowded, *and* we had to wait in line for a table.
Don started the work, *but* Sam finished it.

But when a conjunction is not used, a comma is not a strong-enough mark to separate the two parts. **A semicolon is used between the two parts of a compound sentence when they are not joined by a conjunction:**

The restaurant was crowded; we had to wait in line for a table.
Don started the work; Sam finished it.
We waited until ten; then we gave up and went home.
Dad liked the new Chevrolets best; in fact, he ordered one.

EXERCISE 13 Read the following compound sentences and decide whether a semicolon or a comma should be used between the two parts. On a sheet of paper, write the number of each sentence. After it, write the punctuation mark needed in the sentence and the words that precede and follow it.

1 Grace isn't conceited she is just shy.
2 The bottle had been left open and the ether had evaporated.
3 The men in the rolling mill despised Clark he reported to the foreman everything that happened.
4 I wasn't interested in his problems I had enough of my own.

5 At the police station Miss Finch did all the talking she was the only one who could speak French and German.

6 No guns can be taken into the park the only shooting permitted must be done with a camera.

7 An accident had snarled traffic and we missed the first act.

8 With one eye a chameleon can scan the ground below with the other eye it can search the branches above for insects.

9 His mother approved of his ambition in fact she took in washing to pay for his music lessons.

10 Lincoln Steffens's family was well-to-do and he was given an expensive education.

11 The ball tottered on the rim for an endless instant and then it dropped through the net for the winning two points.

12 You will have to work fast the clay hardens quickly.

DASHES

WITH APPOSITIVES

As you have already learned, commas are ordinarily used to set off an appositive:

> Boise, *the capital*, is the largest city in Idaho.

But if the appositive consists of a series of items separated by commas or the appositive phrase itself has commas in it, dashes are used instead:

> Three Norwegian writers—*Henrik Ibsen, Sigrid Undset, and Knut Hamsun*—are well known through translations.
> Several of the schools—*for example, Bragg Junior High and Morton Senior High*—are badly overcrowded.

Using the dashes makes it easy for the reader to see where the appositive word group begins and ends.

Dashes for emphasis. Occasionally you may want to call special attention to an appositive that you think is quite important. You can do so by using dashes instead of commas to set it off:

> Nine of the parents—*eight mothers and one father*—voted against the motion.
> Only one thing could have made Carol scream—*a mouse.*

As you can see, the dashes emphasize the appositives; they stand out more clearly than they would if set off by commas. When this emphasis is what you want, use dashes. Otherwise use commas.

EXERCISE (14) Read the following sentences and decide where punctuation marks are needed to set off appositives, to separate items in a series, and to set off parenthetical words or items in addresses. On a sheet of paper, write the number of each sentence. After it, write the punctuation marks that are needed (dashes and commas) and the word preceding each.

1 Many exports tobacco cotton nuts raisins and figs are grown in the coastal regions of Turkey.

2 Saint Sophia first a church later a mosque and now a museum is one of the most beautiful buildings in Istanbul.

3 Twenty members of the Science Club eighteen boys and two girls made the honor roll.

4 Many of the books on the list *Beau Geste* for example and *The Sea Wolf* will appeal particularly to the boys.

5 Two cities Flint Michigan and Chicago have been suggested.

6 The little boy proudly handed her the money he had saved three quarters five dimes six nickels and fourteen pennies.

7 The program committee Ed Stearns Rob Nacky and Kay Finch had planned to have an outside speaker.

8 We had forgotten only one thing the key.

9 Five Iroquois tribes the Mohawks Oneidas Onondagas Cayugas and Senecas formed a confederation.

10 A huge chunk of whale nearly half a ton of slithery meat bones and blubber slid across the deck.

11 Some of the games for instance coffee pot and hangman's noose were games her grandmother had played as a girl.

12 She won the prize most valued in Hollywood the coveted Oscar.

467

UNDERLINING

FOR TITLES

Titles of books, pamphlets, movies, radio and TV programs, and plays and poems published as separate volumes are printed in **italics** (a type in which the letters slant to the right). In handwritten or typewritten papers, these titles are **underlined**.

BOOKS:	The World of Bees	Great Caesar's Ghost
PAMPHLETS:	Safe Driving	Your Tax Dollar
MOVIES:	The King and I	The Ten Commandments
TV PROGRAMS:	Father Knows Best	Meet the Press
LONG PLAYS:	The Merchant of Venice	Auntie Mame
LONG POEMS:	John Brown's Body	Hiawatha

The names of newspapers and magazines are also printed in italics but underlined in writing or in typed papers:

NEWSPAPER: the Chicago <u>Tribune</u> (or) the Chicago <u>Tribune</u>
MAGAZINES: <u>Senior Scholastic</u>   <u>Photoplay</u>

Note: You may have noticed that most newspapers and some magazines do not italicize titles. In your school writing, you will be expected to italicize them, following the style used in most books and in the more carefully edited magazines.

EXERCISE (15) On a sheet of paper, write the number of each sentence. After it, write the words in the sentence that should be italicized. Underline these words as you would if you used them in a theme.

1 You will find it interesting to compare the editorials in the Sun-Times with those in the Herald-American.
2 Good Morning, Miss Dove is a novel about an old-fashioned teacher.
3 Hundreds of children read Peter Pan and The Wizard of Oz after seeing the TV versions.
4 Both Holiday and Life had special issues on London that you should read.
5 Person to Person and Youth Wants to Know were his favorite TV shows.

EXERCISE (16) **REVIEW** This exercise is a review of the comma rules explained in this chapter. The page reference in parentheses after each sentence tells you where you can find the explanation of the rule that applies to that sentence. To see how well you have mastered the rules, work out the exercise without referring to the explanations. Your corrected paper, showing you which sentences you have not punctuated right, will tell you which rules are still not clear to you. Rereading the explanations and studying the examples will help you to understand these rules and to avoid future mistakes.

On a sheet of paper, write the number of each sentence. After it, write any commas needed in the sentence and the word preceding each. Three of the sentences do not need commas.

1 Whales which are shaped like fish and live in the sea are mammals. (459)
2 Next June August and Frank will both graduate from high school. (457)
3 Persuaded by the salesman's glib talk Mrs. Countz ordered three brushes. (457)
4 Harrison on the other hand enjoys criticizing people. (453)

5   The firm now has branch offices in London Rome Calcutta and Algiers. (450)

6   William Tell paying no attention to the tyrant's hat walked calmly across the square. (461)

7   No one wanted to leave but Clayton reminded us of our promise. (451)

8   Old Mr. Clooney who is immensely wealthy contributed twenty thousand dollars. (459)

9   Sergeant Matthews the radio-gunner was seated at the control panel. (455)

10   He turned on the flashlight moved the beam over the panel and saw that the fuel gauge was still working. (450)

11   Mr. Martin Greenow 737 Plaza Place Newton Nebraska is the owner of the stolen car. (456)

12   Grabbing up a shotgun Dr. Schweitzer fired a blast at the sky to frighten off the cannibals. (457)

13   Dynamite has helped to build roads bore tunnels through mountains clear land and open new lodes of ore. (450)

14   Remember you pessimist that last year we beat West High in spite of the odds. (454)

15   The spectators who had left the game early missed the most brilliant forward pass of the season. (459)

16   The shirt and the coat were too tight but the shoes fitted him almost perfectly. (451)

17   No writing a long report is hard work. (453)

18   As he played the melody brought back memories of the carefree days on the ranch. (457)

19   He took a letter and a photograph from the file and handed them to the reporter. (452)

20   Paul's uncle in Racine who owns a garage had offered both of us a summer job. (459)

21   The Braves won the World Series in 1957 didn't they? (453)

22   Because of the fog all planes were grounded. (457)

23   As soon as he left the office buzzed with gossip. (457)

24   On May 16 1930 Gilbert La Bine discovered the richest source of radium and uranium in the world. (456)

25   In the fourth ward for example only 435 out of 796 registered voters went to the polls. (453)

26   Do you want to climb up Dave and see the view? (454)

27   On June 6 1944 the Allies invaded western Europe. (456)

28   Halley's Comet probably the most famous of all comets will next be seen in 1986. (455)

29   He forgot Mother but will send it tomorrow. (454)

30   The Imlers who had traveled in Chile showed films. (459)

REFERENCE SECTION

PUNCTUATION CHECK LIST

USE PERIODS—

1   with abbreviations:

   Mr. Carl F. Jenkins, Jr.   47 B.C.   9:30 p.m.   etc.

2   after a statement, a command, a request, or an indirect question:

   Carnegie started out as a bobbin boy in a cotton mill.
   Don't forget to turn off the oven.
   Will you please return the IBM card with your check.
   Dad asked me what I had done with my report card.

USE A QUESTION MARK—
after a direct question:

   What did you do with your report card?
   Carnegie started out as a bobbin boy, didn't he?

USE AN EXCLAMATION MARK—
to show strong feeling:

   Good grief!   What a tightwad he is!   He must be joking!

USE COMMAS—

1   to separate items in a series:

   Peter, Paul, and Mary gave a concert there last week.
   He heard the noise, looked up, and screamed.

[Note: Commas are not needed when all the items are joined by coördinating conjunctions: The radiators rattled *and* sputtered *and* clanked all night.]

2   before the coördinating conjunction that joins the main clauses of a compound sentence:

   Nora voted for Alan, and Tom voted for himself.
   He may be a good lawyer, but he's no Perry Mason.

[Note: If the clauses are short and there is no possibility of misunderstanding, a comma is not needed: He showed the slides and I gave the commentary.]

3   to set off parenthetical expressions:

Little girls, supposedly, are made of sugar and spice.
Common sense, it seems to me, is just as important as brains.

4   to set off a noun of address:

Speak for yourself, John.
But surely, ma'am, you can see what a bargain it is.

5   to set off an appositive:

Clayton Smith, our star quarterback, is only a sophomore.

6   to set off the second and all following items in a date or an address:

On Friday, June 13, two more stores were robbed.
Send the check to Mrs. Jacob Jones, 32 Elm Street, Russell, Minnesota, before the end of the month.

7   after an introductory adverb clause:

When bop came in, Count Basie's old-style jazz went out.

8   after an introductory participial phrase:

Hoping to make Mme. Loire feel at home, Mother fed her snails and crêpes suzette.

Irritated by Sandra's moodiness, we decided to give her a taste of her own medicine.

9   to set off a nonrestrictive adjective clause:

Uncle Bill, who is color-blind, lets my aunt pick out his ties.

[Note: *Restrictive* adjective clauses are not set off: Any man *who is that color-blind* should let his wife pick out his ties.]

10   to set off a nonrestrictive participial phrase:

My parents, sitting in the front row of the balcony, could hear every word.

[Note: *Restrictive* participial phrases are not set off: A boy *sitting in the front row of the balcony* was throwing popcorn over the railing.]

11   after the closing in a letter:

Respectfully yours,   Sincerely,   With love,

12   after the salutation in a friendly letter:

Dear Tom,   Dear Evelyn,   Dearest Grandma,

13 to set off a speaker's directly quoted words from the rest of the sentence:

Ronnie said, "I told you so."   "I told you so," said Ronnie.
"Why didn't you listen," said Ronnie, "when I warned you about his temper?"

14 for clearness:

After that, Bertram's dad started charging him rent.
[To prevent: After that Bertram's dad started . . . .]

USE A SEMICOLON—
between the two parts of a compound sentence when they are not joined by a coördinating conjunction:

The committees did the work; the officers got the credit.

USE DASHES—
1 to set off an appositive phrase if the phrase has commas in it:

The Big Three—Churchill, Roosevelt, and Stalin—met at Yalta in February.

2 to call attention to an especially important appositive:

The money in his piggy bank—fifty-seven cents—would not buy her much of a present.

USE A COLON—
after the salutation in a business letter:

Dear Sir: Dear Miss Bradford: Gentlemen:

USE QUOTATION MARKS—
1 to enclose the exact words of a speaker:

"Wendy," I confessed, "I don't have a cent in my pocket!"

[Note: Quotation marks are not used in an indirect quotation: I finally told Wendy that I didn't have a cent in my pocket.]

2 for titles of stories, articles, chapters, songs, short poems:

"The Tell-Tale Heart"   "Home on the Range"   "If"

USE UNDERLINING—
for titles of books, magazines, newspapers, pamphlets, movies, radio and TV programs, plays, and long poems:

Ivanhoe   Newsweek   Chicago Tribune   Evangeline

CAPITALIZATION CHECK LIST

USE CAPITALS FOR—	BUT NOT FOR—
the **Astor Hotel** on **Elm Street**	a **hotel** on a busy **street**
the **Yosemite National Park**	several **national parks**
overlooks the **Ohio River**	overlooks a peaceful **river**
in the **Squibb Building**	an **office** in this **building**
at **Wilson High School**	at our **high school**
signed up for **Chemistry 201**	signed up for **chemistry** and **art**
is taking **Latin** and **Greek**	is taking **algebra** and **physics**
will take **American History II**	will take American **history**
the **Science Club**	a **club** for **science** students
invited to the **Junior Prom**	invited the **juniors** and **seniors**
a novel of the **South**	turned **south** at the corner
lived in the **Northwest**	a **northwest** wind
became a **Westerner**	a **western** exposure
trips to **Mars** and **Saturn**	the **earth**, our **planet**
a **Friday** in **April** and **October**	a **month** in **spring** and **fall**
the **Fourth** of **July** and **New Year's Eve**	the **fifth** of the **month**, on the **eve** of the battle
bought it for **Mother**	wrote to his **mother**
with her **Uncle Clement**	with her **uncle** and **aunt**
telephoned **Grandpa**	telephoned my **grandpa**
from **Mayor Hyatt** of **Alton**	the new **mayor** of our **town**
Thank you, **Mayor**.	He thanked the **mayor**.
spoke to **Director Wellman**	a **director** named Wellman
for **Superintendent Ryan**	the **superintendent** of schools
the **President** of our country	the **president** of our council
for the **Democratic** candidate	the king's **democratic** views
a **Ford Thunderbird**	a Ford **convertible**
in **Victorian England**	in a Victorian **novel**
asked **God** for **His** help	to Zeus, the **chief** of the **gods**
Dear Sir:	My **dear** Mr. Barnes:
Sincerely yours,	Yours **sincerely**,
Yours very truly,	Very **truly yours**,
"The House We Live In"	**"A Pig in a Poke"**
"And So It Goes"	**"Hansel and Gretel"**
World Without Hate	Life with Dora
Then she asked, **"Where is he?"**	**"Where,"** she asked, **"is he?"**

473

INDEX

A or *an*, 397

Abbreviations, 448–449; in heading and addresses of letters, 203, 211, 212; punctuation following, 449

Accent marks, 160–161

Active participles, 279–281

Active verbs: defined, 244 *footnote*, 285; effective use of, 285–286

Addresses: commas to set off items in, 455–456; in business letters, 210–211, 212; in friendly letters, 202, 203–204

Adjective clauses, 298–300; as sentence fragments, 323; avoiding misplaced, 303–304; for improving sentences, 300–302; punctuation of, 458–459

Adjective phrases, 267–268

Adjectives, 262–263; after linking verbs, 255–256, 385–386; as predicate complements, 255–256; choosing between adverbs and, 383–384, 388; comparison of, 389–391; defined, 262; distinguished from adverbs, 265–266; position of, 263; proper, 405; shifting position of for emphasis, 288; special adjective problems, 397–399; using comparative and superlative forms, 392–393

Adverb clauses, 294–295; as sentence fragments, 322–323; for improving sentences, 296–297; punctuation of, 456–457

Adverb phrases, 268

Adverbs, 264–266; choosing between adjectives and, 383–384, 388; comparison of, 389–390; defined, 265; distinguished from adjectives, 265–266; distinguished from prep-

ositions, 268; relative, 299–300; shifting position of for emphasis, 288; with two forms, 384

Agreement: of demonstrative *this* and *these* with noun, 398; of pronoun and antecedent, 378–380; of subject and verb, 353–363; *see also* Subject-verb agreement

All, number of, 361

Alphabet, importance of in looking up words, 155

And: overuse of compound sentences with, 316–317; when to use in compound sentences, 312

Announcements: at club meetings, 227; making, 184–185

Anybody, number of, 379

Anyone, number of, 361, 379

Apostrophes: in contractions, 443; not used in possessive pronouns, 375; to form plurals of letters, signs, etc., 412; to show possession, 413–415

Appositive phrases, 274

Appositives, 273–274; as sentence fragments, 323; for improving sentences, 275–276; punctuation of, 274, 454–455, 466

As, form of pronoun after, 373–374

Atlases, 121

Author card, 116

Be: as helping (or auxiliary) verb, 244; as linking verb, 256

Biographical reference books, 120

Bread-and-butter letters, 206

Bring and *take*, 347–348

Business letters, 210–220; arrangement on page, 210; envelopes for, 212; folding, 213; of complaint,

474

475

479

phrases, 461; of nouns of address, 454; of parenthetical words, 453; of statements, questions, and commands, 446–447; of the parts of a business letter, 211–212; of the parts of a friendly letter, 202–203; of titles, 467–468; *see also* Colon, Commas, Dashes, Exclamation marks, Italics, Periods, Question marks, Quotation marks, Semicolons

Question marks, 446–447; with quotation marks, 463–464

Questions: determining the subject of, 249–250, 359; punctuation of, 446–447, 463–464

Quorum, defined, 224

Quotation marks: for direct quotations, 462–464; for titles, 464; with question marks and exclamation marks, 463–464

Quotations, books of, 121

Quotations: direct, 462–464; indirect, 464

Raise and *rise*, 345

Readers' Guide to Periodical Literature, 125–126

Reasons, paragraphs developed by giving, 14–15

Reference books, 119–121; atlases, 121; biographical references, 120; books of quotations, 121; encyclopedias, 119–120; yearbooks, 120–121; *see also* Dictionary

Reflexive pronouns (*myself, yourself*, etc.), 375–376

Regular verbs, 338

Relative adverbs, 299–300

Relative pronouns, 298–299; defined, 298; determining use of in clause, 298–299; formal and informal usage of, 376–378

Repetition of key word, as sentence linking device, 31

Reporting a news event, 187–188

Request, letters of, 214–216

Restrictive adjective clauses, 458–459

Restrictive participial phrases, 461

Revising compositions, 150–151

Rise and *raise*, 345

Run-together sentences, 321, 328–330; causes of, 328–329; ways of correcting, 330; words to watch in avoiding, 329–330

Salutations: in business letters, 211; in friendly letters, 201, 202

Scarcely, avoiding double negatives with, 396

School subjects, when capitalized, 406

Seasons, not capitalized, 406

Self, selves, pronouns ending in, 375–376

Semicolons, 314–315, 465

Sentence errors, 320–330; fragments, 322–324; run-together sentences, 328–330

Sentence fragments, 322–324; common types of, 323–324

Sentence patterns, 240; varying for emphasis, 253, 287–290

Sentences: complex, defined, 304–305; compound, defined, 310; simple, defined, 272, 304–305; test for recognizing, 241–242; without subjects or verbs, 326–327; *see also* Complex sentences, Compound sentences, Sentence fragments, Simple sentences

Series, punctuation of items in, 449–450

Set and *sit*, 345

Signatures: in business letters, 212; in friendly letters, 201, 203

481

483

Even a cursory examination of the tables of contents of the various ninth-grade composition books on the market would show that all the books cover more or less the same topics. What distinguishes the books primarily, then, is not the subject matter that is presented, but the *way* in which it is presented. The thought uppermost in our minds as we worked on GUIDE TO MODERN ENGLISH, Grade 9, was to present basic concepts of composition and grammar in such a way that both students and teachers would find the book truly useful.

To be truly useful, a textbook must do more than *tell*; it must *teach*—that is, it must lead students to a clear understanding of what it tells. It is not enough, for instance, merely to tell students that "a nonrestrictive adjective clause should be set off by commas" and to display two or three illustrative sentences, correctly punctuated. Unless students understand what makes a clause "nonrestrictive" and how nonrestrictive clauses differ from "restrictive," the rule is of little or no practical help to them in dealing with their own punctuation problems. On the other hand, if the textbook—through a step-by-step explanation—helps students arrive at a clear-cut understanding of the concept of nonrestrictive modification, they may forget the exact words of the rule, but they won't omit the necessary commas in their writing.

485

To guide us in determining how much explanation it would be best to give for each topic and what form the explanations should take, we did two things: (1) relived our own past experiences in reaching an understanding of the concepts and (2) recalled the difficulties our students have had and how we went about helping them resolve these difficulties. Doing so proved valuable time and time again. For example, a vivid memory of how baffled we had been by the last part of the definition "a verb is a word that expresses action or *state of being*" suggested the wisdom of finding another, clearer way to teach students to understand that words like *is, was,* and *will be* are predicating words even though they do not express action. And remembering that when a student's compositions were poor it was usually because he had done the writing without first doing the necessary thinking and planning indicated the importance of teaching composition as a process to be done one step at a time and explaining—in concrete terms and through specific examples—just how to handle each step.

Though the primary purpose of this book, like that of the others in the *Guide to Modern English Series,* is to give students practical help in improving their skill in speech and writing, it has a second important objective: to encourage in students a willingness to accept this help, to put it to use—not only in working out the exercises and assignments to satisfy the requirements of the year's course, but in all situations, present and future, in which they use language. Knowing that the first step in achieving this goal is to earn the students' confidence in the soundness of the teaching, we did our best to avoid statements about language which would, on careful reflection, prove unrealistic. For example, to make the statement "There is no such word as *hisself*" would inspire little confidence among students, many of whom hear the word constantly, often from people they admire and respect.

A more effective way to deal with this nonstandard pronoun, we felt, was to start with the fact that *hisself* does exist, to point out that it is a quite "logical" form (certainly if we say **my**self and **her**self and **your**self, it would seem logical to say **his**self), but logical as it is, it is a form *not used in standard English* and is therefore to be avoided.

This sort of approach not only makes the usage problem clear, but it also helps students get into the habit of observing their language —to see for themselves how it works. And once students acquire this habit, they will do much on their own to improve their skill in the use of language.

Often students fail to make effective use of what is taught them because they do not realize in what way it is useful to them. Many, in fact, never do realize that the principal reason for studying grammatical constructions (the appositive and the participial phrase, to name only two) is to improve the sentences in their own speech and writing. In GUIDE TO MODERN ENGLISH, Grade 9, we have tried to make students aware of this point. For instance, just before appositives and participial phrases are explained, students are told that they are about to learn several ways in which they can turn dull, childish sentences into interesting, adult-sounding sentences. Then, immediately after explaining each of the constructions, we show students how it can be used to communicate ideas more effectively. By relating the grammar instruction directly to sentence improvement, we can lead students to realize the purpose and value of the grammar study.

Flexibility. The order in which the chapters appear in the book is merely one of many in which they might be used. The most effective order in which to present the chapters in a particular class can be determined only by the teacher, since only the teacher knows the ability and needs of her students, the specific objectives of the year's course, and her own preferred methods of teaching. Teachers will find that the flexible organization of the book will make it easy for them to use the material in what seems to them the most desirable sequence.

For example, in classes in which the primary emphasis is to be on composition, some teachers may prefer starting the year's work with Chapter 1, "Writing Good Paragraphs." Others may prefer to start with Chapter 6, "Writing a Composition," having found that they can teach writing most successfully by beginning with the whole composition and then moving to paragraphs. Since each of these chapters, like the others in the book, is a self-contained unit, teachers can safely start with the one of their choice.

Sometimes the needs of a particular class will suggest the most desirable time to present a chapter. In the course of a class discussion, for instance, the students may reveal that they badly need help in distinguishing between facts and judgments and in avoiding faulty generalizations and stereotyped thinking. This would be an excellent time to turn to Chapter 2, "Clear Thinking," in which students are introduced to the study of semantics.

Some of the chapters can be used effectively while teaching the literature part of the course. For example, the major emphasis in Chapter 4, the vocabulary chapter, is on increasing vocabulary through learning to use context clues. Since most of the selections assigned for reading will give students excellent "contexts" to work with, it would be valuable to study the chapter first.

The last thirteen chapters deal with subjects of importance for all classes: grammar, improving sentences, avoiding sentence errors, usage, spelling, and punctuation. Here too the needs of students will determine in great part how much time and emphasis to give to each chapter. Some classes, for example, will be able to sail through the usage chapters; others will need to spend a great deal of time on them, perhaps repeating the drills in certain sections. Students whose writing reveals a strong "sentence sense" will hardly need the work on avoiding sentence errors; for others, constant reference to the chapter may be necessary. The material in all these chapters is so organized that teachers can easily make provision for these student differences.

The exercises. The exercises, as carefully prepared as the explanations, are an integral part of the text, since they are designed to reinforce the teaching, to help clinch the students' understanding of points in the text. Students will find that though the exercises are challenging and require thoughtful work, they do not present problems the text does not help them solve. One of their chief values, in fact, is that they will lead students to restudy portions of the text they did not fully grasp the first time.

Special features.　While it is highly important to be serious about the teaching of so essential a subject as English, it is also important to make the teaching attractive.　Students will welcome the colorful chapter-head illustrations and the marginal sketches used throughout the book, both for their humor and ingenuity and for their help in driving home various points made in the text.　Teachers will find that each of the three picture stories, by reinforcing *visually* the students' understanding of certain concepts, makes a valuable contribution to the book.

Spoken English, an album of two long-playing records to accompany this text and its tenth-grade companion, provides listening experiences in four subjects especially suited to an aural medium— discussion, pronunciation, semantics, and standard American English dialects.　These records should increase interest in the subjects and may be used at any time in the course.

Acknowledgments.　The authors and editors wish to acknowledge the aid of the following teachers, who contributed many valuable criticisms and suggestions while the work was in progress:　Mrs. Sanford Hanson, Sturgeon Bay High School, Sturgeon Bay, Wisconsin, and Mr. John Maxwell, Consultant in Language Arts, Racine Public Schools, Racine, Wisconsin.

Special thanks are due also to the following for their assistance in making arrangements for the photographs used in the picture stories:　Mr. S. R. Friedman of the American School of Beauty Culture; Miss Karin Julian of Edgewater Hospital; Mr. Walter Weiner and Mr. W. A. Robinson of the DeVry Technical Institute; Mr. Stanley Lyman and Miss Emily Manz of the Bureau of Indian Affairs; Mr. Robert Rietz, Miss Susan Kelly, and Mr. Richard Poweshiek of the American Indian Center—all of Chicago; Mr. Keith Hutchison of the Greer Technical Institute, Braidwood, Illinois; Mr. Clarence Barnhart, Mr. William Halsey, and the editorial staff of the Thorndike-Barnhart dictionaries, Bronxville, New York.

The Authors and Editors

488

Photographs.　Credit for the following original photographs, used in the picture stories, belongs to:　Kenneth Heilbron, p. 60; Charles Bacon of Bacon-Tirschel Associates, p. 65 (left top and bottom), pp. 68–69; Joseph Zortea of Krantzen Studio, Inc., p. 65 (right top and bottom), p. 66; Wayne Miller of Magnum Photos, Inc., p. 67; Rene Burri, p. 173; Kenneth Heilbron, pp. 174–180.　Credit for the cover photograph belongs to M. Halberstadt.

3　4　5　6　7　8　9　10 — 69　68　67　66